Policy and Action

*Essays on the implementation
of public policy*

Policy and Action

Essays on the implementation of public policy

edited by Susan Barrett
and Colin Fudge

METHUEN
London and New York

First published in 1981 by
Methuen & Co. Ltd
11 New Fetter Lane, London EC4P 4EE
Published in the USA by
Methuen & Co.
in association with Methuen, Inc.
733 Third Avenue, New York, NY 10017

Photoset by Keyset Composition, Colchester
Printed in Great Britain by Richard Clay,
The Chaucer Press, Bungay, Suffolk

British Library Cataloguing in Publication Data

Policy and action.
1. Political science – Addresses, essays, lectures
I. Barrett, Susan   II. Fudge, Colin
320'.08   JA41

ISBN 0 416 30670 5
ISBN 0 416 30680 2 pbk (University paperback 756)

Contents

Preface

This book is about the relationship between public policy and action, the processes at work within and between agencies involved in making and implementing public policy and the factors affecting those processes. As a working approximation we suggest that the term 'public policy' may be defined as the implicit or explicit intentions of government and the expression of those intentions entailing specific patterns of activity or inaction by governmental agencies. Public policy provides the framework within which agencies of government operate to control, regulate or promote certain facets of society in the interests of national defence, law and order, economic and financial management, social welfare and the like.

In recent years, professional and academic concern with problems of public policy implementation – translation of policy into actions – has increased, and this concern relates to wider anxieties about the effectiveness of public policy and government in general. At one level, concern with effectiveness forms part of wider ideological debates about the role of the state in society and about the 'governability' of an increasingly complex industrial society, in which, it is argued, interventions are likely to have unforeseen or counter-intentional results.

Whilst public policy emanates from the 'public sector' – including both the institutions of central and local government and state created agencies such as water or health authorities, commissions and corporations – it may be implemented through and directed at a wide variety of individuals and organizations which may or may not be part of the state apparatus, and which may be to a greater or lesser degree independent of state influence or control. In the past, studies have been dominated by institutional, public administration or policy analysis perspectives and have tended to concentrate on the substance of policy, the process of its formulation and its effectiveness in terms of impact. Concern with effectiveness is now being extended to include a closer look at what actually happens to policy 'in the hands' of implementers, that is, the processes of implementation, the factors affecting those processes and their relationship to policy formulation and change.

Our own interest and involvement in the subject area stems in part from this general environment of growing concern with different aspects of public policy 'effectiveness' and in part from our own experience and role as teachers and researchers in the field of policy studies. As ex-practitioners ourselves from central and local government, and latterly as teachers-of-practitioners in our work at the University of Bristol School for Advanced Urban Studies, we have shared awareness of the public criticism of 'bureaucratic ineffectiveness' often levelled at those in the public sector, and the concern, even frustration, felt by many at their inability to 'get things done'. What actually happens may appear a long way short of policy intentions, or innovative action seems to be thwarted by restrictive policy or practice imposed from above. At worst, the sheer multiplicity of agencies that have to be involved in the formulation and implementation of a particular strand of policy, the complicated interaction between policies, and the difficulty of identifying clear objectives and priorities for action against a background of changing political, social and economic circumstances combine to produce an environment of uncertainty, if not impotence, for the individual 'actor' in the process.

These rather different perspectives have led us, along with several of our colleagues, into the study of implementation aimed at understanding the relationship between policy and action. Over the past few years, individuals at the School for Advanced Urban Studies have undertaken a number of studies of the process of implementation or impact of specific public policies. At present a team of researchers (including three of the contributors: Michael Hill, Susan Barrett and Tom Davies) is undertaking research supported by the Social Science Research Council on Implementation in the Central-Local Relationship. This body of work and the debate generated within the School have provided the background to some of the material included in this volume.

Although we are close to the world of practice, we are aware of the power and dominance of practitioner ideologies and debates. Consequently, in this volume we have attempted to allow the contributors and ourselves to develop ideas that are distinct from those used in the practice of government. That is, we hope we have been able to get some distance on the world of practice and present an analysis from a somewhat more detached stance.

Acknowledgements

Inevitably, given a collective enterprise like this, we have incurred many personal and intellectual debts since we first began, and a preface provides a formal opportunity for acknowledging at least some of these. Whilst we alone take full responsibility for the shortcomings of this collection, we are very much indebted to our colleagues at the School for Advanced Urban Studies and others for the quality of debate and comment which has stimulated and contributed to our work, as well as to those making specific contributions to this volume. Our particular thanks go to Tony Eddison, Ken Young, Michael Hill, Tom Davies, Robin Means and Rod Rhodes, whose comments on early drafts have been invaluable. Last but not least, the whole enterprise would have foundered without Sheila Wolfenden, who read through and corrected the final manuscript, and Penny Buckland, who, together with her team of research secretaries, typed and kept track of successive versions of the manuscript. To these, and to other friends and colleagues, many thanks.

Susan Barrett   Colin Fudge
January 1981

Guide to reading the book

In assembling this collection of case studies and essays we have been influenced by some of the problems experienced in our teaching and research activities.

In teaching, we are particularly conscious of the gap between theory and highly personal, anecdotal accounts of specific experience. Though these provide a real and live picture of specific interactions between people with varying opportunities, constraints, motivations and interests, it is very difficult to relate them to existing bodies of theory or draw out generalizations of wider relevance. There is a need for material which brings together a *range* of case study material, and relates the specific instances and issues to wider and more general themes.

From our research work, a second and related issue is the problem of selecting the appropriate level of analysis in the study of public policy. This issue is reflected in the existing literature. On the one hand (and simplifying the differences), we find general analyses using models drawn from the realms of economic and political theory. These often take the form of 'normative' conditions for effective implementation or shopping lists of variables. On the other hand, we can draw on detailed case studies tracing the implementation of a specific policy but which may or may not offer insights that are more generally applicable.

In an earlier paper to the Social Science Research Council, Michael Hill (Hill *et al*. 1979) discussed the issue of implementation under four headings: the nature of policy, centre-periphery relations, characteristics of implementing agencies, and characteristics of the policy environment. The paper by Hill concluded that it was important to avoid the shopping-list approach and to focus on interactions *between* factors on the dynamics of the policy process and on the characteristics and impact of environments, and that research was needed in several modes:

★   case studies of specific policy addressing the variety and complexity of the real world in detail,
★   comparative studies of issues *across* policy areas to look at commonalities and differences,
★   synthesis from both in the context of alternative theoretical perspectives.

The structure and content of the book reflect these suggested approaches. Its main purpose is to provide a range of case study material and perspectives, but it also seeks to draw out key themes and issues, and relate them to different ideas that might be used to conceptualize the implementation process.

Last, but not least, much of the existing published material on implementation is North American. Given the growing interest in Britain from academics, practitioners and students, we have aimed to contribute a body of British material to the debate.

The case studies and essays contained in Part Two form the backbone of the book. They are introduced and their main themes highlighted at the beginning of Part Two. Each represents a self-contained essay reflecting the concerns and interests of the author(s). In seeking contributions we tried to follow the logic of our approach to the study of implementation by taking variety and complexity as a starting point. Each contributor was asked to write on the basis of her or his experience and perspective. We did not attempt to prescribe the issues to be addressed, or provide a conceptual model into which the essay should be fitted. However, in taking this approach we have given ourselves problems; both in *presenting* the material in a volume of this kind, that is, grouping the material in a way that helps the reader to pick up common issues but does not overly constrain the reader, and in trying to *interpret* the material and relate it to wider concepts. Attempting to cope with these self-imposed problems has led us to the structure of the book.

Part One, the Introductory Review, provides a background to the study of implementation and a general review of the literature. More importantly it aims to take the reader through different but not exhaustive ways of viewing implementation as seen from different perspectives. It is intended as a backcloth to Part Two, the individual essays themselves.

In Part Two, we have presented a range of policy case studies and essays. The first group in a sense mirror the 'top down' or 'policy centred' approach to studying implementation, with each one adopting a rather different stance or focus for the analysis of the issues: the problems facing central government in implementing cuts in public expenditure, the problems of local agencies' interpretation and response to central policy in the land field, the negotiation of policy between public and private sector agencies, and the dual problems for a local authority attempting to develop and implement innovative policy in the employment field in the absence of any clear responsibility for activities in this area. The second group includes four chapters focusing on different groups of actors and interactions between actors involved in implementing policies. These look at the involvement of elected members in the implementation of their political manifesto, the activities of local officers involved in detailed planning case work, the interaction between different professionals in the process of briefing architects for designing educational buildings, and the organizational issues involved in introducing a new approach to caring for the mentally ill. The final two contributions to Part Two are somewhat different in character. Both stand back from specific cases and address in very different ways the question of rationality in the policy process.

Part Three, the concluding chapter to the book, looks at the relationship between the case material and some of the ideas outlined in the introduction, discusses particular themes and issues that seem to emerge from the individual contributions, especially those which have not been given previous attention, and looks at some of the implications of these issues for the reconstruction of the field of analysis and further work on implementation.

Notes and references are provided at the end of each chapter and an extensive bibliography concludes the volume. We make no claims to offer in this book a 'theory' of implementation or 'recipes' for policy success. Rather, we have attempted two things: first, to review some of the prevailing views about the subject and raise questions and criticisms on the basis of our evidence; and, second, to pick up a number of themes and issues illustrated by the contributors which seem to have been neglected in current literature and which seem to us to have a bearing on the way in which the policy-action relationship is viewed. Clearly what we perceive as important or interesting is coloured by our own experience and view of the world. Readers ultimately have to make their own sense of the material presented. We hope we will have been of some assistance in providing ways of interpreting the material and practice which readers can revise and develop in the light of their own experience. The book is offered as a contribution to the continuing discussion of public policy.

Part One

Introductory Review

Examining the policy-action relationship

Susan Barrett and Colin Fudge

Public agencies often tend to be viewed as rule-bound and inflexible bureaucratic machines which grind on regardless of changing problems and circumstances, concerned more with their own procedures than with the public they are intended to serve. It is easy to find anecdotal horror stories: examples of 'buck-passing' between welfare agencies, exasperating delay in obtaining planning permission, or housing allocation rules applied to the level of absurdity. Public agencies cannot expect to be immune from public scrutiny and criticism, and failure or crisis is inevitably more newsworthy than adequacy, efficiency or success. However, it is not easy to find ways of measuring the relative incidence of 'failure' among the whole range of activities and services performed satisfactorily by public agencies. As far as the more routine services are concerned, these may only be noticed when something goes wrong – or they fail to be provided. At the same time, the image is perhaps symptomatic of a more fundamental anxiety about the effectiveness of public policy and government in general. Government, whether national, regional or local, appears to be adept at making statements of intention, but what happens on the ground often falls a long way short of the original aspirations. Government either seems unable to put its policy into effect as intended, or finds that its interventions and actions have unexpected or counter-productive outcomes which create new problems. Blame for the ineffectiveness of government intervention tends to be directed either at those responsible for policy-making, for constantly producing the 'wrong' policy, or at the implementing agencies for being, apparently, unable or unwilling to act.

At one level, concern about effectiveness centres around the question of the role and scope of government in an advanced industrial society. This includes differing ideological positions about the role of the state in society and debate focusing on the appropriate level of intervention assuming the continuation of a mixed economy. Even from the latter point of view, it has been argued that government is trying to influence and control more than it has the material or political resources to achieve, resulting in diminishing marginal returns and policy failure.[1] It has also been argued that uncertain or counter-productive policy outcomes can be attributed to increasing social and economic complexity and inter-relatedness of activities in society.[2] At a more prosaic level, lack of effectiveness is equated with incompetence and inefficiency. It is suggested that the bureaucratic structure and style of government agencies are intrinsically unsuited to many of the tasks such agencies attempt or are expected to perform.[3] Alternatively, it is argued, lack of competence, resulting in unresponsiveness or inappropriate responses, is due to an absence of appropriate skills and adequate management in the public sector,[4] or, at worst, the fact that public agencies provide a protected environment for the inept.

Two distinct themes run through debates about government effectiveness. On the one hand, concern centres on the appropriateness of public intervention and the relevance of public policy in relation to problems and issues, implying the need for a better understanding of the implications of public intervention and, thence, 'better' policy. On the other hand, criticism focuses on the *processes* of policy-making and administration, implying the need for increased policy-making skills and better management and co-ordination amongst public agencies.

This is our starting point. In this introductory review we begin by looking at the way in which practitioners and academics have responded to criticism and these expressions of concern and at how, through developments in the study of policy, policy-making processes and the management of public sector organizations and agencies,[5] attention has become focused on the 'problem' of implementation and the processes of putting policy into effect. We then go on to examine in more detail some recent approaches to the study of implementation with reference to selected literature, and to consider how well the conceptualization of implementation as 'putting policy into effect' seems to fit with what happens in practice. We argue that much of the existing literature tends to take a 'managerial' perspective; the problems of implementation are defined in terms of co-ordination, control or obtaining 'compliance' with policy. Such a policy-centred or 'top down' view of the process treats implementers as 'agents' for policy-makers and tends to play down issues such as power relations, conflicting interests and value systems between individuals and agencies responsible for making policy and those responsible for taking action. In the final sections of the chapter, we introduce two alternative ways of viewing the policy-action relationship: as a negotiating process and as a process of action and response. We suggest that, rather than treating implementation as the transmission of policy into a series of consequential actions, the policy-action relationship needs to be regarded as a process of interaction and negotiation, taking place over time, between those seeking to put policy into effect and those upon whom action depends.

This chapter is intended to form a background for the individual contributions which follow in Part Two. In the concluding chapter (Part Three), we attempt to draw out some of the themes and issues raised by the contributions and to suggest some avenues for further work.

Effectiveness, administrative efficiency and the development of policy studies

Those in government, whether elected representatives or employees, are only too aware of their public image and share at least some of the above concerns about the effectiveness of government. Over the last ten years or so, increasing attention has been paid within government agencies to improving and enhancing what might be termed the 'policy content' of government decision-making; to improving decision-making processes and the co-ordination of policy and to streamlining management structures, administrative operations and service delivery. For example, in the mid-1960s, the Planning Advisory Group's[6] review of the land use planning system resulted in the introduction, in the Town and Country Planning Act of 1968,[7] of the concept of a strategic plan that was a statement of reasoned policy, rather than a map of land use zones. Similar developments have occurred in the field of social services, transport, the health service and housing.[8] Policy 'capacity' has been increased by the employment of research staff in both central and local government, whose function is to review, evaluate and formulate alternative courses of action (whether in a service department or in special Research and Intelligence Units). Within central government, these developments are exemplified by the post-Fulton creation of departmental Policy Units, the establishment of the Central Policy Review Staff (CPRS) within the Cabinet Office, and the development of Programme Analysis Review (PAR) in the early 1970s.[9] At the same time there has been an increasing tendency for central government to require or ask for statements of policy and a reasoned justification of the public programmes carried out at local level, as a basis for resource allocation decisions – for example in Housing Strategies and Investment Programmes.[10]

The explicit linkage of policy objectives and resource allocation derives from the Planning Programming and Budgeting System (PPBS) concept developed in a number of American business schools and the Rand Corporation and used first in the public sector in the United States Defence Department in 1961.[11] PPBS was aimed at improving both the *rationality* of public decision-making and the *effectiveness* of action via the purposive direction of expenditure towards clear objectives and the monitoring of performance in relation to those objectives. These ideas, and the techniques imported with them, have had a strong influence on the whole approach to managing British central and local government activities, for example in the corporate philosophy which blossomed in the early 1970s,[12] and which was endorsed in the Bains report.[13]

Corporate planning and management also attempted to improve awareness of the interconnectedness of public policy and the co-ordination of service delivery. Corporate plans – the comprehensive statement of an agency's policies and programmes – aimed not only to provide an explicit statement of policy against which performance could be measured and evaluated (and policy thereby improved), but also to avoid problems of contradictory policy being operated by different departments and to assist in the dovetailing of interdependent programmes.

Opinions vary about the effects and effectiveness of these developments.[14] There may be more rational processes, but it is argued that through the proliferation of planning activity more energy has been expended in producing plans and programmes and in reorganizing management structures than in actually getting things done or paying attention to fundamental questions of policy relevance.

So far we have focused on government's attempts to respond to criticisms of its effectiveness by placing more emphasis on policy development, on increasing the rationality of decision-making processes and on administrative efficiency. The same concerns have also been taken up in the academic arena and are reflected in the development of 'policy studies' as an academic and applied subject for study and research.[15] Perhaps three main dimensions of intellectual concern can be identified, although these overlap, are interconnected and are not necessarily as clearly distinguished as the categorization would make them appear:

1 *Policy analysis*, concerned with understanding and explaining the substance of policy content and policy decisions and the way in which policy decisions are made, and including the prescription of methodological frameworks and techniques for improving the substance and process of decision-making.
2 *Evaluative studies*, concerned with the understanding and assessment of policy outcomes and impacts as a basis for evaluating policy performance – its relevance and effectiveness. This area embraces the development of economic and social indicators, performance measures, evaluative techniques, for example, cost benefit analysis, and issues concerning the methodology of evaluative research and its application in political decision-making environments.
3 *Organizational studies*, concerned with understanding the operation of political and administrative organizations, the relationship between structures, functions and systems of management, the behaviour of individuals and groups within organizational frameworks, and inter-organizational relationships and behaviour. This area, too, includes the prescription of organizational and management structures and styles of administration aimed at improving performance.

Heclo has identified three sources of impetus for the study of policy: 'downwards from a comparative politics seeking to become more empirical, upwards from a decision making approach seeking to become more generalized, and across from either disciplines seeking to become more truthful to the complexity of events'.[16] Whilst economics and political science can be regarded as the key 'parent' disciplines of policy studies, more recent commentators point to the need for a synthesis of the various theoretical strands contributing to explanatory developments, involving the interaction of political, economic, environmental and organizational variables.[17] This kind of approach to the study of policy is associated with a shift in emphasis from comparative studies, which provide explanations of relationships at a high level of generality, to the use of detailed case studies of particular policies or events. Such studies examine in detail the origins and objectives of a particular 'piece of policy' and seek to explain how and why decisions came to be made, or events turned out the way they did.[18] Inevitably, by turning to the detail of events, such studies point to the need for theories that take account of individual and group behaviour within institutional settings. Similarly, they focus attention on administrative structures and the way in which individuals respond and behave in bureaucratic organizations, involving issues such as accountability, rewards and incentives, organizational and professional 'cultures' and limits of authority and control. They also raise questions about the environment in which policy is being made – the context of physical, economic, political and social circumstances – and the individuals, groups and interests upon which policy impinges.

In the field of applied policy analysis, analysts concerned to prescribe for the improvement of public policy-making still espouse concepts of rational choice as an ideal for professional policy-makers and administrators, perhaps, notably, in the case of Dror.[19] At the same time, various attempts (starting with Charles Lindblom's ideas on incrementalism)[20] have been made to relate the process of decision-making to its political and organizational context, and to take on board theories about political and organizational behaviour and response. Ideas about strategic choice and coping with complex interagency inter-dependence,[21] or Etzioni's 'mixed scanning' approach to decision-making,[22] can be regarded as attempts to find *practical methodologies* that utilize more behavioural explanations of the policy-making process.

Concern with complexity and the capability to respond have perhaps been the other main stimuli for development in the prescriptive field. Two main directions can be distinguished: a cybernetics approach, and a behavioural approach. The cybernetics approach applies systems theory to organizational and political systems, and also embraces theories of organizational behaviour. Its prescriptions seek to achieve efficient and effective responses by creating organizational and management structures and processes that are capable of dealing with the variety of demands placed upon them. On the one hand, the cybernetics approach has been taken up by political scientists interested in exploring models of political communication and control;[23] on the other hand, it is associated with developing the technological capacity to assimilate, process and communicate information through the use of real-time computer systems, for example, as advocated by Beer.[24] An alternative perspective is that taken by such people as Vickers or Schon[25] and, on a more prescriptive note, by Etzioni and Friedman.[26] They are really arguing that responsiveness is a matter of attitude – individual and organizational – and that new attitudes and patterns of behaviour are required to shake off conventional bureaucratic responses. Much of the prescriptive content is concerned with altering systems of rewards and incentives in order to effect changes of this kind.

A number of points seem to us to emerge from developments in the policy studies field which have particular relevance for our consideration of implementation and the policy-action relationship. First, the study of policy indicates the complexity of the policy process. Its elements might be described as:

1   an environmental system, from which demands and needs arise, and upon which policy seeks to have an effect
2   a political system in which policy decisions are made
3   an organizational system through which policy is mediated and executed

The problem is to understand and explain how these systems operate and interact – what influences what, when, and how. Since each system is dynamic, the nature of interaction will also vary over time.

Second, there is a distinction between explanation and prescription. It may be difficult to find robust explanations which hold in a wide variety of circumstances, but it is even more difficult to prescribe in a way which accommodates reality without merely mirroring its ineffectiveness.

Third, linked to this is the question of methodologies and perspectives. Allison summarizes the problem thus:

Conceptual models not only fix the mesh of the nets through which the analyst drags the material in order to explain a particular action; they also direct him to cast his nets in select ponds, at certain depths, in order to catch the fish he is after.[27]

If what you see depends on where you are standing and which way you are looking, then a pluralist approach – both in the use of conceptual models or theories and in type of studies undertaken (comparative as well as in-depth case studies) – seems an essential prerequisite to understanding what is going on, especially if it is complicated.

Fourth, and of most significance to the study of implementation, until recently most policy analysts (whether operating in a descriptive or prescriptive mode) have tended to equate policy *decisions* with action.

Decisions are seen as the outputs of the policy process, the assumption being that once made they will be translated into action. Only lately (and largely through the influence of detailed case studies of the type cited earlier) have policy analysts started to focus on what practitioners are only too well aware of, and what Dunsire has termed the 'implementation gap'.[28] Policy does not implement itself, and attention is now being directed beyond policy *making* towards the processes by which policy is translated into action and the factors influencing those processes. This leads on to our last point.

A great deal of research and a huge literature exist on the analysis of organizations: understanding the way they operate, prescribing administrative structures, examining the behaviour of groups and individuals in an organizational setting. Dunsire has pointed out that some of this literature recognizes a distinct implementation process, and that many of the issues and ideas currently being seized upon as 'new' by policy analysts and practitioners have actually been around for a long time.[29] However, therein lies part of the problem. Much of the organizational literature treats the implementation of policy as a separate process more or less in a vacuum. Policy is made somewhere else and handed in, so to speak, to the administrative system which then executes it. The implementation process is seen as inextricably bound up with organizational structures and processes, that is, policy comes in at the top and is successively refined and translated into operating instructions as it moves down the hierarchy to the 'operatives' at the bottom. The desire to separate 'politics' and 'administration', whilst in many ways discredited at an intellectual level,[30] still forms part of the conventional wisdom among professionals and administrators in the public service. Similarly, the stages of implementation tend to be associated automatically with a hierarchical 'chain of command' and this association has no doubt had an influence on the way in which the process of policy implementation is perceived, by practitioners and researchers alike, and hence the tendency to take it for granted as an automatic follow-on from policy decisions. Whilst the literature has much to say about such matters as the way in which controls and incentives operate to ensure compliance or the operation of discretion, behavioural issues tend to be dealt with in terms of a single organization whose basic purpose is to administer policy or to carry out specific functions. Thus implementation is regarded as a matter of communication, channels of communication and control systems to ensure compliance.

Weberian ideas about hierarchical organization and management are so firmly embedded in the conventional wisdom of public organizations that it is difficult to stand back and examine critically some of the assumptions being made. Many of the attempts to improve the performance of public agencies follow the logic of organizational studies, assuming that if management structures and processes, channels of communication and clarity of communication are 'right', effective action will be assured.

Implementation and action

So, how do we start to look at the problem? What is meant by 'implementation'? Pressman and Wildavsky, in their study of the attempts of the US Economic Development Agency to implement a job creation programme in Oakland, California, initially defined the process thus: 'Implementation may be viewed as a process of interaction between the setting of goals and actions geared to achieving them.'[31]

However, they qualified the definition in the following terms:

> Implementation does not refer to creating the initial conditions. Legislation has to be passed and funds committed before implementation takes place to secure the predicted outcome. . . . To emphasise the actual existence of initial conditions we must distinguish a program from a policy. . . . A program exists when the initial conditions – the 'if' stage of the policy hypothesis – have been met. The word program signifies the conversion of a hypothesis into *governmental* action. The initial premises of the hypothesis have been authorised. The degree to which the predicted consequences (the 'then' stage) take place we will call implementation.
> [emphasis added]

They go on to say:

> Programs make the theories operational by forging the first link in the causal chain connecting actions to objectives. Given X we act to obtain Y. *Implementation, then, is the ability to forge subsequent links in the causal chain so as to obtain the desired results.*[32]
> [emphasis added]

We have quoted their definition at some length because it embodies assumptions most commonly held about implementation.[33] First, they assume a series of logical steps – a progression from intention through decision to action – and clearly see implementation starting where policy stops. Second, they distinguish two steps in formulating intentions: policy-making – their 'initial conditions' – and the creation of programmes which form the 'inputs' to their implementation process.[34] We shall return to this point presently. Third, they see implementation as a process of putting policy (or in their case, programmes) into effect, mainly concerned with co-ordinating and managing the various elements required to achieve the desired ends.

Other definitions follow a similar logic. For example, Walter Williams says: 'The agency implementation process includes both *one-time* efforts to convert decisions into operational terms and continuance of efforts over time to raise the quality of the agency's staffs and organisational structure in the field.'[35] And later, in the context of implementation as a research question, he states: 'In its most general form, an inquiry about implementation capability . . .

seeks to determine whether an organisation can bring together men and material in a cohesive organisational unit and motivate them in such a way as to carry out the organisation's stated objectives.'[36] This is echoed by Van Meter and Van Horn in an article which reviews the field and attempts to provide a conceptual framework or model of the implementation process: 'policy implementation encompasses those actions by public and private individuals (or groups) that are directed at the achievement of objectives set forth in prior policy decisions.'[37]

One immediate issue is raised by comparing Pressman and Wildavsky's definition with the others. They take programmes – the means or proposed activities by which intentions are to be translated into action – rather than policy (in the sense of a statement of intentions or objectives) as inputs to the process. They state that implementation cannot start until policy has been made operational through the passing of legislation and the committing of resources to it, whereas the others refer more loosely to 'decisions' and 'objectives'. Pressman and Wildavsky thus explicitly exclude from the implementation process what they nevertheless refer to as 'governmental action' to convert policy intentions into programmes. Williams, on the other hand, explicitly includes 'efforts to convert decisions into operational terms' in the implementation process. This is not merely semantic juggling, but raises some fundamental questions about the definition of policy itself. What is being implemented and where does policy-making stop and implementation start?

What do we mean by policy? A political intention as expressed, say, in a political party manifesto? A formal decision expressed as legislation or a local council resolution? Operational policy expressed in government circulars, managerial statements or detailed administrative procedures providing 'rules' for the carrying out of specific tasks? Clearly, policy is all these things and where policy stops and implementation starts depends on where you are standing and which way you are looking. To some politicians, policy is synonymous with the party manifesto and everything that follows is implementation. For executive officers involved in local service delivery, administrative procedures may well appear to be policy in so far as they comprise the framework governing the scope for action. On this basis, implementation is the process of successive refinement and translation of policy into specific procedures and tasks directed at putting policy intentions into effect. In any study of implementation, it seems important to examine the various stages in this process, who is involved, in what roles and with what motives. It is particularly important to investigate what is happening to policy as it is successively refined and translated. How far do detailed frameworks for action – legislative, administrative, procedural – reflect or relate to original intentions; that is, what exactly *is* being implemented? If what is being implemented is different from the original policy intention, is this 'good', for example, demonstrating that policy was flexible enough to be tailored to the local circumstances, or 'bad' in that the original policy goals have been distorted in the process?

These questions are considered, directly or indirectly, in several of the contributions to this volume, notably in the chapters by Barrett (examining local authorities' implementation of the Community Land Act 1975), Fudge (focusing on local elected members' experience in implementing a political manifesto), and Bishop (looking at the process of briefing architects for school building programmes). Indeed, Hill returns to the theme of the policy-implementation distinction for a more general examination of the validity and implications of attempts to conceptualize implementation as a 'rational' process of putting policy into effect. Even where studies are undertaken to evaluate outcomes in relation to policy intentions, there is no guarantee that the results of such studies will be utilized by policy-makers. Smith, in his chapter, discusses how and why this situation arises.

Our discussion has so far centred on this definition of implementation: a policy-centred approach, by which policy is the starting point, the trigger for action, and implementation a logical step-by-step progression from policy intention to action. This approach might be defined as 'the policy-makers' perspective', since it represents what policy-makers are trying to do to put policy into effect. As noted earlier, this perspective tends to be associated with hierarchical concepts of organization; policy emanates from the 'top' (or centre) and is transmitted down the hierarchy (or to the periphery) and translated into more specific rules and procedures as it goes to guide or control action at the bottom (or on the ground). However, in our view this perspective is open to question. It assumes that policy comes from the top and is the starting point for implementation and action. This, we would argue, is not necessarily the case: policy may be a response to pressures and problems experienced on the ground. Equally, policy may be developed from specific innovations, that is, action precedes policy. Not all action relates to a specific or explicit policy.[38] The hierarchical view of implementation also implies that implementers are agents for policy-makers and are therefore in a *compliant* relationship to policy-makers. But in many instances – especially in the public policy field – those upon whom action depends are *not* in any hierarchical association with those making policy. By definition, public policy is often aimed at directing or intervening in the activities of private interests and agencies. Implementation agencies will thus, in many instances, be autonomous or semi-autonomous, with their own interests and priorities to pursue and their own policy-making role.

We would thus argue that it is essential to look at implementation not solely in terms of putting policy into effect, but also in terms of observing what actually happens or gets done and seeking to understand how and why. This kind of action perspective takes 'what is done' as central, focuses attention on the behaviour or actions of groups and individuals and the determinants of that behaviour, and seeks to examine the degree to which action relates to policy, rather than assuming it to follow from policy. From this perspective, implementation (or action) may be regarded as a series of *responses*: to ideological commitment, to environmental pressures, or to pressures from other agencies (groups) seeking to influence or control action.

Distinguishing between a 'policy-centred' and an 'action-centred' approach to implementation also points to the importance of the interaction between those seeking to influence the actions of others and those upon whom influence is being brought to bear to act in a particular way, whether within or between organizations. This involves considering implementation in terms of *power relations* and different mechanisms for gaining or avoiding influence or control.

In the next section, we look in more detail at what is involved in 'putting policy into effect' before moving on to consider alternative ways of conceptualizing the implementation process.

Implementation as putting policy into effect

This is what policy-makers are concerned about; what they are trying to do. It is, therefore, not surprising that much of the implementation literature, particularly that using policy case studies, takes policy as its starting point and considers implementation in terms of the problems or factors that 'get in the way' of its execution.

So what is involved in putting policy into effect? Take, for example, building a house extension. The task will require money, materials, skills and time; it will also involve obtaining building regulations consent. In some circumstances it may involve obtaining planning permission or complying with public health regulations; it will certainly demand planning and management to make sure that the job is done effectively. Only the most intrepid DIY expert is likely to tackle such a job him or herself. Most people would hire a builder, in which case the task will involve communicating what is wanted to the builder, deciding how much discretion will be left to him or her in the execution and deciding whether and how to check or control performance.

Putting policy into effect is therefore basically dependent on:

1 knowing what you want to do
2 the availability of the required resources
3 the ability to marshal and control these resources to achieve the desired end
4 if others are to carry out the tasks, communicating what is wanted and controlling their performance

Just thinking for a moment about what can go wrong in the execution of this kind of job provides a useful starting point for the more general consideration of implementation issues. In the first place, the householder's aspirations may exceed the resources he has available to carry out the job. In public policy terms, it is certainly not unknown for central government to pass legislation (apparently) without considering the manpower implications for the local agencies which will be responsible for its implementation, or for inadequate financial resources to be allocated in relation to the original policy goals. For example, in her chapter, Barrett argues that one of the reasons for local authorities' lack of activity in buying and selling development land under the Community Land Act 1975 was the low level of financial resources devoted to the scheme by central government. Another example might be the low level of local authority activity in response to the part of the Control of Pollution Act 1974 which empowers them to obtain and make public information about emissions to the air from industrial processes. This was included in the Act in response to suggestions from a Royal Commission, an official committee and various pressure groups, yet it is costly for local authorities to implement and the government provided no new resources for this purpose.[39] Indeed, it is frequently argued (particularly in central-local government debates) that 'central' policy-makers show a certain duplicity in exhorting local agencies, or in passing legislation which requires local agencies to provide services which the 'centre' knows are unlikely to be afforded, at the same time as other policy is being promulgated to cut public expenditure or reduce manpower. Such an argument, of course, raises further questions about the nature and role of policy, and reinforces our argument that implementation cannot be treated as an administrative process in a vacuum. Indeed, the issue of policy intentions crops up in several of the contributions and we return to this theme in our concluding chapter.

Linked to the availability or provision of resources is the 'legitimation' or obtaining of clearance for action. Going back to the house extension, what if planning permission is refused? It is quite probable that the householder's original ideas do not comply with some public policy or regulation and he will have to negotiate a compromise and modify his original intentions. Alternatively, his neighbour may object to the proposed extension and put pressure on the householder to modify his plans. Government policy, too, is likely to come up against problems of obtaining a mandate, and the process of legitimizing action is also likely to involve compromise and modification of the original intentions, either as a condition for obtaining an electoral or parliamentary mandate, or as a result of pressure from powerful interests affected by the policy concerned. The chapter on the Community Land Scheme again provides a useful example. The policy was highly controversial, both ideologically and in terms of development industry interests potentially affected. The original intentions (as set out in the Land White Paper) were substantially modified during the drafting of legislation and the passage of the Bill through Parliament as a result of pressures stemming from these sources.

It is interesting in this context to recap on Pressman and Wildavsky's definitions, whereby they regard both the legitimation and provision of resources as 'starting conditions' *preceding* implementation proper. We would argue, certainly on the basis of the material in this volume, that what happens during these processes is fundamental in helping to explain subsequent actions and reactions, and should therefore be included in any study of 'implementation'. Montjoy and O'Toole go even further, to argue from an analysis of evidence of implementation problems in the US General Accounting Office's reports that: 'From one perspective it appears that the surest way to avoid intra-organisational implementation problems is to establish a specific mandate and provide sufficient resources.'[40] By 'mandate' they refer to the legitimizing and operationalizing of policy objectives.

Assuming that Pressman and Wildavsky's starting conditions are satisfied, the process is then a matter of assembling, co-ordinating and managing the resources necessary to implement the policy or purpose. To organize the building of the house extension, it will be necessary to assemble the appropriate skills for the job to be done, to co-ordinate them in the correct sequence and to programme the activities over time. If a small builder is being used, he will probably employ bricklayers, plasterers and decorators, but may need to subcontract specialist parts of the work, for example, joinery, plumbing or electrical installations. He has to sort out the best way in which to order the various tasks involved in the job, to co-ordinate manpower and materials and to programme the whole series of activities over time. He also has to instruct or brief all those involved. The example demonstrates that even a relatively straightforward job involves a considerable amount of planning and co-ordination where a variety of 'actors' or implementation agencies is involved. The situation would be even further complicated if the house owner in fact owned several properties, was attempting to improve them all at the same time, and was operating through a firm of managing agents. Obvious parallels can be drawn with public policy implementation: many of the problems of putting policy into effect stem from the multiplicity of agencies involved in implementation. Such problems have been well illustrated in Pressman and Wildavsky's study referred to earlier.

Pressman and Wildavsky argue that one of the key reasons for 'policy failure' is that policy-makers generally underestimate the complexity and difficulty of co-ordinating the tasks and agencies involved in implementing programmes. One reason may be the tendency to equate implementation with the execution of policy in a hierarchical organizational context – the 'top down' model already referred to. Both Hood[41] and Dunsire[42] have shown how difficult are the problems of organizational control, even within unitary hierarchical organizations. It therefore follows that these problems will be multiplied by inter-organizational complications.

Lack of co-ordination often tends to be equated with lack of, or inadequate, *communication*; the assumption being that if intentions are spelled out clearly, and the right organizational channels established for the transmission of policy to those responsible for its implementation, then the policy will be put into effect. It is certainly true that one of the most frequent complaints from those 'in the field' is that it is difficult to tell what a particular piece of policy really means. For example, development controllers in a local authority planning department may find it difficult to operate the planning policies set out in the development plan if these are presented as general intentions such as 'to safeguard local employment opportunities', rather than being spelled out in terms of how the development controllers are expected to act when faced with applications for development, for example: 'priority should be given to applications for extension or rebuilding of existing industrial concerns'. Some of the problems of interpreting policy at the 'street' level are discussed by Underwood in her chapter on development control.

However, pleas for better communication or 'briefing' often mask more fundamental issues, such as policy ambiguity; conflict of value systems between professions or agencies; ambiguity of roles and responsibilities between individuals or agencies; scope or limits of discretion. This is well illustrated in Bishop's chapter on the briefing of architects for educational building programmes in a sample of local authorities, and in Towell's account of attempts to implement improvements in the psychiatric services of a large mental hospital. Indeed, we shall presently be arguing that these more 'political' aspects of interpersonal and interagency relations are crucial in explaining policy outcomes or understanding the implementation process.

However, communication figures strongly as an implementation issue not only in terms of making it clear to implementers what they are supposed to do, but also because of the *view* of implementation as separate from policy-making, in which policy is made by the policy-makers and has to be transmitted to those responsible for carrying it out, who may be in a variety of different agencies. Hence the association of communication with co-ordination. Dunsire points to the importance of distinguishing a hierarchy of *tasks*, meaning the 'unbundling' of policy into the whole collection and sequence of tasks necessary for its execution (which he sees as a progression from the general to the specific), from a hierarchy of *authority*. He refers back to the ideas of March and Simon, who distinguished between hierarchies of command related to the central functions of an organization, and the co-ordination of activities to execute particular programmes.[43]

For example, going back to our house extension, the householder or builder who is subcontracting the various parts of the job sees each task as part of an interconnected programme. However, those to whom the tasks are being assigned will tend to see the tasks as separate jobs to be fitted in to their own programmes and priorities. The builder wants the electrical wiring to be fitted in after the basic structure is completed but before the plastering and joinery.

The electrical contractor, however, does not organize his business around the building of house extensions, but takes on a wide variety of electrical installation jobs. He will have his own 'rating' of different jobs, his own problems of managing skills and manpower to meet different requirements. He will thus assign an electrician to the house extension job according to where that job sits in his 'queue' of work and when the particular skills required become available. Successful co-ordination of the electrical work into the whole building will thus require not only communication, in the sense of transmitting to the electrician what is wanted and in the feedback of information about the electrician's workload and capability to take on the job, but also co-ordination and perhaps compromise to arrive at a mutually satisfactory programme. Pressman and Wildavsky place a great deal of emphasis on this idea of implementation as a complicated assembly job of tasks and agencies, which Dunsire refers to as:

> creating and establishing links between separate bodies – *making* a chain, not just using one; a chain which, in principle, might be made up of different sets of bodies for each implementation exercise, though the more often a chain is 'forged' the more easily it is 'forged' the next time, until it may be virtually permanent.[44]

From this view of the process, the main thrust of the argument is that things have to be *made* to happen. Implementation will not automatically follow from policy decisions but needs to be treated as a positive, purposive process in itself. The theme is echoed by Bardach; one of the main conclusions he draws from the study of a relatively successful programme of mental health reform in California is that substantial effort and continuity of effort is required to follow policy through from intention to action – to keep up the momentum and maintain the 'links in the chain'.[45] These aspects are highlighted, in particular, in two of our contributions: Davies' account of the development and implementation of employment policy in a local authority, and Fudge's account of local council members' involvement in the implementation of their party manifesto. Whilst written from very different perspectives, both these contributions focus on policy *innovation* and implementation at the local level and both point to the importance of actively seeking out or *creating* resources, maintaining or *re-creating* legitimacy and motivation during the implementation process, even where these factors were present when the policy was initiated.

So here we have a view of the implementation process as a sequence of events 'triggered off' by a policy decision, involving the translation of policy into operational tasks to be carried out by a variety of actors and agencies, and substantial co-ordinating activity to ensure that resources are available and that things happen as intended. This conceptualization strongly underlies some of the more recent literature which has shifted from the diagnosis of policy failure to attempts to identify ways in which failure can be prevented. For example, Williams exhorts policy-makers to pay more attention to 'implementation capacity' and sets out a checklist of questions:

(a) How well articulated is the policy to the implementers?
(b) How capable are the policy-makers of developing meaningful guidelines for and assistance to implementers?
(c) How capable are the implementers to develop and carry out new policy?
(d) How much ability/power do either have to change the other?[46]

Sabatier and Mazmanian take an even bolder line in an article entitled 'The conditions of effective implementation: a guide to accomplishing policy objectives'.[47] They identify five conditions which must be satisfied if implementation is to be effective:

1. The program is based on a sound theory relating changes in target group behaviour to the achievements of the desired end state (objectives).
2. The statute (or other basic policy decision) contains unambiguous policy directives and structures the implementation process so as to maximize the likelihood that target groups will perform as desired.
3. The leaders of the implementation agencies possess substantial managerial and political skill and are committed to statutory goals.
4. The program is actively supported by organized constituency groups and by a few key legislators (or the chief executive) throughout the implementation process, with the courts being neutral or supportive.
5. The relative priority of statutory objectives is not significantly undermined over time by the emergence of conflicting public policies or by change in relevant socio-economic conditions that undermine the statute's 'technical' theory or political support.[48]

This article demonstrates only too clearly the weakness of this 'recipe book' approach; the sort of 'conditions' for effective implementation prescribed are precisely those which empirical evidence suggests are not met in the real world. The authors' underlying argument is that problems can be avoided by anticipating complications and difficulties in advance. But this assumes that those responsible for administering policy are in a position of total and 'rational' control, that implementation takes place in a static environment and in a politics-free world.[49]

Looking, for example, at Sabatier and Mazmanian's list of conditions, expressions like 'desired end state', 'unambiguous policy directives', 'statutory objectives' rightly imply that if only policy goals are unambiguous then implementation will be easier. However, there are many good reasons for expecting ambiguity. Even when policy-makers are able to express their policy goals clearly, relating means to ends, they are likely to face a policy-making process in which compromise with other actors and their interests undermine this clarity. Many of the features which Sabatier and Mazmanian identify as essential for 'good' policies are precisely those which political processes are likely to undermine. Sabatier and Mazmanian themselves refer to many of the leading American implementation studies dealing with issues like air pollution control, job creation, urban renewal and education reform. These are all issues which were controversial from their initial introduction into the political agenda, and have remained so throughout their history. To suggest that there could have been better policies if attention had been paid to Sabatier and Mazmanian's prescription is to say that they should have been depoliticized. This is like the plaintive cry often heard in Britain that politics should be 'kept out' of education or planning or the health service. Little account appears to be taken of the political processes already referred to earlier by which policy is formulated and 'legitimized'. These processes do not stop when initial policy decisions are made, but continue to influence policy during implementation in terms of the behaviour of those implementing policy and those affected by policy. This is one of the main themes of Barrett's chapter on the implementation of the Community Land Scheme, and is also discussed in Boddy's account of the relations between central government and the Building Societies between 1974 and 1979.

In particular, the presumptions skate over the whole question of consensus, either in a party political or ideological sense, or in terms of organizational/ sectional interests affected by policy. Whilst Chase,[50] in a recent article, does recognize the difficulty of obtaining compliance where policy or a programme is to be implemented by agencies whose interests do not necessarily coincide with those of the policy-makers, solutions to this difficulty are seen in terms of:

* gaining credibility
* reference to higher authority
* financial incentives

He still tends to ignore the relationship between interests, politics and the balance of power between those making, implementing and affected by policy.

We have discussed at some length the concept of implementation as putting policy into effect, since it is the prevailing perspective from which implementation and its problems tend to be viewed – reflecting, perhaps, the origins of concern with 'policy failure'. Seeing implementation as a series of logical steps from intention to action also provides a useful heuristic device through which to identify issues and questions about 'what is going on'. We have thus attempted in this section both to outline the conventional wisdoms and to point to the strengths and weaknesses of this view of the process. Although we have been critical of the 'recipe book' approach presented in some of the recent literature, its analysis has helped us to sharpen our own focus and pinpoint more clearly alternative avenues of investigation. First, it has focused our attention on the need to examine more closely the whole question of consensus, control and compliance as essentially a *political*, rather than *managerial* issue. Second, it has led us to re-examine the conceptualization of the implementation process itself.

If we are faced with the phenomenon of agencies upon whom action depends, but which are ideologically hostile and/or not susceptible to direct control, then implementation must be considered in terms of the nature of inter- and intra-organizational power relations, the interests of implementing agencies and the people in them. At the same time, it is clear that the political processes shaping policy have an important bearing on what actually gets done, when and by whom, and we need to look more closely at what might be termed the 'politics of policy'. In the remaining two sections of this introductory chapter, we put forward some ideas about alternative ways of conceptualizing implementation

*   as a negotiating process
*   as action and response

and look briefly at the issues that come to the fore from these different points of view. In doing this, we are raising questions for readers to take forward to Part Two, rather than offering the kind of critical review undertaken so far, and we return to a more detailed discussion of the issues in our concluding chapter.

Implementation as a negotiating process

The preceding conceptualization suggests that control over policy execution or the ability to ensure compliance with policy objectives is a key factor determining implementation 'success' or 'failure'. We have already made reference to one or two examples of the substantial literature that exists on questions of administrative control and compliance within and between organizations. Some of the literature oriented towards public administration focuses specifically on issues such as the range of controls available to government and factors affecting their choice, the choice of appropriate agencies to execute policy, the limits of control and how to cope with discretion.[51] However, much of this material tends to treat problems of control or compliance as purely administrative and 'policy free'. Lack of compliance is seen as recalcitrance, a deliberate and 'natural' reaction to authority. It is assumed that those subject to an administrative system will tend to try to avoid interference with their freedom of action and will look for ways of outwitting the system.[52] It is assumed that control or compliance can only be achieved by producing the 'right' incentives, or through recourse to sanctions and enforcement mechanisms. On this basis, the 'limits' of control depend on the amount of power (resources, legitimacy, authority) to operate sanctions and incentives possessed by one agency *vis-à-vis* those it is seeking to control. Hence, many of the problems which arise in the implementation of public policy arise because much public policy is dependent for its execution on a variety of actors and agencies which

> whether or not they all belong to a single organisation, exhibit a degree of independence, a relative 'autonomy' as among themselves: either because they are specialised, by skill and equipment or by jurisdiction, and so not substitutable for one another, or because they have their own 'legitimacy' or lines to the outside.[53]

But we would argue that compliance is not only a matter of control, and that compliance in this sense needs to be distinguished from the issue of *consensus* – the degree to which different actors and agencies share value systems and objectives and are thus more or less willing to support and execute particular policies and programmes. For example, going back to the house extension, getting the builder to comply with the specification for the extension may be a matter of incentives and sanctions; but gaining acceptance (or consensus) for the proposal or avoiding conflict and resistance from the next door neighbour is quite a different matter.

Both issues, however, involve notions of negotiation, bargaining and compromise. In order to gain acceptance for his proposal, the householder may have to negotiate and make compromises with his neighbour. Similarly, he may need to bargain with the builder over what will be done for how much. Without total control over resources, agencies and the whole implementation 'environment', those wanting to do something may be forced to compromise their original intentions in order to get any action at all.

If implementation is defined as 'putting policy into effect', that is, action in conformance with policy, then compromise will be seen as policy failure. But if implementation is regarded as 'getting something done', then *performance* rather than conformance is the central objective, and compromise a means of achieving performance albeit at the expense of some of the original intentions. Emphasis thus shifts to the *interaction* between policy-makers and implementers, with negotiation, bargaining and compromise forming central elements in a process that might be characterized as 'the art of the possible'.

What do we mean by negotiation? Who is bargaining with what, for what? Different commentators appear to use the terms in different ways. Pressman and Wildavsky see bargaining as a method of obtaining compliance in the sense of arriving at a shared purpose, that is, consensus:

> Since other actors cannot be coerced, their consent must be obtained. Bargaining must take place to reconcile the differences, with the result that the policy may be modified, even to the point of compromising its original purpose. Coordination in this sense is another word for consent.[54]

Dunsire similarly looks at bargaining as a means of resolving conflicts of objectives or surmounting opposition to a particular course of action. For him, bargaining is a process of negotiation where objectives are *traded*, taking place in the interests of reaching agreement when 'none wishes to sacrifice any objectives, yet all have interest in resolving the conflict in the group'.[55] He goes on to say: 'Continuing conflict is acknowledged but immediate problems are resolved without destroying the group.[56]

Thus, these writers see bargaining as a specific form of negotiation which takes place in a context of shared purpose or in recognition of the need to work together. Similar ideas about the exchange or trading of resources within a framework of interdependence underlie recent analyses of intergovernmental relations in Britain.[57] Government agencies are operating, by and large, within a formal or constitutional framework of interdependence which, at least, specifies the distribution and general scope of functions (*intra* and *ultra vires*). Whilst the 'balance of power' inevitably rests with central government (in terms of its constitutional right to establish, disband and determine the functions of other public agencies), it is argued that central government is, nevertheless, dependent on local government agencies of one kind or another to carry out its policy, both by virtue of the autonomy and discretion granted to such agencies by statute, and because of the political and informational resources 'possessed' by the periphery.

Yet Dunsire (referring once more to the ideas of March and Simon) also distinguishes negotiations involving the bargaining or trading of objectives from those aimed at *persuading* some of a group to relinquish voluntarily some or all of their objectives, and from a process of *recourse to power* in which:

> Resolution of an impasse is sought by enlarging the group, or (the same thing) taking the issue out of the small arena into a larger arena, each interest seeking alliances and combinations in the larger arena on the strength of whatever persuading or bargaining counters they hold, perhaps to do with quite other issues than the one in dispute.[58]

The distinctions made here between persuasion, bargaining and 'power games' aimed at increasing leverage (or ability to enforce compliance) are important ones to which we shall return presently. Nevertheless, it must be noted that Dunsire is explicitly writing about implementation within a bureaucratic context. He takes a 'top down' view of the process and sees implementation problems as essentially problems of policy control in a bureaucracy (indeed, this is the title and focus of his second volume). He discusses at length different systems of controls, sanctions and incentives which may be brought into play to achieve compliance with policy; whilst the resolution of conflict features as an aspect of this, it is treated rather as a side issue to the main concern with establishing an effective administrative system.

Bardach, in his book *The Implementation Game*, takes a more machiavellian view of the implementation process. He sees this as:

1) a process of assembling the elements required to produce a particular programmatic outcome, and 2) the playing out of a number of loosely interrelated games whereby these elements are withheld from or delivered to the program assembly process on particular terms.[59]

In other words, whilst viewing implementation as an assembly job, he sees the interaction between the parts as a struggle for influence going on between one set of actors trying to put policy into effect by influencing and controlling the actions of others, and another set of actors trying to avoid being influenced or controlled, except in so far as it fits in with or furthers their own interests. Bardach, too, regards 'control' as a central concept, but defines control as being: 'exercised through bargaining, persuasion and maneuvering under conditions of uncertainty. "Control", therefore, resolves into strategies and tactics – hence the appropriateness of "games" as the characterisation of the "control" aspects of the process.'[60] Basically, the games which he identifies relate to the administrative processes and procedures usually employed to gain compliance, or to promote activity among implementation agencies, and the way in which both policy-makers and implementers attempt to 'play the system' to their own advantage. The importance of this approach is that it sees implementers not as passive *agents* on the receiving end of policy, but as semi-autonomous groups actively pursuing their own goals and objectives (i.e. engaging in self-interested behaviour) which may or may not be in accord with those of the policy-makers.

Whilst talking about 'bargaining, persuasion and maneuvering' (similar to Dunsire's categories discussed earlier), Bardach characterizes the interactions between agencies as a struggle for control or self-determination. This differs from the earlier conceptualizations where interactions are, by and large, seen as means of resolving conflict. The distinction hinges around whether or not consensus is regarded as important or necessary, which in turn depends on the view taken of inter-agency relations. Both Dunsire and Pressman and Wildavsky assume a degree of interdependence and recognition of the need to work together between those negotiating or interacting. Bardach assumes that the more powerful will act in a self–interested way; strategies and tactics are aimed at preserving or enhancing autonomy and power, regardless of the degree of organizational interdependence in a formal sense.

In practice, this apparent distinction between power play (zero sum games in which goals have to be sacrificed by the less powerful) and bargaining (the more gentlemanly exchange of resources or search for a mutually satisfactory compromise) may not be so clear-cut. We have already referred to literature concerned with the limits of control, even within highly 'rulebound' and formally structured situations. Bardach himself illustrates the power games played by actors in governmental settings *within* a formal framework of interdependence and apparently 'shared purpose'. Perhaps less attention has been given to the converse situation, where the possession of power does not always appear to be the most relevant factor in setting the rules of the game, or a necessary 'bargaining counter' to achieve compliance with a specific policy. Agencies which are not apparently dependent on one another seem in certain circumstances to behave as if they were. Questions of this kind are raised in a number of contributions to this volume (notably in Stewart and Bramley's examination of the implementation of public expenditure cuts and in Boddy's chapter concerning the relations between government and the Building Societies).

This paradox has been central to much of the work carried out by Strauss and leads to his analysis of negotiations.[61] He suggests that 'social orders' – the framework of norms and rules within which groups and individuals operate (including organizational contexts) – are changing all the time, and argues that negotiation plays a big part in the process. From detailed studies of psychiatric institutions he concluded that, even in a highly institutional setting operated in accordance with formal rules and hierarchies, negotiations were constantly taking place (overtly and covertly) which basically set the pattern of *actual* organizational relationships. His later work has extended this thesis to inter-organizational and even international situations.

As well as arguing that social order is 'negotiated order', Strauss points to the importance of the context within which negotiations take place; the limits which different structural situations may place on the room for manoeuvre, and the influence of such factors as power, 'stakes' or interests and experience with the issues and with negotiations, in determining both the negotiation processes and their outcomes.

These aspects seem particularly relevant to the concept of implementation as a negotiating process. It may be useful to view what goes on between actors and agencies in the policy/action arena as bargaining *within* negotiated order. Specific issues may be haggled over, but within broader limits. The limits themselves will vary both in kind and over time, and are themselves subject to negotiation in relation to the wider social setting. For example, at one end of the spectrum limits may be provided by a formal constitutional/legal frame-work (as in central/local government relations). At the other, there may be no formal rules or sanctions, but limits of operation are set by accepted (or negotiated) 'norms' of behaviour.

A specific event or a specific policy may not 'fit' into the current negotiated order and require renegotiation. The question is how far the policy itself is 'renegotiated' – modified or compromised – to fit in with the existing order, or whether it is the order itself which is renegotiated in order to get policy implemented. We return in Part Three to a further discussion of Strauss's concepts and their application to the policy-action relationship.

Ideas about negotiation and bargaining between actors and agencies involved in the policy process lead to a redefinition of 'implementation'. Policy cannot be regarded as a 'fix', but more as a series of intentions around which bargaining takes place and which may be modified as each set of actors attempts to negotiate to maximize its own interests and priorities. Interests and pressures may alter over time in relation to changing circumstances and in response to the way that continuing activities of the organizational environment impinge on the 'outside world'. Thus it becomes difficult to identify a distinct and sequential 'implementation process' which starts with the formulation of policy and ends with action. Rather, it is appropriate to consider implementation as a policy/action continuum in which an interactive and negotiative process is taking place over time, between those seeking to put policy into effect and those upon whom action depends. Diagrammatically, the process can be seen in Figure 1.

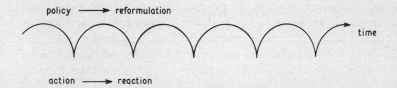

Figure 1 *The policy-action relationship*

This is more appropriate than a simple linear progression indicated by the 'conventional' formulation:

policy $\xrightarrow{\text{time}}$ action.

At any point in time it may not be clear whether policy is influencing action or whether action is influencing policy.

For us, the value of a 'negotiating' perspective for the study of implementation is that it suggests a new way to operate the policy/implementation dichotomy. If we take implementation to describe the day-by-day working of an agency (whether it involves relations between organizations or relations within organizations), then policy-making may be seen as attempts to structure this operation in a way which limits the discretionary freedom of other actors. As such, it may be seen either from a top-down or a bottom-up perspective. It is the former which is most frequently identified as policy-making: the setting of parameters (perhaps by means of the law) by actors at the 'top', who have the power to constrain those 'lower down'. But we may also identify the phenomenon the other way round, when lower level actors take decisions which effectively limit hierarchical influence, pre-empt top decision-making, or alter 'policies'.

This perspective also necessitates changing the way in which implementation 'success' or 'failure' is viewed: if policy is modified as a result of inter- or intra-agency negotiation, then how can 'conformance' or 'compliance' be judged? What may appear to be failure in the policy-makers' terms may be regarded as success by the implementing agencies in negotiating a policy which fitted their own definition of the problem or situation. This raises questions about the possibility of evaluating outcomes in any 'objective' sense. Who is undertaking such studies and for whom are they being undertaken? Again some of these points are developed by Smith in his chapter.

Implementation as action and response

We have identified a need to consider implementation as an *interactive* process whereby the response may itself influence and change policy in the course of implementation, particularly where co-operation or compliance can only be achieved by negotiation and bargaining. We would thus argue that under-standing the relationship between policy and action also requires an *action* perspective, which takes what is going on as central, seeks to understand how and why, and from that base explores the different kinds of frameworks within which action takes place.

To understand actions and responses we need to look at the groups of actors involved, the agencies within which they operate, and the factors which influence their behaviour. We need to consider actors and agencies, not just in single roles as the makers of policy for others to implement or the im-plementers of someone else's policy (which tends to be the case when taking a policy-centred perspective or implementation), but in a *combination* of roles, including a third, that of interested parties affected by the outcomes of policy made and implemented by themselves or others.

Thus the focus of attention shifts from policy to the organizations them-selves (or parts of organizations), to what is going on, who is doing it and why? Some activities will be dependent on policy innovation (either from within the organization or from outside), other activities will not. Day-to-day activities do not necessarily appear to relate to explicit or purposive policy and may appear to operate without control or the need to refer to a higher level of the organization. Agencies also respond to crises or to *ad hoc* issues and events without necessarily first formulating a 'policy'. Within what kind of frame-work do such activities take place?

We also need explanations for:

1 Why apparently similar agencies respond differently to the same policy.
2 Why some agencies innovate and others do not.
3 Why there is variation in priorities at the operational level for different issues.
4 Why some organizations succeed in inter-agency co-ordination and others do not.

26

To answer some of these questions, it is necessary to 'get inside' organizations or agencies and to look at the way in which goals and priorities are arrived at, the interests being promoted or protected by different groups and to try to build up a picture of the way in which practice or the particular way of doing things has evolved. In other words, we are saying that, since actors and agencies operate in a variety of roles, the factors which shape their *own* decisions and actions will also be important determinants of their response to the policy or actions of others.

Two themes seem particularly important to explore as a basis for under-standing action and response:

1　the differential scope for autonomous action amongst agencies
2　the use made of it

Scope for action includes such factors as: the functions, responsibilities and statutory power conferred upon agencies from 'above'; political structure and accountability; environmental pressures and constraints – social, economic, physical and political; access to resources – constitutional, legal, hierarchical, financial, technological and information (in other words, bargaining power). Such factors provide the setting within which groups of actors are operating: the 'formal' limits of responsibility or control which one group may have *vis-à-vis* another; the structural relations and interdependency between agencies and machinery for communication; the contexts for negotiations. As such these factors are the focus of attention in most studies of organizational behaviour. However, much of the material tends to be holistic and 'policy free' in the sense of taking the organization as the unit of analysis.[62] As we have discussed earlier, policy and its implementation are likely to involve specific groups of actors and parts of organizations, the 'forging of links' and creation of instances within and between parts of organizations which are distinct from the 'chain of command' within an organization or the formal structural relations between organizations. The scope for action in any particular policy area may well depend on a variety of contexts devised from the different configuration and combination of 'limiting' factors affecting the different organizations or parts of organizations involved. Lewis and Flynn, in their study of the implementation of urban and regional planning policies,[63] pointed to the variety of modes of action adopted by central government for the implementation of different policies emanating from the same department. This analysis points to the need for more attention to be paid to the interaction between the subject matter of policy (and thus the specific groups and interests likely to be involved in or affected by it) and the organizational contexts in shaping the scope and limits for action.

However, the existence of opportunities for action does not necessarily mean that action will be taken, or determine the nature of action or response. We therefore also need to consider what factors may determine action or inaction in a given situation. Three aspects seem of particular relevance:

1   perceptions of the scope for action
2   perceptions of the need for action
3   motivation to act

Different values, attitudes and experiences combine to form the 'perceptions of the situation' held by different groups of actors which will shape their whole approach to defining problems and issues and to determining whether or not action is needed or cannot be avoided.[64] How far are attitudes and values shaped by political ideology, professional education or the organizational environment? Similarly, attitudes and values at both individual and agency level will affect the way in which different individuals or groups perceive and interpret their scope for autonomous action. For example, is the local authority lawyer's caution in interpreting a particular legal clause as an enabling framework due to his lawyer's training, his own reluctance to act in this particular instance because he doesn't agree with the proposal, or a reflection of the prevailing 'culture' in the authority as a whole which tends to wait and see what others do, rather than initiate or break any new ground? These considerations open up the whole field of theories and ideas about perception, motivation and the 'institutionalization' of ideologies.[65] They also lead back to political theories concerning the determinance of action and non-action.[66]

The way in which different 'actors' perceive and make sense of the world helps to explain organizational behaviour and response. Individuals and groups of actors, via the rules they establish (or absorb) for their own behaviour and the roles they occupy in organizations, not only influence the specific decisions of those organizations, but also 'embed' institutional structures with certain values and norms which will result in a distinctive organizational 'culture' and a tendency to promote certain interests rather than others. These phenomena are illustrated in Davies's description of the attempt to introduce and implement a workers' co-operative within a district authority, and are discussed further in Underwood's chapter on development control, Bishop's chapter on the briefing of architects for educational building and in the chapter by Towell on the implementation of improved services for the mentally ill.

Concluding note

In this chapter we have tried to do three things; to review some of the approaches to policy analysis and the study of implementation, with reference to existing literature; to suggest alternative views of the implementation process and the questions which such approaches bring to the fore; and to raise questions about how well the 'conventional wisdom' seems to fit with what goes on in reality. We have thus dealt in some detail with a 'rational model' of the policy-action relationship – the steps involved in putting policy into effect and have used this analysis as a basis for pointing up key issues of importance in understanding implementation processes

* multiplicity and complexity of linkages
* questions of control and coordination
* issues of conflict and consensus

From this we have suggested that the policy-action relationship needs to be considered in a political context and as an interactive and negotiative process taking place over time between those seeking to put policy into effect and those upon whom action depends. From this perspective, more emphasis is placed on issues of power and dependence, interests, motivations and behaviour, and we suggested the need to consider a third perspective, focusing on action itself, factors affecting individuals' and agencies' scope for action and the perception and use of that scope.

These different perspectives do not necessarily introduce entirely distinct issues; rather, they each place more or less emphasis on particular issues and thereby help to widen the avenues for exploration. We do not regard them as mutually exclusive conceptualizations, but rather as complementary approaches to understanding the policy-action relationship and, in the context of this book, as providing a 'backcloth' against which to look at the cases and themes discussed in the detailed contributions forming Part Two.

Perhaps one further point needs to be made before moving on to Part Two. Throughout our own discussions, whilst assembling the material for this chapter, we have found ourselves coming back again and again to the question of policy as the 'key' to the whole debate about implementation. Policy has been seen as the starting point for action, the focus of negotiations, or the expression of values, stances and practices which frame organizational activity. Most of the contributions in Part Two raise questions, albeit in a variety of ways, about the nature of policy – what it is, where it comes from, how it is used. We have, therefore, deliberately left discussion of this important theme to our concluding chapter.

Notes and references

1 For general arguments about 'government overload' see, for example, King 1975: 162–74; Rose 1978. See also Brittan 1975: 129–60.
2 See, for example, Forrester 1969; La Porte 1975.
3 See, for example, Crozier 1964; Perrow 1972; Litwak and Meyer 1974; Beer 1974.
4 These kinds of assumptions underlie many of the prescriptions and recommendations to be found in 'official' reviews and reports such as the Fulton Report on the Civil Service (HMG Cmnd 3638, 1968), the Redcliffe-Maude Report on the reorganization of local government in England (HMG Cmnd 4040, 1969) and the Bains Report on the management of reorganized local government (DoE 1972), and

in many of the management reviews undertaken by consultants for individual agencies, e.g. that carried out by McKinsey & Company Ltd for Sunderland as part of the Department of the Environment's three towns initiative in the early 1970s (DoE 1973).

5 The term agency implies a body or organization acting as an agent to carry out specific tasks on behalf of another body. However, throughout the book we shall be using the term in a looser sense as a shorthand for any body or organization or part thereof involved in the policy-making relationship.

6 Ministry of Housing and Local Government 1965.

7 Town and Country Planning Act 1968.

8 These systems were introduced in the following circulars: DHSS Circular 35/72, 1972; DoE Circular 104/73, 1973; DHSS Health Circular (76)30, 1976 (introducing the DHSS Manual entitled *The NHS Planning System* issued at the same time); DoE Circular 63/77, 1977.

9 For an account of these developments and their origins see Chapman 1975; McDonald and Fry 1980: 421–37. Programme Analysis Review (PAR) (along with the Public Expenditure Survey Committee) originated from the recommendations of the Plowden Committee on the Control of Public Expenditure (HMG Cmnd 1432, 1962). The introduction of PAR – a form of PPBS – into central government departments tended to reinforce the need for the kind of policy planning units recommended by the Fulton Report (HMG Cmnd 3638, 1968). These were intended to be concerned with long-term policy planning and their major objective was envisaged to be to provide a capacity for assessing the longer term implications of day-to-day policy decisions.

 The Central Policy Review Staff (CPRS) was established as part of the proposals set out in the 1970 White Paper (HMG Cmnd 4506, 1970).

10 The key HIPS circular was listed under (8) above. For an appraisal of the HIPS system, see Bramley, Leather and Murie 1980.

11 This 'orthodox' version of the antecedents and purpose of PPBS is challenged by Harvey Sapolsky. He argues that PPBS was the creation of the US Defense Department and that its real purpose was to provide a smokescreen around a new weapons development agency. Sapolsky 1972.

12 See, for example, Stewart 1970; Eddison 1973; Skitt 1975.

13 DoE 1972.

14 See, for example, Wildavsky 1979; Stewart 1969: 313–19; Armstrong 1969: 454–66; Cockburn 1977: 5–40.

15 Gordon, Lewis and Young 1977: 26–35.

16 Heclo 1972: 83–108.

17 For a comprehensive review of the field, see Jenkins 1978.

18 Notable examples of the case study approach are: Meyerson and Banfield 1955; Selznick 1966; Derthick 1972; Allison 1971; Crenson 1972; Pressman and Wildavsky 1973; Hood 1976; Hood 1968.

19 Dror 1968; Dror 1971.

20 Lindblom 1959; Lindblom 1965.

21 Friend and Jessop 1969; Friend, Power and Yewlett 1974.

22 Etzioni 1967: 385–92. See also Etzioni 1968.

23 See, for example, Deutsch 1966.

24 Beer 1971; Beer 1975.
25 Vickers 1965; Vickers 1970; Schon 1971.
26 Etzioni 1968; Friedman 1973.
27 Allison 1971: 4.
28 Dunsire 1978a: 18.
29 Dunsire 1978a: chapter 2.
30 Dunsire 1978a. For a discussion of this issue, see chapter 1.
31 Pressman and Wildavsky 1973: (Preface) xiv.
32 Pressman and Wildavsky 1973: xv.
33 However, it is important to point out that these definitions are only the starting point of Pressman and Wildavsky's study. They go on to say 'We oversimplify. Our working definition of implementation will do as a sketch of the earliest stages of the program, but the passage of time wreaks havoc with efforts to maintain tidy distinctions' (xv). 'The study of implementation requires understanding that apparently simple sequences of events depend on complex chains of reciprocal action' (xvii).

   Wildavsky has subsequently revised his conceptualization of the implementation process, in Majone and Wildavsky 1978.
34 The American literature uses the term 'program' to describe the means and proposed activities by which policy intentions are to be translated into action. Unless quoting directly from literature, we use the British spelling of the word in this context – programme.
35 Williams 1971: 131.
36 Williams 1971: 144.
37 Van Meter and Van Horn 1975: 445–88.
38 See, for example, Keeling 1972; Hill *et al.* 1979.
39 For discussion of the implementation of the Control of Pollution Act 1974, see Hill 1980; Levitt 1980.
40 Montjoy and O'Toole 1979: 465–76.
41 Hood 1976.
42 Dunsire 1978a.
43 Dunsire 1978a: 48. On this point, Dunsire refers specifically to p. 161 of March and Simon 1958 and their use of the ideas in Bakke 1950.
44 Dunsire 1978a: 85.
45 Bardach 1977.
46 Williams 1971: 147–8.
47 Sabatier and Mazmanian 1979: 481–3.
48 Sabatier and Mazmanian 1979: 484–5.
49 These points are developed further in Gunn 1978: 169–76.
50 Chase 1979: 385–435.
51 See, for example, Griffith 1966; Lewis and Flynn 1979: 123–44; Hood 1976; Hill 1972; Argyris 1960; Burns and Stalker 1961; Dunsire 1978b.
52 Hood 1976, especially chapter 5.
53 Dunsire 1978a: 85.
54 Pressman and Wildavsky 1973: 134.
55 Dunsire 1978b: 106.
56 Dunsire 1978b: 106.

57 See, for example, Rhodes 1979 and Rhodes 1980: 289–322.
58 Dunsire 1978b: 107.
59 Bardach 1977: 57, 58.
60 Bardach 1977: 56.
61 Strauss 1978.
62 For a critique of this approach, which we return to in our concluding chapter, see Hjern and Porter 1980.
63 Lewis and Flynn 1979.
64 See, for example, Young 1979 and Young and Mills 1980.
65 See, for example, Berger and Luckman 1966.
66 See, for example, Bachrach and Baratz 1970.

Part Two

The Case Studies

Introduction

The individual contributions forming the main body of the book have been chosen to illustrate different aspects of the policy-action relationship, from a variety of public policy spheres and involving different kinds of intergovern-mental relationship. At the same time each is a self-contained and self-explanatory essay; each author has chosen his or her theme and the perspective from which it is addressed. Whilst we encouraged contributors to focus or enlarge on particular issues that seemed to be emerging as the work pro-gressed, we did not attempt to predetermine the issues discussed or try to force contributors into a common mould. The following ten essays, then, represent a variety of perspectives on the policy-action relationship, reflecting the different interests, professional disciplines and experience (research, teaching and practice) to be found amongst the contributors.

To help the reader we have ordered the contributions and placed them in three groups. The first group includes four case studies of specific public policies and issues relating to their implementation. These case studies start from the formulation of a specific policy, and in that sense mirror the 'top down' or policy-centred approach to studying implementation, but each adopts a rather different stance or focus for the analysis of issues. First, Glen Bramley and Murray Stewart examine the public expenditure cuts which took place in 1975 and 1976 and associated changes in the pattern of central government controls over local government expenditure. This case study takes the classic 'top-down' perspective, starting with the policy and policy intentions and focusing on the scope and limitations of the means available to central government to effect, influence and control the implementation of their policy through a range of implementation agencies. The authors highlight the apparent ambiguity of policy intentions, show how this is reflected in problems of operating systems to control and monitor implementation, and point to the contradiction between the apparent difficulty of establishing effective control and the relatively high degree of compliance achieved in practice.

Next, Susan Barrett takes the subject of the implementation of the Community Land Scheme by English local authorities. Whilst representing another example of attempts to put central government policy into effect via local agencies, this case study focuses on the nature of the reasons for local

35

authority response during the first two years of the Scheme's operation, based on research carried out in a sample of authorities. It looks at the way in which policy intentions were modified, both in the process of translating the intention into legislation and during implementation, and the effects of these changes on local authorities' response to the Scheme. It also looks at local authorities' own objectives, priorities and practices in the field of land development and the way in which these influenced their interpretation of and expectations about the new policy. Finally, questions are raised about the relationship between the nature of policy and the system of controls and incentives adopted by the centre for its administration, and about problems of identifying and evaluating implementation 'success' or 'failure'.

In the third case, Martin Boddy looks at the changing relations between government and the Building Societies during the period 1974–9. Against the background of Labour Government policies to widen opportunities for home ownership in Britain, and the dominant role played by relatively autonomous Building Societies in the financing of home ownership, he examines government attempts to enlist the voluntary co-operation of the Building Societies in the implementation of national housing policy. He does this with particular reference to the creation of the Joint Advisory Committee in 1974 and the subsequent establishment and operation of the Local Authority Support Lending Scheme. This case study centres on the limits of public policy intervention and impact where implementation is dependent on relatively autonomous agencies pursuing their own interests and priorities. However, in discussing the reasons why the Building Societies were prepared to negotiate agreements with government, it also raises questions about perceptions of power and autonomy and the degree to which co-operation must be regarded as a strategy to preserve autonomy rather than compromise or compliance.

The final case study in the first group shifts the focus to the local level of government. Tom Davies documents the process of developing and implementing employment policy in a district authority, and further emphasizes the interactive nature of the policy-action relationship. In contrast to the first three cases he is looking at *local* policy innovation: policy initiated by the local authority without any specific statutory or policy framework provided or imposed by central government. At the same time he points to some of the tensions between the 'centre' and the 'periphery' about who is or should be the policy-makers in this field. This case study looks in particular at the process of legitimizing policy from a 'bottom-up' perspective – the mobilization of support for the initiative from inside and outside the authority – and at how resources, powers, finance and skills were assembled in order to carry it out. Whilst taking a somewhat different perspective from the first three cases, this study indicates the commonality of problems faced by agents for change in getting intentions acted upon by other agents with varying perspectives, interests and priorities, regardless of whether they are within the same agency or outside it. This example of employment policy initiated at a local level contrasts with Pressman and Wildavsky's study (cited in the Introductory Review) of the implementation of federal job creation policy via the Economic Development Administration in the USA.

The second group (cases 5 to 8) consists of four contributions focusing on different actors and interactions between actors involved in implementing policies. In case 5, Colin Fudge examines the role of local politicians and the party political system in shaping and influencing policy decisions and outcomes, with reference to a study tracing the formulation of the political manifesto in a London borough, its translation into operational policy, and progress in implementation. This essay raises questions about the relative influence of elected members and officers on operational policy and procedures, and the degree to which members are effectively in control of policy and outcomes or able to evaluate the effectiveness of 'their' policy and are accountable to the electorate and party activists. The next contribution (case 6) shifts attention to the 'coal face', and the process by which individuals, responsible for delivering a service to the 'client', interpret or mediate policy and formulate their own rules and procedures to produce outcomes that may bear little relationship to the formal policy framework. In discussing the work of development controllers in a London borough, Jacky Underwood introduces the whole theme of discretion: as 'given' by the statutory planning system to the local authority as planning authority; as given by elected members and chief officers to officers at the individual level; and as it is *used* in practice by those dealing with applications for planning permission for the development of land. She picks up the question of professional 'cultures' but also considers the conflicting and competing demands placed on officers by the policy system, the local political system, the legal system (involving rights of appeal) and by their clients.

Case 7 returns to the theme of translating intentions into action with reference to research carried out by the author on the process of briefing architects for educational building projects. Jeff Bishop looks at the roles played by different professional groups involved in the process, the inter-actions between them, and problems of communication arising from differences in discipline and perspective. Above all he raises the question of who actually 'makes' policy in the sense of setting frameworks for action, and suggests that briefing, although normally regarded as a 'low level' implementation task, is in reality the focus of a very fluid process whereby policy is constantly being remade as it is translated into specific projects.

In the final contribution to this group, David Towell describes how, through an action-research relationship with a Regional Health Authority, he and others shared with full-time staff in the struggle to find effective ways of taking on board the implications for mental health services of government policies requiring a shift from institutional to community care for the mentally ill.

(There are interesting comparisons here with Bardach's case study of mental health reform in California, *The Implementation Game*, cited in the Introductory Review.) He examines the problems of implementing new policies in a situation where real change requires co-ordinated developments across a wide network of local agencies and significant modifications in the attitudes of both managers and practitioners. The main focus of the essay is on how established views and motivations can be harnessed positively to embrace innovation and change despite the existence of strong pressures towards what Schon has described as 'dynamic conservatism' (see Bibliography).

The final two contributions are somewhat different in character. Both stand back from the more specific policy-oriented or actor-oriented cases and address in very different ways the question of rationality in the policy process.

Michael Hill examines the distinction between policy-making and implementation, and asks why both practitioners and those studying public policy seem to attach such importance to it. His essay attempts to answer this question by analysing three factors which affect the extent to which real situations may come close to or diverge from the 'rational model' in which policy and action are logically separable. The factors considered are the influence of different topics or issues, the influence of political and administrative structures and the impact of different interests. In discussing the question, Hill draws on a range of different case material and concludes by asking whether the demand for active government is bound to lead in corporatist directions or whether concepts of democratic intervention can be developed which come to terms with what he argues to be the inherently inter-related character of policy-making and implementation.

Evaluative studies can be regarded as a way of putting pressure on the system – or achieving greater responsiveness to environmental realities and needs. This is the subject of the final essay, in which Randall Smith discusses the problems associated with getting the results of such studies implemented or acted upon. As well as looking at some of the difficulties of assessing implementation success or failure, he is using the example of evaluative studies as a way of focusing on the process of getting new information recognized and accepted by government agencies. He raises questions about the politics of information – whose information, who is trying to influence whom for what purpose – and from this viewpoint offers an alternative perspective on issues covered by other case studies concerning the attitudes, values and 'cultures' to be found among different agencies and professional disciplines engaged in getting things done.

1
Implementing public expenditure cuts

Glen Bramley and Murray Stewart

Introduction

This chapter examines the process of implementing large scale cuts in public spending in Britain. At the time of writing – late 1980 – the Conservative government is deciding on, and putting into effect, major reductions in public expenditure as a central part of its economic strategy. There is heated debate both about the wisdom of the underlying strategy and about where the axe should fall, but questions can also be raised about whether the cuts can or will be implemented and what will be their true extent and impact. Whilst some references are made in what follows to these recent developments, we take as a case study an earlier episode – the series of cuts imposed by the previous Labour administration during the period 1975–7. There are of course some differences between these earlier cuts and those pursued in 1979–80, but a study based on the experience of the earlier period offers the benefit not solely of hindsight about the general nature of the implementation process but also of specific evidence about what actually happened to public spending following the cuts.

This chapter is not, however, primarily an analysis of the public expenditure system; it is rather a case study in policy implementation. Public expenditure planning and control is a centralized, visible, sophisticated, well resourced activity attracting extensive attention from the very top of the policy hierarchy – the Cabinet. There is a vast administrative machine supporting the planning and control processes and a battery of controls at central government's disposal. One might expect, therefore, a reasonably precise relationship between 'policy' established at the centre and communicated to the periphery and 'implementation' effected by the many spending bodies throughout government. Our study demonstrates that this picture is misplaced and that considerable uncertainty pervades the system. We seek to illustrate this in the three main sections of the chapter. In the first section we present a statement of the 1975–7 spending cuts, attempting to distinguish between planned reductions on the one hand and actual outturn on the other, and identify the considerable mismatch between the two. In the second section we discuss, albeit briefly, two of the elements central to the policy implementation debate. First there is the question of the aim of expenditure policy in the context of broader economic policies. In this context we emphasize the considerable ambiguity in policy during the period in question. Second we describe the administrative structures formal and informal and processes within which expenditure planning and control is carried out. In section three we unpack the implementation process itself and discuss the processes of finding and effecting cuts as well as looking in more detail at two key features – the role of the cash limits system and the position of local authorities. Finally we offer some tentative conclusions.

Throughout the chapter we are concerned with a contradiction. The evidence on policy, on the administrative machinery, and on the operation of the various forms of control suggest a policy system ill-suited to the implementation of public expenditure goals – and indeed the actual outcomes of expenditure policies in the period demonstrate considerable variations between intention and outcome. At the same time, we recognize a system which induces conformance and compliance, a system which almost in spite of itself produces outputs which are acceptable to most of those involved. It is these contradictions between autonomy and control, freedom and compliance, administrative flexibility and bureaucratic rules, that this chapter seeks to illustrate.

The cuts

Planned reductions

Early in 1975 the Labour government's first White Paper on public expenditure[1] was published showing plans for a 2.8 per cent annual growth in real public spending up to 1978. This growth was required to implement a range of social and industrial policy developments. In the context of a deepening economic recession and accelerating inflation, these plans attracted criticism from various quarters for the unrealism of their growth assumptions and the apparent divergence of actual spending from previous plans.[2] The pressure of events on the economic and financial front over the next two years led to a series of cutbacks in these plans, resulting in a major change in postwar public expenditure trends.[3] Simultaneously, and in part for the same reasons, considerable innovations in expenditure control, centred on cash limits, were put into operation and these played a key role in the implementation of the cuts.

The cuts were decided upon and announced in four main stages. These were (1) the April 1975 budget, (2) the 1975 expenditure survey, the results of which were published in the 1976 White Paper, (3) the measures of July 1976, and (4) the 'IMF cuts' of December 1976. Table 1 summarizes these changes, at constant prices,[4] by showing the total reduction over previous plans for each of three financial years distinguishing between the four stages of the cuts. The table shows that the second stage was the most important and that the main impact was to fall one or two years ahead, on the financial years 1977–8 and 1978–9. As in most numerical analyses in this chapter, nationalized industries and debt interest have been excluded, because as well as being inherently unstable they were affected by important definitional changes during the period in question.

Table 1 *Summary of expenditure cuts 1976–7, 1977–8 and 1978–9*

	1976–7	1977–8	1978–9
Announcement (date)	(£m at 1977 survey prices)		
1975 budget (4–75)	1347	—	—
1976 White Paper (1–76)	340	2459	3891
July measures (7–76)	27	899	128
IMF cuts (12–76)	—	1617	1557
Total	1714	4975	5576

Source: See note 5 at end of chapter.

It is important to realize, however, that these cuts were not the only factors affecting expenditure during the period. There were also policy changes which increased planned expenditure (e.g. by £1969m in 1976–7 and £2478m in 1977–8), re-estimation of the cost of existing policies, changes of definition and classification affecting particular programmes (about 40 between 1975 and 1979) and, of course, major changes in prices (of the order of 50 per cent). Such changes make it difficult to disentangle the effects of particular elements after the event and in our view contributed at the time to uncertainty, even inside government, about the policy being pursued. The cuts were not imposed uniformly, although none of the main programmes emerged entirely unscathed. Expressed as a percentage of the announced plans for 1976–7 and 1977–8 in Cmnd 5879, the main programmes most subject to cuts were agriculture, forestry and fisheries (16.6 per cent and 35.3 per cent), roads and transport (7.9 per cent and 20.4 per cent), other environmental services (5.5 per cent and 18.7 per cent) and overseas services and aid (5.8 per cent and 10.3 per cent). Programmes escaping relatively lightly in 1976–7 but being subject to major cuts in 1977–8 included trade, industry and employment (40.8 per cent) and education (18.7 per cent). Programmes only lightly affected by the series of cuts included social security (nil and 0.1 per cent) and Northern Ireland (1.5 and 2.8 per cent).

We have already mentioned that during the same period as cuts were being agreed, policy decisions were also being taken to increase spending on certain programmes. In total these increases were substantial, greater in fact than the cuts in 1976–7 and half as large in 1977–8. This puts a slightly different complexion on the process, suggesting a redirection of resources as much as an overall reduction. These decisions to increase expenditure tended to be made at different times from the cuts, to be scattered through the period, and for the most part to be charged against the planned contingency sum.[6] The pattern of increases across main programmes was broadly consistent with the cuts in that programmes more heavily cut were less favoured by increases, although trade, industry and employment was an exception with large cuts in 1977–8 more than offset by very large increases.

Actual spending

If we compare the government's original plans (from Cmnd 5879 of 1975) with what actually happened (from Cmnd 7439 of 1979 and Cmnd 7841 of 1980) and identify the main components of change, all at the same price base, we get a picture for total main programmes which is summarized in Table 2. 'Estimating changes' are in principle changes in the cost of existing policies due, for example, to unforeseen demographic change or different take-up levels.

Table 2 *Differences between original plans and actual expenditure for 1976–7, 1977–8 and 1978–9*

	1976–7	1977–8	1978–9
	(£m at 1977 survey prices)		
Original plans (Cmnd 5879)	57,470	58,286	60,500
Outturn (Cmnd 7439 and 7841)	56,341	53,650	56,033
Difference	−1,003	−4,642	−4,467
Comprising:			
Cuts	−1,705	−4,882	−5,576
Policy increases	+1,969	+2,478	+3,911
Estimating changes	+406	−395	+614
Official shortfall	−1,817	−2,405	−1,979
Residual	−16	+562	−1,437

Not all such changes can be separately identified from particular White Papers. The official definition of 'shortfall' (underspending) changed between the 1978 and 1979 White Papers.[7] The 'residual' encompasses shortfall, estimating and policy changes not specifically identified in the White Papers, definitional

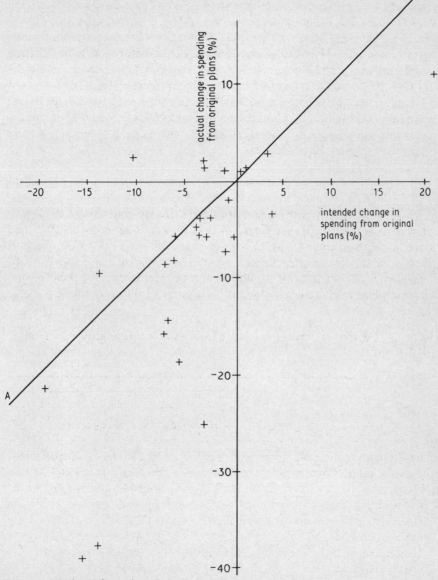

Figure 2   *Actual against intended change in spending for fourteen main programmes in 1976–7 and 1977–8*

changes, and the possibility of the authors' own errors in repricing and calculation.

The most striking feature of Table 2 is, of course, the scale of shortfall, which was of the same order of magnitude as the policy changes. This is particularly striking when we remember that nationalized industry lending and debt interests have been excluded from the table, for these tend to be the least predictable elements of public spending. Shortfall very considerably exceeded the margins previously allowed for it in successive White Papers, and it was only in the 1979 White Paper that allowances began to be made which were realistic in terms of the 1976–8 experience.

That there was a divergence of actual expenditure changes from policy intentions becomes more apparent when we consider the individual spending programmes. Figure 2 plots the actual percentage expenditure change relative to 1975 plans against the intended change represented by announced policy changes (increases minus cuts) for fourteen main programmes in 1976–7 and 1977–8. If actual and intended changes had coincided precisely all the points would lie on the diagonal AA, but the very wide scatter of points reveals that this was far from being the case. In fact the correlation between actual and intended change was only 0.46, implying that just over one-fifth of the variance in actual changes could be 'explained' by policy changes (i.e. $r^2 = 0.21$). This measure of policy ineffectiveness may be a little harsh, as the unexplained residual variance does include estimating changes[8] as well as shortfall and other changes unaccounted for in the White Papers. On the other hand, it could be argued that some estimating changes represent weaknesses in the planning of expenditure. Of course, if the main aim of policy was to reduce expenditure in total without regard to precision of outturn or to the distribution between programmes, the policy was undoubtedly successful.

Policy and administration

Policy ambiguity

Evaluating the effectiveness of a policy of cutting public expenditure ideally requires some clarification of the aims of the policy. In practice it is extremely difficult to determine what were the government's precise objectives in this instance, and space precludes a full analysis of the underlying economic policy.[9] It is evident, however, that economic policy in the period 1975–7 was highly ambiguous, containing elements of at least four partially contradictory strategies each of which had differing implications for the level, composition and control of public spending. These strategies ranged from traditional Keynesian demand management, through industrial restructuring and regeneration, to action to counter inflation reliant either on prices and incomes policies on the one hand or monetary control on the other.

The combination of inconsistency and interaction between different strategies (which were often being pursued simultaneously) poses real difficulties in identifying even retrospectively the desired policy outputs and the best means of achieving them. Thus it is not clear which was more significant, the level of public expenditure in real terms (and thus its effect on demand in the economy) or the amount of cash required to finance it. Was the public sector borrowing requirement the crucial variable? How far did the definition and presentation of public expenditure figures matter (bearing in mind the major changes instituted in 1977)?[10] How significant were sectoral or individual programme targets and was it important that each and every specific cash limit was adhered to? Was underspending a measure of success or failure in terms of the economic policy being pursued and was the emphasis in policy on the immediate financial year ahead or in the medium term?[11] Was it central to public expenditure policy that local authority current expenditure financed from local rates be controlled?[12]

Even clear and consistent macro-economic policies would produce a variety of answers to these questions. Given the ambiguity in economic policy, what was in practice required of the public expenditure system was far from clear. In addition this policy ambiguity stemming from the economic aims of policy was almost certainly compounded by difficulties in interpreting guidelines on expenditure policy, particularly changes in plans, as set out in the White Papers and elsewhere. When describing the cuts themselves, we pointed out the difficulty of untangling these cuts from price changes, estimating changes, policy increases, classification changes, and so on. It is scarcely surprising, therefore, that considerations relating to the effectiveness of the implementation process in relation to economic policy objectives (performance considerations) disappear, with emphasis instead being laid on the achievement of administrative objectives relating to the successful operation of the system (conformance considerations). As far as implementers were concerned the 'policy' or framework for action was concerned not so much with public spending programmes in the context of economic, industrial, prices and incomes, monetary, or whatever policies, but rather on the need to be seen to conform to the spirit and/or letter of a cutting exercise. In the light of this it is important to recognize the processes and mechanisms of implementation as a complementary influence to the apparent aims of policy, and to balance administrative goals against economic policy goals.

Formal and informal structures

The planning and control of public expenditure demands extensive administrative resources and, since the Plowden Report of 1961[13] which provided the impetus for the development of the present public expenditure planning system, a complex administrative structure has gradually developed. It is possible to map this structure in two ways. One approach is to identify the various departments and agencies and specify their particular function and role. Seen in this way the structure embraces Parliament, the Treasury, other central government departments, public corporations, local authorities, semi-independent bodies (quangos) and the private sector (as recipients of grants and subsidies and as generators of revenue), each taking their place in a largely hierarchical system. Such a simple organizational map, however, implies a homogeneity of activity and singleness of purpose that simply does not exist, and it is more useful to map the administrative structure on a functional basis, that is by defining the various processes – of planning, allocation, spending, and control – and identifying the extent to which such processes occur both within and between agencies. Thus planning is undertaken in a variety of agencies in a variety of forms and the national expenditure planning statement – the annual White Paper – is the product of such multifarious planning activity. Similarly, control is exercised at many levels throughout the system. The consequence is that individual departments or agencies cannot be easily typecast. Thus whilst the Treasury is predominantly (though not solely) an allocative and controlling ministry, other departments (Environment, Health and Social Security, Education) undertake all four functions and in consequence undergo a variety of internal tensions. Furthermore, most central departments exercise allocative and control functions in relation to other public bodies – local authorities, nationalized industries, other public corporations – which themselves in their turn have to resolve their own internal spending/control tensions.

This co-existence of often conflicting functions within organizations in the public sector, allied to a clear hierarchical structure spreading outwards from the Treasury, produces considerable complexity in administration. This is accentuated by the inevitable existence of professional and administrative loyalties crossing organizational boundaries and significantly blurring the definitions of organizational responsibility and accountability. On the other hand it can be argued that such loyalties go some way to reduce the impact of variety in administrative function and role, in so far as they help to reinforce a common culture and value system in the planning and control of public spending. Heclo and Wildavsky[14] have identified 'the Whitehall village', where loyalty and trust, particularly between senior administrators in the role of finance officers, play a major part in allowing the system to operate and where the unwritten code of conduct supersedes any manual. Whilst Heclo and Wildavsky directed their observations largely at central government it is clear that the administrative village culture extends in some measure to a number of outlying settlements (e.g. quangos). There are also important professional groups working in central departments, local authorities and private practice with a common interest in particular policy areas (e.g. architects, engineers, town planners). Our emphasis on compliance as a major feature of the implementation system relies to a large extent on the recognition of this loyalty ethic in various parts of the public sector.

However these behavioural factors affect the implementation of public spending decisions there nevertheless does remain a formal mechanism of planning and control which gives shape to the system. This stems from the annual public expenditure survey and White Paper to which estimates and cash limits are linked. Figure 3 summarizes the PESC (Public Expenditure Survey Committee) cycle – in an ideal form since in practice the dates usually slip by a month or more – and illustrates the sequential tasks of planning, spending and control over a period of some forty months.[15] In the context of this simplified picture of the PESC process, certain features of the system which are of particular interest in the context of implementation should be stressed. First, as Figure 3 demonstrates, the process is a lengthy one. Even if the accounting and planning cycles are shortened, there remains an extended period of some two-and-a-half years from survey to outturn. The correct forecasting of changes in the likely cost of programmes over that period is a central element of the system undertaken in part by 'spenders' rather than 'planners', to use the role distinctions made at the beginning of this section. Consequent upon the length of the process and the inevitable changes which arise, PESC is not merely a roll-forward exercise – the addition of an extra year to the plans – but also a revision of the estimates for the current and previous years. Thus the White Paper of January 1978, for example, not merely produced plans for 1981–2 but radically altered the outturn figures for 1976–7 and the estimated outturn for 1977–8. Third, the very fact that PESC involves four-year forward planning reflects the reality that political, legal and financial commitments build up to become major factors in effecting or inhibiting changes to planned programmes. Finally it is evident that the PESC process and the White Paper are becoming more significant documents in public debate. Despite the fact that in some areas PESC sets out government plans where it has no formal control (e.g. local authority current spending), PESC figures are increasingly being taken as guidelines by spending agencies.[16]

These points about PESC illustrate both the complexity of the process and the difficult but necessary task of relating short-term decisions and action about public spending to a longer-term framework of implementation and monitoring. Cutting spending is like stopping an oil tanker, as a lot of power needs to be applied to alter the momentum of ongoing programmes.

The combination of these two main themes – a complex organizational system influenced by behavioural features as well as structure, together with relatively sophisticated processes of planning and control – produces an administrative system which combines formal and informal relationships. On the one hand there is an array of rules, conditions and procedures which govern the way in which funds are provided, used and accounted for, and in all public

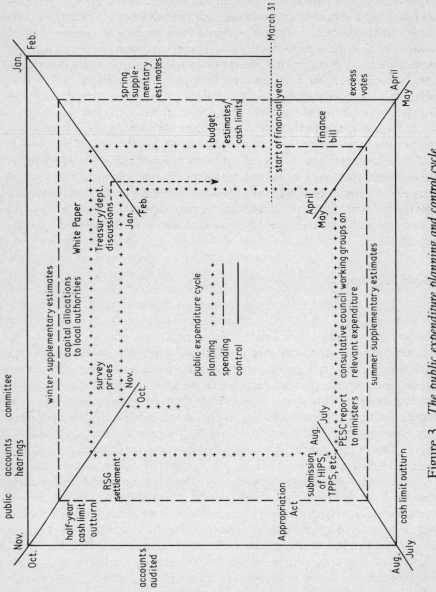

Figure 3 *The public expenditure planning and control cycle*

organizations there are necessarily officials whose prime concern and responsibility is to operate those procedures correctly. At the same time there are others, often within the same organizations, whose concerns are with planning and managing spending programmes, and the inherent uncertainty in these latter tasks demands a system within which discretion – to overspend, underspend, switch funds from project to project and in general operate autonomously – is important. The statutory relationship between controlling agencies and spending agencies – for example the central/local government relationship – whilst embracing the formal procedures, normally involves much of the informal as well. The expenditure planning system is in consequence characterized by a significant amount of consultation and bargaining (e.g. via the Consultative Council on Local Government Finance and its working groups, or less publicly within Whitehall itself) and whilst we would argue that much of the consultation is in fact 'tokenism' and that the bargaining when it does occur is between like-minded negotiators, nevertheless the mixture of formal and informal relationships bring a complexity to the expenditure planning system which an over-simple centre/periphery model overlooks.

Implementation

Finding the cuts

Following the policy decisions to reduce public spending, the process of implementation starts with the search within government for acceptable packages of cuts. Indeed in some respects this process may precede the final policy decisions to cut, thus illustrating the interdependence of policy and implementation. This section is not directed primarily at a discussion of the highly political process of finding cuts and in any case evidence on what happened in 1975–7 is obviously limited. Nevertheless, it would appear that several factors influenced the choice of where to cut expenditure programmes. First, the immediacy with which cuts were required varied from one episode (e.g. the 1976 White Paper) to another (e.g. the December 1976 'IMF Cuts'), thus probably affecting the extent to which systematic evaluation of options could take place. Second, despite policy ambiguity the thrust of economic policy did influence the choice of areas for growth and savings. For example, policies for manpower and industrial development received some priority, as did subsidies towards housing and food costs in the early stages of the counter-inflation policy. Political priorities were reflected in the growth of employment-related and social security spending. Third, it is possible to detect the significance of micro-politics – the influence, commitments and tactics of particular ministers and/or departmental officials – whilst external factors were also important and used to advantage (as with the refinancing of Export

Credit)[17] or coped with as necessary (as with the escalating cost of EEC contributions).

Of most interest in the context of this section, however, is the extent to which implementation considerations influenced the choice of cuts. Some evidence suggests that feasibility factors were very important. Thus, social security and other expenditures were deemed to be demand-determined and escaped not only direct cuts but also the imposition of cash limits. The feasibility of the legislation necessary to reduce commitments here must surely have been a weighty consideration. A second major example is the way cuts fell disproportionately on capital rather than current spending: this much criticized[18] tendency can be explained by the higher political cost of measures to withdraw existing services and/or reduce public sector employment[19] despite the inevitable by-product of a general bias against capital-intensive programmes such as housing, transport, water, and local environmental services. In other senses, however, implementation considerations were not given primacy. For instance, a lack of direct control over spending agencies other than central government did not result in their being spared, and indeed local government bore a disproportionate share of the cuts, as Table 3 (p. 58) indicates. It can also be argued that inaccurate estimates of likely actual spending levels on certain programmes rendered arguments about feasibility misleading. For example, Cmnd 6721 (February 1977) estimated housing expenditure for 1976–7 as £200 million in excess of February 1976 plans, but a year later Cmnd 7049 revealed an outturn £300 million lower. With such an information base, either the cuts themselves or the arguments used to support them seem somewhat spurious.

Effecting cuts

Having agreed a set of cuts in planned spending, how were these new targets imposed on spending agencies? We are more concerned here with inter-agency relationships, and particularly with controls exerted by the centre on peripheral organizations, than with detailed management inside spending agents like local authorities.

The Public Expenditure Survey, though increasingly important up to the mid-1970s, was not an effective instrument of control. Indeed it had been sharply criticized in the period immediately preceding the cuts for failing to control expenditure growth.[20] With its emphasis on the volume of services at constant prices, on a four-year programme, and on policy areas rather than spending agencies, it was not well developed for control purposes.[21] An earlier established system, the Supply Estimates procedure, had co-existed with PESC as a control framework, albeit an incomplete and in some respects outmoded one. While formally the mechanism for Parliamentary approval of expenditure, the real significance of Estimates is as the basis for Treasury control of spending departments' activities.[22] Estimates represent funds legally allowed to be spent by particular agencies for particular purposes within one financial year. They are sub-divided into Votes and Sub-Heads, and Treasury approval is required to exceed or switch between even the latter category. Clearly, the number and structuring of such compartments is important, small specific ones fostering more direct control and accountability whilst large general ones foster flexibility and discretion. Traditionally, Supply Estimates have erred on the side of accountability in this respect, producing very large quantities of paper which Parliament and others have found quite indigestible.[23] This issue has been brought into sharper focus by the development of cash limits.

Cash limits

A cash limit is a budgetary allocation which is not to be exceeded whatever happens to wages, prices or other factors affecting the cost of a programme. The planned spending on a programme is taken from PESC and 'enhanced' by an amount to cover inflation up to the end of the relevant financial year, and this becomes the agency or programme limit. Cash limits were introduced and applied extensively in 1976–7 and now cover around three-fifths of total public expenditure directly or indirectly.[24] Although not all Estimates are cash limited the scope of cash limits is wider than central government spending, bringing in local authorities through Rate Support Grant and capital programme approvals, nationalized industry borrowing from central government and the capital programmes of certain other public corporations. The main exceptions to cash limit control are programmes like social security where a legal commitment exists which is open-ended to the extent that take-up may increase.[25] For economic policy, cash limits offered particular advantages in terms of limiting the government's financial requirements (monetarism) and/or attacking cost inflation directly (incomes policy). And, as we show below, cash limits have also facilitated expenditure monitoring, which is in itself a crucial aspect of control.

When cash limits were first set up they appeared to be a separate system tacked on to the two previously existing systems of PESC and Estimates. A new set of about 100 compartments known as 'cash blocks' were defined, coinciding with neither previous system. The weakness of Estimates as controls was that Supplementaries (extra amounts to cover price increases, etc.) became so inevitable in a period of inflation as to be routine and unquestioned.[26] The aim, and to a large extent the practice, with cash limits has been to avoid any supplementation or, failing that, to question any such request very closely. This made the size and structuring of blocks much more crucial, so a new approach was adopted. In general, the choice favoured relatively larger units implying a strong pressure from some departments for discretion and flexibility in managing their programmes. However, some very small blocks (e.g. about £0.5 million for the Trustees of the Wallace Collection) co-existed with the giants (e.g. £5000 million for the National Health Service), suggesting a mixture of principles being applied. The figures for actual spending against cash limits reveal that smaller cash blocks underspent more than larger ones, an interesting piece of evidence that flexibility and discretion may be a more effective strategy in achieving precise control.[27]

The co-existence, on different price bases, of PESC, Estimates and Cash Limits was so confusing[28] that from 1979–80 the Estimates and Cash Limits systems have been substantially merged on a cash limit basis.[29] This introduces a new element of Parliamentary scrutiny and control which at the time of writing it is too early to evaluate, but does not alter the basic nature of the cash limit system.

The introduction of cash limits highlighted the need for an effective monitoring system, something which had been in large measure lacking in central government previously. Monitoring requires a forecast of the scale and pattern of spending (an expenditure 'profile'); regular collection of information on actual spending; matching of spending to profiles to identify 'exceptions'; and the ability to explain exceptions (e.g. in terms of price or demand changes) and to take remedial action where appropriate. Prior to the introduction of the Treasury's Financial Information System (FIS) in 1976–7,[30] only the second of these features was present, and then not in a comprehensive, consistent and up-to-date manner. FIS produces monthly reports on actual spending and quarterly analyses against profiles, and thus represents a significant advance. It should be stressed that FIS is a partially decentralized system in that 'in nearly all cases the information on the returns is based ultimately on the views of the spending officer'[31] – this applies to original profiles, timing and estimating changes, and price changes. Local authorities and other spending agencies were perhaps less backward than central government in this monitoring capability in the mid-1970s, but have progressed less since that time, although there are significant models for the development of 'best practice'.[32]

The existence of financial information and monitoring systems, however, does not remove the inherent shortcomings of cash limits in relation to plan implementation. These are that, whilst they increase confidence in the given figure not being exceeded, cash limits offer no precise control over how far short of the ceiling actual spending falls. To some extent this 'inevitable' shortfall reflects behavioural considerations, such as the degree of caution of managers and their perception of the 'costs' of overspending or underspending. It also reflects the technical problems of controlling certain types of inherently uneven programmes, particularly the timing of capital projects, and of forecasting the precise time profile of spending through a year.

At the national level debate has focused more on the effect of a divergence between actual inflation and the rate assumed in the cash limit, the latter being susceptible to politically inspired underestimation. Under these circumstances, adherence to the cash limit would imply a cut in the volume of expenditure (notional level of service), possibly of greater magnitude than the planned year-to-year change or the 'cuts' previously debated.[33] While this might be interpreted as a built-in contradiction in the implementation process, this depends upon the precise policy being pursued. For example, in terms of the alternative economic strategies mentioned in the first section of this chapter, an unplanned volume cut would be unfortunate for Keynesian demand management (greater unemployment, slower growth, etc.) but irrelevant for the incomes policy or monetarist strategies.

It is possible that inflation has affected the outturn in an additional way arising from managerial and behavioural factors similar to those discussed above. If programme managers (including local authority treasurers) believed that the inflation assumptions in the cash limits were over-optimistic, they would cut back in real terms in anticipation.[34] This would lead to a shortfall in cash terms as well, and such shortfall in fact occurred.[35] Thus central government cash limits were 97.4 per cent spent in 1976–7 and 97 per cent spent in 1977–8, while more significant underspendings have been experienced in some local authority capital programmes (e.g. housing, transport) and in nationalized industry lending (26 per cent underspent in 1977–8).[36]

There is, however, nothing new about shortfall in public expenditure, although it reached higher levels in total in 1977–8 than in previous years.[37] If a causal relationship existed between cash limits and underspending we would expect PESC programmes which were more subject to cash limits to have underspent relatively more. In fact, as Figure 4(a) shows, there is little apparent relationship between underspend and the proportion of the programme cash limited. This need not surprise us, though, because certain programmes are inherently more prone to underspending, as is shown by their past (pre-cash limits) record, examples including overseas aid, trade and industry, transport and Northern Ireland. Figure 4(b) allows for this, by plotting the increase in underspending coinciding with the introduction of cash limits against their extent of application. Again, no relationship can be discerned, suggesting that the popular view of cash limits may be exaggerated. This is on the face of it a surprising finding, but it should be remembered that cash limits have only been applied to certain 'controllable' programmes and thus do more to reinforce existing controls than to introduce controls to new areas. In addition, the sharp cuts of the 1975–7 period combined with the momentum of established programmes may have temporarily lessened the chances of underspending in certain cases. Figure 4(b) also shows no negative relationship, but that is no evidence that cash limits increased the precision of expenditure control – 'blunt instrument' is the term often used.

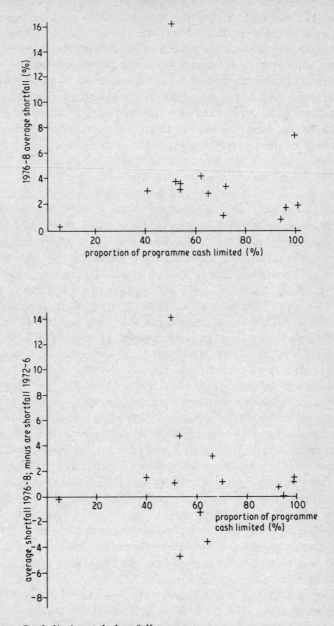

Figure 4   *Cash limits and shortfall*
(a) 1976–8 average percentage shortfall by proportion of programme cash limited
*(b) Increase in average shortfall, 1976–8 compared with 1972–6, by proportion of
programme cash limited*

We have discussed supply estimates and cash limits as the centre's main instrument of control. Although we can see a clear attempt at increasing or restoring control in this period, what is more striking is the ultimate limit to control inherent in any system of this kind. There is the tension between large accounting units which give the centre less detailed grip of the precise mix of expenditure, and small ones which are too complex and, by stifling discretion, lead to less effective or precise control, particularly in relation to under-spending; there is the conflict between volume and cash control in a period of uncertain inflation, both real and perceived; and there are technical problems in controlling certain types of spending, for example capital projects, at the best of times.

Spending agencies

The discussion so far has tended to assume a hierarchical inter-organizational structure. In fact, some of the major spending agents have significant autonomy, the two main categories involved being nationalized industries (and other public corporations) and local authorities. Relations between government and the *nationalized industries* are complex and often fraught, involving many considerations beyond the public expenditure field including pricing, investment strategies, employment protection, technology and so forth.[38] As such they go beyond the scope of this chapter. Lending to these bodies has been (and is) subject to cash limits but it is unclear whether these limits affected the corporations much, given their generally favourable cash flow during the period in question. The most noticeable feature of government lending to nationalized industries is its volatility, because it represents that part of their capital spending which cannot be financed from trading profits, that is, internally financed. This figure is a difference between much larger flows of income and expenditure and hence is liable to fluctuate sharply and unpredictably. Again, the theme of limits to control applies here. Some other public corporations (e.g. regional water authorities, Scottish Development Agency) are more directly controlled by cash limits, but we do not examine these more specialized cases further.

Local authorities come within the mainstream of public expenditure and account for just over a quarter of the total. Even accepting the central government view that local authority spending should be treated in this way, important issues of discretion in a decentralized system of local politically accountable units are raised. Although at the time of writing this principle is under ever increasing pressure, local authority revenue expenditure remains free of direct control. Central government must exert its influence indirectly if it wishes to achieve its spending objectives. Several channels of influence are open to it, of which the most important is the Rate Support Grant (RSG), which meets about three-fifths of net revenue expenditure overall. The annual

RSG settlement is decided by central government, after extensive consultations, and contains two figures which together exert very strong leverage on local government, namely the total amount of relevant expenditure (the level of which is worked out as part of the PESC process) and a grant percentage. To implement the cuts of 1975–7 the total spending figure – whose status is very unclear but which is consistent with PESC – was reduced but so also was the grant percentage. This had the effect of forcing up local rates sharply except where spending was cut back. The leverage was reinforced by cash limiting RSG. However, it should be stressed that these measures have impacted differently on different authorities, depending on the amount and composition of grant received and the simultaneous operation of complex distribution arrangements. In general, authorities more dependent on grant are more affected by its restriction, because it has a greater 'gearing' effect on the rates.[39] But this was somewhat modified by two features of the distribution system operating in 1975–7. First, the 'resources element' of grant was open-ended so that more spending attracted more grant,[40] while the use of a regression analysis of expenditure variations to determine the 'needs element' opened the possibility of groups of similar authorities attracting higher grant by spending more.[41] Recent legislation – the Local Government Planning and Land Act 1980 – introduces a different distribution system, known as Block Grant, which involves reduced grant support for 'high spending' authorities.

The other channels of influence over local authorities are the PESC White Paper, exhortation through circulars and other media, and capital controls. Until recently, the first of these was not as influential as it might have been for a number of reasons. These included the uncertain status of the figures, the structuring of the White Paper in terms of programmes rather than agencies, a lack of consultation on authorities' spending priorities, and the problem of adjusting national targets to local circumstances. Local authorities have been reluctant to budget more than one year ahead, in part because of the uncertainties generated by national policy changes and by the distribution arrangements for RSG, and this has further limited the usefulness of PESC as a medium-term planning guideline. Exhortation has played an important role, particularly in 1976–7 when a series of circulars expressed grave concern about over-spending and contained thinly veiled threats about the consequences.[42] More generally, however, central/local communications have suffered from an in-built contradiction which stems from the conflicting roles of the policy-sponsoring departments (DES, DHSS, parts of DoE, etc.) and the financial control departments (Treasury, mediated through the local government finance divisions of DoE). Thus, while the latter issued circulars urging restraint, the former were still issuing circulars urging authorities to develop certain policies or provisions further.[43] This illustrates the complexity of the system, the co-existence within departments of different roles (planning and control) and the significance of policy conflicts heightened by the cuts.

Central government has always had the power to control local authority borrowing and hence to control most local capital programmes. The general experience in public services is that capital schemes generate extra revenue expenditure (loan charges, staff and running costs) rather than savings,[44] so that capital controls are an indirect means of limiting revenue expenditure growth. This relationship can also work in the opposite direction, with authorities feeling so constrained on the revenue side that they may be unwilling to take up the permissions to borrow (loan sanctions) which central departments offer. This in turn makes the task of central departments allocating loan sanctions more difficult, for these departments want the resources in their programmes to be fully used and hence must decide, on often inadequate evidence, how much particular authorities will take up of the permitted borrowing. Attempts are often made to hawk unspent permissions around different authorities late in the financial year, when the prospects of spending on additional capital works are slight.

Local capital programmes are cash limited, but the way this is done has varied considerably from case to case and over time. The general trend has been away from the traditional pattern of giving individual scheme approvals towards a system of block approvals, often responding to rolling programme bids from authorities. In the period in question, individual loan sanctions were still required in some cases before schemes could start, whilst other programmes (schools, social services) moved to a block control of starts, payments (housing), or borrowing (locally determined schemes).[45] There was considerable local discretion in respect of this last category of projects since many were funded from revenue or capital receipts, although this clearly depended on the local availability of spare resources. While the shift to block controls is claimed to increase flexibility and discretion while retaining strategic and financial control at the centre, in practice difficulties have arisen, particularly with annual payments limits, given the difficulty of forecasting or controlling cash flow on capital schemes. These block planning and allocation systems perhaps suffered from being introduced at a time of severe restraint, and certainly the immediate drive to implement capital cuts in 1976 used very crude expedients including a general moratorium on new starts and additional individual scheme approval procedures. Whilst the principle of block programmes has been reinforced by the system of comprehensive block capital expenditure allocations introduced in April 1981, crude expediency in restraining local authority expenditure has also been clearly in evidence in subsequent years since 1976 with the 1980 moratorium on housing expenditure an obvious example.

How did this complex system of central-local relations perform in the cuts crisis? Table 3 summarizes the total change in public expenditure from what had originally (in 1975) been planned for the years 1976–7 to 1978–9. It shows separately the shortfall (underspending) element of this difference, comparing

Table 3 *Expenditure changes and shortfall: central and local government capital and current expenditure performance compared, 1976–7 to 1978–9*

		Central govt current	Local govt current	Central govt capital	Local govt capital
		£m at 1977 survey prices (% of original plans in brackets)			
Overall changes compared with original (1975) plans	1976–7	−538 (−1.5%)	−364 (−2.9%)	−103 (−2.7%)	−229 (−5.1%)
	1977–8	−1113 (−3.1%)	−720 (−5.7%)	−1630* (−42.9%)	−938 (−21.3%)
	1978–9	+398 (+1.1%)	−576 (−4.5%)	−980 (−25.3%)	−1596 (−35.9%)
Shortfall (−)/ excess (+) of actual expenditure compared with adjusted plans	1976–7	−877 (−2.5%)	−320 (−2.6%)	−262 (−6.8%)	−182 (−4.1%)
	1977–8	−1149 (−3.2%)	−425 (−3.3%)	−974 (−25.6%)	+7 (+0.1%)
	1978–9	−890 (−2.5%)	+135 (+1.1%)	−564 (−14.6%)	−495 (−11.1%)

* exceptional factors involved
Sources: HMG Cmnd 5879, 7049, 7439, 7841

the capital and current spending of central and local government. The main conclusion to be drawn from the table is that, although local government bore a larger share of the cuts, it managed to conform reasonably closely to plans, more so than central government in the case of capital spending. Local authorities as a whole neither overspent nor underspent dramatically. This finding somewhat contradicts the popular view of local government as uncontrollable, profligate spenders. More central to our concern here is the point that local government behaved in this way *despite* the very considerable shortcomings in central government's means of control. We have depicted a complex, indirect system of control with major scope for discretion and a number of inbuilt contradictions. Yet local authorities in general obliged with the right level of cuts. This singular result illustrates one of our main themes – compliance in the system – and suggests that its extent was greater than could be explained solely in terms of formal controls. Various explanations are possible, not least the fear of loss of autonomy which might result from non-compliance. We would judge that in part compliance was achieved because key actors (politicians, treasurers) in local authorities shared the centre's view of economic strategy, however woolly. But we would also suggest that compliance in total spending can conceal a subversion of other policy goals, including territorial equity (e.g. non-compliance by high-spending authorities and over-compliance by low-spending ones) and the balance between different programmes.

Conclusion

Our assessment in this chapter is that the straightforward top-down model of policy implementation is an over-simplification. In the 1975–9 period there was a lack of clarity and an ambiguity about objectives at the general and the operational level which makes it almost impossible to judge the extent of policy 'success' or 'failure', although it can be argued that on some grounds and for some policies, e.g. the reduction of aggregate spending for a monetarist strategy, policy was implemented. The absence of clear policy guidelines was reflected in the process of actually finding cuts, a process probably influenced at least as much by environmental and technical factors and by micro-political considerations as by the thrust of economic policy objectives. Arguably, expenditure reduction became an end in itself rather than a means to an end, and the justification and legitimacy for cuts was administrative rather than political.

We suggested that the administrative system was a complex one – a mixture of the formal and informal combining behavioural characteristics with procedural ones – and we demonstrated that there exists at certain points some element of discretion for 'spenders' to influence both the imposition of cuts and the way they are implemented and monitored, a discretion which we consider to have been reinforced by the absence of clear policy guidelines for implementers. It also seems that the expenditure reduction process was undertaken on a very uncertain base of information about actual spending trends. Cash limits and other controls are subject to inherent limitations, and expenditure monitoring is characterized by the fact that the most sophisticated system (FIS) is applied to those areas where central government has most control anyway, its own programmes.

In summary we have outlined a case where the conditions for straightforward, speedy, unambiguous implementation of national policies appear not to be fulfilled. The exercise of reducing public spending was, in 1975–7, riddled with lack of clarity from the top downwards and administrative flexibility from the bottom upwards. Public expenditure control in retrospect appeared not to conform to the tidy model we set out in our introduction, with the pattern of actual expenditure changes across programmes not conforming closely to planned shifts.

The fact remains, however, that despite the relative absence of the conditions required for easy, top-down implementation, cuts were made and indeed there was a significant level of underspending. In other words, the system was highly compliant in a situation where lack of compliance would be possible, due to the policy vacuum and administrative flexibility. Moreover the compliance seems to have been greater in those areas where it might have been expected to be less – for example, local authorities. Several explanations suggest themselves. There may have been a good deal of fat in the system anyway due to overbudgeting, optimistic forward planning and the like. In consequence, a squeeze caused no great problems. Another version of this explanation suggests that spending agencies are chronically incapable of spending up to budget limits (particularly cash limits) and that underspending was thus inevitable. We did not find strong support for this in the pattern of underspending. A different view would be that spending agencies do not wish to be seen to be troublemakers and that compliance with a cuts policy is a price to be paid to win more local discretion over the detailed implementation of the cuts. Finally, we can return to the Heclo and Wildavsky model, but widen its applicability to all those parts of the administrative system connected with the 'government of public money'. We would argue that the networks which they alleged to operate in Whitehall in fact extend into a variety of public agencies and that the responsibility ethic is encouraging conformity with government guidelines and caution in forward planning. Accountability within budget ceilings in practice spreads throughout the public sector as a whole and we have observed an implementation model which is not so much top-down or bottom-up as all-in-together. Conformance is the pervading ethic.

Notes and references

1 HMG Cmnd 5879, 1975.
2 Particular attention was drawn to the overspending issue by Wynne Godley's evidence to the Expenditure Committee in 1975 that there had been an unplanned increase of £5 billion in the four years to 1974–5, discussed in HC 69–11, 1976: 212–54.
3 Table A (ii) in Goldman 1973 shows that public expenditure (in real cost terms) grew at an annual average rate of 2.9 per cent between 1952 and 1970; from 1970–1 to 1974–5 the rate was 7.5 per cent; from 1974–5 to 1977–8 it was 2.1 per cent. The latter figures, repriced as in (4) below, are from HMG Cmnd 5879, 1975 and HMG Cmnd 7049, 1978.
4 Public expenditure White Papers present nearly all figures at constant prices so as to emphasize real changes in the level of public services, technically referred to as 'in volume terms', so discounting all changes in prices. However, each White Paper uses a new set of constant prices. Thus, '1977 Survey Prices' means those used in the 1977 survey, published in 1978 as Cmnd 7049, but in most cases referring to November 1976. The figures in this chapter have all been repriced to the same base by comparing, for each of fifteen main programmes, past outturn figures for the same year (e.g. 1971–2) given in different White Papers. This is only an approximation. See HM Treasury *Handbook* 1972: chapter IV, for further

details of prices bases.

5 Each White Paper presents near the end a summary in varying detail of changes to planned spending since the last White Paper, distinguishing cuts, increases, 'estimating' and other changes broken down by programmes. The figures in Table 1 and elsewhere in this chapter are derived from these analyses in HMG Cmnd 6393, 1976; HMG Cmnd 6721, 1977; HMG Cmnd 7049, 1978 and HMG Cmnd 7439, 1979, repriced to a common base by the method outlined in (4) above.

6 For example, HMG Cmnd 6393, 1976: Table 1.4 allowed a contingency reserve of £700 million for 1976–7, £900 million for 1977–8, £1200 million for 1978–9 and £1400 million for 1979–80. In principle, any policy changes requiring increased resources decided between surveys would be charged against these notional figures, although no table analysing the use of this reserve was published and, as the figures quoted show, gross increases exceeded the planned reserve. However, internal procedures governing the use of the contingency were tightened during this period, as was revealed to the Expenditure Committee in 1976 (HC 718, 1976).

7 Up to 1978, HMG Cmnd 7049, 1978 'shortfall' was the difference between estimates made early in the spending year and outturn as estimated shortly after the end of the year, one year later. In HMG Cmnd 7439, 1979, shortfall was redefined as the difference between plans prevailing six to nine months before the start of the year and the outturn revealed two years later. This latter measure is a truer one but figures for earlier years than 1977–8 are not available on this basis.

8 HM Treasury's *Handbook* 1972: 40 gives as examples of estimating changes the effects of demographic changes, delays to road programmes or changes in demand affecting nationalized industries.

9 For extensive rehearsals of competing arguments, see the evidence submitted to the Expenditure Committee in HC 69–11, 1976 and HC 257, 1978. The bases of government policy at the time are most clearly seen in the discussion in Part I of the White Papers of 1976 (HMG Cmnd 6393) and 1977 (HMG Cmnd 6721). For further discussions see Posner 1978 and Bacon and Eltis 1976.

10 Self-financed investment by the nationalized industries and debt interest covered by trading income or subsidies were removed from the definition of public expenditure in 1977.

11 Compare, for example, the emphasis in HM Treasury's *Handbook* 1972: 4, paras 11–12, with the Treasury's 1976 *Memorandum* HC 718: 2, para. 6.

12 See Jackman 1979.

13 HMG Cmnd 1432, 1961.

14 Heclo and Wildavsky 1974.

15 A full description of the public expenditure planning system can be gained from the reports of the Expenditure Committee over recent years. In addition, the annual White Papers have contained increasingly large statements on definitions and methodology and the 1979 White Paper (HMG Cmnd 7439) contains an extended section on the PESC system.

16 Blackburn 1979.

17 The government was able to persuade the clearing banks to undertake a larger share of the refinancing of export credit, and to encourage foreign currency financing of export credit.

18 HC 257, 1978.
19 Treasury evidence to the Expenditure Committee (General Sub-Committee 2 Feb. 1978) acknowledged the relative ease of cutting capital as opposed to current spending, HC 257, 1978.
20 See (2).
21 See Godley's evidence to the Expenditure Committee, HC 69-11, 1976: 212–23.
22 Wildavsky 1975: chapter 19.
23 In 1977 the Supply Estimates ran to about a thousand pages: HC 661, 1978: para. 26.
24 HC 661, 1978: Appendix 9.
25 See (24).
26 HC 299, 1978: paras 22–3.
27 In general, expenditure on the central government cash blocks has tended to be closer to the cash limits in the larger blocks. The provisional outturn figures for 1977–8 indicate that, on average, about 98.5 per cent was spent of the cash limits of over £500 million. For the cash limits between £250 million and £300 million the average was around 94 per cent; and for limits below £250 million, around 90 per cent. HC 299, 1978: Appendix II, para. 15.
28 See HC 299, 1978 and earlier reports referred to therein.
29 The method of alignment is described in HC 299, 1978 and HC 661, 1978.
30 Butler and Aldred 1977 and Aldred 1979.
31 Aldred 1979: 95.
32 The Local Authority Financial Information System (LAFIS) being developed by Oxfordshire County Council with certain other authorities and ICL is the major example, but the range of current local practice is well described in CIPFA 1980. An interesting approach to forecasting and monitoring capital payments by health authorities is described in Hudson and Maverick 1978.
33 While this possibility has been a great source of concern to outside commentators, the Treasury have been guarded in their response; see HC 661, 1978: 38, para. 6 and pp. 103–4.
34 See reference in (35), and Prentis 1979: 16–17.
35 HC 661, 1978: 103–12.
36 ibid.
37 HC 257, 1978: Appendix 17.
38 The relationship is extensively analysed in NEDO 1976.
39 For example, an authority with grant equal to 80 per cent of net expenditure would have to increase rates by 20 per cent to offset a 5 per cent across-the-board cut in grant ($80 \times 0.5 \div 20$), whereas an authority only 20 per cent dependent on grant would only face a 1.25 per cent rate increase.
40 Resources element is paid to authorities below a standard level of rateable value per head of population so as to put them in the same position as authorities with a rate base equal to the standard. The government in effect acts as a rate payer on the local deficiency in the rate base and must pay more grant as the local authority increases its rates to balance increased spending.
41 The regression formula in effect assumes that authorities which spend more have greater needs and thus should receive greater grant, to the extent that this higher spending shows a systematic statistical relationship with a set of objective needs

indicators (e.g. numbers of single-parent families). Individual authorities have insufficient weight to affect the regression formula significantly, but groups of authorities having similar objective characteristics may all tend to spend more and hence receive appreciably more grant over time. London boroughs may have been a particular example because of their special treatment in the regression. This potential feedback relationship has been widely recognized and may have affected spending decisions, along with the actual receipt of higher grants. The regression system and this potential result are explained in Jackman and Sellars 1977. For further discussion see Rhodes and Bailey 1978 and the reply by M. Rose 1978.

42 Particularly DoE circulars 45/76, 1976 and 84/76, 1976.

43 Compare, for example, DoE Circular 120/76, 1976: paras 35–62, with Circular 45/76 and 84/76.

44 HC 257, 1978: 37–9.

45 A wide variety of local capital projects (e.g. town halls, recreation centres, smaller highway schemes) were not controlled by the relevant central departments through the 'key sector' arrangements but, since 1970, fell into the locally determined sector (LDS) block. See DoE Circular 66/76, 1976.

2
Local authorities
and the Community Land Scheme

Susan Barrett

Introduction

The first part of this book referred to the tendency for implementation problems to be viewed as either a failure of policy design or the result of the failure of implementation agencies to carry out policy intentions. These perspectives, however, were seen to incorporate a number of important assumptions about the policy-action relationship. The first, 'policy analysis', perspective assumes not only that the 'right' policy can be identified, but also that, once formulated, it will automatically be implemented. In other words, it assumes that the compliance of (if not consensus between) all the interests and agencies concerned in policy-making and implementation can be assured. The second, 'managerial', perspective also embraces this latter assumption insofar as failure of implementation agencies is attributed to incompetence or inefficiency, rather than to dissensus or pursuit of other objectives.

Both perspectives tend to assume a distinction between policy-making and implementation activities, and a sequential policy-action process: the 'top-down' model, with policy emanating from the 'top' or 'centre' and being executed by agents lower down the hierarchy or located at the 'periphery'. Above all, the very concept of implementation as a problematical issue assumes that it is possible to identify and evaluate implementation 'success' or 'failure'. This chapter attempts to explore some of these assumptions with reference to the British Community Land Scheme and its implementation in the public sector by local authorities.

The subject area itself sets the scene in terms of the actors, interests and issues involved. The Community Land Scheme was essentially concerned with the extension of public control over the process and outcome of land development and over increases in land values arising in that process. As such, it was highly controversial for two main reasons. First, the questions of state intervention versus the market as an allocative mechanism and public versus private control over land – its ownership, use and value – are key ideological issues separating the major parties, and have been so more or less throughout the twentieth century.[1] Second, any attempt to change the balance of control between the public and private sector, and particularly the incidence of benefits from changes in land values, was bound to be resisted by those with financial interests in land and property including the major investors, such as insurance companies and pension funds, and those obtaining their livelihood from the development process – developers and contractors – as well as landowners themselves. The existence of political controversy and the influence brought to bear by these actors played an important part in shaping the Community Land Scheme, and together raise interesting issues about the 'implementability' of the policy that emerged from the process.

The subject matter could, perhaps, be described and treated as a classic example of central government policy innovation implemented by local agencies. This chapter focuses on one group of implementation agencies – the local authorities – looks at how these agencies *responded* to the policy emanating from central government, and postulates some explanations for their responses based on research carried out for the Department of Environment in a sample of English local authorities.[2] It illustrates:

1   implementation issues and problems arising from the nature of the policy and the local authority activities upon which it impinged
2   issues concerning the interpretation of policy by implementation agencies
3   issues relating to the nature of the central-local government relationship (including control mechanisms) established for the operation of the Scheme

From this particular (and admittedly partial) view of the Community Land Scheme in action, the following issues seem to emerge which may be of wider interest and significance in the study of implementation. These form the key themes around which the chapter has been structured; they will be returned to at the end. First, the notion of laying 'blame' for implementation problems solely at the feet of either policy-makers or implementers seems too simplistic. In practice, the process of translating an intention into action is difficult to unravel and is certainly not a simple transmission of a fixed policy into a number of consequential actions. In the case of the Community Land Scheme, policy *evolved* over time. Responses and reactions were shaped as much by historic expectations and perceptions and by actors' own objectives and attitudes as by the actual policy being communicated. It is difficult to determine where policy-making stopped and implementation started. For example, the production of operational procedures was seen as part of its administration by central government personnel, but operational procedures appeared as 'policy' to those actually buying and selling land. What was the policy or, rather, what was being implemented? Second, experience with the

Land Scheme suggests that the nature of policy intentions and the methods chosen for execution also carry implications about the appropriate degree and type of control exercised by those seeking to put policy into effect. This theme will be developed further in the concluding section.

Last but not least is the whole issue of evaluating implementation. The problems of distinguishing policy and action in any straightforward manner make it difficult to assess whether a policy has been implemented – and if so, which policy – let alone to evaluate 'success' or 'failure'. The chapter takes this last theme as its starting point. The next section describes briefly the origins of the Community Land Scheme and the main provisions of the legislation as a base for looking at what happened in practice and the question of its success or failure during the first two years of operation.

The Community Land Scheme

Origins

The origins of the Community Land Scheme are inextricably entwined with the postwar history of British land use planning. The 1947 Town and Country Planning Act introduced across the country as a whole a system for regulating the development and use of land.[3] The Act gave local planning authorities (then, County and County Borough Councils) responsibility for assessing the land use needs of their areas and preparing development plans; it also nationalized development rights and vested them in the local planning authorities. Where a local planning authority enhanced land value by granting planning permission for development, the increase in value thereby created ('betterment') was to accrue to the community as a whole rather than to the individual landowners concerned, via a 100 per cent tax on betterment called the Development Charge. However, in practice, the Development Charge deterred private owners from bringing land on to the market and virtually halted private development activity.

In 1954 the subsequent Conservative government repealed the Development Charge provisions, though they left the regulatory aspects of the planning system intact. The next Labour government had another try, with the Land Commission Act 1967. The Land Commission was established with powers to trade in land (including compulsory purchase powers) so as to enable a supply of land for development to be provided. It also had the responsibility for collecting Betterment Levy, a new version of the Development Charge, which was intended to be ploughed back into land purchases and development. The Levy was charged at only 40 per cent, in an attempt to ensure that owners were not discouraged from putting land on the market.

Even at the time of its introduction, the Land Commission Act was shadowed by promises of repeal from the Conservative party. It is difficult to assess how far political uncertainty, rather than the existence of the Betterment Levy itself, was responsible for a repeat drying-up of the market in development land and the escalating prices which followed.[4] The Land Commission Act was, in its turn, repealed by the 1970 Conservative government on the very grounds that it had been introduced by the previous Labour administration, that is, in the interests of ensuring land release for private development activity.

One further factor is important in understanding the context of the Community Land Scheme. The early 1970s saw a major boom in property development with substantial land speculation and (in the eyes of the public) profiteering, particularly in urban redevelopment for offices.[5] This came to be regarded by all parties as 'the unacceptable face of capitalism' – a phrase coined by Edward Heath, then Prime Minister of the Conservative government. The Conservatives themselves introduced a Development Gains Charge (another version of betterment levy), so that by the time the Labour government came to power in 1974 there was, for the first time, a measure of cross-party support for at least the principle of taxing betterment.

The Land Scheme

This, then, is the background to the Community Land Scheme. Not surprisingly, the Labour party, in its manifesto for the 1974 election, pledged itself to reintroduce measures to tackle the related questions of betterment and control over the supply of development land, though the proposals were themselves a compromise between differing views held within the Labour party.[6] The White Paper *Land*, published in September 1974, referred to the two previous attempts thus:

> Despite their repeal neither Act was in vain . . . the operation of both schemes provides valuable experience from which the following lessons may be drawn:
> a) the key to positive planning and to a successful attack on betterment problems is acquisition of land by the community;
> b) a central agency is too far removed from people and from those responsible for planning decisions; and
> c) an inflexible scheme can only be self defeating.

It went on to spell out the objectives of the 'new' scheme:

> a. to enable the community to control the development of land in accordance with its needs and priorities;
> b. to restore to the community the increase in the value of land arising from its efforts.[7]

Two pieces of legislation were passed to give effect to these aims, the Community Land Act 1975[8] and the Development Land Tax Act 1976.[9]

Together they form the Community Land Scheme (referred to hereafter as 'the Land Scheme' or 'the Scheme').

The Community Land Act 1975 (CLA) gave new powers for the public acquisition of land suitable for development, and empowered the disposal of land for private development. In England and Scotland the powers and duties were vested in both county and district local authorities. In Wales a separate agency, the Land Authority for Wales, was established to operate the scheme.

The new acquisition powers involved *inter alia* an important change in existing compulsory purchase procedures, by which objection to the principle of public purchase was no longer a valid objection to a compulsory purchase order under CLA. Consent was required from the Secretary of State, Department of the Environment, for the disposal of any land owned by local authorities – whenever, and by whatever powers, they acquired it. However, individual consent was not necessary, provided that the basis of disposal accorded with the terms of a 'general consent'. This covered disposal of land leasehold up to a maximum of 99 years' lease, plus the freehold disposal of housing land, on condition that safeguards were included to ensure that the freehold passed to individual owner-occupiers.[10]

The 1975 Act also included duties which varied at different stages of the Scheme. In the *first stage*, which came into operation on 6 April 1976 (the First Appointed Day), authorities had a general duty to 'consider the desirability of bringing development land into public ownership',[11] having 'regard to' the land needs of all sections of the community.[12] In the *second stage*, the general duty was to be replaced by a specific duty to pass all land designated in what were termed 'duty orders' through public ownership before development could take place. Duty orders were to be introduced gradually, and only when the patchwork was complete for all types of development in all areas would the *third stage* be reached with the declaration of the Second Appointed Day.

The CLA powers and duties were linked to the provision of the Development Land Tax Act (DLTA). This introduced yet another version of the betterment levy; this time a tax on *realized development value* – the excess of the net proceeds of disposal over base value.[13] The rate of tax was established in 1976 as 66 and two-thirds per cent on the first £150,000 and 80 per cent on the remainder of realized development value above a basic annual threshold of £10,000. Local authorities were themselves exempt from paying DLT and also collected the tax payable on land they purchased (by purchasing at market value *net* of DLT). In theory, then, the Scheme aimed to enable (and later require) local authorities to take positive steps to buy land needed for development and release it in accordance with its priorities for the location and timing of development. In the process they were expected to benefit directly, in the form of cost savings on the purchase price, from any development value (betterment) accruing to the land concerned.

However, authorities were not free to buy and sell any land they chose.

First, the definition of development land included only land 'needed for relevant development within 10 years'.[14] Second, some categories of development were excluded from the scheme (relevant development being the remainder).[15] Authorities were also required to justify their land purchases to the Secretary of State on the basis of identified needs (set out in a Land Policy Statement) and in accordance with current development plans.

The financial arrangements further limited the scope of local authority actions. It was originally envisaged that the Land Scheme would ultimately be self-financing, receipts from the disposal of land coupled with the continued creation of development value (and thereby 'profits' derived from net of tax purchasing) more than offsetting the costs of land acquisition. On the assumption of ultimate profitability, there was a Ministerial pledge not to put any burden on the rates – even in the early stages when costs would inevitably exceed returns. The whole financial system was designed on this basis. All activity under CLA – land purchase, debt servicing, provision of on-site infrastructure, staff and administration costs – was to be funded by borrowing, the debts accruing on any individual site only being repaid when the land was actually sold for development. Authorities were thus required to keep separate land accounts, the operation of which was subject to special accounting procedures (discussed in more detail later in the chapter). A new Key Sector public expenditure head was established for the initial CLA funding and the original arrangement was for each local authority to submit annually, to the Department of the Environment, a five-year rolling programme setting out its expected expenditure and receipts. On the basis of this programme, the Department would issue a block loan sanction (permission to borrow money) to cover the authority's land purchases for the next financial year.

A general Circular was produced in December 1975, giving initial guidance on how the Scheme was to operate.[16] This included the following advice, which, as we shall see later, turned out to be one of the major points of issue between local and central government in the Scheme's implementation:

> Availability of money resources should be an important consideration in authorities' initial selection of land outlays. Purchases for private development will not fall on the rates and will in due course be recouped on disposal. Nonetheless, they will add initially to total public expenditure and their selection and turnover will affect the speed with which land accounts move into profit. *It will therefore be essential for authorities to concentrate initially on those programmes that, consistent with planning objectives, contribute most to necessary development and can yield returns within say two to three years.*[17]

The above paragraphs outline the main provisions of the Scheme, at its inception, of particular relevance to this case study.[18] Before turning to implementation, two further points are worth making. First, by the time the Land Scheme was launched in April 1976, the property boom of the early

1970s had collapsed and the development industry was in a state of slump and inactivity. This was in part associated with the general economic recession of the mid 1970s – which itself led to the severe cuts in public expenditure of 1975 and 1976. Second, even at its inception the Land Scheme was overshadowed by Conservative pledges to repeal the Community Land Act and reduce the level of DLT if and when they were returned to government. At the time of writing, this is indeed happening. A Conservative government was returned in the May 1979 general election. Almost immediately upon assuming office the Secretary of State for the Environment issued instructions curtailing further expenditure on the Scheme and promising repeal of CLA as soon as practicable; the government's first budget reduced the level of DLT to 60 per cent and increased the threshold for tax liability from £10,000 to £50,000. The Local Government, Planning and Land Act,[19] enacted in November 1980, repealed the Community Land Act; the wheel has once again turned almost full circle.

Implementation: success or failure?

Looking back to the origins of the Scheme and concerns about the supply of land for private development, it is not surprising that the key criteria used to measure the progress of the Scheme were the acreages of land bought and sold by local authorities and the amount of money spent in relation to what was available. In the first financial year (April 1976–March 1977) English local authorities bought 1570 acres of land, using approximately £14 million of Community Land Key Sector (CLKS) loan allocations, and sold 36 acres, with receipts of about £0.3 million. The acreage of land exceeded central government expectations (based on loan sanction available and a notional average price per acre of land), and Department of Environment officials hailed the first year as a satisfactory, cautious start. However, expenditure by authorities represented only about half of the total borrowing power made available (around £27 million for England).

In the second year, the acreage dropped to 766, and underspend increased, with only £10 million spent, despite roughly the same overall allocation of public funds. Land *sales* increased to 178 acres, with receipts estimated at around £4 million, but, by the end of the second year, the Scheme was widely regarded as a failure, or at least as a non-event.

Many local authorities blamed central government – the DoE and Treasury – for not making adequate funding available (notwithstanding the level of underspend) and for lack of financial incentives. Local authorities and private sector agencies alike castigated the Scheme for being over-complicated, excessively bureaucratic and basically unworkable. Some commentators associated lack of activity among local authorities with political hostility to the Scheme. Others, notably those representing building and development

71

industry interests concerned about land supply for private development, criticized local authorities for not fulfilling their responsibilities under the Scheme, tending to equate inactivity with incompetence or lack of experience in land dealing.

So what went wrong? How did these views arise? Were they an extension of intrinsic hostility to the Scheme in principle, or the result of practical experience? What really happened? Was the Scheme a 'failure'? In whose terms and why?

In this rather confused picture of blame and counter-blame, perhaps three main arguments can be identified as the basis for allegations of implementation failure:

1 The Scheme had not been implemented as intended.
2 It was unworkable.
3 It had no impact.

Underlying the first of these criticisms is the basic association of failure with lack of land trading activity among local authorities, with the implication that authorities were not doing what they were supposed to do. But what were authorities supposed to do, and in terms of the criterion of land trading activity, how much land should they have bought and sold?

During the first stage of the Scheme, whilst authorities had *powers* to buy and sell development land, there was no mandatory obligation to do so. The CLA in section 17 required authorities only to 'have regard to the desirability of bringing development land into public ownership'. It was quite legitimate for authorities to decide that, in their opinion, public acquisition was not necessary to meet local development needs. Thus the amount of land bought and sold cannot be used as a basis for judging local authorities' implementation of the legislation. Even if no land had been transacted, authorities could justifiably have claimed that they had simply exercised the discretion granted to them under the first stage of the Scheme. Given this discretion, it could be argued that authorities politically hostile to the Scheme had no need to 'rebel' against the legislation; they could simply choose not to use it. It might therefore have been expected that only Labour-controlled councils would actively engage in land dealings under the Community Land Act; indeed, one of the reasons put forward for the low level of local authority activity was the deliberate avoidance of action by Conservative-controlled councils. In practice, once the legislation was in force all authorities, regardless of political colour, complied with the letter of the law in setting up land accounts and establishing organizational procedures for decision-making. Further than that, although there were clearly individual cases of inaction on purely party political grounds, across the country as a whole as many Conservative as Labour controlled councils actually bought land under the Scheme.[20]

Thus, in a strictly legal sense, the Land Scheme was certainly operated by

English local authorities. As far as the level of activity is concerned, central government was at great pains to exhort local authorities to take it slowly and cautiously in the first few years. The original PESC allocations envisaged a modest start to land purchase, rising steadily over several years.[21] Thus, what critics regarded as a low level of activity could be interpreted as:

1   Adherence by local authorities to central government policy and guidelines, i.e. a 'cautious' start, or
2   A reflection of the current state of the land and property market; the prudent use of public funds at a time of uncertain markets for development land.

So why did people regard the Scheme as a failure? The clue lies in considering the term 'implementation' not in a literal or legalistic sense, but as the achievement of intentions or the realization of expectations. Clearly, in its critics' eyes the Land Scheme did not live up to expectations, either as a piece of policy (unworkability thesis) or in execution (lack of impact/effect). The rest of the chapter explores how and why this was so, as far as the implementation agencies, the local authorities, were concerned.

Initial expectations

The whole history of the Land Scheme, and the intentions behind it, gave rise to differing expectations (or fears) amongst the 'actors' involved in land dealing and property development. Space forbids a detailed discussion, but it is useful to highlight the following points that have a particular bearing on attitudes towards and within the local authorities as implementation agencies for the Scheme.

First, the Land Scheme did not introduce concepts that were new or unfamiliar. As indicated earlier, it represented the third major attempt since World War II to extend public control over development land and to tackle the related question of betterment; many practitioners in the planning and estates professions had been through it all before. Second, the history of ideological controversy itself created a certain amount of cynicism among protagonists and antagonists alike about the longevity of the Scheme and expectations of repeal in the event of a change of government. This tended to result in a cautious 'wait and see' attitude amongst experienced professionals advising either private sector clients or local authority politicians. Third, those involved in the development industry were concerned about land supply and profits. Hostile to the Scheme in principle, they expected local authorities to deliver the goods at once in terms of getting development land on to the market; in a sense they were just waiting for the chance to 'prove' that authorities had failed.

Turning to the local authorities themselves, at a more specific level their initial expectations about the nature of the Scheme and how it would work derived in part from the original *Land* White Paper and in part from their own past experience of land trading and development activity. In the White Paper, two key elements were emphasized:

1   positive planning
2   local control over the Scheme's operation.

The Scheme was put forward as a means of extending and strengthening the existing planning system, the public ownership of development land enabling local authorities positively to implement plans rather than having to wait upon the action of private landowners or developers. The *Land* White Paper had also pointed to the experience of the Land Commission as a reason for placing powers and duties in the hands of local authorities (in England and Scotland), arguing that local agencies were better able to assess local community needs and priorities than a central agency. It is, therefore, not surprising that local authorities gained the initial impression that the Scheme would be very much 'their own show' and, specifically, a means of implementing local authority priorities for development.

At a practical level, some authorities already had substantial experience of land and property dealing and involvement with the private sector development process, in a variety of ways and using a variety of powers.[22] Whilst such experience was not universal, it certainly affected local authority attitudes and expectations about the whole structure and objectives of the Land Scheme. First, the Scheme was seen as a measure to universalize practice previously confined to relatively few authorities. Second, existing experience contributed to expectations about the nature and scale of activity that might be anticipated under the Scheme, and the level of funding required for local authority activity to have a significant impact on the land and development market. In particular, both professionals and elected members in those local authorities already involved in land and development activities and dealings with the private sector came to the Land Scheme with built-in assumptions and expectations about:

1   objectives – what the Scheme should be used for
2   practice and procedures – the ways of going about land dealing activities
3   financial arrangements – management and accounting procedures based on their own activities and ways of doing things in the past.

Reality and reaction

In practice, the Scheme did not turn out as they had anticipated. First, the level of funding allocated to the Scheme was substantially lower than expected. For 1976–7, £31 million was allocated in total for England, Scotland and Wales. Authorities quickly did pro rata calculations and realized that this represented approximately £61,000 per authority, only enough for very small scale activity in the first year, even assuming that not all authorities would make land purchases. By the time the PESC report[23] announcing the allocations was available, most authorities had already made decisions in principle about the degree to which they intended to use the Scheme and some assessment of potential land purchases. Authorities intending to make substantial use of the Scheme – generally those with programmes of development activity already in hand or in areas of substantial development pressure – were immediately disillusioned about the prospects for a major change in the scale and scope for local authority intervention (the 'positive planning' anticipated in the *Land* White Paper). This was exacerbated by the public expenditure cuts which occurred in November 1976, in which the Community Land Key Sector allocation was halved for the next financial year.

Second, the structure and administrative framework of the Scheme was more restrictive than had been expected on the basis of the White Paper or from the experience of previous practice. The Excepted Development classes[24] – especially Class 2 relating to land already held by builders and developers – effectively took much of the immediately available development land outside the scope of the Scheme. In particular this affected the scope for local authority activity in the provision of housing land. Most of the land allocated for private housing in existing development plans (and much more) was already in the hands of house builders anticipating the grant of planning permissions.

The use of compulsory purchase powers under the CLA was firmly tied to the existing statutory planning system. In order to get central government loan sanction for land purchase, authorities had to demonstrate that the land in question had been allocated for development in a development plan and, in order to get confirmation of a compulsory purchase order, authorities had to demonstrate either that planning permission existed for development or that the plan in question had been subject to full public participation under the Town and Country Planning Act 1971. This meant that authorities could not buy land substantially in advance of requirements – common practice in the private sector housebuilding industry, and indeed amongst some authorities prior to the Land Scheme (empowered usually by local Acts).

Perhaps most significant for authorities with previous involvement in supplying land for private development, the financial arrangements and procedures for the Scheme provided less room for manoeuvre than had been the case previously, both in relation to obtaining loan sanction for land purchase and in relation to the use of disposal receipts and any overall profits. Previously, activity such as town centre schemes, industrial regeneration or expansion on the urban fringe, was very much a matter of local discretion as far as the decision to take positive action was concerned. As indicated earlier, authorities were empowered to buy and sell land under a variety of legislation, and such activity was generally funded out of the Locally Determined Sector

(LDS) of public funds, or from authorities' own capital funds. Debt charges were funded annually out of revenue, and capital receipts ploughed back into further activity or held as a capital fund.

The Land Scheme introduced a completely different system of financial accounting. All the operating costs of the Scheme were funded by borrowing (including loan charges); all land purchase had to be subject to new loan sanction; all receipts from land disposal had to be paid into the separate land accounts established for Land Scheme activities. At the end of the financial year, any cash surplus was distributed – 40 per cent to the Treasury, 30 per cent to a 'redistribution pool' – and only 30 per cent retained by the authority itself. Thus authorities were not able to build up capital funds from disposal receipts in the way they had previously, and were not able to plough back disposal receipts directly into new land purchase.

The detailed central control over loan sanction turned out to be particularly irksome to authorities. As noted earlier, it had been intended that authorities should receive block allocations of loan sanction relating to broad programmes of land purchase reflecting local policy and development priorities. Central government would 'vet' these programmes but programmes would not be site specific, and authorities would be free to manage the use of the block loan sanction for the purchase of individual sites as they chose. For the first financial year, however, a system of individual site-by-site loan sanction was operated, supposedly as a temporary measure until authorities could get programmes organized. However, following the November 1976 public expenditure cuts, programmes were 'postponed' and individual loan sanction continued, coupled with the introduction of specific guidance on the criteria to be used by central government in the allocation process.[25] These criteria by and large restricted loan sanction to the purchase of land which could be sold within eighteen months for housing and two years for industry, and which could show a profit on disposal.

The procedure for granting loan sanction thereby first established and maintained detailed central government control, on a site-by-site basis, over the purchase of development land and, second, introduced strict financial criteria for the allocation of loan sanction, which in the main took precedence over local development priorities. As well as finding the procedures time-consuming and bureaucratic, many authorities regarded this as the restriction by central government of what had previously been an area of local autonomy.

The net result was that many local authorities lost interest in the Scheme, or tended to regard it as marginal to their overall activities. Those generally hostile to the Scheme in principle were happy to make only occasional use of it, or none at all, but authorities which had started out with enthusiasm were generally disillusioned and disappointed. Most authorities felt that there were inadequate incentives in the Scheme to compensate for the extra bureaucracy and central control (as compared with previous land trading activity). Indeed, some of those previously active in the land market felt that the Scheme was actually preventing them from maintaining, let alone expanding, their former level of activity. Far from the Land Scheme fulfilling its objectives and enabling local authorities as representatives of 'the community' to 'control development in accordance with its needs and priorities', it had turned into a finance-led instrument of central government.

Theory into practice

So what had happened to the Scheme and why? To look at these questions, it is necessary to turn attention to central government and the process of turning the political intention into operational policy. Space forbids a detailed discussion or speculation about the various influences – technical, professional, financial or political – brought to bear on this process via different agencies and interests. However, perhaps three factors had a particularly important influence on the scope and structure of the Scheme as it turned out in practice:

1 pressure from the development industry
2 concern about local authority competence and local accountability
3 the assumption that the Scheme would be self-financing and the ministerial pledge to keep the Scheme off the rates

The Scheme was heavily dependent for its success on a healthy development industry as the 'market' for development land. In the transitional first phase at least, it was also dependent on the continued operation of the land market and the continuing role of private sector actors and agencies to initiate the development process in parallel with local authorities. Leaving aside their intrinsic ideological hostility, the development industry (i.e. developers, builders, funds and advisers) argued, as they had with previous attempts, that the effect of the Scheme, in the short term at least, would be to dry up the supply of land for development with a consequent collapse of the development industry. On the one hand, DLT would discourage landowners from putting land on the market and prohibit private sector land banking (which was an important buffer in the housebuilding industry against fluctuation in land supply and overall profitability of development). On the other hand, they feared that local authorities would be unable or unwilling to provide an adequate supply of land to meet developers' 'needs', at least during the early stages of the Scheme.

Both the exemptions and exceptions from the CLA were a response to these pressures, aimed at cutting down on unnecessary intervention by local authorities in minor development and ensuring continuity in the development industry until such time as local authorities were geared up to take on a major land supply role. Similarly, the basis on which DLT was calculated, various tax exemptions and a transitional lower rate of tax were all introduced with the aim of reducing the short-term disincentive effect of the new tax on landowners and developers alike.

Fears about local accountability centred around the potential conflict of interests between the local authority as *planning* authority with power (and responsibility) to determine what development should take place where, and the 'new' role of landowner introduced by the Scheme. It was feared that financial motivation – especially profits to be made via net of tax land purchasing – would override planning considerations and that authorities might be tempted or pressurized to make planning decisions on the basis of their own financial interests as landowners. Local authorities themselves were extremely sensitive to the corruption issue, and were concerned to maintain their integrity in both planning and financial matters. Professional planners, in particular, were also concerned about the potential for by-passing public participation and consultation procedures established in the planning system, via land purchase under the Scheme.

As a result of these fears and pressures, the operation of the CLA was firmly placed within the context of the existing statutory planning system as far as the statutory definition of development land was concerned, as well as the procedures for identifying such land and obtaining loan sanction for its purchase. This was also reflected in the early Circulars, which emphasized that the Scheme should be 'planning led'[26] and elaborated the planning backing required for land purchase under the Scheme. A logical progression from policy to action was clearly envisaged; from the preparation of a development plan through its translation to a land Policy Statement setting out priorities for land purchase, the rolling programme bid for finance, acquisition and finally to disposal and development.

The whole financial structure of the Scheme resulted from the promise that it would not be a burden on the rates or, in the longer term, on the Exchequer (i.e. that it would be self-financing), combined with concern to ensure public accountability at all levels. In order to do this, the financing of the Scheme had to be kept separate from other local authority accounts.[27] The result was the system outlined earlier, which was in a sense a national accounting system for the Land Scheme operated in a series of local 'branch' accounts.

So much for the design of the Scheme. In practice, the government faced additional problems in launching the Scheme at a time of economic recession and severe restraint on public expenditure. The Treasury was reluctant to sanction additional local authority spending without evidence of adequate central control over local expenditure and evidence that the Scheme could and would be self-financing. There were certainly fears that local authorities, released from their 'normal' accountability via the rates, would use the Land Scheme to undertake unprofitable schemes on the 'never never' with increasing debts piling up in the land accounts for central government to underwrite at taxpayers' expense. This attitude was further reinforced by the November 1976 public expenditure cuts, and DoE officials found themselves in a difficult position between political and financial masters; a conflict between the political objective to obtain maximum impact as fast as possible, and the vulnerability of the Scheme as an obvious target for public expenditure cuts (there was little *committed* expenditure to be sustained).

The main objective for the DoE, then, became the *survival* of the Scheme; to ensure that it maintained financial backing long enough to prove its self-financing capability. The emphasis of operational policy changed from concern with the policy framework for local authority activities, and with keeping the Scheme firmly 'planning led', to emphasis on

1 financial returns – profit and quick turnover – as indicated in Circular 26/76 and strengthened to the point of 'rules' in GNLA 12[28]
2 maintaining central government control via the retention of individual loan sanction procedures for each site purchased

The strategy was to avoid investment likely to lead to an ever widening gap between overall costs – purchase, interest charges, etc. – and eventual returns from disposal. By restricting activity to schemes likely to break even or be profitable in the short term and those able to be turned over quickly, it would be possible to generate more resources for the Scheme from the recycling of borrowing power (and profits), without adding to the call on public funds.

All this sounds eminently sensible – and certainly some authorities were sympathetic to the problem facing DoE. However, the prevailing reaction was disillusion with the Scheme, the nub of which was the *interpretation* placed by local authorities on central government action. In particular, the shift from a planning to financial orientation is a good example of 'goal displacement',[29] whereby the original policy intentions were 'distorted' by the practical realities of the implementation environment. Central government regarded this as a necessary means of obtaining the long-term ends – or even keeping those ends in view. Local authorities, on the other hand, interpreted central government emphasis on financial returns as a shift from means to an end in itself, hence the disillusion (at least among many) about the direction in which the Scheme was going.

Assumptive worlds and appreciative gaps

The situation described above might be interpreted from a 'centralist' stance as a simple conflict between central control and local autonomy. On this basis, it could be argued that local authorities were disenchanted with the Scheme as it turned out in practice because they had wrongly assumed that it would give them power backed up with unlimited funds to 'do their own thing'. This is an over-simplistic view of central-local relations, but it incorporates an important grain of truth, insofar as it reflects the way in which local authorities perceived the Scheme in the context of their overall responsibilities.

For central government, the Scheme was a national policy initiative, to be implemented at local level. Central government set the legislative and policy framework and procedures for its administration, within which local authorities were expected to operate. By and large, it was expected that authorities would accept (if not agree with) this framework, and the control systems established were intended to ensure that this happened. There is nothing very unusual in this typical 'top down' approach to policy implementation. However, it does assume that the implementation agencies, in this case the local authorities, concur with or at least share an understanding of central policy objectives and priorities.

In practice, local authorities not only came to the Scheme with built-in assumptions and expectations about its scope and objectives, but also *interpreted* central government policy in the light of their own particular 'assumptive world' or local perspective.[30] Local values, perceptions, motivations and priorities were not necessarily coterminous with those of central government.

First, the Land Scheme was one of several government policy initiatives being 'pushed' from the centre. Authorities had to assess the relative importance given by central government to the implementation of the Land Scheme as compared with, say, the Industrial Strategy, Inner Cities, or the new Housing Strategies and Investment Programmes. In the absence of any clear directive (given that authorities were also being told to cut back expenditure and not to employ extra staff), the money being allocated to the Land Scheme in comparison with other policy areas was as good a way as any to judge the strength of central government intentions.

Second, local authorities were not special agencies set up to operate the Land Scheme (by contrast with the Land Authority for Wales). As autonomous political bodies, local authorities are policy-makers as well as implementers, setting their own priorities for action according to their own interpretation of the area's needs and opportunities. The Land Scheme was just one more function added to the list of their responsibilities, to be 'fitted in' with other policy and priorities, and with existing practice and procedures making up the total spectrum of local authority activities.

In practice, there was remarkable commonality of objectives in the land and development field between authorities of differing political complexion. By and large, most were concerned with land trading and development activity, not as an end in itself – or purely as a commercial enterprise – but as a means of achieving broader economic and social objectives, such as providing housing and jobs for the people in the area, improving the environment and economic base. At the same time, authorities varied enormously in the way that they saw the Scheme being used to further these kinds of objectives, depending, for example, on traditional attitudes to intervention and positive action. The degree of priority accorded to the Land Scheme at local level was therefore a function of the

1 political stance
2 perception of central government priority
3 relationship to local policy and priorities
4 prevailing attitude towards intervention or activism

If this rather different view is taken of local authorities as separate political bodies with existing policy systems into which the Land Scheme was 'thrust' from above, it seems less surprising that authorities did not share central government's emphasis on financial benefits or their concern with national 'book balancing'. Whilst central government was looking for short-term returns as a means of generating financial growth, local authorities were looking to the longer term benefits to arise from development itself – partly financial, but also economic and social. Thus there was also conflict over the time horizon for expected benefit from the Scheme. Authorities' perceptions were clearly also coloured by their normal accounting horizons for other public schemes – normally expecting to clear capital debt over thirty years or more.

Last, authorities perceived the management of the Scheme as essentially a local affair – it was supposed to enable *them* to control development according to *their* priorities. This was not just a matter of taking the White Paper objective literally, but, as indicated earlier, very much an expectation based on past experience of freedom and local discretion in this area. There was thus a major appreciative gap between central government 'policy-makers' and local authority 'implementers'. What the DoE regarded as sensible survival tactics were seen by local authorities as restrictive practices and a distortion of the Scheme's objectives. What local authorities regarded as sensible long-term investments – or getting on with urgent local priorities – were viewed by DoE as attempts to use the Scheme for irresponsible, loss-making schemes.

Further implications

This chapter has suggested that the political controversy surrounding land policy and the long history of attempts to extend public control in this field played an important part in shaping the Community Land Scheme and responses to it. At the same time, it has focused mainly on the reactions and responses to the Scheme observed among English local authorities and the relationship between local and central government in the implementation process. This focus suggests that some of the 'problems' experienced in operating the Scheme stemmed from differing expectations, and the intrinsic differences in interests and priorities between them, rather than from any 'conspiracy' on the part of central government to take the Scheme out of the hands of local authorities, or particular reluctance in local government to implement the legislation.

At the beginning of the chapter, two specific issues were introduced concerning the relationship between central and local government as 'policy-makers' and 'implementers':

1   The inappropriateness of viewing implementation as a simple transmission of policy into action.
2   The need for a 'match' between policy intentions, the world of the implementers and the system of administration and control adopted to give effect to policy.

In the case of the Land Scheme, the legislation clearly defined the local authority as the implementation agency, and yet in practice it is not so simple to distinguish roles or to determine where policy-making stopped and implementation started. If the *Land* White Paper is taken as the statement of government policy, then all that followed could be regarded as 'implementation' – including the process of translating the original intention into legislation, the production of operational policy and procedures as well as action by the local authority. This perspective fits with the way in which central government officials viewed the Scheme and their responsibility for putting it into effect. Their task was to get the Scheme off the ground. The various modifications and adjustments made both in drawing up the legislation and in subsequent Circulars and advice notes were a necessary part of the process of making the scheme workable in the face of operational constraints.

However, from the local authority's 'implementer' viewpoint, implementation was a matter of actually doing something on the ground (or deciding not to), while policy was the framework which actually shaped or controlled its actions. At a practical level, the original White Paper intentions were less relevant as a policy framework than the detailed administrative 'policy' and procedures controlling what land might or might not be purchased and the availability of finance. If this 'implementer's' definition of policy is taken, the policy-making process continued in parallel with implementation. Policy evolved in the early stages mostly in response to external circumstances (such as the public expenditure cuts) but later very much in response to experience in implementing the Scheme. No less than ten Circulars and nineteen Guidance Notes emanated from the DoE during the three years of the Scheme; each reflecting changes to, or guidance on the interpretation of, policy and procedures. The policy-implementation relationship might better be described as a process of action and reaction.

However, this itself raises questions about who actually made the policy in the case of the Land Scheme and what sort of objectives or criteria actually shaped local authority action. Politicians clearly initiated the Scheme, but civil servants were responsible for operational policy and procedures. The chapter has discussed the kinds of pressures brought to bear on these officials and the problems they faced in getting the Scheme off the ground during an economic recession. However, the criterion which appeared to dominate the administrative system was public accountability – especially the control and stewardship of public funds. In a book about the use made of social policy research in the US War on Poverty programme,[31] Walter Williams concludes (among other things) that government administrators tend to be preoccupied with public accountability rather than with the effectiveness of outcomes: 'In carrying out his public trust with public funds, a program operator likes to be able to open his books and to show that he spent all his money, and that he spent it in a responsible and prudent manner.'[32]

Williams goes on to comment that, for new social programmes, preoccupation with public accountability also extends to control, the concern being: 'that the whole program might run wild and cause a public scandal'.[33] The administrative system adopted for the Land Scheme clearly displayed these tendencies, and it is interesting to speculate how far this would have been the case regardless of the economic circumstances in which the Scheme was launched – which at the time were used to justify the need for strict central control over local authority activities. In any event, the important point is whether the emphasis on control was appropriate. Local authorities were under no obligation to buy and sell land, nor were they dependent on the Land Scheme to justify their existence. Performance therefore depended largely on their own motivation to act. Yet the administrative system was designed to control and regulate rather than to promote or encourage local authority activity.

Contrary to their expectations, authorities found that they were neither in control of what land might be bought where, nor able to gain a great deal of direct financial benefit from land trading activity. In effect, they were being asked to act as 'agents' for central government but without the request being backed by either the means to coerce them to act, or incentives to make it worth their while. The net result can be summed up as overkill and underspend. Underspend itself threatened the survival of the Scheme (funds not spent were taken away) and the DoE began to think in terms of *incentives* to activity. During 1978, the financial criteria for loan sanction were relaxed, and authorities offered greater freedom of manoeuvre via the reintroduction of block loans and rolling programmes and more latitude in the use of disposal receipts.[34] Unfortunately the effect of this more 'promotional' approach cannot be tested; before these measures had time to take effect the Scheme was overtaken by the general election.

Finally, what of success or failure? The chapter as a whole demonstrates the difficulty of making an 'objective' assessment of the Scheme. It all depends who you are, where you are standing and which way you are looking. Given the whole spectrum of 'policy' – White Paper, legislation, Circulars, advice notes –

there are many different objectives or criteria against which the Scheme might be judged. For example:

1 profit on individual land transactions
2 physical achievement of development on sites according to plan
3 occupation of development with the right kind of tenant, for example, employers creating new jobs
4 full spending of a year's loan allocation
5 speed of transactions – no 'delays'
6 fulfilling programme targets for acreages of land bought and sold
7 facilitating the release of land for private housebuilding
8 the extent of the contribution to the solution of specific local planning problems, e.g. vacant urban land

Different actors will have different perceptions of success or failure depending on the priority they accord to different objectives. The question is, which objectives took priority – and whose were they?

This chapter has pointed to the tension between the original idea of a scheme based within the framework of local priorities and central government's concern with overall financial control and accountability. To a certain extent, the latter was achieved at the expense of the former, and at the expense of a high level of land trading activity. Although the chapter shows how and why this was the case, in the final analysis it was the result that counted. As far as the outside world was concerned, the Scheme appeared to have little or no impact in terms of action on the ground. Ironically, the very measures designed to protect the development industry and to ensure the proper use of public funds became the butt of criticism, some of it from those interests. The Scheme was seen to have no impact because it was bogged down in bureaucratic and 'unworkable' procedures. Most of this chapter has been concerned with trying to understand and evaluate the *process* of implementing the Land Scheme. Perhaps the final lesson to learn from this experience is that process and procedure cannot be a substitute for outcomes.

Notes and references

1 See, for example, Ashworth 1954; Cherry 1972.
2 For a full description of the research see Barrett, Boddy and Stewart, 1979.
3 A detailed account of the origins, objectives and provisions of the 1947 Town and Country Planning Act is contained in Cullingworth 1975.
4 For a discussion and evaluation of the Land Commission experience see Drewitt 1973; also Cox 1980.
5 See, for example, Marriott 1967, and Ambrose and Colenutt 1975. Both books examine the development of the property industry since World War II and the roles of different actors and agencies involved in it. Marriott concentrates on the 'boom' of the 1960s, whilst Ambrose and Colenutt focus on the situation in the early 1970s.

6 There was considerable pressure within the Labour party for complete land nationalization; see, for example, Brocklebank *et al.* 1973, and Battersea Redevelopment Action Group 1975. The political context surrounding the introduction of the *Land* White Paper is discussed in chapter 8 of Massey and Catalano 1978.

7 HMG Cmnd 5730, 1974, paras 15 and 16.

8 Community Land Act 1975.

9 Development Land Tax Act 1976.

10 The General Disposal Consent was included as Annex D to DoE Circular 26/76, 1976.

11 Community Land Act 1975, section 17.

12 Community Land Act 1975, Schedule 6.

13 Base values were derived either from the cost of the land to the vendor or 110 per cent of current use value (whichever was higher) with additions in respect of other items, e.g. certain improvements. Development Land Tax (DLT) was chargeable on a disposal of land by sale or lease, or when development commenced (in which case a disposal at market value was 'deemed' to have occurred). There were also several categories of exemptions and deferments and complex interactions with other taxes, e.g. Capital Gains.

14 Community Land Act 1975, section 2.

15 *Exempt* development, set out in Schedule 1 to the Act, was excluded entirely from the powers of the Act, and covered development for which planning permission was granted by virtue of a general development order under the Town and Country Planning Act 1971 and development on land used for agriculture or forestry for the purpose of that use (including the winning and working of agricultural minerals, but excluding the building of houses).

   Excepted development, specified by Regulation, was excluded from the *duties* of the Act, but included in the scope of the general power of acquisition contained in section 15 (though special justification was required if authorities wished to acquire land for development in these categories). In summary, excepted development covered *inter alia* three main groups:

   1 development in the 'pipeline', i.e. development for which planning permission had been granted or for which land had been acquired by a residential or industrial builder/contractor prior to 12 September 1974.

   2 minor developments – up to a threshold square footage
                              – changes of use
                              – alterations and extensions

   3 the building of a single dwelling house

   For full details of Excepted Development Classes see Schedule to Community Land (Excepted Development) Regulations 1976. In all cases the term 'development' is as defined by the 1971 Town and Country Planning Act.

16 DoE Circular 121/75, 1975.

17 DoE Circular 121/75, 1975, para. 60.

18 For a fuller summary of the Scheme see Barrett, Boddy and Stewart 1979: 106–112, or DoE Circular 121/75, 1975.

19 Local Government Planning and Land Act 1980.

20 See Gazzard 1978.

21 The original estimates for total expenditure in England, Scotland and Wales on 'Community ownership of development land' in the Public Expenditure Survey Committee report published in February 1976 were:

	1975–6	1976–7	1977–8	1978–9	1979–80
£m at 1975 survey prices	1.0	31.3	76.7	102	102

(HMG Cmnd 6393, 1976: 73).

22 New Towns and expanded town developments are the most obvious examples. For a detailed account of the activities of one local authority using the Town Development Act 1952 see Harloe 1975. During the 1960s a number of the larger urban authorities gained experience with town centre redevelopment, often in partnership with development companies. Many local authorities have been involved in the provision of land for industrial development using powers under The Local Authorities (Land) Act 1963, special local Acts, or more latterly, general enabling provisions contained in the Local Government Act 1972.

23 HMG Cmnd 6393, 1976.

24 See (15) above.

25 DoE GNLA/12, 1976, issued to Chief Executives of English local authorities, Joint Planning Boards and New Town Development Corporations.

26 DoE Circular 121/75, 1975, see particularly para 12; and DoE Circular 26/76, 1976: paras 4–7 and Annex A.

27 This meant:

  1 providing public funding to get the Scheme off the ground
  2 finding a means to service debt charges that did not use rate revenue
  3 establishing a means of keeping track of expenditure and receipts for both national and local accounting purposes – and for the calculation of net borrowing requirements for the Scheme as a whole

28 DoE GNLA/12, 1976: paras 11–13. Para. 13 starts, 'These criteria are tough, particularly as regards the short-term financial considerations.'

29 The concept of goal displacement is discussed in a variety of contexts in Hill 1972: chapter 5.

30 See, for example, Young 1979 and Young and Mills 1980.

31 Williams 1971.

32 Williams 1971: 135.

33 Williams 1971: 135.

34 See DoE Circular 44/78, 1978: DoE GNLA/19, 1978.

3

The public implementation of private housing policy:
relations between government and the building societies in the 1970s

Martin Boddy

Support for home ownership and for its continued expansion has become a central component of government housing policy in Britain. The Conservative government's White Paper *Fair Deal for Housing* argued in 1971 that:

> Home ownership is the most rewarding form of house tenure. It satisfies a deep and natural desire on the part of the householder to have independent control of the house that shelters him and his family. It gives him greatest possible security against the loss of his home; and particularly against price changes that may threaten his ability to keep it. If the householder buys his house on mortgage he builds up by steady saving a capital asset for him and his dependents.[1]

In 1973 the government, observing that 'most people want to own their own home', declared its intention to 'reinforce the momentum towards home ownership'.[2] This objective may be readily identified with the Conservative ideal of the property-owning democracy; but by the 1970s the Labour party was as firmly committed to home ownership as were the Conservatives in *Fair Deal for Housing*. According to the Labour government's Green Paper *Housing Policy* in 1977:

> The Government welcome this trend towards home ownership which gives many people the kind of home they want . . . [and] . . . reduces the demands made on the public sector. . . . The Government will therefore promote measures to widen still further the opportunities for home ownership.[3]

Policy and Action

The crucial role of the building societies in furthering this policy was recognized in the Green Paper, which observed that they 'occupy a pivotal position in the growth of home ownership'[4] and, more generally:

> Their dominant role in financing home ownership is probably unique among countries where home ownership is the largest tenure, and places their operations at the centre of housing policy. . . .[5] The Government hope and expect that the building societies will be ready to shoulder still greater responsibility and to extend their voluntary co-operation with central and local government in the expansion of home ownership within the framework of national housing policy.[6]

The Green Paper identified as the main obstacles to the steady growth of home ownership the problems of, first, entry into home ownership and the terms on which mortgages are made available and, second, securing a stable and adequate supply of mortgage funds.[7]

The extent to which these problems may be overcome and the general policy aims of central government relating to owner occupation realized is, however, dependent upon the activities of the building societies themselves and a range of other agencies operating in the private sector; these are autonomous, in a formal sense, from the public sector and pursue their own diverse aims and objectives. The extent to which government can actively seek to implement policy in this field, rather than simply identify a preferred course of events, is therefore dependent on the nature of its relationship with these agencies; and as Murie *et al.* have observed, policy in relation to home ownership 'is characterised by government attempts to influence and enable rather than control'.[8] This chapter analyses the relationship between government and the building societies, focusing in particular on the period of Labour government from 1974 to 1979. It identifies the growth and development of closer working relations between government and the building societies in the 1970s, seeks to explain this growth and the particular character of the relationship which has developed, and examines the significance of this changing relationship in relation to the aims of government housing policy and the objectives of the building societies. Two specific examples of closer working relations are looked at, the first relating to the supply of mortgage funds and the second to the problem of entry into home ownership.[9] First, however, it is necessary to sketch in, briefly, the role and objectives of the building societies and the nature of the legal framework within which they operate.

The building societies

Building societies are the main source of loans for house purchase in Britain. Local authorities, banks and insurance companies also provide loans, but in the 1970s the societies accounted for 80 per cent of all lending for house purchase by these four institutions. Local authorities accounted for a further 12 per cent, banks 6 per cent and insurance companies 2 per cent. Since most households borrow in order to buy a house, the societies are thus the major overall source of finance for house purchase.[10] The societies are also major financial institutions in their own right, raising funds from the personal sector in competition with a range of other institutions. With, collectively, total assets at the end of 1978 of £39,538 million,[11] they are second only to the insurance companies in terms of asset size.

Role and objectives

Building societies' objectives are a combination of asset growth, concern for the security of investors' money, 'social responsibility' as a form of enlightened self-interest, the promotion of thrift and home ownership and, finally, freedom from government control. Building societies are non-profitmaking mutual institutions, equivalent in status to friendly societies, but they act in many respects like commercially orientated financial institutions; the general manager of the Bristol and West Building Society is reported as saying that 'societies are run as commercial enterprises and not as extensions of the welfare state',[12] and Williams has suggested that, in the pursuit of asset growth, 'investment has become the primary concern with lending on mortgages being an outcome of it'.[13] Being 'mutual' institutions, societies do not distribute profits, nor do they need to demonstrate growth in order to attract subscribers to new share issues. They do, however, strive for commercial efficiency, minimizing the operating margin between mortgage and share rates in order to offer investors the maximum return and thus to attract investment: 'the time-honoured concept of building societies as part of the self help movement is steadily giving way to more businesslike considerations'.[14] The fact that building societies base particularly long-term lending on short-term deposits, the bulk of their funds being withdrawable on demand or at very short notice, makes societies particularly concerned to emphasize the security of their funds, in order to maintain and attract investment; hence they adopt an 'investor-oriented safety first ethic'.[15]

While at a practical level societies may, as indicated above, be 'run as commercial enterprises', social functions remain an element of the societies' business ideology: 'Although building societies compete with each other and strive for commercial efficiency, they conceive of their function as partly a social service.'[16] They ration mortgages through their allocation rules and procedures, rather than by allowing the mortgage rate to be bid up to a market clearing price; and they also go to great lengths to ease the problems of borrowers with arrears. However, as Harloe *et al.* have also observed,[17] 'social responsibility' is in the long-term interest of the societies. Leniency in dealing with arrears avoids the adverse publicity surrounding possession orders and evictions. Rationing mortgages administratively, rather than through market forces, and keeping down the mortgage rate below a market clearing level encourage favourable treatment from the government (see next section); these practices also allow societies to be more selective about borrowers and the property they accept, thus maximizing the security of their mortgage funds. [18]

Societies are also motivated by their belief in the 'promotion of thrift and home-ownership'. On a practical level, they have a strong vested interest in the maintenance and extension of the private housing market since this represents their field of investment. [19] This is overlain by a strong political and ideological commitment to private home ownership. To quote one society, 'We believe profoundly in the ideal of a property-owning democracy, and it is our purpose to play a part in translating the ideal into a reality', [20] and their role was recognized by the Secretary General of the Building Societies Association (BSA) in 1976, when he observed that: 'The point where more than half the houses in the country have become owner-occupied was a significant milestone because even a small stake in the country does affect political attitudes. The greater the proportion of owner-occupiers, the less likely were extreme measures to prevail.' [21]

Finally, the societies' commitment to private enterprise and the free market is expressed in their great concern to maintain their own autonomy and freedom from government regulation and control. Strong opposition is mounted to specific legislative measures which threaten the societies' autonomy. More generally, they work through the influential BSA to promote a favourable image of the societies and their activities in the housing system, counter criticism and oppose arguments and proposals which might imply the erosion of their autonomy.

Government control and the legal framework

Government control and the legal framework within which building societies operate are primarily concerned with the stability of the societies as financial institutions. They provide mainly prudential controls concerned with safeguarding investors' money. The legislative framework is concerned with building society lending policies only insofar as they affect the security of funds invested in the societies. In 1960, for example, societies were forbidden to lend more than 10 per cent of their funds as 'special advances', loans for investment purposes, to corporate bodies, or greater than a specified size to individuals; this was done in order to curb practices which threatened societies' financial stability and led to the collapse of the State Building Society in 1959. The legal framework, and the powers of the Chief Registrar of Friendly Societies which it establishes, are not therefore concerned with lending in relation to housing or social policy. The role of the societies in the housing system is defined as providers of mortgage finance, primarily to individuals buying houses for owner occupation. But the legal framework does nothing to allow government to specify societies' lending policies in terms of the characteristics of borrowers and property or to control interest rates, the level of mortgage lending or the volume of societies' liquid (as opposed to mortgage) assets.[22] As the Secretary General of the BSA commented in 1978:

> Looking around the world, the British building societies must be the least controlled of all such institutions. In many countries the Government dictates rates of interest, limits branching, insures investment accounts and mortgages and provides a tedious regulatory system.[23]

In a formal sense, societies thus retain complete discretion over their lending policies, interest rates and level of mortgage lending, and the government can only seek to implement policy through influence and persuasion. In terms of Orren's threefold classification of 'policy modes',[24] the legal framework may be characterized primarily as 'enabling'; it authorizes the use of funds in a particular way, but with no legislative intent of controlling the cost, volume or pattern of allocation of these funds. This may be contrasted with 'inducing' laws, such as federal and state guarantees in the USA on mortgages granted on cheaper housing, or 'mandatory' laws which might require lending to certain categories of borrowers. As Orren points out, 'enabling' laws are mainly concerned with investors, whereas 'inducing' and 'mandatory' laws relate to a wider constituency such as lower income housebuyers.

It is, however, insufficient to analyse government influence purely in terms of the nature of the legal framework and the formal 'policy mode' which this represents. We have already seen that the building societies are particularly concerned to maintain their autonomy and freedom from government regulation. Consequently, the threat of more formal control over the societies gives government significant power to influence and persuade the societies in accordance with its policy objectives.

Additionally, the government allows the building societies certain privileges over other financial institutions, which it justifies largely in terms of housing and social policy. First, the special arrangement under which societies settle investors' liability to basic rate income tax gives them roughly a one-and-a-half per cent competitive advantage over their rivals;[25] for a given rate charged to borrowers they can offer investors an interest rate one-and-a-half per cent higher than if they were subject to the same tax arrangements as most of their rivals, such as the banks, and they can therefore attract a greater volume of funds for mortgage lending. The special arrangement does not involve any element of government subsidy, nor was it specifically originated to benefit the building societies in this way; nevertheless, it does give them a significant practical advantage over other financial institutions which is condoned and maintained despite growing criticism, particularly from the banks who see it as an unfair financial advantage. Second, building society lending has been specifically excluded from credit restraint as an element of monetary policy to which banks and other financial institutions have periodically been subject. Furthermore, the societies received direct government support in the form of a bridging grant in 1973 and a £500 million loan in 1974 to help them maintain the level of mortgage lending without raising the mortgage rate, and the government requested the banks to limit interest on deposits under £10,000 for a period in 1973–5, in the hope of limiting competition against the societies.[26] Finally, societies continue to enjoy equivalent status to friendly societies. Societies pay a lower rate of corporation tax on their gross financial surplus than companies and banks and, like trustee and national savings banks, they pay no corporation tax on gains from selling government securities held for at least twelve months. The societies are particularly concerned to preserve these various privileges and have frequently defended them.[27] Since the preservation of these privileges is largely dependent on the continuing goodwill of the government towards the societies and its belief that the privileges are justified, the threat of their withdrawal represents a further source of government power to influence and persuade the societies.

The formal policy mode adopted by central government in relation to the societies was characterized earlier as primarily an 'enabling' mode. We can, however, identify two further sources of government influence over building societies, derived from the societies' desire for autonomy and their desire to maintain their privileged status as financial institutions. These are, respectively, the threat of mandatory legislation, and the threat that privileges will be withdrawn. These sources of government power and influence represent two further policy modes used by government to attempt to secure the compliance of building societies with government policy. But, in contrast to Orren's *formal* policy modes, which she defined in relation to the existing legal framework, these additional policy modes, which it is necessary to distinguish, are essentially *informal* and non-legal in character. It is these informal policy modes, which played an important part in the new relations developed between government and the building societies in the 1970s to which we now turn.

Co-operation between government and the building societies

While the legislative framework within which societies operate remains enabling rather than coercive, non-legislative formal links between government and building societies have been developed and a much closer working relationship has been established in the 1970s, based on voluntary co-operation by the societies. This new relationship has arisen from the interaction of the aims of government housing policy regarding owner occupation with the objectives of the building societies. The context for interaction was both the general growth of owner occupation and the importance of the building societies in the housing system, and the more specific developments in the housing market in the 1970s. The purpose of the remainder of this chapter is to analyse and explain the origins of this changing relationship, focusing on two key elements: the Joint Advisory Committee on Building Society Mortgage Finance, established in 1974, and the Local Authority Support Lending Scheme, which originated in 1975.

The joint advisory committee

In the 1950s and 1960s building societies became increasingly important in the finance and housing markets. By the end of the 1960s, home ownership accounted for 50 per cent of households, having almost doubled since World War II, and societies' total assets reached over £10,000 million compared with £756 million in 1940.[28] As one building society commentator describes it, the societies in this period 'went reasonably quietly about their task of raising funds from the saving and investing public and lending them to those who wanted to borrow to buy homes'.[29] It was a period of 'solid progress', during which there were no formal links between government and building societies or the BSA. There was, however, increasing public and political outcry when it became necessary to increase mortgage rates in order to offer investors a competitive rate in the face of general increases in short-term interest rates and thus maintain the supply of mortgage funds. And there was increasing contact between the government and representatives of the BSA at times when a rise in interest rates seemed likely.[30]

In the early 1970s, by which time owner occupation was the majority tenure group, conditions in the finance and housing markets under which societies were operating changed rapidly. In 1972 and 1973, strong underlying demand for house purchase was fed through to the housing market by a major increase in mortgage lending by the building societies, whose interest rates were particularly competitive in the finance market at this time. Chasing a limited supply of housing, this resulted in the notorious hyper-inflation of house prices which rose on average about 31 per cent in 1972 and 35 per cent in 1973.[31] Towards the end of 1973, however, the general level of interest rates, against which societies compete to raise funds, started to rise. Bank Minimum Lending Rate rose from 7.5 per cent in June to 13 per cent in November. Societies increased their rates to investors in an attempt to retain their competitiveness, which in turn pushed up the mortgage rate from 8.5 per cent in March to 11 per cent by September. Despite this move, the societies remained uncompetitive and receipts fell quickly, leading to a sharp cutback in the rate of new house building and to serious financial problems for many building companies.

This rapid 'feast and famine' cycle thus threw up a series of specific problems in quick succession: rapid house price inflation, which put house purchase out of reach for many aspiring owners; a major increase in the mortgage rate, which raised the ongoing costs of existing owners, particularly recent buyers with high mortgage payments to meet; a mortgage famine, which resulted in first-time house buyers, and many existing owners who wanted to move, being unable to raise a loan; and, finally, a major slump in the house-building industry and related trades, leading to bankruptcies, unemployment and a severe cutback in house building. The situation was complicated by the contradictory nature of this set of problems: while rapid price inflation hits first-time buyers, existing owners benefit from it and a high rate of house building is encouraged; similarly, raising the mortgage rate allows the societies to pay investors more and attract more funds for mortgage lending, but raises the housing costs of existing owners.

At a general level, these problems conflicted with the government's desire to support and increase home ownership. More specifically, their obvious political sensitivity demanded a public policy response. For, as Murie *et al.* have observed 'we now take for granted the government's ultimate responsibility for the success or failure of housing policy'.[32] The building societies were, for their part, particularly sensitive to the considerable criticism and blame levelled at them, particularly for fuelling the initial rise in house prices, but also for failing to stabilize the level of mortgage lending. As one building society commentator observed:

> Needless to say, with housing being such a sensitive political issue, these developments gave rise to considerable public and political concern with building societies being singled out as the scapegoat.[33]

The reasons for the situation which developed in the housing market at this time are not at issue here; more significant is the effect these events had on relations between government and the building societies.

Initially, a series of meetings took place between government and the building societies and, to quote a building society account, there grew from these:

> a realisation on both sides that building societies occupied a special position in the social and economic fabric of the country and that an attempt should be made for Government and the building societies to work together in an effort to avoid or at any rate to mitigate, the alternation of feast and famine in the supply of mortgage funds.[34]

In October 1973, a Memorandum of Agreement between the government and the societies was drawn up, stating the agreed objectives of both parties as follows:

1 to continue to support owner occupation;
2 to produce and maintain a flow of mortgage funds to enable the house-building industry to plan for a high and stable level of housebuilding for sale;
3 to contribute towards stabilisation of house prices;
4 to maintain an orderly housing market in which, subject to 3 above, sufficient mortgage funds are available to allow purchasers a reasonable choice of owning the sort of house they want.[35]

The Memorandum also provided for the setting up of a Joint Advisory Committee which would meet monthly and which would provide the BSA Council with an estimate, normally for a period one year ahead, of the level of receipts needed to realize the agreed objectives and to provide 'an agreed analysis and review of the current situation with particular reference to changes in interest rates in the economy generally, the inflow and outflow of building society funds, advances to first-time purchasers, housing starts and completions and house prices'. The JAC, which first met in 1974, is composed of representatives of the BSA, Department of the Environment, the Treasury, the Bank of England, and the Chief Registrar of Friendly Societies or his deputy. A Technical Sub-Committee (TSC) was subsequently set up to consider analyses and forecasts of the housing market.

In 1975, a further agreement was reached on the stabilization of mortgage funds, whereby each six months the TSC calculates the appropriate level of lending to maintain a healthy housing market, while avoiding excessive increases in house prices. This reflected the government's view of events in the early 1970s, set out in *Housing Policy*:

> The implication is that when the building societies' interest rates are especially competitive and the inflow of funds to them is large, there is no automatic mechanism that would ensure that they did not enable to become effective a greater demand for houses than could be met without undue increase in house prices. The further implication is that if the amount lent is to be matched in such circumstances to what the markets can take, it has to be done deliberately.[36]

Initially, the agreed levels of mortgage lending exceeded what the societies could achieve without an excessive increase in the mortgage rate. In early 1978, however, it appeared to the government that prices were rising threateningly; the quarterly rate of increase in new house prices which averaged 3.5 per cent over 1977 rose to 4.8 per cent in the first quarter of 1978 and reached 7.4 per cent over the third quarter. In the face of strong government pressure, societies agreed to limit their intended level of lending for house purchase by £70 million to £610 million a month from April to June, increasing to £640 million a month from July and to £700 million for the first quarter of 1979. The societies

95

gave in to government pressure with considerable reluctance and there was widespread disagreement with the government view that house prices were rising at an unacceptable rate, expressed officially by the BSA chairman who stated, 'We are not convinced that there is a take-off in house prices.'[37] The societies were particularly aware that the cut in lending 'would lead to frustration amongst would-be home buyers' and were concerned at the criticism levelled at them as a result.

The JAC and associated agreements have established formal linkages between government and the societies and fostered a closer working relationship. The government has sought by this means to manage and influence the relationship between mortgage availability, house prices, the mortgage rate and the rate of new housebuilding, and in particular to stabilize housing demand. Linkages between government and the societies remain, however, non-coercive; government may seek to influence the societies through the medium of the JAC, but still depends on the voluntary co-operation of the societies.

The establishment of formal linkages and the societies' agreement, albeit reluctant, to reduce lending in 1978 might suggest some increase in government influence over societies. In part, this doubtless reflects the fact that societies are anxious to avoid a repetition of the 1972–3 boom and slump and to counter the considerable criticism and scapegoating which they suffered. But the voluntary nature of their new relationship with government is crucial, for their willingness to co-operate with the government undoubtedly minimized pressure, if not actually heading off a more formal stabilization arrangement and an increase in government regulation of building society lending which would directly threaten their autonomy. To quote the BSA Council deputy chairman's account of these events:

> Numerous ideas were put forward during this period, including the possibility of setting up a form of Stabilisation Fund under Government auspices, and the suggestion that there should be a greater formal regulation by Government of building society policies. Happily, commonsense prevailed and there emerged instead the idea of bringing into existence a Joint Advisory Committee.[38]

From a technical point of view, it is likely that analysis of the housing market and management of mortgage lending have improved to some extent as a result of the JAC. The improved public image of the building societies since the events of the early 1970s and the societies' desire to avoid being the scapegoat again have probably marginally increased government influence over them, although the significance of their agreement to limit lending in 1978, the main tangible evidence of this influence, must not be overestimated. From the building societies' point of view, however, the main function of increased voluntary co-operation in determining the level of mortgage lending has been to counter the threat of more formal government regulation and erosion of autonomy. This argument is amplified in the second example of increased co-operation.

The local authority support lending scheme

The second example of closer working relations between government and the building societies relates to detailed mortgage lending policies, rather than the aggregate flow of funds on to the housing market, and concerns the arrangement whereby building societies were intended to compensate for the cutbacks in direct local authority mortgage lending from 1975. Local authorities have played a small but significant role through their mortgage lending activity. There has been considerable overlap between the lending patterns of local authorities and building societies in terms of the characteristics of borrowers and the property they purchased. Furthermore the scale and nature of mortgage lending activity has varied considerably between different authorities. But local authorities have, nevertheless, tended to operate rather more liberal lending policies than the societies. Local authorities tend to lend proportionately more to those buying older and cheaper housing, in lower income and age groups and to first-time buyers: in 1975, for example, 30 per cent of local authority borrowers purchased pre-1919 housing costing under £6000, compared with only 4 per cent of building society borrowers; and 87 per cent of local authority borrowers were buying for the first time, compared with 47 per cent of building society borrowers.[39] Local authorities also tend to lend more generously in relation to incomes and house prices, grant longer mortgage terms and provide more 'low-start' mortgages. Local authority lending has thus been particularly important in facilitating the entry into owner occupation of lower income households and, through facilitating the purchase of older housing, encouraging the improvement of the older housing stock.

The volume of local authority lending has, however, been subject periodically to severe monetary restraint, economic policy overriding considerations of housing policy. In the period 1971–5, these constraints were lifted and the volume of local authority lending rose rapidly in 1974 to nearly a quarter of net lending by the four main institutional sources, compensating to some extent for the building society mortgage famine in 1973–4. Monetary limits were, however, reintroduced in 1975 and tightened in succeeding years, and net lending fell from £620 million in 1975 to £570 million in 1978.[40] Following the cutback in direct local authority lending in 1975, the government negotiated with the BSA a scheme whereby building societies were intended to fill the gap, which became known as the local authority Support Lending Scheme (SLS). Under the SLS, individuals apply to a local authority for a loan and, if the

97

authority considers it would have granted a loan had it had funds available, it nominates the applicant for a building society loan under the Scheme. The societies initially earmarked £100 million to be loaned in this way, £176 million for the financial year 1977–8 and £300 million for 1978–9.

Although the Scheme was slow to start, due primarily to administrative problems and misunderstanding between building societies and local authorities at the local level, £160 million had been loaned by March 1977 and a further £106 million was loaned in 1977–8.[41] The volume of lending under the SLS has been argued by the societies, and to some extent accepted by government, as indicating the success of the Scheme, but, in themselves, these indices have little significance. It is more meaningful to consider what changes in the structure of building society lending, in terms of the characteristics of borrowers and the property they purchase, have been achieved through the Scheme. Little direct evidence is available. It appears, however, that the societies have indeed expanded their lending in that part of the mortgage market where considerable overlap had developed between building society and local authority lending patterns. There was an appreciable 'up market' extension when the volume of local authority lending expanded in the early 1970s, followed by a retraction down market from 1976. For example, the average local authority loan in 1972 of £2956 represented 57 per cent of the average building society loan of £5200; this proportion rose to 90 per cent in 1974 then fell back to 63 per cent in 1977.[42] Building societies have thus increasingly granted loans to those who, in the early 1970s, would have obtained local authority loans; furthermore, the proportion of building society loans granted on pre-1919 houses has significantly increased in the 1970s, rising from just over 18.5 per cent of the total over the period 1971–5 to 24 per cent in 1978.[43] However, it is unlikely that the societies have been lending as generously in relation to house prices and borrowers' incomes, or have been as willing to grant long-term loans, as the local authorities.

While the societies have increased lending in the 'lower' categories of their existing lending range, there is little evidence that they have extended or liberalized their lending range to embrace borrowers and property which are more exclusively the domain of the local authorities. In Leeds, for example, a study suggests that societies had granted loans on property which, previously, would more likely have been purchased with a local authority loan; but they were not prepared to lend on 'back to back' terrace houses which, in 1974–5, accounted for nearly 30 per cent of local authority loans in the city.[44] The crucial point, as the societies themselves have pointed out, is that: 'it has always been axiomatic in the Scheme that the societies would apply and preserve the appropriate criteria on the basis of which they would be prepared to lend.'[45] In other words, 'the Scheme has always operated under societies' normal lending criteria'.[46] This was the source of much of local authorities' initial 'misunderstanding' of the Scheme. Any replacement of local authority lending has thus taken place within the societies' traditional lending range and criteria. Furthermore, given the extent to which local authority lending had expanded and had extended up market in the early 1970s, much of this so-called 'replacement' would undoubtedly have occurred in the natural course of events, without the elaborate formal arrangements, as happened following the earlier cutback in local authority lending in 1965. With the cut in local authority lending, would-be borrowers would automatically have turned to the societies – many indeed by-passed the formal SLS as it was. Furthermore, in the normal course of events societies would have increased their down-market lending as their funds became more plentiful after the 1974–5 famine.[47]

Although negotiated at a national level between the Department of the Environment, the BSA and the local authority associations, the SLS established formal links and fostered a closer working relationship at the local level between building societies and local authorities. The evidence suggests that the SLS has had little specific effect on building society lending patterns and policies and that 'replacement' of local authority lending would largely have occurred in the normal course of events. More important in a practical sense is, probably, the fact that the SLS 'has proved to be the catalyst for increasing cooperation between building societies and local authorities – both at national and local levels – across the whole of the housing market'.[48] Mutual awareness of objectives and constraints, exchange of information and increased contact may have furthered housing policy at a local level in relation, for example, to the improvement of older housing areas, without compromising building societies' emphasis on mortgage security. The increase in lending on older property, reflecting the end of large-scale housing clearance since the late 1960s, the success of revitalization policies in some areas, and increased demand for older, cheaper housing, may well have been encouraged by this closer working relationship.

In practical terms, the Support Lending Scheme has done little to replace cuts in local authority loans to borrowers and on property which building societies have traditionally been reluctant to accept. Although a closer working relationship has been established between local authorities and building societies, it is based, like the JAC agreement on mortgage funds, on voluntary co-operation by the societies rather than on coercion. Furthermore, as the societies pointed out, the preservation of societies' existing lending policies and criteria was 'axiomatic' to the way the SLS operated. The Scheme was, however, particularly valuable to the building societies at a time when their lending policies were the target of increasing criticism, popular, political and informed. A number of reasons for this may be identified. Following the cutback in local authority loans, an increasing number of would-be buyers of inner city housing were turning to the societies and being frustrated by their lending criteria; furthermore, an increasing proportion of younger and first-time buyers were seeking cheaper, older housing in the inner city following the rise in house prices in 1972–3, which left traditional new 'starter homes' beyond their financial reach. Considerable evidence emerged relating to building society lending practices, and 'red lining', the alleged denial by building societies of loans to buy property in particular areas, entered the vocabulary of discussions of building societies' lending practices in older areas. Finally, increasing emphasis was placed on the spread of owner occupation in older housing areas in the context of government policy to improve the inner city. In this context, the major function of the SLS, from the building societies' point of view, was to counter the threat of more formal government regulation of their lending policies, by demonstrating their willingness voluntarily to co-operate with the government in a scheme which apparently achieved considerable success in replacing local authority lending.

In particular, the proposal that building societies should make a block loan of 10 per cent of their mortgage funds to local authorities, which would then on-lend them to individual borrowers, gained increasing support in the Labour party and was the subject of two (unsuccessful) private member's bills. Under this scheme, local authorities would have guaranteed interest and capital payments to the building societies. This would have effectively guaranteed the security of what is currently the riskiest 10 per cent of societies' mortgage lending, benefiting building society investors by increasing the security of their capital, with minimal administrative effort from the societies, while simultaneously absolving them from responsibility for, and criticism of, their policies towards the lower end of the market. But fear of creeping nationalization and erosion of their autonomy led to general opposition from the building society movement. According to the General Manager of the largest society, the Halifax:

> building societies do not like what amounts to direction of their members' funds in a way which they, the societies, cannot control themselves and that, of course, is what direct investment with the local authorities would amount to. One must always beware of the thin edge of the wedge.[49]

As William Clarke MP, a vice-president of the BSA, said when opposing this measure in 1978, 'Mr. Allaun says that we should direct the investment of building societies to the tune of 10 per cent of their advances, but who is to say that next year that figure will not be 20 per cent, 40 per cent or 60 per cent?'[50] Opposing the measure, the Chairman of the BSA argued that the government's aims 'could best be achieved by close co-operation between building societies and local authorities'.[51] Societies were also concerned that the Scheme allowed local authority nominees to jump the societies' queuing system which gives priority to applicants who are investing in a society or are introduced by an 'agent' who has channelled money into the society, this priority system being used by the societies primarily to generate investment.[52] The societies were aided in their opposition to this measure by the fact that block loans to local authorities would, under current Treasury regulations, increase public sector borrowing which the original cuts in direct local authority lending were specifically designed to reduce. In practice, however, the effect on the economy would be little different if local authorities rather than the societies allocated this 10 per cent of building society funds and a similar scheme was in fact set up in Northern Ireland through the Housing Executive. It therefore seems most likely that if the societies had supported the block lending scheme the Treasury could have been persuaded to change its definition of public expenditure in this case. It should also be noted, however, that although the 1978 private member's bill received a second reading, the measure was developed and supported by the Labour party's National Executive Committee, broadly speaking, the left of the party, and did not receive enthusiastic support or parliamentary time from the government or the Environment Secretary, who had negotiated the voluntary Support Lending Scheme and fostered co-operation with the building societies. The government appears to have used the SLS to some extent as a means of managing its reduction in direct local authority lending in the face of strong criticism from the left of the party and other, extra-parliamentary, bodies such as *Shelter*, the national housing pressure group.[53]

Conclusion

Private housing is now too significant in political and social terms to be left to the private market. The spread of owner occupation and government support for its continued expansion, coupled with the crises in the housing market in the 1970s, have brought private home ownership squarely within the domain of public policy, and the crucial role of the building societies has put their activities in the centre of housing policy. Consequently, in the 1970s we have seen the development of closer working relations between government and the building societies at both central and local levels. This has centred in particular on the JAC and the agreement on stabilizing mortgage lending, and on the local authority Support Lending Scheme. But although formal working relations have been established they are firmly based on the voluntary co-operation of the building societies. The legal framework and 'policy mode' remain 'enabling' in character, rather than 'inducive' or 'mandatory'.

It has been argued, however, that in practice these new working relationships have had little tangible impact on building society activity and there has been little furtherance of government housing policy. From the building societies' point of view the main function of co-operation with the government has been to counter the threat of more formal regulation of their activities or erosion of their privileges at a time when they have been subject to increasing criticism. The government took the view that: 'We are in favour of a policy of co-operation, not coercion, because the societies have shown a readiness to develop relevant policies in consultation with Government.'[54] The societies' demonstration of goodwill and of their willingness voluntarily to enter into co-operative working relations with the government has served to pre-empt government initiatives to pursue its policy objectives through mandatory legislation, adopting a mandatory policy mode, and to justify continued favourable treatment by government.

While, however, the societies entered into co-operative working relations 'voluntarily', in that they were not subject to coercion, their actions undoubtedly reflected the government's informal powers of influence and persuasion derived from the threat of mandatory legislation and the withdrawal of privileges. There can be little doubt the societies would have preferred to avoid the development of co-operative working relations, bringing closer contact with government; but, under the circumstances, the moves they entailed were necessary in order for the societies to manage their relations with government. Thus concessions were made by the societies in response to non-formal government influence and persuasion; the societies were drawn closer to government. But the working relations developed involved no compromise of the societies' major objectives identified earlier, in particular formal autonomy, asset growth and security. The experience of relations between government and the building societies in the 1970s suggests that although government may achieve minor concessions through non-formal policy modes involving influence and persuasion, the practical results of these concessions are minimal and their main effect is to counter the effective implementation of government policy. The form and strength of the societies' objectives, in particular their commitment to autonomy, are such that mandatory legislation will be necessary to achieve any real control over their activities. This would imply, however, a much greater commitment to state intervention and control than was displayed by the Labour government in the 1970s.

Notes and references

1 HMG Cmnd 4728, 1971.
2 HMG Cmnd 5280, 1973.
3 HMG Cmnd 5851, 1977: 45.
4 HMG Cmnd 5851, 1977: 68.
5 HMG Cmnd 5851, 1977: 50.
6 HMG Cmnd 5851, 1977: 68.
7 HMG Cmnd 5851, 1977: 51 reiterated by the Secretary of State for the Environment, speaking to a BSA Conference following its publication: Shore 1978: 30–3.
8 Murie, Niner and Watson 1976: 238. The role of *local* government in relation to the private housing sector, embracing both the general functions of planning and a range

of more minor functions, including mortgage lending and building for sale, etc., must also be borne in mind.

9 Much of the detailed background to the argument in this chapter may be found in Boddy 1980, which is a comprehensive account of building societies, home ownership and housing policy in Britain, describing how building societies operate in the finance market and the housing system.

10 *Financial Statistics*, HMSO; HMG *Housing Policy Technical Volume* 1977, Part I: 83.

11 Financial Statistics, HMSO.

12 Harloe, Issacharoff and Minns 1974: 82.

13 Williams 1976: 30.

14 Building Societies Institute 1970: 9. On the issue of efficiency, see, however, the comments of the 'Wilson Committee' HMG Cmnd 7937, 1980: chapter 8.

15 Harloe *et al.* 1974: 85.

16 Revell 1973: 367.

17 Harloe *et al.* 1974: 88.

18 For a wider discussion of the setting of building society interest rates see Boddy 1980: 59 and 87–8.

19 *Building Society Management* 1970: 22 speaks of societies as being 'vitally concerned with properties for owner occupiers' and building society spokesmen have frequently argued that home ownership should be encouraged, for example M. Boléat, 'Home ownership may not reach 70 per cent if the council house programme continues', *Building Societies Gazette*, December 1977: 1256–7.

20 Temperance Permanent Building Society (now the Gateway BS) 1973.

21 Griggs 1976.

22 The legal framework does define a minimum reserve ratio as a condition for the granting of 'trustee status' to societies, allowing them to accept investment held on trust and taken as a hallmark of security.

23 *Building Societies Gazette*, March 1978: 238.

24 Orren 1974: 19–20. This excellent and detailed analysis of the social impact of life assurance investment and mortgage lending in Illinois and relations between the industry and government presents many similarities to the present study and represents useful parallel reading. In particular Orren demonstrates the industry's political strategy aiming to thwart coercive direction of life assurance funds by government.

25 Explained fully in Boddy 1980: 46–8 and 81–3. The latter section describes in more detail the privileged position of the societies in the finance market.

26 It should be noted that the societies have generally argued that the £500 million loan and limit on bank interest rates were ineffective and that this government action was unnecessary if not indeed unwelcome. The fact that the societies accepted the loan, however, casts some doubt on the argument that it was of no benefit to them.

27 See for example 'Taxation of building society interest', *Building Societies Gazette*, January 1979: 60–4; BSA 1978a; 'Mr. Stow replies to bank critics of societies' competition', *Building Societies Gazette*, May 1978: 470.

28 And more than doubling in terms of real purchasing power over housing. The proportion of the housing stock owner occupied in the United Kingdom rose from 50 per cent in 1970 to 54 per cent in 1978, *Housing and Construction Statistics*, HMSO (quarterly).

29 Williams 1978: 3.
30 Williams 1978: 3.
31 *Housing and Construction Statistics*, HMSO (quarterly). Figures are at mortgage completion stage.
32 Murie *et al*. 1976: 235.
33 Williams 1978: 3.
34 Williams 1978: 3.
35 Boléat 1979: appendix.
36 HMG *Housing Policy Technical Volume* 1977: Part II, p. 51.
37 Press statement reported in *The Times*, 11 March 1978.
38 Williams 1978: 3.
39 HMG *Housing Policy Technical Volume* 1977: Part II, tables VII.7 and VII.8. A fuller analysis of local authority and building society mortgage lending patterns is contained in Boddy 1980: chapter 5.
40 *Financial Statistics*, HMSO.
41 The Scheme is described in Spalding 1978: 12–18.
42 *Housing and Construction Statistics*, HMSO (quarterly).
43 *BSA Bulletin*, BSA.
44 Harrison 1977. See also McIntosh 1978: 44–7.
45 Spalding 1978: 15.
46 Boléat 1978: 31.
47 For example, Lambert found when interviewing estate agents that it was normal practice for the societies to clamp down on older areas when funds were low: Lambert 1978.
48 BSA 1978b: ii ('Foreword').
49 Spalding 1978: 13.
50 Reported in *Building Societies Gazette*, March 1978: 358.
51 Statement reported in the *Guardian*, 23 March 1978.
52 The societies priority system and the function of agents are explained fully in Boddy 1980: 32–4, 51–78.
53 The general discussion of government/building society relations and the specific argument that the societies have been particularly concerned to preserve their autonomy and privileges has centred on the JAC and the SLS. The argument is supported by negotiations and relations between government and the building societies, focusing on a number of other issues. These include: the building societies' opposition to the development of local authority mortgage guarantees, arguing that their commercial scheme negotiated with the insurance companies is superior; the societies' argument that the £500 million loan and limitation of interest rates on bank deposits, discussed earlier, was ineffective and contrary to the wishes of the building societies; and the societies' opposition to government participation in any agency which might be developed to secure adequate mortgage funds in the long term.
54 Shore 1978: 30.

4

Implementing employment policies in a district authority

Tom Davies

This chapter deals with the implementation of a new set of policies and, in particular, with attempts at innovation in the modes of behaviour adopted by the organization concerned. Chandler and Templeton[1] have recently discussed the nature of implementation by local authorities in the employment planning field, pointing out that most resort to activities which do not challenge the *status quo* within their own structures. This chapter describes an attempt to break away from this general principle.

What follows is an attempt to recall, from the point of view of a participant observer, some of the events surrounding the implementation of employment plans for a district authority in a conurbation, Alphaville, which exhibited mainly inner urban characteristics. Employment is a non-statutory function for local authorities and has been marked by a certain reluctance by both central and local government to face up to the need for local government to play a part in the structuring of the local economy. However, many local authorities now have employment policies, mostly concerning factory building, office development and infrastructure. It is an area in which, because of its nature, economic goals conflict more with social goals than they do, perhaps, in most policy areas. The legitimacy of social goals is, therefore, difficult to achieve and, as a result, policy formulation on the social side of local employment planning is in its infancy. Moreover, there are already operating in this field major national organizations, notably the Manpower Services Commission and the Supplementary Benefits Commission, who are jealous of their territory.

Alphaville is a second-tier authority, the county council being the strategic authority. It has a population of almost 200,000 and is one of a number of such districts in the county. It has had a history of changing political administrations which makes for instability, but also for innovation in policy. The planning department, which only a few years ago had been part of the equivalent of the architects' department, had become independent and grown to a staff of approximately ninety in the period leading up to the creation of the employment policy and the conditions for its implementation.

Any account of events from one point of view must be partial and biased. However, what follows gives some idea of the complexity of interaction involved in implementing the series of individual policies which make up an employment policy at the local level.

The chapter commences by examining the process of formulating the policies and, within this stage, the relationship between the members and officers. It shows how the apparatus and process of implementation started before the policy existed and built up through the policy-setting stage to become fully operational by the time the policy emerged in its first 'fully grown' state. The chapter then proceeds by examining four issues or events in the process of implementation selected from a very complex policy field:

1   The attempt to stop the displacement of firms by the housing development process, in which it raises questions of intra-departmental relationships between different groups of professionals following different policy goals.
2   Co-operatives policy, in which it looks particularly at inter-departmental, but also at central local relationships between a quango and trade unions on the one side and the local authority and the potential co-operators on the other.
3   Leasing policy, in which it examines the difference between two professional ideologies and their impact on implementing social versus economic policies.
4   The search for powers – a General Powers Bill – a case of central government being reluctant to give powers to local authorities to carry out certain economic policies.

Setting the policies

This book deals with the implementation of policies, and so I will not deal in detail with the policy formulation process in Alphaville. The process itself presents a confusing picture, difficult to unravel, and is perhaps best presented historically.

In 1972, under a Conservative council, a document analysing the need for employment policies had been produced in the planning department, with a number of physically orientated recommendations. These were accepted by the council but were not implemented, save for the appointment of an officer concerned with the relocation of small firms displaced by the development of housing sites for the council. Small plots of land were made available for those firms who could afford to build their own premises.

In 1975 and 1976 two factors materially influenced things: a concentration of energies by the planning department research officer on the decline and closure of firms in Alphaville, and the start of the process leading to the production of the District Plan under the statutory structure planning procedure. In addition, a new management team had taken over the planning department, and the Labour party was in power in the Town Hall.

A series of committee papers drawing attention to the already high and rising unemployment rate in the district and to the pattern of plant closures were produced. The reports pointed out that the ownership of many of the factories being closed was from outside the district, and as a consequence called for a state factory building programme within Alphaville. This was, in effect, to call for the implementation of one of the 1972 policies. This proposal was for a rolling programme of factory building, designed to replace the loss of jobs from closures. At the time of these reports, a small number of recently elected backbench councillors became closely involved in the policy work and in convincing the leadership of the importance of the policy area. Their role was crucial in the process of policy formulation and implementation which followed. They could be said to belong to the 'Bennite' wing of the party and thus seized particularly on the issue of ownership of the local economy. The party leadership eventually agreed with their argument and set up the equivalent of a parliamentary commission, a policy review sub-committee on employment, to examine the question. The planning department played an important role in producing basic evidence for this committee.

The committee produced a document which laid the blame for Alphaville's economic decline squarely on the shoulders of the private sector. It produced a set of over thirty policies concerned with building an 'alternative' economy which, besides the acceptance of the rolling programme of factory building, included policies for industrial co-operatives, municipal industry, 'planning agreements' at local level on the model of the national policy, the use of the council's own personnel policy as a major employment planning instrument, and the adoption of government training programmes. The report received considerable press coverage and established Alphaville's reputation, at least in the employment/planning field, as a 'Red' authority, half-jokingly referred to among the cognoscenti as 'Red Alphaville', on the model of Red Bologna which was then acquiring popularity among planning students.

The inner area Consultative Employment Group

During this period, Alphaville had also been active in the establishment of a pressure group to publicize and formulate policies for the economic plight of the inner urban areas of the county. The Consultative Employment Group was not the first such group in the county, but it became the first to have a wider role than that of promoting its area as a site for the location of economic activity and to see itself as a part of the implementation process for employment policy. Alphaville realized at an early stage that it could not effectively implement its own employment policy if there were not like-minded authorities throughout the county and if the county authority were not sympathetic and active. The reason for this was that the inner areas of the county were interdependent. Policy in adjacent districts, particularly the central city, had considerable impact on the economy of Alphaville, in terms of direct loss or gain of jobs. The inner districts needed to speak as one if they were to overcome central government's attitude that they were at the heart of one of the more prosperous regions in the UK and, therefore, not a problem area in themselves.

The Consultative Employment Group, consequently, became a strange amalgam of rich Tory districts, Labour districts of traditional stance or actively anti-industry, 'radical' districts and pressure groups of the Left, the County Association of Trades Councils, and, on the right, the Chamber of Commerce and Industry and the CBI. Alphaville chaired the first meeting, instituting the procedure of rotating chairman. Alphaville officers and members have always been active in the Group's work, and the secretariat has remained in Alphaville, enabling such activity to have considerable effect.

A series of officers' working groups reported to members on finances, powers, land and buildings, training policies, offices, co-operatives, information for small firms, leasing policies for industrial buildings and so on. Pressure group activities included conferences and seminars.

The beginnings of implementation

Implementation had, of course, been continuing during this preliminary process through the activities of the relocation officer and the start of the industrial development rolling programme, with the commencement of the building of a three-storey block of small factory units. The latter was initiated and co-ordinated by the planning department through an employment working party on which representatives of the development, finance, engineering, valuation, and solicitor's departments sat, and which was chaired by the planning department. This working party was the scene of much departmental in-fighting, and was itself the product of previous dog-fights which culminated in the establishment of the legality of own-factory building and a budget. These events had set much of the tone of the inter-departmental relationships, with which I shall deal in more detail below.

The backbench committee's report was presented to each of the main committees for whom it had relevance and was referred back to the officers for a report on the feasibility of implementation. Unfortunately, responsibility for all the recommendations was not given to the planning department, and so policies on personnel and direct labour, for example, were implemented by other departments, where they received varied treatment. This would, anyway, have been politically difficult to achieve with other departments already jealous of the innovative and co-ordinating role taken by planning.

Each of the policy recommendations was, then, examined for powers, for finance required, for implementing organizations and for staffing implications. In effect, this meant that implementation was commenced, at least in terms of making connections, on each one. All the policy recommendations were accepted as being 'feasible', although there were qualifying reports by the finance and solicitor's department warning of difficulties. The report was accepted by the council and became the basis of an appreciable section of the council's employment policy. One of the immediate outcomes of this process was the establishment of the Employment Development Office in the planning department. The Office consisted of the existing relocation officer, a senior employment development officer concerned with industrial and office development and in overall charge of 'implementation', and an employment liaison officer responsible for the implementation of co-operatives and small firm policies.

The estates and valuation department made a late bid to have the Office in their department, a bid which they lost partly through the members' view of them as hostile to their policies, and partly through their having relinquished responsibility for factory building to the planning department.

The district plan

The next stage of the process of policy formulation was the amalgamation of the above policies into a wider set of policies to deal with the overall problem of employment planning in the district. If you like, this was the officers' response to the backbench members: 'We accept your policies, but they are only a part of the answer – here is the rest.'

Shortly after the feasibility document was presented to the council, a policy document proposed a revival of some of the 1972 policies, such as a relaxation of development control procedures for industry, and the addition of others, such as industrial improvement areas, aid for the expansion of existing industries, and finance for conventional small firms as well as co-operatives. Its analysis of the employment problem pointed out that private sector manufacturing had declined, but that its decline was matched by other sections of private industry and also by the public sector, notably British Rail, gas and electricity.

Policies for firms were distinguished from policies for employees in an attempt to show that one did not automatically help the other, and to show the need for specific policies for the placement of the unemployed and the disadvantaged. Land, buildings and finance policies were viewed as 'support' policies for the major goals of reviving the economy and alleviating unemployment and poverty.

The policy was couched as a series of intentions to act. This was due mainly to the philosophy of the deputy director of planning, whose energies were devoted to converting the normally rather academic process of statutory planning into a tool for action. These intentions to act were then accepted by the council, providing legitimacy for those officers concerned to see the policies implemented.

At the end of this period, the stage was set for formal implementation to begin. In fact, of course, it had already begun in the process of setting the stage. The planning department now had three full-time officers in the Employment Development Office concerned with implementation, two full-time officers in forward planning concerned with employment policy, one officer concerned with land and buildings policy, who co-ordinated implementation in that field, plus local planners and district planners, much of whose work was to be concerned with employment. The development of this situation, from that where the entire employment planning team had been composed of one relocation officer, took approximately eighteen months.

Summary

This section shows how the policy developed incrementally from a small effort at relocation towards the traditional planners' view of the need for physical development. This was followed by members' intervention, to ensure the acceptance of radical and socially-oriented policies, then by the professionals re-establishing their legitimacy by expanding the field to cover further economic and physical policies and establishing the policy in the District Plan formulation process. It shows how the deputy director of planning's view, that policies should be implementable, influenced what followed, including the early establishment of a relatively large implementation staff in the planning department, despite opposition from the valuer's department. It also shows how an inter-local authority and inter-agency group became an important tool for implementation, establishing legitimacy for the development of policy.

Housing *v.* employment

The implementation of the policy for the halting of proposed housing development on sites containing significant employment provides excellent case material to illustrate the problems of intra-departmental conflicts in implementation. One of the 1976 committee reports had shown that the council was responsible for the destruction of premises which had housed several hundred jobs, of which only about 10 per cent had been relocated by the council. The relocation officer had, on the basis of this, been able to command more resources, and had had his status raised, but the problem remained. The concern about this loss of jobs coincided with the running down of the council's redevelopment programme, and so few future sites where this might happen could be identified. However, a policy was formulated which clearly stated that development of a housing site containing industrial and commercial firms could not proceed until the firms had been satisfactorily relocated. If that was not possible, development would be halted. In the process of implementation, the policy was extended to include development for educational, open space and even retail use.

The policy was strongly supported within the planning department by the deputy director, the employment liaison officer and the employment policy analyst: it was opposed, at varying times, and with varying intensity, by the director of planning, and the town centre local planners, in whose areas lay most of the sites concerned.

Meetings between groups who were for and against the policy were, at the beginning, heated and negative: the issue had, in the absence of detailed information about the firms concerned, an element of 'moral' argument which precluded a meeting of minds. However, one particular case was mutually agreed to be crucial and became the focus for implementation. The site, on the fringe of one of the five small 'town centres' in the district, was owned by British Rail and contained some twenty-five to thirty firms on leases of varying duration. The site was a former goods yard, unsightly, without made-up roads, and many of the firms were involved in vehicle maintenance, plant hire or haulage. In addition, therefore, to being a proposed council housing site, it was seen by the town centre planners to be environmentally unsatisfactory.

After much argument about the 'rights' of maintaining jobs of this sort, it was agreed that the town centre team would find out exactly how many jobs were involved, and of what type. It transpired that 300 jobs were involved, many of them drivers' and maintenance workers'. It was argued by the pro-housing group that many of these jobs were 'off site' and therefore did not count, a curious argument which was countered by showing that if the 'site' did not exist, then neither did the 'off-site' jobs. The principle referred to here by the pro-housing group was that of density of employment (jobs per acre), which in turn referred to the principle of 'efficient use of land'. Eventually the town centre team reluctantly agreed that the jobs had to be preserved, but suggested, as per the policy, that they could be relocated elsewhere. They immediately produced a schedule of the firms, showing sites where each could be located throughout the district. This raised several interesting questions and demonstrates how attempts at implementation of one policy can lead to the generation of new policies.

The question arose of whether the firms needed to be in that particular part of the borough, or in locations with street frontages, as many were specialist hire businesses. However, many of the new sites were chosen because of the environmentally intrusive nature of the firms concerned and were, therefore, in inaccessible locations, some with no direct access to the site. The lead-in times to having these sites ready to receive relocated firms were in some cases too long to meet the start-date for the housing development. In any case, some of them were already earmarked for other use.

Although British Rail received a good income from the site, many of the firms were paying relatively low rents, which raised the problem of how to achieve such rents on the new sites. This meant that the owners of the new sites would have to be prepared to accept low rents, thus ruling out most of the prime industrial land in the district, and pointed to land purchase by the council to provide low-rent sites for these firms.

During the thinking and discussion surrounding this site, it became clear to the employment policy analyst that the firms in question were typical of similar firms on similar sites across the district and that the existence of all of them was threatened by the thrust for other sorts of development and for higher environmental standards, now gathering pace. Scrap merchants, demolition experts, oil and other storage yards, plant hire and haulage firms were essential to the local economy and also provided jobs, many of them being well-paid semi-skilled jobs open to local residents and with opportunities for 'perks', overtime, commission, etc. It was therefore suggested that a policy be developed to ensure the rationalization of their siting in areas where they were relatively isolated from residential areas. This led to further conflict, with the director of planning's statement that 'we don't want these crap firms, they can go elsewhere'; a sentiment no doubt echoed by every adjacent district. The other side of this argument was: 'If we provide sites for these sorts of firms, all the crap industry from adjacent districts will come to Alphaville.' However, patient argument and some conflict eventually established the right for such a policy to exist: but in this case the policy had to be backed up with a schedule of the firms involved and possible sites for such industry.

This was eventually achieved by the policy analyst's team and one of the sites identified was the original British Rail housing site. Discussions between the planning and housing departments meanwhile had reached a stage where Housing had recognized that the members would be against any embarrassing removal of firms from a housing site, and had decided to relinquish it. Planning then commenced discussions with British Rail for the purchase of the site under the Community Land Act, and plans were in preparation for the landscaping of the site and its more rational layout. The inevitable conflicts with the valuer's department about rents to be charged to firms when the site came under council ownership were gathering pace, when the Conservative council achieved office and the whole policy was delayed as the Conservatives favoured such activities taking place in the private sector.

This short example, then, illustrates the nature and complexity of the intra-departmental factors surrounding implementation. In writing it, it has become obvious to the author that the reasons for the resolution of such conflicts are not always clear, even if one is a key actor in the conflict. Obstacles melt away, to be replaced with others, events are overtaken, arguments appear to be accepted for no good reason, only to be dismissed at a later stage; decisions about one policy's implementation lead to the need for further policies.

Co-operatives

One of the more controversial policies introduced under the new employment policy was the encouragement of industrial common ownership. Before the publication of the backbenchers' report, the policy had been put forward for adoption by the planning committee, following research by the planning department into existing initiatives, including the Cumbria CDP experiments, the Industrial Common Ownership Movement and Fund, and the then new co-operatives of Meriden and Kirkby. One of the backbenchers, a community worker, was particularly keen on the policy. Implementation started before the publication of the document. There are three aspects of the implementation process which are of interest: intra-organizational conflict over the interpretation of powers, intra-organizational conflict over the goals of the policy: central-local conflicts over the use of finance for the policy.

On the basis of existing precedent, the planning department decided to go ahead with the presentation of a co-operative for funding from the council under Section 137 of the 1972 Local Government Act. This clause, summarizing, allows the product of a 2p rate, in the case of Alphaville approximately £1 million, to be used for the benefit of all or some of the inhabitants, or all or part of the district. The power had been used to finance school milk and law centres in Alphaville. However, the district solicitor was of the opinion that, despite interpretations elsewhere, it was not clear whether co-operatives came under the heading of 'benefit of all or some' and, in his concern to avoid the disapproval of the district auditor and the danger of councillors being surcharged, refused to let the co-operative be funded.

By the time this conflict had reached a head, the employment liaison officer had been appointed. She was a member of the Industrial Common Ownership Movement, a parliamentary candidate on a number of occasions and familiar with the process of parliamentary lobbying. She had a considerable array of contacts and moreover a formidable personal style. Her commitment to the cause of co-operatives, added to the already conflictual style of inter-departmental relationships which had led to the solicitor taking his stance, produced an escalating situation where distinguished lawyers were employed who were willing to counter the solicitor's interpretation and posed a threat to his professional identity. The outcome was recourse to counsel's opinion: a process which produced a remarkably opaque document which could be interpreted in whatever way one chose and which allowed the solicitor to retire from the field with his professional skills of interpretation intact.

Policy and Action

The goals of the policy

There were two conflicting goals for co-operative policy which did not become explicit until the process of implementation had demonstrated their opposition to each other. Co-operatives in Alphaville were seen as a way of directly employing unemployed Alphaville workers who would then have control over their own working lives, and they were also seen as an experiment of national importance, where co-operative policy could be shown to work. The members of the first co-operative to come forward were drawn from the ranks of the unemployed by the Employment Services Division of the Manpower Services Commission. They were a mixed group of electrical installation engineers from the construction industry, many of whom (the younger element) had been unemployed for a short period only and were constantly looking for other jobs. Others (the older element) were into their second year of unemployment. The problems presented by this group were: how to educate them in the 'art of co-operating', how to generate enthusiasm and commitment for the emerging co-operative, and how to keep the group membership stable.

The process of meeting these problems turned out to be time-consuming in terms of officer and member personnel, and was achieved only to a limited extent: most of the livelier younger workers found employment elsewhere during the preliminary work. At the same time, much potential co-operator time was involved in market research, raising finance and goodwill, a considerable commitment; whilst endless meetings about cash flows, break-even points and two-year cash projections continued for weeks. Many innovations were created as a result of this experience, not least how to 'create co-operators'; but the achievement of the goal of establishing a viable co-operative was seriously hampered. It later proved to be the case that those without experience of work, or those about to be made redundant, and therefore with commitment to their work and each other, were preferable raw material for the policy.

Central-local relationships

The co-operative experiment is instructive for relationships with central organizations on two planes: central government/local authority and trade union headquarters/co-operators. Co-operatives were only partly financed by the council. The greater part of their finance, the co-operators' pay, was supplied by the Manpower Services Commission from a fund retained for special projects under the then Job Creation Programme. Two criteria were laid down by the MSC: the enterprise had to demonstrate its ability to break even after the period of assistance was over, and it had to show that it did not compete with other businesses 'in the area'. The former demand meant that the co-operators and officers were immediately involved in complicated prediction and market procedures, in which they were assisted by the local further education college business school, where enthusiasts were found who would offer their expertise at a nominal rate. The latter demand meant that the co-operators were not able to use their existing skills because an electrical installation co-operative would have created subsidized competition in a fast declining market. They were, therefore, reduced to concentrating on the maintenance of domestic electrical equipment and to contracts for electrical work which the council itself could place. In other words, they had to enter a protected market. The lessons learned from this experience eventually led the council to set up a market research group whose function was to seek out new products and market research them so that co-operators could be introduced to packages which fulfilled the criterion of the MSC.

The TUC, which has representatives on the MSC's structure for approving projects, insisted that all members of co-operatives belonged to a trade union, a requirement which led to a number withdrawing from the project. However, in the case of Alphaville's first co-operative, there was personal animosity between the General Secretary of the union concerned and the chairman of the co-operators, who would, incidentally, not have been a working co-operator. He resigned, but too late to save the co-operative, which foundered before its voyage commenced. Later co-operatives were more successful, but the above case history shows how implementation of employment policies can consume the time and energy of officers in establishing the appropriateness of the activity.

One of the most interesting aspects of the implementation procedure here was the conflictual style in which it was carried on. Many of the early meetings, regarding powers and finance and, later, premises, were carried on in a climate of high drama, with the employment liaison officer playing a highly charged aggressive role, the deputy planning officer playing a higher status, supporting, though more reasoning role, the policy analyst playing the go-between role, and the director of planning playing the adjudicating role. Throughout the process, one of the junior councillors played a 'progress chasing' role, visiting the department frequently, particularly on crisis days, attending meetings of the co-operators and calling in the chairman of the planning committee when officers from other departments were, in his view, being obstructive.

This section has shown how a socially-oriented policy, in seeking successful implementation, has to become involved in a series of negotiations and compromises to become established and resourced. In particular, the relationship with the resourcing body – in this case, both the local authority itself, defended by the solicitor's department, and the Manpower Services Commission – presents an especially difficult series of negotiations where the nature of compromises forced from the implementers can change the outcome of the policy.

Leasing policy

After the first eighteen months of the new employment policy, Alphaville had built, and had let, one block of small units and had purchased, converted and partially let one large ex-packing factory. Three further small blocks of units were in the process of construction. Two events came together to produce pressure for control over the sort of firm that should occupy the premises. The first was pressure from the local Trades Council, the second a problem of finding premises for a co-operative.

The Trades Council had become concerned at the quality of the firms occupying the flatted factories and, together with council community development workers and backbench members, set out to show that some firms were responsible for low pay and in particular, the employment of homeworkers at low rates. This concern was then taken up by planning department officers who perceived that it ran counter to one of the council's policies as set out in the draft district plan, concerning pay and conditions of work. The leases were about to be signed for the factory involved, but the solicitor felt that they could not be held up at such a late stage. The community development team in the chief executive's department then proposed to members that a leasing policy be created which would ensure good working conditions and rights of union membership. The policy was to be drafted by the planning department.

The second event to reinforce this bid was the culmination of a local expression of a conflict based on professional ideologies. Since the beginnings of implementation of the policy, one element of it, the density policy, had led to disquiet among the valuers, who were responsible for the letting of council property. They felt that to insist on a specified ratio of jobs to floorspace was to interfere with the free operation of the market, by which property should go to the highest bidder. They reinforced this argument by showing that the law required them to behave in a 'businesslike manner' and that the district auditor could make them responsible for deviations from this rule. In addition, they felt that, anyway, the situation feared by the planning department would not arise because high-paying tenants were likely to employ satisfactory numbers of employees. However, there came the inevitable case where the social goals of employment policy conflicted with the economic goals of estates policy: the valuer had to choose between a small co-operative employing seven and an antiques storage firm who were prepared to offer more for the premises.

The principle of marketing, then, was challenged from two positions. The solicitor again had recourse to the advice of counsel, who showed as regards the co-operative that it was possible to behave in a businesslike way, whilst specifying the type of user who would occupy the premises, for example co-operatives. He also said that a lease with clauses similar to those suggested by the council was not illegal but was unlikely to be enforceable. The co-operative got its premises. A lease was drawn up and was about to be implemented in selecting tenants for the second block of units, when the Conservative party took office in the Town Hall and as one of its first acts withdrew the lease. Incidentally, the valuers took this opportunity to take their philosophy to its logical conclusion and let the premises to the highest bidder, rather than at fixed rent levels, as they had themselves decided under the previous administration.

It is interesting to note that one of the last acts of the outgoing administration was to bring its leasing policy to the notice of the inner area employment group, where it was presented after the elections to a membership with a much larger Tory representation. The report from the honorary solicitor echoed counsel's report to Alphaville and left it to the districts concerned to choose whether to implement it or not. As few had at that time built their own units the choice was delayed, but some evinced interest.

Here we have an attempt in the implementation process to advance head-on into the conflict between economic and social goals. These are represented in professional ideologies by the valuer and the social planner, a professional conflict which is, in turn, echoed in political conflicts between, for example, the Treasury ministers and the ministers with responsibility for social services. This conflict is central to the implementation of a comprehensive employment policy: policies to aid the market process rely on the creation of sufficient long-term growth to allow redistribution; the problem may require an earlier solution.

The General Powers Bill

Alphaville had experienced major problems, as we have seen, in the implementation of its employment policies because of lack of specific powers. The General Powers Bill in question was drafted when the Labour party was in power in the county and included several clauses giving the county and the districts, if they wanted them, powers to aid industry. The clauses involved giving financial assistance to industrial firms for both building and working capital. The county interest in these powers arose mostly from their involvement in a major development site outside Alphaville, but Alphaville was happy to make use of them, particularly those involving aid for working capital. Unfortunately, the Conservative party came to power in the county just before the Bill was to go through Parliament and withdrew most of the industry clauses from the Bill, leaving the clause providing the power to advertise the delights of the county as a location for industry.

At the time of the withdrawal, the inner area employment group was chaired by a councillor from a district other than Alphaville, who was particularly interested in employment matters. This district had recently announced a fund for industrial policy of several million pounds, and they were also anxious to have the powers in the Bill. They therefore suggested that the districts petition to have the industrial clauses reinstated and a number, including Alphaville, agreed. This involved the preparation of an immense amount of evidence, and the briefing of counsel for presentation at a House of Commons Special Committee. The county was not pleased about the petition, arguing against it at member and officer level in the employment group meetings, but they agreed not to oppose the petition in committee.

We now add the variable of central-local relations between central government and the districts. Both the Department of the Environment and the Department of Industry opposed the petition. The Department of the Environment argued that the principle of universality of powers would be breached. They acknowledged that other local authorities had similar powers, but noted that they would lapse soon with the forthcoming review of special powers. They added that they were anyway contemplating general legislation on such powers. This was actually a reference to the Inner Urban Areas Act, which in fact established a principle of non-universality, but one which was centrally determined.

The Department of Industry was implacably against the Bill as a breach of regional policy. They foresaw the powers being utilized to provide incentives for large firms to locate in the county's major development site rather than in the Assisted Areas, and, indeed, this was largely what the county administration had had in mind. Alphaville, on the other hand, with a smaller budget and a policy for aiding co-operatives, small firms and local firms, was more concerned to use the powers for small disbursements to small firms. It argued, on the basis of academic work, that such firms were unlikely to move to the Assisted Areas anyway, and if allowed to grow in the inner areas of the county, would eventually provide branch-plants for the mobile industry policies of the Department of Industry. This eventually became the argument of the petitioners, although there was some resistance to accepting it from some districts in which lay the aforementioned development site; they would have preferred to take the Department of Industry head-on.

The Committee was made up of MPs from the Assisted Areas and shire counties, two Labour and two Conservative, with a Conservative chairman. The petition was successful, partly at least because of the evidence of the employment liaison officer from Alphaville, whose political experience and passionate commitment to Alphaville and to co-operatives were obvious to the MPs. However, it was defeated in the House, largely due to the efforts of the ministers concerned.

Alphaville eventually gained some of the powers under the Inner Urban Areas Act, where it has third-tier designated status, but still has no specific power to loan or grant working capital to small firms. However, the employment liaison officer and the research director of the Alphaville planning department were successful, with their colleagues in the movement for co-operatives, in having a clause included in the Inner Areas Act which enabled assistance to be given to co-operatives.

This example demonstrates how central government attempts to control the efforts of local authorities to equip themselves with the means to implement policies which central government feels run counter to the principles of its own national policies. The above example can be described as part of central government's implementation of its regional policy and its attempt to deal with the inner areas of cities outside the areas assisted under that policy without wrecking the concept of priority regions. It also illustrates some of the problems faced by one local authority in attempting to take advantage of alliances with others.

Conclusion

The recently published report of the RTPI Working Party on implementation included in its recommendations the need to make sure that the implementation of policies was clearly allocated to one or more officers to 'turn that decision into action, by whatever means are available and appropriate'.[2] The evidence from the case study of Alphaville suggests that this is probably a difficult recommendation to achieve in practice because the situation is, in fact, much more complicated than it would need to be if clear allocation was to work. Clear allocation might, in fact, have been disfunctional because it was not always apparent, until implementation was achieved, exactly who had the competence to carry out the task. The Working Party also states that policies should be 'clear, simple and relevant' in order to be 'understandable to a wide variety of people'.[3] However, again, the evidence quoted above suggests that although clarity, simplicity and relevance may make for wider understanding, the outcome from that understanding does not necessarily lead to 'implementation'.

In effect, some of the policies in Alphaville emerged *after* the process of implementation had begun. Others, however, emerged from the political process within the members' context. All were then brought together and, in this case, presented as a coherent policy package. At that stage, Alphaville's employment policy was, in fact, a series of simply and clearly stated policies, relevant to the economic situation in Alphaville in a political sense at least, and allocated to specific officers in the planning department. What followed was an almost unchartable mêlée which might, in the absence of the introduction of a new set of policies when the administration changed to Conservative control, have led to implementation.

However, what would have been implemented? In fact, the things 'done on the ground' were not necessarily those in the politicians' minds when they formulated the policies. The co-operatives turned out to be very different from the 'alternative sector' which the politicians had in mind: the factories were occupied by different sorts of firms from those which the politicians really wanted, and so on.

The process described by Schon had, in fact, taken place at local level.[4] The politicians and the implementers had produced something, but in so doing had learned something new, something unexpected, which the triggering policy no longer accurately described. So perhaps one lesson which can be drawn from these examples is that implementation is unlikely to lead to the originally desired outcome, although the outcome may, of course, be desirable under the new conditions.

One of the characteristics of the process which has been described is the immense importance and complexity of the networking process, both within the organization and outside it. This has also been taken up by the RTPI Working Party formally, in a suggestion for the need for a task force and informally in a reference to a redrawing of the organizational map. However, the attempt to formalize the networks is, perhaps, to be resisted. The extreme dynamic of a situation of implementation suggests a combination of conflict and alliances with no lasting structure. The formalization of any structure will, indeed, either lead to the demise of the implementation process or its re-emergence elsewhere in a new informal structure.

Recent work on implementation has also pointed out the importance of these networks, referring to them as 'implementation structures' which cut across the hierarchies beloved of organizations and the theories which describe their operation.[5] However, there is a tendency in Hjern and Hull's paper, too, to suggest that general rules which are simple and replicable can be discovered as to the operation of these structures. I suspect this may not be true.

However, one of the main characteristics of the kind of implementation I have been describing is the by-passing of rules, for instance in the case of the lettings policy on factories, or the use of Section 137, and even the destruction of rules. Now it is true that you require a certain type of person, or perhaps just motivation, in order to achieve this. However, the interesting question is: what is it that provides the legitimacy for this sort of implementation? The answer must surely lie with the nature of the political problem which is being faced in Alphaville and places like it. Heydebrand has drawn our attention to the importance of external crisis in triggering off the sorts of rule changes and innovatory networking described in this chapter.[6] Certainly, it could be said that if the economic problems had not been so obvious in Alphaville, then the legitimacy for the implementation of even the most conventional of the policies would have been lacking.

I suppose the question which remains is, how far could implementation have gone? Could the bulwarks of lawyers, finance department, surveyors' professional ethics, inter-departmental rivalries have continued to crumble? This might, perhaps, have depended upon the continued interpretation of the political crisis as a priority and the evaluation of the implementation achieved as inadequate. However, given those conditions, what could have been prescribed?

The author here finds himself in agreement with Fay,[7] that there is a danger of assuming that implementation is based on a rationality which can be scientifically understood, and that rules for the game can be produced. Structures, even if they are called 'implementation structures', are characteristic of consensus and agreement: they may even be symptoms of 'yesterday's policies' being accepted. Implementation may imply the constant breaking down of structures, of rules, of sacred areas, or their use only as objects to achieve their own destruction. It is possible that implementers, if they get 'caught' in the new structures which they may set up to replace the old ones, will end up as bulwarks against the next wave of implementers.

Implementers, then, may be not so much structures as individuals, who break free from, or, in the case of Alphaville, never become part of the existing structure. They then pursue their own action career, constantly making alliances and breaking them, bringing outside legitimacy into the organization if necessary, using political legitimacy where accessible. Members may, themselves, be implementers, as in the case of the co-operatives policy, networking with officers and taking the initiative themselves.

Perhaps one of the most important characteristics of the implementers is a lack of reverence for the 'implementing organization' and its rules, and those of its context, in this case, for instance, the Departments of Industry and Environment and the House of Commons.

However, outside a situation of 'putsch' or takeover, the implementer is always 'used' by another, for example, by a chief officer or a senior member, as a convenient front – a 'hit-man'. The implementer may take the policies a bit further than 'the other' would originally have expected, or wanted, but eventually they have to be controlled if the organizational hierarchy is to survive. Sweeping innovation is, thus, unlikely within this model.

Notes and references

1 Ideas embodied in Chandler and Templeton 1980.
2 Royal Town Planning Institute 1979.
3 Royal Town Planning Institute 1979.
4 Schon 1971.
5 Hjern and Hull 1980.
6 Heydebrand 1977: 83–107.
7 Fay 1979.

5

Winning an election and gaining control:

the formulation and implementation of a 'local' political manifesto

Colin Fudge

> The Labour Group requests that at its next meeting the Chairman of the major committees should present a progress report on the implementation of our manifesto commitments and an outline of a future programmed time-table for carrying out those commitments which still remain outstanding.[1]

This motion was proposed and agreed in the Labour party group one year after their successful campaign to retain control of the London Borough of Brent Council, following the May 1978 elections. The manifesto[2] it refers to and, in particular, the path to its implementation during the first year and sub-sequently are the subject of this chapter. The motion suggests that in Brent the Labour politicians hold certain assumptions about the nature of local auton-omy, their ability to govern and the role they need to play to obtain control locally.

It is the aim here to trace – from familiarity but not propinquity – the formulation of political objectives at the local level, their consolidation in a document – an election manifesto – and the use of this framework by the party group, individual members and officers in the execution of these objectives. The account is partial and derives, not from a concerted research effort, but from impressions acquired somewhat haphazardly from a variety of sources: recorded semi-structured interviews, documentation, meetings and political gossip. The choice of the inquiries and issues pursued, however, has been informed by a strong base of experience with the world of local government and its politics.

In reflecting on the experience of the first year, what will be stressed is the importance of raising, in the study of implementation, questions about whether *local* policy-making really is *local* or merely a reflection of stereotyped ideological responses to issues and problems; and whether elected members are really involved in shaping, deciding and executing the policies of the authority. These questions raise issues about the *limits* of member involvement and local politics, prescribed by the changing context of local government, the non-local forces of policy change and by the nature of the councillor's job.

The Borough of Brent

The Borough of Brent was formed in 1965 by the amalgamation of the former boroughs of Willesden and Wembley. It lies in the north-west quadrant of Greater London and straddles the middle section of a radial line running from London's centre to the Green Belt edges of the city beyond Harrow.

In the field of contemporary British politics it has some minor claim to fame in that many readers, perhaps unknowingly, will be familiar with parts of the Borough and its politics. Within its boundaries are the parliamentary seats of Rhodes Boyson, the current Minister of State for Education and Science, on the one hand, and Reg Freeson, the ex-Minister of State for Housing and Construction, on the other. It is also the 'home' of English soccer. Wembley Stadium sits in the middle of the administrative area and, without realizing it, many people may have travelled, via television or in person, through the area to the stadium. However, on such occasions one's perception of the place bears little resemblance to reality. Brent on any other day has no strongly remembered form, nor any distinct social or physical entity of its own. Brent is a somewhat arbitrary slice of north-west London which happens to be administered by the London Borough of Brent.

In terms of acreage, the dominant use is housing, the urban structure having developed primarily as residential suburbs to London. The broad pattern is one of Victorian and Edwardian terraces and semi-detached houses in the old Borough of Willesden and of twentieth-century 'suburban' houses in Wembley. Willesden is more densely developed, with few open spaces or other breaks between the housing; Wembley has a lower density, much more open space, broken by some larger housing estates. These open spaces, together with the North Circular Road, major industrial estates, individual housing estates and railway land, form the main physical divides between residential areas.[3]

Brent today contains a range of metropolitan characteristics: a considerable diversity of environments, housing types and conditions, and social and ethnic groups. The Borough's population, arguably the largest mixture of people of all income groups, occupation, races, languages, religions and cultures in London, is falling and changing. The housing varies considerably in age, type, condition, tenure and occupation density; and half of the population has to travel out of the Borough to find work. The historical development of the area has led to the creation in many minds of a stereotyped division between 'working-class Willesden' and 'middle-class Wembley'. This perception, it has been argued,[4] may affect the personal decision-making of families and the political decision-making of parties and the Council.

Political and administrative structure

Three parliamentary constituencies were formed at the time of Brent's own creation in 1965. They are:

1   Brent North (comprising a large part of the old Borough of Wembley)
2   Brent East (comprising the northern part of the old Borough of Willesden, between Church End, Queens Park and the Edgware Road)
3   Brent South (comprising the southern part of the old Borough of Willesden, plus Wembley Central, Barham and Alperton wards)

Brent North has had consistently Conservative majorities since it was formed; Brent East and Brent South have had consistently Labour majorities. Voting at the General Elections of 1974 and 1979 is shown in Table 4.

Table 4   *Voting results for the 1974 and 1979 General Elections*

	Brent North		Brent East		Brent South	
	1974	1979	1974	1979	1974	1979
Conservative	24,853	29,995	11,554	14,008	10,558	12,562
Labour	17,541	18,612	20,481	20,351	21,611	24,178
Liberal	8,158	5,872	4,416	2,799	3,929	2,859
National Front	1,297	873	1,096	706	1,388	811
Other	—	—	382	290	—	—

Source: *Guardian*, 5 May 1979

These results illustrate the general balance of political loyalties throughout the Borough, and suggest that there are limitations to the stereotypes of 'Labour Willesden' and 'Tory Wembley'. What is particularly noteworthy is the way in which the Labour vote held or increased from 1974 to 1979 at an election where in London and the South-East generally the swing away from Labour was remarkable.

The Borough Council[5] has a strong party political character. The political complexion of the council is polarized around the two major parties and control has swung between them. Labour controlled the council in 1965, following the reorganization of London government; in 1968 there was a change to Conservative control, along with a general swing to the Conservatives in London; in 1971 it returned to Labour and has remained so ever since. Voting at the local elections of 1978 gave the Labour party 39 seats on the council and the Conservative party 27 seats.

Until the last couple of years, the decision-making behaviour might have been characterized by strong political control within each main departmental area, with the chairman and chief officer jointly providing a strong lead; but with rather less apparent interest or development in inter-departmental working and little political demand or machinery for corporate management or planning. Over the past two to three years, there has been a growing awareness among some members and officers of the desirability for improvement in the council's handling of the needs of the diverse communities, families and individuals in the borough.

Formulating policy: the manifesto

About eighteen months to two years before the May 1978 London borough elections, some members of the Brent Borough Labour party started to exchange ideas about the forthcoming election campaign. At a meeting of the Local Government Committee,[6] it was decided to formulate a political manifesto as a platform for the election campaign and, in some people's minds, as an operational framework to guide policy development and action subsequent to a successful election result.

The purpose of the manifesto

During discussions with councillors and Labour party members involved at the time, four main reasons for having a manifesto emerged:

1   The manifesto would provide a platform upon which to fight the election. There was a desire for a comprehensive and convincing document, more detailed than those in the past, which would unify the work of the party activists in the election and encourage them to go out and convince the people of Brent that the local Labour party was worth returning to power. As a by-product it was thought that the election address would be more convincing and easier to write if it was based on a broader, more thorough document.

2   If the Labour party were returned to power, the manifesto would be used as a guide to action. This purpose, although suggested and agreed in discussion, may also have been subject to different interpretations. For example, it is not clear whether it was established how much discretion the leadership and councillors would have to reinterpret or adjust the mani-

festo as circumstances changed; how the document would stand up to changes over the four years in office; whether it represented a binding contract with the party; or whether councillors would be expected to be accountable for their actions to the party, and by what process.

3   Having a manifesto, and therefore having to prepare the content, would provide opportunities for the lay and council members of the local Labour party to comment on existing policies and practice and participate in policy development. This kind of opportunity was seen as an important contribution to moves to improve Labour party democracy at the local level and allow a greater number of its members, whether they be councillors, party activists or simply party members, more of a say in shaping future policies for Brent.

4   The spelling out of policy objectives clearly, across a broad range of issues and in one document satisfied two further, possibly opposing, objectives. On the one hand, it provided the leadership with a device for channelling commitment, maintaining solidarity and achieving control. On the other hand, the institution of broad targets against which progress could be measured would be of particular concern to some party members and backbenchers interested in accountability in the party group and the party generally.

Content

The manifesto 'Forward together . . . with Labour' is divided into ten different chapters, each dealing with a different aspect of policy.[7] The policy discussion is couched in fairly simple terms and the policy objectives – 'Labour will do' – are lists of objectives of varying magnitude. Some are very specific and detailed:

> 6.2.6   (Labour will) Call for a bus service from Wembley Park Station along Fryent Way to Kingsbury.[8]
> 4.4.6   (Labour will) Devolve management of allotment sites to the Allotment Societies where they wish as we have with Lower Place.[9]

Others are broad and wide ranging:

> 9.1.15   . . . when re-elected, Labour will seek to press Central Government to provide these funds. We will campaign openly at national and local levels with all Labour groups and forces who are willing to join us whilst continuing our policy of using existing finance to ensure, as far as possible, that privilege is eliminated and that all citizens of Brent are given the chance to achieve a decent standard of life.[10]

Although the various policy areas are generally self-contained, there is some discussion of inter-departmental or between-committee problems, for example in the Social Services chapter:

> 3.4 Co-operation with other Council Departments; (Labour will) continue to encourage links recently established with Housing and Education Services, to highlight priorities and areas of great need in the future and tackle problems in a flexible way.[11]

It is quite noticeable that many of the objectives, if they are to be successfully implemented, require not only co-operation between departments but also the support and action of other agencies in both the public and private sectors.

There is very little discussion of how the various policy intentions will be achieved, merely the assertion that 'Labour will do'. The manifesto items have not been costed; the finance section provides little guidance on how objectives and resulting financial commitments will be met; and there is no overall view of priorities either within or between policy areas. It can be argued that such refinements would make the document more complex and unsuitable for its basic purpose as a platform upon which to fight an election. However, in terms of the other reasons for the manifesto, particularly its use as a guide for action once elected, some of the refinements might have been quite useful. Perhaps the main point is that one document simply cannot satisfy all of the purposes for which it is required.

Formulation

The process by which the manifesto was formulated was similar for most of the policy themes; that is to say, it was carried out by working parties of party members. The performance of these groups varied, as did the number of meetings or working sessions they held. In the case of social services, no group met, leaving a member very interested in social services to put together the section on his own over one weekend. This was an exception, however, and it is perhaps more useful to trace through the stages followed by the rest of the working parties.

First, a paper would be prepared by a member of the Brent Labour party in consultation with the existing chairman of the relevant committee. Work on these papers was started in May and June 1977. The information used in this first paper was drawn from a number of different sources, some of which were: previous manifestos; chairman's personal position statement; views held in the party; the council's position statements published in 1977.[12] This paper was then used as the basis for debate at the first meeting of the working party. The working parties were open to all members of the Brent Labour party, but generally consisted of current chairmen of committees, other councillors and party activists. The meetings to discuss the 'opening' paper usually took place at weekends.

Second, following the first meeting it was possible to see broadly where there was agreement and where not, and ways in which a consensus might be obtained. Building on this position, one member from each working party drew up a first draft statement on the particular policy theme. All of these first drafts were then put together to form a draft manifesto which formed the basis for discussion at a one-day 'policy conference' of the Brent Labour party convened by the party's Local Government Committee. This took place in November 1977. The one-day conference, which filled the council chamber, allowed other Labour party members not involved in the working parties to have a say in policy development and the preparation of the manifesto.

Third, each working party met again to discuss the views expressed at the conference and to make revisions of their sections of the manifesto. A second draft manifesto containing each working party's latest revisions was then put together and copies sent to each ward party for discussion at their next monthly meeting. Most of these discussions took place in January 1978, about four months before the election.

One of the three constituency parties wished to make a number of revisions to the manifesto, as a result of grassroots feelings within their wards, and these amendments were considered at the meeting of the Local Government Committee in late February. The constituency party wishing to make amendments turned up in full force (the Local Government Committee is open to all Brent Labour party members) and with their significant majority carried the day, much to the annoyance of the other two constituency parties. However, if the latter were a little tardy in entering the final debate, this soon galvanized them into action. Important negotiations followed between the various groups concerned, with full attendance from all quarters! Following these negotiations within the party, only a couple of months before the election, a 'rough' version of the manifesto was agreed. The word negotiation screens some important tactical moves, bluffs and counter-moves within different groups of the party, which for an outsider are difficult to disentangle and yet are recognized as being highly significant. The rough, third draft of the manifesto was rewritten for publication and a format was adopted which demonstrated: what the party had achieved since the elections in 1974; the problems still to be faced; and the party's policy objectives if re-elected.

Earlier, four main reasons for having a manifesto were suggested. From observation, a fifth can be cautiously added. It is one that is significant to both the formulation of policy and its implementation. By experiencing a concerted, but fairly informal, process for arriving at the manifesto, the committed in the party, many of whom were later to be either re-elected or become councillors for the first time, would have had the opportunity to work together, to develop a deeper understanding of each other and to identify more closely with the main thrusts of party policy and the tasks ahead. Thus the *process* of developing policy, that is, the way in which people worked together to prepare the manifesto, may be an important contributory factor in subsequently dealing with the problems of implementation.

It must be acknowledged, however, that local parties vary and that in some the process might not be as open as the one in Brent appears to be. In these circumstances, the working parties could equally be used in a more manipulative way to maintain existing policies and political stances, to stifle criticism and debate, and to bring the unconvinced into line. Further examination is therefore needed to establish to what extent the process allows existing policy and previous performance to be reviewed and new or revised policies generated.

Implementing the manifesto: the first year

By the early hours of 5 May 1978, the members of the Labour party in Brent knew that they had been returned to power. This was a time for celebration, but soon the euphoria would die away and the majority party would get down to business: electing its officers, sorting out the committee responsibilities, starting to fill up their diaries, dealing with some of the issues that had arisen during the election period and thinking about direction and action over the next four years. This section turns to the implementation of the manifesto and asks, what status does the manifesto have now that the election is over? How do they start? How do they maintain their commitment and direction in the complex world of urban government?

Getting started and keeping going

We might speculate on the role of the manifesto once the election has been won. There will, of course, be varying individual attitudes within the group. For some councillors, perhaps those who are concentrating on ward problems or special schemes or projects left over from last time, the manifesto has done its job – the party and, most of all, they themselves are back in power again. Others bear it in mind and see it as a broad guide, but recognize that in reality they may have to adjust their actions and also the manifesto itself in the time ahead. For others still, particularly those most passionate in upholding democracy and open government, the manifesto may represent a binding contract to be adhered to throughout the life of the administration. New members may be finding the whole experience of being a councillor for the first time so overwhelming that the manifesto might represent, on the one hand, a lifeline or, on the other, merely another document littering the sitting-room floor. For the eager backbencher, the manifesto might represent an important lever to use in group to gain access to the policy arena. The manifesto, then, may be perceived by different people in different ways and, indeed, may be used by the same person in varying ways, depending on the nature of the issue at stake. Given this variety of perceptions and positions, how does the majority party start to govern? At a general level, the manifesto is implemented in two ways:

1 Through the leader, deputy leader and committee chairman communi-cating the policy objectives to the chief officers, such that they all have it in mind when carrying out their functions and duties.
2 Through the party group having it in mind and acting as a kind of memory-cum-conscience. In addition, both of these groups are also accountable to the Brent Labour party as a whole and to local party activists who might monitor and check progress, via the Local Government Committee.

At a more detailed level, getting started is seen as being primarily the responsibility of the leadership and the committee chairmen. The leader or deputy leader was responsible for ensuring that the ideas contained in the manifesto as a whole were embedded in the collective mind of the officers as early as possible via the town clerk, but the responsibility in each policy or departmental area was left largely to the chairmen. Individual chairmen approached this task in different ways. Most of the chief officers were given copies of the manifesto or the parts that were relevant to their service or responsibility. The example of leisure services is one illustration of what could happen.

The chairman of the Leisure Committee arranged two meetings at weekends with the members of his committee, during which the manifesto was dis-cussed. In these meetings they studied the parts of the manifesto relevant to the activities they foresaw as being the responsibility of their committee. For example, they looked at and discussed the sections on race relations, employ-ment, youth and community work and education, as well as the specific section on leisure. They also spent time arriving at a view, albeit in fairly simple terms, of the priorities for action. They achieved this through a high/medium/low ranking of objectives from the manifesto, based on interpretations held by different councillors. Thus, before having their first formal committee meeting, they had already done quite a lot of work sorting out their priorities, knowing what direction they wanted to go in, providing guidance for the chairman and developing a capability in working together and a commitment and feel for the policy area.

Following this, that is prior to the first official meeting, the chairman met his chief officer and some of the section leaders in the department and used the occasion to hand over the relevant parts of the manifesto as it affected the department's activities. Once again, this briefing included drawing the officers' attention not only to the parts of the manifesto which were of direct concern to them, but also to the other parts which should affect their work. In addition, the chairman briefed the officers about priorities. This, then, was the start of the chairman's relationship with the chief officer and section heads.

As the year progressed, the chairman maintained his links with the chief officer by allocating a certain number of days in the year during which progress on manifesto items, amongst other matters, could be discussed. These discussions would include questions about how the officers were doing on manifesto items and also the methods they were using to achieve the objectives. In this particular service, the chief officer had developed a practice of providing the chairman with draft items for the agenda some time before it would become more widely known in the authority, and this practice also provided an opportunity for further discussion from both sides concerning the manifesto and other material. Through this semi-formal communication and through the chairman's ability to 'be around' and 'pop in', a watch over and involvement in the implementation of manifesto items was maintained.

The leisure example presents a somewhat misleading view of the apparent ease of getting involved in aspects of policy implementation and seemingly overcoming implementation problems. To take a second example, this time from the Education section of the manifesto:

> 2.3.6   Corporal Punishment: Abolish corporal punishment in our Schools after consultation with teachers and parents,[13]

a different and perhaps more common view is presented.

This example illustrates more closely for many the reality of implementation: a process of negotiation and bargaining carried out over a fairly long period, requiring patience, stamina and skill from those involved, who may or may not be councillors. Many people involved politically in Brent, including councillors and party activists, thought that this objective would be achieved more or less overnight. The policy has proved to be far too controversial for such a quick result, and at the time of writing the council is still negotiating with the educational profession. For a majority party like Brent Labour party, committed in their terms to a programme of radical changes, expansion and development of services and improvements to the quality of public intervention, they have to consider the process through which manifesto statements can be turned into working practices, whilst at the same time maintaining the strength of the original policy intention. If the only way certain policy intentions can be achieved is by negotiation and bargaining with the officers of the council, the question of who should be involved in this kind of process and what skills and information are required needs to be addressed.

A further example may provide an answer. The leadership and the party group realized that if they were to achieve the various objectives they wished to pursue, then they would have to face up to the problems of industrial relations. What was needed was for somebody, preferably of some seniority in the group, to agree to get involved in industrial relations in the council setting. This person would need to develop a specialism in industrial relations to be able to cope with existing problems and, especially, new problems which might occur as Brent expanded its services and introduced new policies and practices. The deputy leader took on the job and developed a peripatetic role assisting in negotiations between the officers and the unions.[14] In a similar way, the housing chairmen and deputy leader have spent much time on housing matters both within the council and on outside bodies, such as the London Boroughs Association. Thus there is a strong belief that councillors in Brent should be involved in both policy development and implementation, and should develop adequate skills and be able to draw on appropriate resources to maintain their involvement and improve its effectiveness.

Responsiveness and review

As the first year progressed, there was more and more discussion about 'new' opportunities to be seized and 'new' problems to be faced. In Harrow, just outside the borough, an independent school was facing possible closure, and this was seen by some councillors and interested parties in the borough as an opportunity to provide a school for musically gifted children living in Brent, who at that time had no such provision nearby. The objective of providing educational facilities for gifted children was not contained in the manifesto; hence this was a new project 'outside' the terms of reference of the manifesto. Nevertheless it claimed strong political support and through this was implemented. Now, it is not the intention here to delve into this particular example in detail, but merely to illustrate that new opportunities, like this example, frequently present themselves. The question is, how are they handled in relation to manifesto commitments? In some cases, the leadership or a chairman may use their discretion to decide an issue there and then. Generally, this would be where the objectives of the manifesto were not particularly affected or threatened. However, to move away from the manifesto, or to reinterpret parts of it, would be more difficult and might be on the threshold of the leadership's discretion. In these cases, the leadership or chairman might go back to the party group for their views before making a final decision. Thus new opportunities will arise and can be taken up; new problems will have to be faced and solved; but where possible this should not mean that manifesto items are excluded or omitted.

In the more marginal cases, the Group Policy Committee[15] might take a view on the 'new' issue and report their position to the full party group. In full group, this view might be defended or attacked and the outcome would be that the group takes a view of the issue. If this was politically contentious, the group might then report back to the local party and it would be open for, say, a local ward party, or indeed an individual member, to comment via the Local Government Committee. Thus there are many ways in which new items are managed, ranging from the discretion of the leadership and chairmen to resolution through the various formal, democratic channels. This also raises the question of how responsive the manifesto is to changes over the four-year life of the administration. At the outset, little thought, perhaps, was given to the need to change the manifesto. Although the Local Government Committee meets every two months and holds additional special policy meetings (for example, meetings have been held on falling school rolls, keeping of ethnic records and the rate rise), it was not until their annual general meeting, almost at the end of the first year, that the deputy leader suggested that the manifesto could not remain static for the four years and still be a central guiding document. As a result of this, the Local Government Committee have accepted, as a working principle, that they should review and if necessary alter the manifesto annually; and that all chairmen must be accountable to the Local Government Committee for their part of the manifesto.

Towards the end of the first year there were moves within the party group to have some sort of review of progress in achieving the objectives contained in the manifesto. I referred in my introduction to the motion which was proposed and accepted in the party group and which demanded that a formal review of progress should take place and that each chairman should be accountable to the group and the party for their part of the manifesto. At two meetings of the party group the chairmen provided a brief typed statement relating the progress of the implementation of the manifesto items dealt with by their committee. The review statement on financial resources was not as satisfying to the Labour councillors as the others. This particular review explained the likely financial situation for the next year (1980–1) and made a plea for a rapid appraisal of commitments in the light of an unfavourable (and with hindsight, accurate) prognosis of the future financial context. The chairman of finance went on to suggest that the leader, deputy leader, chairman of finance and chairman of group, in consultation with the chief officers and the chairman of the Spending Committee, should advise on priorities, options and possible contingencies in terms of finance and manpower both in the current and the coming year.

Between 18 June and 25 July, the Labour party in Brent went into action over the proposed cuts as a result of the budget and changes envisaged in the Rate Support Grant (particularly to pay for the Clegg settlement). Policy working parties were reconvened, lay ward members involved, local government trade unions consulted, with the result that within just over a month the majority party had agreed a strategy. As a result of this exercise they also agreed that in future review exercises they would examine more closely the level of quality of existing services in relation to the manifesto objectives and that, if necessary, cuts in some areas may be necessary to finance the new policy initiatives.

By drawing on different issues during the first year of the Labour administration, this section has sought to describe some of the ways in which councillors in Brent were involved in implementing the manifesto. The final section reflects on the ways the councillors operated and suggests that the present system of local government, or at least how it operates, limits their involvement and effectiveness.

Gaining control

It is clear from an examination of the implementation of locally generated political objectives that the determination of politicians in Brent to be involved in the formulation of their own policy and actively engaged in seeing that it is carried through to action is beyond question. The question that many people might ask is why they needed to go to these lengths. Surely, it would be argued, as the majority party and politicians, they are in control and their policies are the ones that are formulated and get implemented. The Brent members' concern to be involved in *all* stages of the policy process suggests that they hold certain views about how local government works and the real power local politicians hold. In attempting to implement the manifesto policies they have had to break a number of conventionally held assumptions about local government, local politics and the role of local politicians.

First, it is quite common to draw a clear distinction between the roles of members and officers. The establishment of general principles governing policy, or simply policy, is seen conventionally as the premise of the councillor, and the implementation of policy or the application of general principles, that of the officer. Although such a distinction has little basis in law, there is strong pressure, institutionalized in local government ideology, to deter the member from intervention beyond a certain level, to define a 'proper' role and to 'defend' some decisions and processes from the member.[16]

Other members, and indeed academics, may well argue that there is no clear dividing line between policy and implementation nor should there be. Given this view, it is the responsibility of locally elected representatives to exercise effective control over the totality of the policy process, disregarding professional or administrative definitions of what is 'technical' or 'detailed' or 'implementation'. One attempt to resolve the problems of the 'proper' role of members and officers sees policy and implementation as a continuum, with members towards the policy end and officers towards the implementation end. A closer model to reality might envisage the senior members and officers at the policy end, with backbenchers and junior officers dealing with detail and implementation. In Brent, as elsewhere, the key question is who has the final say in issues (whether of policy formulation or its execution) considered by the councillors as political? For Brent Labour councillors this means getting involved in implementation.

Second, Labour's attempts within the borough party structure to move towards more rational, anticipatory and participatory processes of policy-making are noteworthy. Although perhaps more modest, their experience is similar to that of the Labour party in Nottinghamshire in 1973, whose experience Gyford suggests 'was almost certainly unique in both its scale and outcome'.[17] A manifesto of the kind they prepared presents a tangible symbol of political initiative and control, providing clear political instructions and a means for monitoring implementation progress. In addition, the *process* by which the manifesto was formulated, the use of working parties consisting of members of the local Labour party, laymen and councillors, provides an experience through which people can learn about each other and the task at hand, resources and expertise can be shared, commitment can be generated and political control attempted. Taken together, they form the necessary 'central driving force' if politicians are to take control and offer a way of overcoming the more common situation where 'the lack of expert advice and the competition from other demands on the time of the amateur politicians tend to preclude all but the most perfunctory of attempts at formulating policies and the steps required to implement them'.[18]

It has to be recognized, however, that the Labour party was already in control of the borough during the policy formation stage. How much of the manifesto is a reflection of the then current policies and how much of 'new' local policy is not known. The answer to this would provide us with a view of policy as either one of continuity and maintenance or one of innovation – an important factor influencing the anticipated success in terms of implement- ation. Another factor which can affect policy-making of this kind is the quality of the process in terms of democracy within the party. This, in turn, is dependent on how the various parts of the party (ward, constituency, local government committee, party group) operate and interrelate. In Brent, the process seems to be fairly open and developing further; in other areas this is not necessarily the case. At a more general level, if a political party was in opposition prior to an election, would this kind of process – the formulation of a comprehensive manifesto through the involvement of party members in 'open' working parties and policy conferences – improve the chances of winning? This in turn raises the still wider question of whether local elections are won and lost on local issues and performance or national factors.[19]

Third, for implementation to be successful in the sense of a policy being carried through to action (though not necessarily successful in terms of outcome), it seems important for there to be an understanding of the character- istics of the policies and from this the ability to select the most appropriate mode of implementation, whether it be by negotiation, argument, discussion, application of force or persuasion.[20] This 'diagnostic' ability within political judgement seems particularly important in recognizing differences between policies, for example, the difference between straightforward projects (build more school kitchens) versus changes in policy emphasis or changes in the quality of service delivery (review of library service).

Fourth, if policies are to be implemented and party government is to be effective locally, then councillors and the party must know their own minds and have the political will and skill to attempt to impose their ideas on the apparatus of government. Of particular relevance here is the relationship with officers. Although the view about councillors making decisions and officers carrying them out has been challenged by some studies,[21] these have had little success in exploring the view that policies and proposals emanate from the officers and particularly the chief officer, rather than the members. The officers' style of management and administration is not necessarily designed to maximize the contribution of the elected member or to enable participation in decisions; both strong departmentalism, as in the case of Brent, and moves towards structured, centrally directed processes of planning resource allocation and decision-making, as in some other London boroughs, can inhibit participation by members, especially newer members, who are presented with a picture of continuity which is difficult and slow to change. In a number of fields the officers' management style is sustained by an appeal to professional training and standards and by increasingly complex and technical methods of presenting, analysing and forecasting problems. The officer appears to have a monopoly of expertise, experience and information. Consequently, the power within some local authorities tends to become centred in particular groups of officers. This tendency can lead to the situation where the political leadership is not 'averse to a clear division of labour between member and officer, and between leadership and backbenchers',[22] a situation where the leadership might consult the party group, provide information and obtain endorsement for policies, but does not involve them in the process of policy-making and implementation.

Thus, in attempting to gain control and implement 'progressive' policies, the majority party in Brent has had to challenge the system of local government in Brent. This has not been easy. As a consequence, the members have had to spend much time and effort preparing their own case (the manifesto), reaching down into the implementation process of the authority, developing different modes of action for implementation, challenging officers and their professional and practice ideologies, and, most of all, throwing off any views about restrictions on the role of the locally elected member.

At the end of the first year, the Brent members felt that they had been relatively successful in achieving many of the manifesto objectives. There was also a belief that by improving the co-ordination of manifesto items, reviewing their policies and practices within the annual budgetary process, establishing clearer policy priorities, obtaining agreement for broader policy goals within which speedier decisions could be made and, of most importance, continuing to develop their understanding of how to get things done, they would get nearer to satisfying their objectives. However, since that time there have been further major changes imposed by central government – cuts in public expenditure, changes to housing allocations and policy, and the withholding of part of the Rate Support Grant. These changes, coupled with continuing resistance from officers to certain policies, seriously question the autonomy of local politicians and suggest that even assertive and active political groups, like the Brent majority party, are seriously *limited* by the broader environment in which they have to operate, the impact of non-local influences and the nature of the councillor's job.

Discussion

Underlying all of these issues is the nature of the local government system. The most fundamental factor affecting the task of the elected member is the nature and extent of local discretion and control. In recent years, it has become widely accepted that central government has extended its controls, especially financial controls, in a manner which leaves local authorities with less room to manoeuvre. The combined effects of the recent fiscal crisis, of centrally determined cuts in public expenditure, the development of cash limits and the Rate Support Grant system, make the financing of local services more complex and more subject to control. The local elected representative is directly affected by these developments and the extent to which they reduce the scope for local decisions. The elected member is also increasingly dependent on local government officials to interpret and explain the nature of controls which are both complex and subject to change. But financial controls are not the only matter in question here. The volume and complexity of legislation, statutory controls and advice emanating from central government places duties and responsibilities on local authorities. These can technocratize decision-making and policy choice such that members are increasingly dependent on other persons – in particular their professional staff.

At the same time as these developments have taken place, and partly as a response to them, the style of management and administration has changed. This is most easily seen in attempts towards a 'business efficiency' approach to government and of a firmly established, centrally directed process of decision-making. These quests for rational control – corporate planning, output budgeting, chief officer teams, chief executives, policy and resources committees – tend to combine to increase the power of local government professionals and those members in a position to keep up with them. The style of management is not necessarily geared to localized problems or to the representative role of councillors. In a number of fields the style of management is sustained by an appeal to professional training and standards and conformity to national local government ideology concerning behaviour and practice. The professional officer appears to have a monopoly of expertise, experience and information which is used to restrict the capacity of the members to participate and achieve change. The power within the local authority tends to become centred in particular groups of officers and particular committees. Member involvement may lengthen the process of policy-making and implementation and conflict with other objectives of the administrative machine.

These management changes have not occurred without local political response. It has been argued, for example, that local government reorganization directly contributed to the increased proportion of councillors elected and operating under a party label. In turn this implies stronger party political involvement, as in Brent. But this may not deal with the problems of participation and involvement. The party group may become more effective and powerful in relation to the officer system but may only engage the administrative machine in a small number of key committees and in direct contacts between party leaders and chief officers. It is not evident that this development necessarily leaves the majority of elected representatives in a situation compatible with the notion of representative democracy. Indeed, Benn[23] argues that rather than increasing opportunities for discussing policy, the system more or less ensures that there is hardly time for politics at all. One way of summarizing all of these trends is to characterize them as centralist tendencies. The increasing financial control of central government, the increasing complexity and scale of activities in local government, and the styles of management developing out of these have the effect of removing policy formation and decision-making from local control. The members' role has changed in consequence. Once the councillor might have been one of eight or ten men on the council, attending evening meetings, serviced by unqualified officers known personally by frequent contact over cases, able to run the authority like a voluntary organization with little party conflict and central government somewhere at a distance. Now the councillor is more likely to be one of dozens on the council, attending meetings both during the day and in the evening, serviced by anonymous, highly qualified officers in an authority run more like a business than a voluntary organization; the atmosphere is one of party conflict, with increasing participation of organized groups outside the authority, sophisticated negotiation and even partnership with central government.

Compared with advice on other aspects of local government, there is very little discussion of the elected member. If it is felt that the elected member does have a contribution to make, some thought needs to be given to how members should be assisted in developing their contributions and what services should be made available to them if they are to cope with their environment and make an effective contribution in spite of the pressures posed by the changes of recent years. Some attention needs to be given to the ways in which this can be achieved. It is complacent and unrealistic to expect support and services to emerge through a 'normal' process without conscious effort. If members are to be encouraged to become involved in decision-making and gain control, some conscious effort is needed to consider what is required in order to achieve this. But a necessary prerequisite for opening up channels and developing support and facilities for the member is some appreciation of the amount of time[24] and energy needed to do the job; a sacrifice which may threaten the member's employment prospects, home life and leisure activities – referred to in one study as the 'predicament of the elected member'.[25]

Without attention being given to these matters, the position of the elected member is likely to become untenable. Predictably, the member will prove unable to cope fully with the business of local government, will be seen as inadequate, and will be increasingly bypassed or relegated to deal with trivial tasks. The consequence of this is a major change in representative democracy, a tendency for local government to become an agency of central government and lacking in accountability to the general public. Issues about the role of the member and sustaining representative democracy have wide-ranging implications. But these problems are already evident. The implications of the development of local government into 'big business' have been fully argued elsewhere.[26] However, it must be acknowledged that many of the key factors influencing and changing local government – notably non-local economic, financial and political pressures – may render any attempts to support the elected member redundant.

The drafting of a local electoral programme and manifesto, the investigation of certain issues in depth, the use of study groups, the convening of delegate policy conferences and the annual review of manifesto commitments and party policy, and the spirit in which these were carried out, go some way towards meeting the 'idealized' special committee's recommendations on the conduct of the Labour party in local government. In addition to their involvement in policy formation and review, the councillors in Brent felt it necessary to engage actively in the implementation of policy. Their concern for, and active involvement in, policy-making *and* implementation demonstrates their understanding of the limitations of the conventional ideology of local politics and local government. What is not so clear, and requires further analysis, is whether their commitment, involvement and sincerity has led to relevant local action in line with local needs as defined by their 'progressive' policy stance, or whether an analysis would show that local politics in Brent is largely a legitimization process for the playing out of the broader social forces in society maintaining the *status quo*.

Acknowledgements

Many councillors and Labour party members have assisted me in preparing this chapter. I am grateful for their interest and encouragement. Of these people I would particularly like to thank John Lebor, George Crane and Terry Hanafin, whose comments and ideas have proved invaluable.

Notes and references

1 Brent Borough Council 1978.

2 Brent Borough Labour party 1978.

3 Dower and Rapoport 1977.

4 Dower and Rapoport 1977: 82.

5 The Borough Council, constituted by the London Government Act of 1965, provides most of the public services in Brent. Political administration is carried out by 66 councillors who act on behalf of the population of approximately 280,000 and many commercial and industrial interests. The main services under the Council's jurisdiction are: education, housing, highways, town planning, public health, building regulation, social services, libraries, refuse collection, local drainage and sewerage, parks and swimming baths, arts and entertainment, inspection of food, shops, drugs and weights and measures. 13,500 employees work for the Council in seven major departments.

6 The Local Government Committee in Brent consists of 51 constituency party members (17 from each constituency), the leader, deputy leader and whip. At the time of writing 12 of the LGC are councillors.

7 The manifesto is a 28 page document containing chapters on housing; education; social services; leisure; direct works and basic public services; transportation; employment; finance; race relations and the ethnic dimension. About 2500 copies were printed and all were either distributed free or sold. Indeed, the demand necessitated a second edition.

8 Brent Borough Labour party 1978: 17.

9 Brent Borough Labour party 1978: 14.

10 Brent Borough Labour party 1978: 25.

11 Brent Borough Labour party 1978: 12.

12 London Borough of Brent 1977.

13 Brent Borough Labour party 1978: 9.

14 The Council has an all party sub-committee to deal with industrial relations. What is important here is that the Labour group thought that this formal arrangement should be supplemented by the informal negotiating activities of the deputy leader.

15 The Group Policy Committee consists of the following councillors: chairman of the group, party whip, leader, deputy leader, all main committee chairmen (9) and three backbench members.

16 Gyford 1976: 46.

17 Gyford 1976: 138.

18 Gyford 1976: 138.

19 Green 1972: 45.

20 Meyerson and Banfield 1955: 304–12.

21 See Dunleavy 1978 and Savon 1973.

22 Cockburn 1977: 30.

23 Benn 1974.

24 The surveys for the Maud and Robinson Committees' reports provide evidence of the time spent by councillors on council business. The average amount of time spent on council business increased from 52 hours per month in 1964 to 79 hours per month in 1976.

25 See Fudge, Murie and Ring 1979.

26 Benington 1973.

6

Development control:

a case study of discretion in action

Jacky Underwood

Introduction

Development control is normally seen as something of a Cinderella in the town and country planning system, at least as far as the town planning profession is concerned. Periodically, however, it becomes the focus of attention – usually in association with upswings in the level of development activity when the system is unable to cope with increased numbers of planning applications and the decision period is therefore lengthened. As the development boom passes, so do the complaints of unwarranted interference and delay and the concern with development control. Over the last couple of years, though, there have been a number of published documents from government and other institutions which have commented critically on the operation of the planning system and of development control in particular. These reports have been accompanied by a polemical debate in the professional and local government press. This unusually extended spate of criticism has produced a revival of interest in development control which has come as something of an unwelcome surprise to the planning profession, provoking some self-examination as can be seen in the reports of the Royal Town Planning Institute's working parties on development control and on implementation.[1] To others concerned with the use and development of land the surprise is more at the neglect of development control in the past, given its function of intervention and control which the rest of the planning system does not have.

Local planning authorities have two basic functions: to prepare a plan which will guide the future use and development of land in the area they administer; and to consider and make decisions on planning applications. The latter development control function stems from a statutory requirement that anyone who wishes to put up, extend or alter a building, or to change the use of land and buildings (within defined limits) must apply to the local authority for permission. The system is based on a perceived need for the state to intervene in order to regulate the use of land in the interests of the public at large. In making their decisions on planning applications, local authorities should therefore take into account the present and likely future competing demands on the land resource in their area, and the 'externality' effects, or potentially adverse repercussions, of a development on the area. The formal authority for decision rests with the elected local councillors who in the majority of cases rely on the recommendations of their development control officers. It is in this part of the planning system, then, that critical decisions are taken that affect what actually gets built, and where, the form of physical development, and the pattern of land use activity.

Implementation and the planning system

Development control therefore has a strong implementation function which, while it rests in statute, is largely administered at the local level. For this reason it provides a useful example of local discretion in action where a 'bottom-up' perspective can shed light on some of the criticisms of 'failure' in the system. This is in contrast to those who argue that greater control by the centre over peripheral agencies will induce 'better' policy implementation. Such a 'top-down' perspective, in the author's view, fails to appreciate the way in which conflicting values penetrate a policy system selectively at its various levels.

A few introductory remarks may prove useful in setting a context for subsequent discussion; these will highlight the differing characteristics of development control and forward planning as regards attitudes towards implementation. During the 1960s the urban design conceptualization of planning with its emphasis on a master plan to control the built form of the future (criticized as idealist and unrealistic) gave way to the systems view of planning.[2] Though the latter conceptualization stemmed from an attempt to recognize the complexities of the real world, its association with the rational decision process model in fact tended to reinforce the previous idealist tendencies in the planning profession by emphasizing professional expertise rather than taking sufficient account of the political values and processes involved. In theory, planning was envisaged as a *continuous process* of control over the actions of others, change in the urban sub-systems being guided towards a future desired state through continuous adjustment against the provisions of a strategic plan which was itself subject to a process of monitoring and review.

In the working out of this theory in practical terms, more attention was paid to the methodology for forward planning than to the realization of the control process. Implementation came to be seen as a final stage in the rational planning and decision process following the setting of objectives, generation of options, and selection of a preferred strategy for the future of the area in question. Strangely, the very criticisms of planning which insisted on a 'process' model served to reinforce a sequential view. Consequently, although the rational model includes a subsequent phase of monitoring and review, methodologies for evaluation have been less well developed and the practicalities of linking policy review to the monitoring of planning application decisions only recently tackled. Only limited progress has been made in developing computerized informations systems which serve both strategic policy-makers and the management needs of development control officers.[3] Forward planners appear to rely on others to take note of their predictions and policies, adopting an advocative stance. Implementation, as far as development planning is concerned, is still a secondary consideration and one which is seen to lie in the hands of other actors than the planners themselves.

The development control process, by contrast, is one of continuous day-to-day activity with little opportunity to reflect on desired options for the longer term future. Although he or she is actually operating the controls of the system, the development control officer is far from being in the position of the confident 'helmsman' visualized by McLoughlin and others.[4] There is rarely time to assemble the amount of information that is needed for the 'comprehensive rationality' required by the ideal model of planning suggested in this literature and 'imperfect' decisions are therefore likely to produce unfortunate consequences. Development control officers, unlike their colleagues in forward planning, are in addition in close contact with applicants and under pressure to speed decision-taking. They are less likely, therefore, to think of 'implementation' as something independent of their role but rather to focus on 'getting things done', keeping the applications moving, and fairly rapidly witnessing the results of their recommendations in the real, albeit imperfect, world.

Criticisms of development control

In principle this might sound like an appropriate set of attitudes for development control officers to hold and one which would bring them into less opprobrium than their colleagues. However, it is clear from the recent spate of complaints that there is considerable dissatisfaction with the way in which the planning system is working and with its results. Much of this criticism is directed at development control which is the interface of the planning system with the public in its various guises.

The case put forward by the House Builders' Federation can be cited as typical of the criticisms coming from private sector development interests.[5] For the house-building industry a recurrent problem has been that of building land availability. The Federation sees the problem as created by the inability of the planning system to respond to changes in market demand which leads to unstable land prices and 'boom or bust' cycles. The main elements identified in the problem are, first, the identification and allocation in development plans of sufficient land which can be guaranteed infrastructure servicing; second, hindrances in the developing control system – the mechanism for 'converting' allocated land into land on which to commence building. The control function is criticized for creating excessive and costly delays due to a lack of clarity in the planning framework and to an increasingly detailed and unnecessary involvement in minor matters which 'should not be the concern of planners'.

Interference in matters of external appearance is particularly resented. Many architects and individual applicants concur in this criticism, seeing aesthetics as a matter for subjective judgement and not amenable to control through the equally subjective appreciations of the development control officer. The Royal Institute of British Architects believes that the proper field in which planning authorities should exercise their responsibilities are land use, mass, density and access, except in conservation areas – the opportunity for comment on matters of external appearance is 'an invitation to planning authorities to intervene in a trivial way' which frustrates and inhibits 'adventurous and high quality design'.[6]

Evidence produced for the House of Commons Expenditure Committee's review of planning procedures,[7] however, shows that this is by no means a universal view. Many representatives of community groups would like controls to be more strict. Such groups are perhaps less concerned with delay than that adequate protection should be given to the environment and to the needs of existing residents. The focus of their complaints is that planning procedures allow insufficient time for effective consultation or participation; planners have, as a consequence, been responsible for allowing or instigating unwelcome changes, damaging the environment in terms of the scale and visual appearance of new developments, and failing to extract benefits for the community through bargaining for 'planning gain'.[8] Such arguments produce a counter-attack that development control has become too 'political', tending to deal with the immediate issues which are of prime interest to local councillors rather than the longer term management of change. For those with this perspective, political 'expediency' has resulted in a 'neighbourhood protection service' and the use of development control as a 'weapon in the fight to aid the disadvantaged' and it is therefore urged that the professional planner should 'check that such a use of power does not create a new disadvantaged section of society', namely the developers.[9]

This range of views could be extended but serves to illustrate the varying expectations which different interest groups have of the planning system and in particular of the service provided by development control. Decisions on planning applications have, of course, always been 'political' in nature, as is inevitable in any process which adjudicates on competing demands – either objectors have felt their representations to be ignored, or refused applicants will have felt their freedom to be constrained. Earlier concepts of planning have, however, tended to stress its technical nature and have masked political aspects in a professional 'mystique'. It is only recently that the extent and complexity of the demands placed on the planning system by different interests has been recognized by the RTPI. Its working party on development control pointed to the significance of changes in the external forces influencing the operation of development control, notably the increasing political influence on development control within local government; the variations brought about by frequent changes in central government policy relating to land and the economy; the growth in public participation and the awareness of the public of their own environment and of the planning system; variations in economic changes including the periodic escalation of land and property values; the growth of concern for conservation of natural and man-made resources; and the suggestion that development control should be an initiator and catalyst rather than a negative, regulatory system.[10] As a result there has been an accretion of objectives, some of which may be in conflict with one another.

The legislative framework

These objectives, which will be discussed further, surround the interpretation of the development control task and it may be worth referring briefly to the functions which are set out in the legislation as a basis for examining the scope for their discretionary interpretation. Part III of the Town and Country Planning Act 1971 (which in essence re-enacts the provisions of earlier acts in relation to development control) sets out the basis for planning control. Section 23(1) provides that 'planning permission is required for the carrying out of any development of land'; other sections and sub-sections define the meaning of development, list exceptions, make provision for conditions to be attached to the granting of permission, and lay out various procedures including those for consultation and the making of representations relating to applications. The Act is largely concerned with procedure and very little direct guidance is given on matters of policy. Section 29(1) states that, in determining applications, the local authority 'shall have regard to the provisions of the development plan, so far as they are material to the application, and to any other material considerations'.

The content of the development plan[11] is therefore one of the key criteria affecting the interpretation of the development control task. Sections 7 and 11 give a broad indication, for structure and local plans respectively, of the subject matter of the plan – being 'proposals in respect of the development and other use of land in that area (including measures for the improvement of the physical environment and the management of traffic)'. The accompanying Regulations[12] give some indication of the list of topics which local authorities may wish to include in the plan, e.g. housing, transportation, open space, but they are essentially advisory. The only overriding legislative requirement (under section 7(4)) is that, in formulating its structure plan, the local authority 'shall have regard to' current policies for regional economic planning and development, to the resources available for carrying out proposals, and to 'such other matters as the Secretary of State may direct'. In relation to development plans, as with other aspects of planning policy, central government policy is normally communicated to local authorities in the form of a circular which is advisory only, rather than by statutory instrument.

The legislation governing the development control system, then, is worded in such a way as to give considerable flexibility and discretion to local planning authorities and by implication to their delegated officers. Both the activities which can be controlled (determined by the definition of development) and the grounds on which decisions can be made are left imprecise. Although the Act contains powers for the intervention of the Secretary of State on policy and procedural matters, the view that the detailed implementation of planning is the responsibility of local government has been strongly held by central government. The chief planner at the Department of the Environment has emphasized the degree of local discretion:

> The planning system was given by Parliament to local authorities. It was not given to the Department of the Environment to delegate to local authorities. We are not, therefore, as a Department in a controlling situation. I am not arguing whether it is right or wrong. That is what Parliament did. So the Department's job is to give advice and press authorities to do the best they can.[13]

There is a check to the discretion of local authorities through the system whereby applicants may appeal against a decision on a planning application (the reasons for refusal or conditions attached to a permission), initially to the Secretary of State and subsequently to the courts. It is here that the second criterion by which authorities are to judge an application, 'other material considerations', becomes significant since the question of what is 'material' is frequently the grounds for challenge. The courts have always emphasized the quasi-judicial role of the Secretary of State in these matters and have accepted that, when they are called on to review the legality of his decisions, the question of whether something is material must be decided from a planning point of view. This, of course, depends on the availability of a definition of the scope of planning and here local authorities and their officers find themselves in some difficulties due to the imprecise guidance given by the Act. As indicated earlier, views have changed substantially over the last two decades both within the planning profession and in relation to the expectations of those who have to deal with the system as applicants, political decision-makers, or 'consumers' of the resulting environment. It would appear that the courts have shown some reluctance to modify their interpretation of the scope of planning to include broader social and economic aspects, and their guidance has often seemed to retain a rather out-of-date emphasis on amenity aspects alone.[14] Some officers would suggest that this is also true of many members of the planning inspectorate who act for the Secretary of State in planning inquiries (though a more common complaint is that they emphasize central government policies above local circumstances). What effect the behaviour of the courts and the inspectorate has on the attitudes of development control officers will be considered further below.

There is a further point to be made here relating to the context for development control provided by the attitudes of the courts. Traditionally the courts have seen their duty as protecting the private individual against the abuse of public powers. The planning system, on the other hand, is primarily concerned with planning for the 'public interest', which inevitably means that in some instances the interests of individuals will be overridden as undesirable or untimely in their impact on others. This is made clear by some of the objectives of the RTPI's working party, where mention is made of the need to protect and manage the built and natural environment and to co-ordinate and promote the efficient use of both public and private investment in the interests of the social and economic needs of the community. These objectives are fulfilled to an extent by the duty to prepare a development plan but their detailed implementation relies heavily on the development control system, especially when proposed changes are being initiated by agencies and individuals other than the local authority itself. There is, then, a tension in the role of the development control officer between the concern of the planning system with the overall public interest and the criterion of protection for the individual which is known to be emphasized by the courts. The presence in the background of the Ombudsman (one third of the cases brought to the Commission for Local Administration are complaints about the planning system) also serves to reinforce in the development control officer's mind the need to tread a legally precise procedural path and to give due weight to the representations made by individuals.

The scope for discretion

In summary, the rules by which development control operates are ones of procedure rather than substance and this allows scope at a number of levels in the system for the discretionary interpretation of what factors are material to a decision. At the 'higher' levels, policy is defined on the one hand through government circulars from the Secretary of State and on the other by case law developed through the courts. The former tends to emphasize national policy concerns, the latter the rights of the individual, with the planning inspectorate sitting uneasily between the two. This dual system has important implications for the operation of development control at the local level where maximum discretion lies. Here the policy framework for development control decisions relies on the presence of a development plan whose policy content depends on the priorities defined by the local planning authority. This framework is frequently unclear because plans are out of date or 'informal' in nature, but even where an authority has a current plan which has been through a process of wide consultation, there is some doubt about how far this can or does guide the operations of development control. Plan policies are not always formulated in sufficient detail for the use of development control officers; in addition the practice of treating 'each case on its merits' and taking account of representations from the locality introduces a further set of considerations. Within the local authority itself, decision-making is often delegated to officers and even where this is not the case the opinions of officers are significant because it is on officer recommendations that most decisions by elected members are taken.

The 'sharp end' of the planning system is therefore by no means a clearly defined stage of planning policy implementation. Instead it is an arena where there is considerable scope for the use of discretion which rests fundamentally in the role of the development control officer. In formulating his or her recommendations on an application, differing weight can be given to a variety of individual or group interests which tend to be supported by the different levels of the planning system. There are tensions within the local situation itself, but these are increased by the duality of the development control system at higher levels.

It is hardly surprising, then, that the complaints about development control indicate a concern with the interests in which the planning system operates and with its accountability. The amount of discretion in the system gives rise to important questions, given the degree of potential public intervention on individual property rights and the potential impact of decisions on the quality of the environment experienced by those living and working in it. Much of the onus for these decisions rests with the development control officer responsible for framing the recommendation and consequently his or her behaviour and attitudes play an important part. Little is known about how the control officer operates in practice, a gap which it is intended to remedy in the remainder of this chapter.[15]

Information sources for development control

It is useful initially to outline the administrative and decision machinery for processing a planning application and reaching a recommendation on it which may then be adopted as a decision of the local planning authority. McLoughlin's study, based on a survey of development control practice in a range of local authorities, though published in 1973,[16] is still probably the best work on this subject. It is particularly useful for the light it sheds on the weight given by development control officers to different information sources.

McLoughlin traces the path followed by an application as it enters the planning office, is checked, registered and made up into a case file by the administrative section. It is then passed to the development control officer who subsequently carries out a series of consultations, discussions and a site visit before framing his or her recommendation on the application; this is the phase of most interest to a study of discretion in action. After checking by a senior officer, the recommendation is passed to the council committee responsible, for discussion and/or decision before the planning authority's formal decision notice is issued.

McLoughlin found a 'remarkable consistency' in the sources and types of information which development control case workers sought in order to frame their recommendations, regardless of the backgrounds of the planning authorities or the areas they administered. This, he suggested, was due not only to the influence of universal statutory requirements, but indicates that case workers share a 'common ideology' or set of principles and attitudes to their job irrespective of the employing authority. One reason for this, he suggests, is that development control officers are carrying out tasks which are routine jobs, dealing with cases and dealing with people face to face. In this they are less like their colleagues in the planning department and more like other 'front-line' workers such as building inspectors, senior clerical workers in a taxation office, and the like. Though the details of individual cases may differ there is something of a 'humdrum sameness' in the routine procedures, a sense of low status and lack of glamour, but at the same time a perpetual level of stress. [17] It is therefore not surprising that caseworkers accommodate to this by on the one hand formalizing their work by seeking 'decision rules' for greater certainty and security, and on the other hand emphasizing their public service role – 'bureaucrats with hearts of gold'. It is therefore these attitudes, together with the more technical aspects or specific objectives of planning, which colour their response to various information sources.

The key information sources are surprisingly 'soft' and are rarely recorded in the case file although they are often crucial to the recommendations. Three such sources are reported by McLoughlin: information about precedents on similar cases gathered through informal discussions with immediate colleagues; telephone and personal discussions with the applicant, which often take the form of negotiation and bargaining whereby initial stances on both sides may be adjusted and proposals modified; and information from site visits, whether visual observations or conversations with people in the vicinity. The second set of sources are 'harder', being the various maps associated with the statutory development plan, the relevant Acts, statutory instruments and government circulars. Less attention was paid to non-statutory plans, often of a 'bottom-drawer' status, or to the written statements accompanying plan maps. This is particularly significant; in the case of informal plans because they are often prepared in the absence of an up-to-date statutory plan to ensure consistency with emerging policies for the area; in the case of written statements because under the new system of structure and local plans, written policies are of considerably more importance than the maps themselves which do not provide the clear 'zoning' guidance of earlier development plans.

This apparent reluctance of development control officers to engage in complicated evaluations of the balance between the often necessarily conflicting policy guidelines which bear on individual cases seems to be confirmed by McLoughlin's findings on the frequency of their consultations with others. He found that, within the planning department, most contact was with colleagues in the design section rather than in forward planning or policy sections; and that external contacts were limited, apart from statutory consultations, largely to highways personnel, being virtually non-existent with other policy-making departments such as housing, education and social services.

Development control in action

These findings are corroborated by the author's own research[18] which again demonstrates the interplay between the search for decision rules and the reliance placed on soft information provided largely through the office 'culture'. An examination of how development control officers in this particular authority approached their task will give some indication of the perspectives which are brought to bear on an application, whether the policies and standards applied are clear, and where and in what form discretionary judgement is brought to bear.

In the authority studied, the development plan was sufficiently out of date that it was not really used except as a technical fallback to support decisions taken largely on other grounds. Pending the completion of a series of district plans (the preparation of which was in hand) control officers were encouraged to treat each case 'on its merits'. Although treated as something of a cliché by planners, this phrase is one which is used frequently by the planning inspectorate and the courts to indicate the need to pay attention to the special circumstances of a particular case and to safeguard individual interests. It is an approach which cannot be carried to the limits since, in the interests of equity, similar cases in the same area must be treated consistently. Because of this, in the authority in question some attempt had been made to codify for internal use the various standards and policies which were currently operated by the authority; these were listed on a standard checklist which was placed in each case file. Most officers in principle appreciated the relative autonomy that treating each case on its merits, and the system of each being responsible for a particular district, allowed them. Nevertheless, under pressure to process applications speedily and constantly interrupted by telephone or callers at the office enquiry desk, the development control officers found themselves slipping into an essentially clerical role, testing each application against the points relevant to it. One officer described himself as a 'fault finder clerk'; another commented on the task of dealing with an application, 'It passes through a cleansing operation if you like, that is the way the forms are laid out – it's like processing a laboratory specimen really.'

The control officers, then, had a series of detailed standards (e.g. for parking, house conversions, conservation areas) to assist them, but little guidance on broader policies. They were, in fact, ambivalent in their attitudes towards the need for a development plan backup to their work. The statutory plan was referred to as 'ridiculously out-of-date', and the caseworkers gave the author a list of topics on which they felt a lack of policy guidance and where they felt the cumulative impact of individual decisions was unsatisfactory: for instance, the problem of the use of vacant premises in declining shopping centres, and the conflict between the need to encourage employment and the principle of refusing applications for non-conforming industry or home-working. Nevertheless, each caseworker felt quite able to continue without a replacement for the development plan. One pointed out that 'generally speaking, so much is little rear extensions, adverts, shop fronts – that's not going to affect anything'. Another stated, 'no, you can still make valid decisions, each decision is valid in itself, but it doesn't make sense as a whole. You need an overall policy of where an area is going – but that is not the same as an up-to-date development plan.' In spite of such comments, the control officers only infrequently consulted their plan colleagues about applications and no attempt was made by the development control section to influence the scope and content of the emerging district plans.[19] One officer admitted, 'to be frank, I don't have a great understanding of what the district plans are and how much they would affect us'.

Without a clear policy framework to guide them, and unwilling to consult their district plan colleagues (partly from feelings of professional jealousy and low status),[20] the development control officers had to rely on their own resources. Clearly, planning education cannot provide the necessary knowledge of local circumstances, but neither does it seem to give adequate preparation for what is likely to be involved in the development control task. Trainees in their first job and doing a day-release course not surprisingly had difficulties and a particularly limited grasp of how their control work related to the work of the planning department as a whole. But a recent planning graduate also commented, 'when I first came here I found decision-making quite difficult – the actual point of saying yes or no. I wasn't able to know all the criteria you would apply.' The most important training for the development control officer consequently appears to be 'learning on the job' through discussions with colleagues, particularly senior officers in the section. Through them an officer comes to develop a feel for what will or will not get approval – the crucial concept of 'precedent' – and most officers seemed quite concerned to 'play safe' by this reference back to past decisions, a tendency which must have a strong bearing on the formulation of development control 'conventional wisdom' (McLoughlin's common ideology). The management of the development control team is an additional factor behind the tendency of officers to codify and routinize their work. In this authority, as in the majority of development control offices, the practice was for the team leader to check recommendations for their consistency and the likely reactions of councillors, which reduced the responsibility of caseworkers but at the same time had the effect of discouraging them from taking risks.

Faced with 'irate ratepayers' complaining over the phone, the little understood complexities of council politics (particularly how much weight to give to pressure from ward councillors when it appears to contradict agreed council policy) and the ever present fear of an appeal, caseworkers are unwilling to make explicit their own judgements and to show themselves as 'political animals'.

> It's just working with other people . . . you pick up . . . it's very difficult to point it out because in a way you must argue for the status quo. That sounds very vague, but it's almost all we've got to go on because we haven't got local plans yet. I don't think development control is negative but when you have to tie it down to policies, unless you can think of a valid reason to refuse it, you have got to grant it. That's the basis on which you make your decision really.

This statement demonstrates the insecurity of the development control officer but masks the amount of personal judgement which is used, especially by an experienced officer. 'It's very much a subjective approach, a common-sense approach. You can recommend a refusal just on your own dislike of a scheme. There is usually some technical infringement you can fall back on – but it's subjective really, though the two do go hand in hand.' Others also remarked that their personal inclinations towards applicants might influence how stringently they would interpret standards, one person for instance mentioning his political dislike of developers who sought to maximize profit from housing conversions regardless of the living conditions which resulted.

The key factor for all officers was that they could justify a recommendation 'from a planning point of view', though they found this hard to define. The substance of planning grounds would appear to relate largely to the effect of a proposal on its surroundings. This can be taken in a narrow, aesthetic sense but all caseworkers interviewed insisted that more was involved – 'what the impact of this thing is going to be, just being there'; a question of whether the proposed development would be beneficial or detrimental to the functioning of an area – 'whether it works'. It is clear that, depending on the type of scale of application, this could require a very sophisticated level of judgement: for instance, of the impact of a complex industrial development not only on the immediate visual environment but also in terms of pollution by noise or effluent, traffic generation throughout the area, and the wider repercussions on the local economy. Although control officers profess to have a good under-standing of how their area functions (and probably do have a better day-to-day working knowledge than other members of the planning department) there must be doubt about the extent of their expertise to make such complex assessments – certainly they have little time to carry out extensive impact studies as a matter of routine.

The pressure of day-to-day life in the development control office means inevitably that most reliance is placed on information which is ready to hand. If *clear* policy statements and standards are available, they will be used. If they are not available, the support given by the collective wisdom of immediate colleagues takes precedence, together with the pressing claims of the appli-cants themselves counteracted by complaints from the locality of the appli-cation site. Authorities vary in their consultation policies, but increasing numbers now circulate information about applications to amenity and residents' groups and to the occupants in streets adjoining the application site. Almost inevitably this reinforces the weight given to aesthetic and amenity matters over policy considerations which might affect a wider area or have broader implications.

The objectives of development control officers

This examination of development control officers' approach to their work indicates that a relatively restricted set of information sources, and perhaps therefore a limited set of values, is drawn on when framing a recommendation on an application. At this point it is worth reviewing the objectives of develop-ment control in comparison with the realities of the practice situation. The objectives discussed below are those listed by a sample of development control officers working in a range of different types of authority[21] and closely correspond to those drawn up by the RTPI's working party. They fall into four groups relating to environmental issues, questions of resource management, the client group being served, and the manner in which the development control task is carried out.

By far the majority of the objectives related to the quality of the built and natural environment. Most were concerned to promote enhancement and improvement of visual quality and design standards, though some people, perhaps more realistically, limited themselves to 'weeding out the mediocre' or 'preventing horrors'. A number of people mentioned the question of con-formity or 'harmonization' with surroundings, but only one appeared to show a realization that this could have a limiting effect, adding, 'but at the same time not losing the brilliant designs, as happens all too often'. A second element of this set of objectives related more broadly to the management of the environ-ment, with mention being made of the separation of incompatible uses, efficiency, convenience and 'ensuring that schemes actually *work* in terms of correct functioning, circulation space, privacy and other criteria'.

The next largest group of objectives was concerned with the efficient use of the land resource including the conservation of natural resources. Here phrases such as 'optimum use', 'maximum benefit' and 'sensible and economic' use of scarce resources were prominent, often with a realization that this might involve the resolution of conflicting demands. This was sometimes coupled with a recognition of the need for more direct measures, for instance, 'to generate development where there is harmful inertia' or 'to direct development pressure to where it will do most good'; and that development control was a 'backup to other interventionist policies such as micro-economic management, housing investment, public health action'.

It was clear that development control is regarded as a public service since virtually everyone mentioned in their list some client group in whose interests they were working. The provision of some kind of public or neighbourhood protection service figured strongly in this group with a concern to prevent 'harmful developments' in inappropriate locations. In the main the client was broadly defined as 'the community', 'society', 'the public interest'. Few officers mentioned specific groups or interests within the community; where this happened it was underprivileged groups and those less able to look after themselves: 'to guide the client (especially a community group or individual) through the local government system'. Two officers came out *against* particular interest groups which they saw as having too much power: 'rampant capitalism' and 'corporate bodies'. One officer, something of an exception, was concerned to 'assist developers' but added, 'to achieve social objectives'.

The last, much smaller group, of objectives comments on the manner in which development control is carried out. Some of these which relate to the idea of 'positive planning', where development control is recognized as a catalytic force for encouraging opportunities for investment and facilitating co-ordination and development, have been alluded to above. Others express a concern with the need to process applications speedily, though the qualifications placed on such aims when mentioned suggest that officers find it difficult to balance them against other objectives.

The first observation to make about these objectives is their very wide range; development control officers would appear to be quite ambitious in the scope of what they aspire to influence. The second point to emphasize is the degree of ambiguity and contradiction contained in their aims, something which is not readily apparent from the categorization given above; many of the objectives as actually written were compound in nature or contained qualifying clauses. Officers are obviously torn between their aspirations to extend their role and take more initiative and the constraints under which they work: 'to try to be positive at the outset for any proposed development, but at the same time maintaining a degree of pragmatism and reality'. An examination of some of the main conflicts revealed, when compared with the case study outlined earlier, will throw additional light on the problems of development control in practice.

This can perhaps best be approached by looking again at the clients of development control, this time in relation to stated policy objectives. As mentioned, most officers referred to an undifferentiated 'community' or 'public interest' and, given that they are chiefly concerned with environmental enhancement and management, control officers will clearly wish to take into account the interests of as many sections of the population as possible. Their public service ethic reinforces this desire as one officer made clear: 'a sense of responsibility, for good or for bad, in the sense that the public tend to understand what development control is about without really understanding "planning"'. This is not, however, an easy responsibility to bear, since a development control officer is often presented with very conflicting opinions about the desirability of a particular scheme, for instance, from other officers, councillors, residents and developers whose concept of the 'optimum' use of any site will vary according to their particular interests and the constraints under which they themselves have to operate (the conflict between council housing policies for local needs as against developers' marketability criteria is a frequently found example).

What weight, then, do different interest groups receive? The predominance of amenity and environmental objectives suggests that it is neighbourhood interests and this appears to be confirmed by the author's case study and McLoughlin's work where it was seen that fewer consultations are taken on 'policy' issues. This pattern does call into question some of the broader aspirations to resource management and co-ordination of public and private investment. The involvement of development control in the implementation of such objectives would require considerable interplay between development control officers and other parts of the local authority and outside agencies. Development control sections in local authorities are, however, notoriously self-contained in this sense and only rarely initiate policy investigations.[22] It is important, though, to distinguish between the behaviour and attitudes of control officers and their impact in practice. Here the actual power of development control officers must be located in relation to the power and influence of the various groups with which they deal.

It was suggested earlier that there is considerable scope for discretion in the operations of development control. In large part this is due to the lack of a clear definition of 'planning grounds' in the legislation, which has enabled a wide variety of often conflicting expectations and objectives to accumulate around the implementation of policies for the use and development of land. In such conditions of uncertainty and conflict there is considerable potential for the intrusion of the values of individual caseworkers. In practice, though, the pattern of organizational and institutional interests constrains the boundaries of development control discretion since only selected interests are amenable to influence.

If influence is to be brought to bear, channels for communication and control are necessary, but the evidence suggests that the networks of the development caseworker are relatively limited, that some are stronger or more frequently used than others. Some networks serve largely for the passage of information, often *to* the control officer who may have limited opportunity to put forward counter-arguments, for example, in the case of statutory consultations, government circulars, or objections from local residents. Other links do have the scope for the exchange of views: discussions with developers often take the form of negotiation and the position adopted by each side may be modified accordingly, though it should be noted that such bargaining requires skills and an understanding of the operations of the private sector that few local government officers possess. Other networks again may be used to transmit normative values or expectations about what stance or policy should be adopted. This latter type of network is significant chiefly because its influence is difficult to observe or measure and may well therefore be denied. The values of local councillors, for instance, may be critical because of their dual role both as locally elected representatives and as employers (the tensions here are evident when officers are called on to present the local authority's case at public inquiry when it conflicts with professionally held views). Equally significant are the judgements passed on similar cases by the planning inspectorate and the courts since they take on the quality of legal 'rules' which can give the control officer a greater sense of security in the face of the uncertainties of his or her job.

Above all, the conventional wisdom of immediate colleagues is a constant reinforcement of what is or is not feasible. This, it is suggested, normally operates on the side of conservatism because of the perceived incontrovertibility of certain interests above others – notably the reluctance of the 'higher levels' of the planning system to engage with social and economic definitions of planning. The appeal system emphasizes amenity and private property rights and development control officers appear to make little attempt to mobilize other networks which might give additional weight to broader policy issues or to the public interest. It is perhaps unsurprising then that development control officers appear to have what one critic has termed a 'garden mentality',[23] since their wider aspirations are often blocked.

Even if they attempt to extend their role it is uncertain how much impact they could have. Other planning colleagues already grapple, somewhat unsuccessfully, to co-ordinate and influence other public sector planning and investment programmes.[24] Influence on the private sector, particularly in relation to large-scale developments, is equally constrained by the reluctance of central and local government to hinder developments which might aid the local or national economy.[25]

Conclusion

Returning, finally, to the complaints levelled against development control, it seems that officers are placed in an unenviable and impossible position. Caseworkers do have a strong public service orientation, and their work in terms of protecting local environments against the worst excesses of individual action are highly valued. But community groups who expect development control procedures to halt large-scale changes in the environment are probably making unrealistic judgements about the powers of development control in relation to corporate interests, whether public or private. Developers, on the other hand, who complain about excessive delay (which generally only occurs on complicated, large-scale applications) are apt to forget that such developments have considerable repercussions on the investment programmes of a number of public agencies and also that democratic standards require a consideration of spillover effects of developments on the environment and local economy. They are also unwilling to recognize that a significant proportion of the 'delay' is produced by applicants themselves.[26] The question of unwarranted intervention on matters of detailed design is more open to argument and can be explained not only by the strength of environmental enhancement objectives in development control, but perhaps also by caseworkers' inability to affect broader matters of principle. It may well be that development control officers do cause some unnecessary delays in this way without unfortunately having any fundamental impact which would justify the time spent. Suggestions for improvements are difficult to make and no attempt will be made here to summarize the proposals for procedural or policy changes that have been made.[27]

Instead, the concern in this chapter has been to shed some light on how the role of the caseworker affects the operation of development control at the local level. Most caseworkers would defend the scope here for the exercise of discretion in the formulation of recommendations from the basis of professional expertise and judgement. In practice, however, as has been shown, the organizational and institutional pressures on the caseworker tend to lead to attempts to regulate the development control task to one where it is possible to work in accordance with rules. This brings a much needed sense of security to a job which is full of uncertainties and the stress of conflicting demands. The way that the objectives of individuals interact with organizational networks and values to produce expectations in the exercise of a particular role is crucial to an understanding of implementation. Without an understanding of these tensions and how they affect the behaviour of caseworkers, it is difficult, in the opinion of the author, to put forward any proposals for improvement which would effect a real change in the operation of development control. One of the key problems is that the development control officer is in effect operating within two separate systems which employ differing concepts of a 'planning point of view' and what is 'material' to this, something which consequently confuses the caseworker's concept of the criteria which should take precedence – those of local democracy or those of the legal context.

At the very least, planning education could help by preparing planners for the potential conflicts they are likely to face, not in abstract and theoretical terms, but in much closer relation to the realities of practice. This preparation might also seek to equip caseworkers with some of the skills needed in their day-to-day work. One of these involves an expertise in negotiation, without which it is difficult to modify the often unsatisfactory proposals of developers and applicants. Effective bargaining requires considerable insight into the strengths and weaknesses of the other, and therefore an understanding of the objectives and constraints which constitute the other's role. Another skill is the neglected one of networking, whereby alliances are consciously made with others who can bring useful resources to a situation. It has been suggested here that development control officers' networks are limited, and in consequence their perspective on problems and hence their willingness to take risks which may in fact be justifiable are constrained. An extension of the networks of development control officers would serve to expose further the conflicts of interest which are latent in the task of managing the environment by bringing into the arena for debate a wider range of interests and policy considerations. This might serve to quiet some of the anxieties about the accountability of the system but, unfortunately, it is doubtful whether it would make the development control officer's task any easier.

Notes and references

1 Royal Town Planning Institute 1978; Royal Town Planning Institute 1979.
2 See Faludi 1973 for various conceptualizations of planning; and McLoughlin 1969 for a discussion of the systems view in particular.
3 This was apparent from discussion at a workshop of the British Urban and Regional Information Systems Association (BURISA) on information systems for development control and land availability (BURISA Newsletter Jan. 1979 and March–April 1979).
4 McLoughlin 1973.
5 House Builders Federation 1977.
6 Memorandum submitted by the RIBA on the government's Response to the Eighth Report of the Expenditure Committee 1976–7.
7 HC 395–1, 1977: para. 45.
8 Ambrose and Colenutt 1975.
9 Report of a conference of the Institute of Chartered Surveyors 'The unacceptable face of development control', *Estates Gazette* 13 January 1979: 138.
10 RTPI 1978 and 1979.
11 Since the 1968 Town and Country Planning Act, the development plan consists of a mandatory structure plan together with local plans prepared if the local authority thinks desirable. The situation is complicated by the delays in introducing this

system due to local government reorganization in 1974 and in many areas development plans prepared under earlier legislation are still in operation. For this reason
the term 'development plan' is used generically in this paper.

12 Town and Country Planning Regulations 1974.

13 HC 395–1, 1977: para. 59.

14 Purdue 1977.

15 The material is derived from research carried out by the author. It involved a
participant observation study carried out in one London borough. Though the study
of development control officers was incidental to the main purpose of the research,
much valuable field data was collected on the operations of the control workers and
this is drawn on here. The research is written up in Healey and Underwood 1978 and
Underwood 1980. Additional material for this paper is drawn from a short survey of
the participants of two one-week Development Control Courses at the School for
Advanced Urban Studies, in February 1979 and March 1980. Forty-five course
members were asked to list the three most important objectives of development
control from their personal viewpoint.

16 McLoughlin 1973.

17 McLoughlin 1973: 106–7.

18 In a London borough (see 15 above). The following quotes are taken from interviews
with development control officers there.

19 These district plans, interestingly, did not include policies relevant to the particular
needs of development control during the time of the author's research, though this
was amended at a later stage.

20 McLoughlin also makes this point, referring to the lower educational qualifications
of the officers in his survey compared with their colleagues in the forward planning
sections. This pattern is likely to have changed in recent years as numbers of
planning graduates have increased.

21 See 15 above.

22 This is confirmed by hearsay evidence on a number of SAUS courses but also by
Healey and Underwood 1976.

23 Roberts 1976: 4.

24 Healey and Underwood 1978 and Underwood 1980.

25 The recent controversy over development proposals for the Coin Street area in
Lambeth is an example of such conflict. The outcome of the public inquiry on
several large commercial applications there has been seen as a test of the planning
system. The recently prepared Waterloo District Plan, which had been through
public participation procedures and therefore has statutory force, contains policies
for local housing and community needs in preference to 'West End' commercial land
uses. Nevertheless, commercial uses will dominate development on the site.
Surveyor, 28 June 1979: 29, *Estates Gazette* 30 June 1979: 1318, *Planning*, 25 July
1980.

26 Simms 1978.

27 HC 395–1, 1977, RTPI 1978; Dobry 1975; measures included in the Local
Government, Planning and Land Act 1980; and codes of practice developed through
the National Development Control Forum.

7

Briefing for implementation:
the missing link?

Jeff Bishop

Introduction

What we wanted was a community centre that happened to contain a school. What we got was a school that happened to contain some community facilities.

This comment by a frustrated education adviser goes straight to the heart of the variety of difficulties associated with design briefing. The adviser had expressed a wish for something to the person actually responsible for preparing the design of a new school and yet this wish was not (in the adviser's judgement) respected. Many areas of policy implementation (although perhaps not policy-making) require that person or group A 'briefs' person or group B to carry out task X. To return to the opening example, one needs to discover whether the 'failure' of the policy for which this adviser was responsible, i.e. community schools, can be attributed to a poorly constructed and communicated policy, to a poorly controlled briefing process with the other educationalists and architects involved, or to poor implementation by 'practitioners'. This chapter will argue that the briefing process is an inadequately studied aspect of implementation and that consideration of its operation, dynamics and tensions helps to link policy-making and policy implementation.

As briefing in general, and design briefing in particular, are likely to be relatively unexplored territory for many readers, the remainder of this introduction will describe the briefing process in design and cover the major reasons why it is considered that briefing can provide insights into policy and action. The second section will summarize the more relevant results from a research project undertaken by the author at the School of Advanced Urban Studies on the briefing process in school design, and reasons will also be given to suggest why school design is a particularly pertinent example to study. Section three is a development of a series of issues raised by the research which have particular relevance to policy-making and implementation. At this stage, the arguments move well away from school design, and even the development process, into policy at a more general level.

The term 'briefing' is not exclusive to building design. In fact, most people probably know the term from the legal usage. Here briefing is the process in which a client says two things to his/her legal adviser: (1) he/she requests the legal adviser to pursue the case (to the best of his/her ability) and (2) he/she makes known to the adviser all the facts of the case. Apart from the assumption that the adviser will aim for the best possible result, nothing is said about the nature of the end product. No further negotiation takes place between client and adviser except to clarify or add certain facts.

Briefing in building design is only now emerging from a period in which the relationship between professional (architect) and client was very similar to that between lawyer and client. A client would approach an architect with a problem which was primarily but not exclusively his own; he would provide a minimal amount of information and the architect would go away to do the best possible job. Briefing as a process therefore barely existed, the key element being 'the brief' – the written or verbal statement of what the client wanted. Changes in the context of building design have exerted considerable pressure on this relationship, in which virtually the only process was the passing across of instructions. The changes have been slow and complex, but four particular aspects deserve to be picked out:

1 Building types have multiplied and for each type the functional complexity has increased at a remarkable rate. Given this change, a once-and-for-all written statement of intentions becomes unwieldy as well as extremely tedious to compile accurately.

2 The single client building a building for himself alone (disregarding servants and workers for a moment) has almost disappeared except for private houses. Nowadays, not only have 'clients' become 'client bodies' with diverse memberships, but a large number of buildings are commissioned by people and organizations who will never themselves occupy those buildings. There is, therefore, an important split between client and user.

3 The role and status of some professionals have been eroded considerably, to the extent that many clients are unwilling to pass over certain decisions to their architect and generally see the architect almost as a technician who carries out, rather than mediates in, the client's intentions. The overlap between the client's and the architect's 'territory' has therefore increased and, at the same time, territories have become blurred.

4 The number of people and organizations involved has increased dramatically and the 'client' has often ceased to be in direct total control of resources – especially money, but also land and people.

No single pattern exists of the briefing process as it operates in building design today, although one can give a very generalized description of the development process and how briefing broadly fits in. Once a decision has been taken that some sort of need exists for a new building (for example an old persons' home), several independent processes begin to operate. Finance is required, and the sources and timing of this finance need to be determined as closely as possible. Clearly, some notion of the size and standard of the building is needed before a sum of money in a particular year can be allocated. Studies are also needed to translate general objectives into more specific requirements, for example, location, size and special features. Third, it is necessary to begin the hunt for an appropriate site and to establish its cost and likely constructional problems. As can be seen, all three of these are closely related and yet not sequential; one cannot determine finance until one knows what one is financing, one cannot know what one is financing until one knows where it will be located, and one cannot abstractly play with location until financial limits are established. One obvious way through this is to refer to previous examples and project forward to suggest costs, likely changes in design practice and any new criteria for site location. In local government, a project might be included at this stage in the building programme, for example, an old persons' home with X places for Y pounds on Z site. According to the Royal Institute of British Architects,[1] it is at this point that the job architect is appointed and the 'brief' should be prepared. It is rare for a brief to be prepared solely by the 'client'; more typically there will be a period of time during which the client will pass over information and instructions and the architect will ask questions both to challenge and extend the information. The end product will be an agreed written brief, and the architect will not start 'designing' until this brief is complete.

From this point onwards there is an expectation that the architect will be working primarily alone (although 'architect' here is shorthand for a mixed professional design team). By default, there will be many points of both detail and general philosophy which the architect will need to clear up, but the principle is that a 'better' brief would avoid this. At several points during the architect's design process, there will be formal presentations to the client (and others such as the local planning authority), but there appears to be an assumption that these presentations are for information rather than criticism. Assuming that no problems occur, a final design is then translated into sufficient detail for the building to be constructed and finally handed over to the client. A nominal mention is made in the RIBA Plan of Work[2] of feedback to further projects, but generally each job is treated as isolated and finite. As with the earlier stages, many questions arise of a 'chicken and egg' nature, and it is these which have led to a challenge of the traditional notion of a full brief.

Having covered the general sequence of development, it remains to describe briefly the main actors in this process. In local government, the client is, to be technically correct, the council of elected members of the authority. There is little clarity about whether this means all the members of the council or just those serving on the relevant committee. In reality, the client who prepares the brief and with whom the architect communicates regularly is the group of officers of the commissioning department. The officers' group will probably include someone from a central department and someone from the 'coalface', for example a head teacher or hostel warden. Within the commissioning departments, those involved may be at several levels in the hierarchy, and there may also be major variations in terms of professional background and status (e.g. between a head teacher and a furniture supplies officer).

Caught between this client body and the architect are an ever-increasing number of people who must be consulted at one or more stages of the briefing process. These include planners, building inspectors, cleansing officers, highways engineers – each of whom will monitor specific aspects of the building design or site layout. At the architect's end there is a group who, more so than the others, can fairly be called a team. Traditionally, the architect leads the team with a quantity surveyor (QS) as an informal second-in-command. The QS, except on very small projects, monitors the projected cost of the building, prepares documents to control the cost and assists in supervision during construction. Other typical members of the team would be a structural engineer, a mechanical engineer (heating, ventilation, etc.), an electrical engineer and perhaps a landscape architect. Few architects work alone within their office; it is usual for a senior person to keep an eye on progress while the 'job architect' does all the major design work, perhaps with one or more less senior architects and a technician. For small projects, the job architect may be young and inexperienced, although his work will be closely supervised.

Although it may appear superficially from the above description that architecture and design are of little significance to broader issues of policy-making, there are some comparisons between the two processes which can provide useful insights into the world of policy. The first parallel lies in the similarity between descriptive models of the two processes. The design process[3] is very similar to that proposed in various models used to describe an idealized policy process.[4] There are elements of sequential decision-making, from broad intentions, through the establishment of a context to detailed objectives, on to the generation of alternatives, the selection and implementation of one of these, and occasionally finishing with some form of monitoring and feedback. Although few examples from either design or policy-making cover all of these stages, the conceptual parallels are significant.

The second comparison is slightly more arguable, suggesting as it does an omission in policy-making and, to a lesser extent, in design. The idea is that it is only in architectural design that a formal but also dynamic and exploratory briefing process operates. Briefing goes on between and within many other groups, but the breadth of the process in design is perhaps unique. Nevertheless, there is also a major weakness in both areas in that they both concentrate their efforts too heavily on the substance of the information to be exchanged during briefing and not upon ways of achieving the effective mobilization of that substantive material.

The third comparison is again more of a contradiction and omission. Architecture, unlike town planning and perhaps policy-making, has concentrated its efforts historically on implementation – getting things built – often at the expense of challenging the objectives, intentions or purposes of the building. By contrast, other areas (especially policy-making) appear to have missed out on the later stages of 'getting things done' and have tended to concentrate instead on objectives and issues.

The final comparison is an important one, although even after the research discussed in the next section it remains somewhat elusive. Briefing and policy-making both involve complex negotiations between people from different professions and different departments. The professional aspects are especially difficult, because departmental agendas become overlaid with professional agendas which may often be in opposition to each other. In particular, different professions will operate with different perceptions of the problem in which they are mediating. These perceptions will often, quite naturally, support the role of each profession, i.e. housing managers will stress the key role of council house allocation, while architects will stress the primacy of the physical environment. Unless problems and priorities are construed in the same way in the early stages of design or policy-making, later argument is almost certain to occur. Even if problems are construed in the same way, professional differences will emerge in terms of how to tackle them.

The research on school design

As a consequence of the author's long-standing interest in briefing, it was decided in 1976 to set up a research project to examine design briefing in operation. As research on briefing for social services buildings was already under way,[5] it appeared that a choice could be made between housing design and school design. The reasons for selecting the latter are important:

1 Since 1945, school design has achieved a reputation as an area in which co-operation between different professions has been close and successful. One was thus studying an area, unlike housing design perhaps, without obvious major tensions.
2 Despite the above, pressure on the good relationship was thought to be coming from the trend towards smaller, more complex and more diverse extension, conversion and adaptation projects, rather than new buildings. This is primarily the result of falling school rolls.
3 One result of the shift to extension and conversion work is that the tight

group involved in the design of a school for which no staff exists is being pressed to expand to take account of the views of a major new element in the 'client body' – existing head teachers, school staff and pupils.

4 A contradictory requirement of current school design is that all subjects in the curriculum must be catered for fully and effectively (necessitating much specialization), and yet the curriculum is changing so quickly that flexible buildings are essential.

5 School design is an area in which interdisciplinary theory is advancing very quickly. In this case it is the burgeoning world of environmental psychology which is contributing important ideas about the relationship between teachers, teaching, children and space.[6]

6 Finally, school design is an excellent example of an area overburdened with information, much of which does not appear to arrive with the right person, at the right time, and in the right form.[7]

Having selected school design, the author approached the Architects and Buildings Branch of the Department of Education and Science, who agreed to support a one-year research project. A team of four (two from the School for Advanced Urban Studies), representing architecture, education, educational administration and organizational behaviour, selected eight English education authorities in which to study briefing. The research was carried out in two stages. In all eight authorities, key people from different departments were interviewed and asked to describe 'how briefing operates in your authority'. In the second stage, three current projects were selected and a wide range of those involved in the briefing process were interviewed, perhaps twelve people from each project. No clear pattern emerged from this study, but between stages one and two the team abstracted certain factors which they hypothesized could account for the variations in practice between authorities. These factors could be related to a broad framework and stage two generally served to reinforce the basic form of this framework. Given that each authority exhibited certain features likely (in the team's terms) to generate varying briefing processes, it was inappropriate to suggest a model of good practice. The final report[8] therefore suggested that those involved in school design should study their own 'profile' in relation to the framework of issues and then refer to a checklist which gave a fairly comprehensive notion of what should be done during briefing, leaving the decisions about how, when and who to each authority. The following notes give a summary of the two sections of the report which describe and analyse what happened during the briefing stages in each of the sample authorities. The first part is a straightforward description; the second picks out major aspects of the framework generated by the team in answer to the question 'why does this happen?'

Analysis of procedures

This section concentrates on discussing some of the factors which emerged as having a significant influence on variations in briefing practice. Limitations on space forbid a detailed description of the research findings on which this analysis was based, but a few points are worth making by way of context for what follows. Throughout the discussion, terms such as 'most' or 'all' refer only to the research sample. The word 'Architecture' is used hereafter as a shorthand version of Architecture department and 'Education' as a version of Education department.

The decision to undertake a particular project is essentially a political one. Although there was considerable input from officers, several architects would have appreciated better briefing on the political implications of their projects and, indeed, greater and earlier involvement in the forward planning of building programmes (especially extension and conversion projects) having major implications for workloads and timing of design work. By the same token, elected members appeared to be involved little in the design process once initial decisions were made.

Once a project had been identified, few authorities produced a clear written statement of educational aims or priorities such as the intention for a particular pastoral system or community use. Half the authorities had set up a group to look at overall problems of school design beyond each separate project, but these did not always include architects. Such groups characteristically produced 'model briefs' of varying detail, but these tended not to contain sections dealing with desired character, ambience or appearance.

In only two authorities was any attempt made to determine the group who would take responsibility for the design of a particular project. Equally, no attempts were made to define all the members of the client 'body'. There were ambiguous attitudes to existing teaching staff and no mention of children, caretaking, secretarial or school meals staff or trade unions as being 'clients' for the product.

During the design process contact between the job architect and client was generally controlled by the education officer in a classic 'gatekeeper' role. The team found no examples of formal procedural systems to ensure the complete and coherent flow of information between designers and clients, though two authorities demanded (but did not always achieve) the completion of 'briefing sheets' for each space or room.

As follows from the above comments, it was no surprise to discover that much of the design process remains a 'black box'. On the one hand, there was little attempt to involve clients in discussion of appearance; on the other hand, selection of furniture and fittings tended to be made by Education with little contact with the architects involved in designing the buildings.

Last but not least, regarding the handover of buildings to users, no authority was undertaking a process of what the team called 'user briefing' and the final question about appraisal and feedback also received a negative response.

In answer to the question 'Why does this authority do X and not Y, or do Z in a particular way?', the research team identified a range of factors that appeared to influence the range of practice found in the sample of authorities. These divide into two main groups, distinguished by the extent to which a single authority can control them. The first group (called constants by the team) are factors which, for any authority, are relatively 'given' or invariable – such as size of authority, control of budget, costs and standards. These provide a background within which the next group (called intermediate by the team) become important. The intermediate group, upon which the rest of the chapter focuses, includes what might be termed 'organizational' and 'professional' dimensions of practice within individual authorities.

Organizational factors

Although organizational issues were divided in the research report into three professional roles, there are a few themes which reappear, albeit in a variety of ways. The first of these is the argument between a system based on *generalization* and one based on *specialization*. Within educational administration the alternatives result in either a system of AEOs (assistant education officers) 'general', who are responsible for all aspects of a section of the education world – e.g. primary, secondary, further – including buildings, or AEOs 'buildings', whose sole responsibility is the programming, design, construction and management of school buildings. In the advisory service the split is less clear; there are advisers who are 'general' in that they are responsible for the same phases as AEOs (general), and there are those who are termed specialist advisers who are responsible for a single subject such as geography or English. (There are also many combinations, such as responsibility for all schools in a small area or one subject authority-wide.) Architectural departments exhibit a relatively clean split although reduced workloads are tending to make specialization impossible to achieve. The difference is very simple – in generalist offices architects get to work on a great variety of building types and in specialist offices they work on one type, for example schools or housing.

The benefits of generalization are the greater breadth of involvement, avoidance of fixed thinking, contact with new ideas and, in career terms, greater job satisfaction and increased promotion prospects. The disadvantages are that school buildings are only one item of concern, and it therefore becomes extremely difficult to reach a level of detailed expertise in that particular design problem. Architects will not get to know about education generally or important individuals in particular, while educationalists will be under great pressure to give precedence to matters considered more central to education than school building. One can thus imagine an architect who has not designed a school for some years working with an AEO (primary) who has recently moved from another phase of educational administration!

Arguments on specialization are a total reversal of those on generalisation. Specialism has the advantage that initiation into the complex and ever-changing detail of school design only has to happen once, time can be saved and 'silly' mistakes avoided. It was, however, a specialist system in an architecture department which produced the example quoted at the start of this chapter – a classic illustration of specialist designers trapped in the conventions of school design. Specialism can therefore also lead to staleness and reduce career prospects. Organizational solutions can be found to temper the extremes of either approach, although specialization is apparently more intractable. It is, however, extremely unusual for all three groups – administrators, advisers and architects – to be organized along the same lines. This is often helpful but can exacerbate issues such as hierarchy-match when a 'generalist' architect (relatively junior) meets a 'specialist' AEO (bristling with detailed knowledge).

The second theme is the general *orientation* taken by individuals to their job. Bolam,[9] in a study of advisers, found two basic orientations and the school briefing team corroborated his findings. Bolam identified those who were 'administration-oriented', who tended to focus on the management of their role, on co-ordination and efficiency, and those who were 'training-oriented', who saw their role as directly improving the teaching standards of the teachers with whom they worked. Using a general terminology of '*admin-orientation*' ('admin' will be used from here on as a shorthand for 'administration') versus '*policy-orientation*', the advisers encountered by the research team tended to exhibit one or other of those orientations, the educational administrators were similar (the split here being admin-orientation and teaching), while the architects tended to split between admin and design.

It is quite common to think of many professionals both in public and private service being 'promoted out of' the substance of their professional concern. Those individuals occupying key roles in school design were mostly in that position, having not gone through the next stage to major positions focusing undeniably on management. Given the pressures that this shift produces, it is perhaps not surprising that many people do not attempt to tackle both aspects of their role but concentrate on one. The difficulty is that school design demands that both skills be brought to bear because it *is* a complex network demanding good management and it *is*, rather obviously, a distinct substantive problem.

As well as personality reasons for the choice of orientation, there are important reasons related to the career structure of each professional group. For AEOs, especially those who have come from teaching, school buildings are not a major area, and therefore a position of AEO (buildings) is not somewhere to be stuck for long, if one's aim is promotion. Thus, although specialization produces greater in-depth knowledge, the ex-teacher who is an AEO (buildings) is just beginning to master the intricacies before moving on to richer pastures. Their teaching-orientation therefore has no time to blossom. By contrast, for those who work their way up through the administration, AEO (buildings) may represent the peak of achievement in those authorities who reserve senior posts for ex-teachers. This is compounded by the fact that, instead of using a long period in one area to develop expertise of all aspects of school design, non-teachers tend to be strongly admin-oriented rather than policy-oriented.

In the advisory service there appears to be a sort of hierarchy in which general advisers are senior to specialist advisers, and this is probably paralleled by a tendency for generalists to be admin-oriented and specialists to be policy-oriented. Suggestions were made to the research team that this hierarchy is reinforced in job descriptions which push each of the groups strongly towards their particular orientation. The career structure for advisers is rather strange; there are not many chief advisers and the next step, if any, is into administration or a headship or (in better times) lecturing at a College of Education.

For architects, remembering that there can be considerable private sector opportunities, career possibilities are less clear. The impression gained was that generalization provides a better base for promotion than specialization although again one questions whether this is because generalists have a wider substantive experience or because they are more likely to have taken, or be willing to take, an admin-orientation. Certainly in the architectural profession there is much stronger resistance than in other professions to the move from, in their case, the 'drawing-board' to the 'desk'. The hierarchical pyramid is much flatter in architecture departments, partly because it is difficult to carve up administrative and design decisions in a horizontal manner.

The third factor in this set is much less important but deserves a short mention. The impression may have been given that all three groups are nothing more than isolated bundles of individuals when in fact certain elements of a *team approach* can be seen throughout, even if simply in the administrative sense of senior personnel overseeing work by more junior staff. The use of related groups of participants (perhaps not as integrated as 'teams') can help to ameliorate the effects of specialization and generalization, and yet although school design is a joint effort, both major professions (teaching and architecture) are notoriously individualistic. The research team found few examples of truly constructive work in Education departments (and these were in departments using a generalist approach), very few within advisory teams (although the word 'team' was often used), and only one short-term, doomed example in an Architecture department. Even 'design teams' rarely exhibited anything more than a tacit understanding about who did what. Interestingly, the better examples of positive teamwork were seen in those authorities in which there was a very powerful and almost charismatic chief officer. As few groups of education advisers had a chief and many architects work under a director of planning or technical services, it is perhaps not surprising that teamwork was undervalued in those groups.

Professional territories

The factor under the 'professional' heading to be dealt with in this chapter is much more elusive, probably because for professionals working in local government it is all too easy to use organizational constraints as a shield to prevent discussion of inter- or intra-professional difficulties. An earlier example described attempts by architects to gain more control over the selection of furniture in schools – an apparent encroachment on to educational territory, an infringement of the teacher's right to control his/her own classroom. At the same time there was a suggestion that educationalists were attempting to become more involved in issues of appearance and character – an apparent encroachment on to architectural territory. There are probably two conflicting reasons for both attempts. First, each profession will have its own notion of what it is about architecture that influences teaching and will want to explore this overlap, and, second, each profession is anxious both to extend and consolidate its own territory in order to justify its existence.

The overlap between architecture and teaching, looked at dispassionately (although recall that the author is an architect), is now being shown by research[10] to be significant enough to warrant good inter-professional co-operation, but not important enough to justify enormous effort. Generally architects tended slightly to overplay the links, while educationalists varied considerably, from the headmistress who said that 'this school determines how I teach' to the headmaster who thought that the design had no influence at all. AEOs and advisers, rather interestingly, seemed to veer towards an anti-determinist attitude, although this can perhaps be attributed to a tendency to feel a professional sense of loss at not teaching any more, accompanied by a parallel tendency to recall and focus upon more central aspects of the teaching role than school design. If some relationship does exist (and current theories[11] tend to talk of architecture as having an 'enabling' or 'prompting' role rather than a 'determining' one), then there does need to be more open debate between professionals to decide what is being 'enabled' and how to 'enable' it. Perhaps the best example of this comes from primary school design, in which a common arrangement now seems to be of relatively small 'home bays' (rather than classrooms) abutting shared areas for individual work, group work or projects shared between classes. An architect briefed to understand the wide variety of ways in which spaces of this sort might be used can design in such a way that teachers can easily use the 'prompts' of walls, fixed furniture *and* moveable furniture to produce the varied arrangements. If, however, furniture arrangement is indeed jealously guarded by teachers, then the architect and perhaps an adviser need to ensure that the teachers (for whom space is probably not a resource they would be taught about at college) are made aware of the potential offered by the design. Careful communication is therefore absolutely essential, and problems are unlikely to be solved by, for example, simply handing over furniture selection to the architect.

Unfortunately the links between architecture and teaching are almost certainly not looked at dispassionately. Local government has a distinct tendency to be rather blunt and apparently cannot deal very successfully with issues which cross departmental or professional boundaries. Thus issues of conceptual overlap between education and design may theoretically be open to exploration by all sides involved, but there will be considerable pressure to carve some line through the middle and allocate issues to one side or another – furniture to Education, appearance to Architecture. Both major groups are, at the moment, under strong pressure from outside to justify their existence. Cuts in capital programmes are making architects redundant; reduced public expenditure and calls for improved teaching standards are focusing many eyes on educational administration and the advisory service. In this case, it is hardly surprising that both groups are jealous about their existing territory and are keen to extend it to include other aspects. It is naïve to expect anybody in the midst of such pressures to view professional boundaries dispassionately, but as this overlap is at the very heart of briefing then a serious difficulty exists.

Issues for policy and action

The introduction suggested some parallels between the worlds of building design and policy-making. These can be summarized as follows:

1   Design follows a process model, from initiation through problem definition to action and evaluation, which is broadly similar to that proposed by some for policy-making.
2   Design, and perhaps policy-making, have concentrated very heavily on the substance of solutions to the point where ideas are running well ahead of the ability to implement them.
3   Design has focused too heavily on the implementation end of problems at the expense of serious thought about purpose and objectives. Policy-making could be said to be currently in the opposite position.
4   Both processes have at their heart a series of complex negotiations between different professions and departments, each with their own perceptions of problems and solutions.

It would be dangerous to pursue the comparison between architectural design and policy-making too far, but the summary of the research should have sparked off thoughts in the minds of those concerned with any other policy

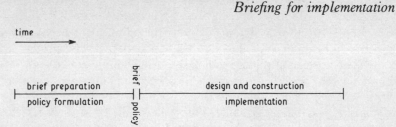

Figure 5 *Traditional model of the relationship between policy-making and implementation*

area which relates directly to their own experience. The analysis of those factors considered to be affecting the briefing process obviously relates to school design but is general enough to suggest why certain things happen and others do not during almost any exchange of ideas and information between professionals or departments. There are, therefore, two major lessons to be learnt from this research relevant to policy-making: first, about the sort of factors influencing professional and departmental behaviour and, second, about the importance of considering briefing in its own right. While lessons about inter-professional working can be applied to many situations, it is perhaps still necessary to convince the reader that some distinct process which could be called 'briefing' is a part of policy-making and implementation.

Inasmuch as written, or even informal, policies may be thought of as briefs given by policy-makers to those responsible for implementation, then the inter- and intra-departmental negotiations necessary for the production of policies can be considered as a briefing process. Particular questions can then be asked about the relationship between those making policy and those allocated to its implementation. A traditional model for this relationship can be seen in diagrammatic form in Figure 5.

It should be clear that the preferred model implicit in the research described earlier (which is not in any way innovative) is more akin to that shown in Figure 6. (An interesting aside at this point is that the architect/builder relationship would also benefit from a shift to the Figure 6 model, but many legal constraints prevent this.)

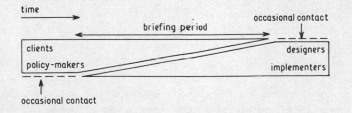

Figure 6 *Model of relationship between policy-making and implementation found in the research into the design of educational buildings*

175

Policy and Action

Purely impressionistically, it appears to the author that much policy-making remains, like design, rooted in the Figure 5 model, despite attempts to move away. The reasons for this are complex, although hints can be drawn from the analysis of factors earlier in this chapter. There are, however, a few key issues which emerge when one considers the implications of a shift to a more interactive, less clearly articulated model. At this stage, they remain implications prompted by the research, rather than researched topics in their own right, but they pose questions which must be faced if what appears to be a 'better' model is to be put into practice successfully. Each of the issues will be dealt with in turn, although in line with other arguments in this chapter, each issue relates closely to the others. None will be dealt with in depth, rather they will be left as questions requiring further work. The issues/questions can be summarized as follows:

1 Are objectives possible?
2 Benefits and disbenefits of a move from brief to briefing.
3 Is design/policy-making strictly sequential?
4 Representation, participation and accountability.

Are objectives possible?

All briefs, however cursory or informal, contain some sort of objectives, as do many policy statements. For a primary school, the objective could be 'the creation of an environment which encourages group work', for a secondary school it might be 'the provision of spaces which can be used in a variety of different ways'. A planning policy might be as follows: 'In industrial areas, applications and uses which generate local employment will be favoured.' Here the objective is an increase in local employment opportunity, but some notion of the means to the end, as well as the end itself, is included. It is often argued (indeed the briefing research does so) that objectives need to be stated but the means of achieving them should be left open. In this sense, the two school design policies appear quite good, until one looks again. The secondary school objective is in fact a physical design suggestion for achieving an educational objective which is not only not given, but which would be extremely difficult to write in a few words. The idea of flexibility in design is, not surprisingly, very important and yet arguments can be put forward to suggest that a variety of different spaces used and programmed carefully is a better way of achieving the educational objectives than the creation of similar but internally adaptable spaces. This brings us to the primary school objective, which does at least give some idea that group work is a desirable component of primary education.

The answer suggested by those comments would appear to be, in school design terms, a strictly educational set of objectives. If, however, there is some overlap between education and school design, then it is surely not possible to

176

write about purely educational objectives except at the level of platitudes. Even if it were possible, one then has the problem of an architect, not trained as a teacher, failing to understand such objectives.

Neither side wishes to be rooted in preconceptions and previous experience, but in the absence of shared professional territory a stalemate will often occur, either because both sides will not approach close enough or because they pass each other by. Given that professional territories are jealously guarded, then it may also be inevitable that preconceptions on both sides are unlikely to be made explicit and hence evaluated and transcended. There are even pressures within professions to avoid explicit objectives. This is particularly true in the educational world in which, according to many teachers, certain concepts of school design (especially open-plan) have been used to impose particular teaching innovations on the profession.

In terms of objectives contained in written briefs, the research team discovered no examples at all which were purely educational without being platitudinous. What was worrying, however, was that the only alternative to broad generalizations conceivable to those interviewed was an extremely elaborate and highly detailed brief. In the one case in which such a brief was used, it proved to be redundant very quickly. Although such a level of detail seems unnecessary, perhaps one could argue that the reason why that particular design proceeded so quickly was precisely because the detailed brief had been prepared as a comprehensive sounding-board against which to test ideas. The problem, then, seems to be to find some level of objectives which will enable all professionals involved to get quickly into the problem, but not too detailed to be either a waste of effort or a restraint on innovation. This leads directly to the next issue, because there is a danger that briefs and objectives will be seen as something finite to be produced by one group at a fixed moment in time.

A brief or briefing?

Contained within the previous discussion of objectives is the assumption that no brief is value-free or solution-free but rather that it implies, if not explicitly contains, answers and end-products. The author finds the literature on policy-making rather ambiguous about whether a policy should or should not contain or determine solutions. Even those who would argue that policies should contain solutions for implementation would probably envisage that such solutions should be very generalized. (This also implies that general solutions are always implementable in detail – the next sub-section aims to refute this.) In the traditional briefing model shown earlier in Figure 5, it was essential that a brief be produced by the client (who then almost bowed out) to hand to the architect (who then worked mainly alone). If clients of any sort – or policy-makers – are rooted in their own professional conception of problems, then if the issue under discussion is any way inter-professional, the objectives and solutions contained in the brief are almost certain to be inadequate. The rather challenging thought floating around during the briefing research was that a brief cannot be written until a project is complete. This is clearly an extreme viewpoint and Figure 6 given earlier suggests the more reasonable notion that work starts within the client body, moves through stages of interaction at first dominated by the client, then evenly balanced, and then dominated by the architect until the client merely takes up an intermittent checking role. The key point here is that at no stage is the definition of a problem the sole prerogative of any single group, but, rather, it is the product of interaction between groups.

If this process is to operate, then some of the research results are very worrying. If the interactive model is to succeed, then participants unfamiliar with either educational principles or architecture need to be initiated into these areas, and people from both sides – especially architects – need to open up their 'black boxes' of techniques, jargon, sketches, etc. These areas cannot be called unexplored; indeed many techniques have been evolved to help to open up this overlapping territory.[12] Generally, the argument used is that design is a form of simulation, an attempt to create in one's mind as real as possible a picture of the actual solution proposed. It is, for all involved, a form of 'action-learning' which makes the absence of coherent attitudes to design, minimal use of published material, lack of in-service training and negligible contact between authorities seem even more reprehensible.

Is design/policy-making sequential?

There are two assumptions within most views of policy-making and design which, on the evidence of the school design research, badly need to be challenged. The first of these is the notion of a progression from general issues to specific issues, from overall aspects to detail. Thus, having formulated some objectives, one moves on to thinking about a strategy for implementing those objectives, then on, perhaps, to a programme of activities within the overall strategy and, finally, on to the individual activities, projects or procedures. Uncertainty has already been expressed about the extent to which the feasibility of implementing policies is considered during their formulation. Similarly, in design one moves from an overall concept into generalized layouts and three-dimensional ideas on to a sketch design, then on to detailed design and finally on to production drawings for use on site. It is probably only at the detailed design stage that all contradictions, compromises and ambiguities are resolved and often they are merely displaced rather than resolved.

In the halcyon days of system building, the detail of a design had to fit the general dictates of the basic structure, and constant repetition enabled a designer to be certain about whether decision A at stage X could be implemented in detail. As school design problems have shifted to more complex adaptations and extensions, and as attitudes towards system building have changed in favour of more localized, one-off and finely tuned solutions, so certainty about the ability to implement early decisions has diminished. This loss of certainty and control could explain the low status given to jobs which nevertheless give architects the contact with user clients to which they continually aspire. What is being suggested here is that some would argue that the only way to ensure that later details do not upset earlier general decisions is to impose highly centralized, inflexible and repetitive, standard solutions. In more general terms of policy-making, however, such approaches are as out of fashion as system building. This lends a further challenge to the idea that broad policies can successfully contain generalized and implementable solutions.

The second assumption, which is almost implicit in the idea of an A to Z sequential progression, from the general to the specific, is the idea that one only goes from A to Z *once*. Clearly, in any process which demands direct physical action of some sort, one cannot actually initiate this action very early simply in order to learn from it. Nevertheless, if, as has just been argued, it is only through reaching a level of detail that one truly begins to understand the nature of any problem, then can one hypothesize some general working model for introducing detail early enough for most lessons to be learnt? There is in fact a model which can be used in combination with, and not in opposition to, the general overlapping triangles of Figure 6. The model is of an iterative process which involves going from A to Z several times rather than once. Clearly, the first stab at a solution is bound to be very poor in detailed terms (indeed the author's attempt to try this approach for the design of a football stadium produced a scheme in which 5000 people could not see the pitch!). Nevertheless, a quick attempt to move into detail can (or it did extremely successfully in the author's case) lead to a major change in basic strategy with a greater certainty of later implementability. In the same way as client and architect shift responsibility in Figure 6, so the level of general and detailed work can shift as design proceeds – little detail at the start, little general at the end. Figure 7 sums this up.

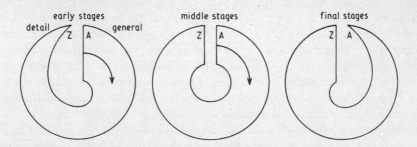

Figure 7   *Level of general and detailed design work throughout the design process*

Policy and Action

Representation, participation and accountability

This last major issue is, of course, an amalgam and its scope is huge. Nevertheless, as soon as one proposes the sort of models either hinted at or suggested specifically throughout this chapter, then questions arise: How, given the likely variation in perception between all interested parties, can any system of representation be devised? Will teachers accept the head as their representative, or engineers accept the architect? If representation is not possible, how can one cope with vast numbers of people in a complex, interactive process?

Once people are involved in school design, how are they initiated into the process, how will they know what to comment upon and how can one resolve the inevitable conflict of views?

If no clear, written briefs exist and people are moving in and out of school design as interactive and iterative processes charge merrily along, how will anybody either within the system, or those outside, discover what is actually happening, who is responsible and perhaps in the end, quite crudely, who to blame? Is a complex, highly flexible system more or less open to manipulation for personal ends than clear if rather ponderous systems?

All of these questions are again not exclusive to school design but have great relevance for policy-making generally. They are also the most intractable. In retrospect the author feels that the research conclusions have little to offer about representation and accountability except platitudes. The team was unable to conclude with any specific idea about representation except inasmuch as authorities are exhorted to be much more explicit about, and give much more thought to, establishing responsibilities, opening up debate and generally spreading the net more widely. What needs to be avoided is the sort of attitude implicit in the superbly ambiguous comment of an education adviser who, in describing who is involved, said 'we talk to teachers and consult with architects'!

In relation to accountability one is really asking questions about the extent to which the process is open to scrutiny by outsiders (or peripheral participants) and about the responsibilities of those more centrally involved. Several of the themes apparent within the research and directly elaborated in this section are about the development of more flexible, responsive and open systems to assist in the creation of more localized, one-off and sensitively designed buildings. During the research the team encountered people who appeared to be manipulating the process for personal or professional ends, and the spectre still haunting the conclusions is that perhaps there remains too much scope for individuals to determine end-products or for a closed caucus to develop to the detriment of the overall end-product. Is it really true that flexibility (and the other themes) are in opposition to accountability?

The final topic in this threesome is participation and here one promising notion did emerge which could also assist the other two issues in this sub-section. The word 'participation' is guaranteed to raise hackles in a large number of people in local government – it can mean wasted time, more frustration and less satisfactory solutions. The research produced a fascinating perspective on the point that participation is bound to mean extra time. On several occasions when negative reaction to a new school was mentioned, little of this reaction seemed to relate directly to particular aspects of the building. There were also occasions on which, once staff had got to know what was involved in the design process, they deliberately chose a minority of aspects upon which they wanted further consultation and a majority on which they were quite happy to let the core group proceed alone. The suggestion being made is that people's satisfaction with an environment can be less a matter of what that environment is actually like in physical terms than of the extent to which those people were involved in its design and will be involved in its continuing management. More than this, if people are given a choice (and actually understand the meaning of that choice) about their involvement in design, then they will not necessarily demand to know about everything but will determine for themselves those aspects they consider most relevant. These conclusions therefore reinforce the need for fuller participation of all parties while at the same time providing the assurance that the feared problem of extra time will not necessarily materialize.

It is said that one aim of research projects is to produce more questions to be answered. The research on briefing certainly achieved that, although this is hardly surprising in an area as little studied as briefing. Some work exists on the subject of overall purposes in design and much more on actual solutions. Briefing is a process which is not discrete but which links objective and solution – it links policy and action.

Notes and references

1 RIBA *Handbook* 1962.
2 See (1) above. The Plan of Work is a model version of all stages of design and construction.
3 Broadbent 1973.
4 Jenkins 1978.
5 By the Social Services Buildings Research Team of Oxford Polytechnic.
6 Durlak *et al.* 1972.
7 A typical example found by the research team was the lack of use by practitioners of 'Plans and People' issued by Lancashire Education Authority (n.d.).
8 DES 1979.
9 Bolam *et al.* 1976.
10 See (6).
11 See, for example, Long *et al.* 1974.
12 See Long *et al.* 1974.

8

Developing better services
for the mentally ill:
*An exploration of learning and change
in complex agency networks*

David Towell

Introduction

In the late summer of 1976 I received a call from the medical officer of an
English regional health authority. He explained that with his colleagues he was
very concerned about achieving improvements in the psychiatric services
based on a large mental hospital in their region. The problems being
experienced in these efforts were such that the region's officers believed it
would be helpful to seek external assistance. In short, he was proposing that a
small independent advisory team, made up of people with relevant professional experience, should be established to work with staff involved in these
services with a view to encouraging informed change. Knowing that I had
undertaken similar *action research* projects, the purpose of his call was to invite
mc to join this team.

In accepting this invitation, I and other members of what came to be known
as the 'Assistance Group' were beginning what proved to be a lengthy, arduous
but rewarding partnership with full-time staff in the struggle to overcome
major deficiencies in the mental health services. For nearly three years, we
shared with practitioners, managers and policy-makers at all levels in the
relevant health and local authorities both the successes and disappointments
encountered in this challenge. Notwithstanding the many difficulties, this
experience has provided an unusual means of illuminating the dynamics of
learning and change in a complex network of public agencies. It has also
permitted some testing of the local strategies necessary to secure informed
innovation in existing patterns of psychiatric provision.

By agreement with regional and other officers, our own involvement in this work was brought to a planned conclusion in May 1979. Over the rest of that summer I had time to reflect on the events of the previous three years and to prepare a first draft of this chapter. Then in May 1980 we were given the opportunity to return to the region and share with officers at all levels in a review of the progress made after our departure. Writing in June 1980, I have drawn on this review to test and sharpen the judgements in my earlier draft and now offer for wider examination some account of what has been learnt from this experience.

'Westville', the mental hospital which was the focus of our attention, is one of the largest in England – still with over 1500 beds – and any league table of financial deprivation would locate it near the bottom. In 1976 this hospital provided most in-patient services to a population of three-quarters of a million people spread over a wide urban catchment area spanning nearly forty miles. Most of this population was in four health districts. These four districts are in two health authority areas, matching a county and a metropolitan borough, with the associated range of social services, housing and other agencies.

At Westville itself, first impressions suggested that despite often dedicated staff, standards of care seemed to have lagged considerably behind modern professional practice. Particularly noticeable were the large wards, poor conditions and few staff – often lacking effective therapeutic leadership – which together shaped the lives of a vast and heterogeneous group of long-stay and elderly patients. Outside the hospital, community-based contributions to mental health provision from the statutory agencies were still at an early stage of development.

These features of the services based on Westville are, of course, by no means unique. Similar complex patterns of agency responsibility and comparable deficiencies in provision are characteristic to varying degrees of much of the English psychiatric services. Indeed, the common problems facing many large mental hospitals became the subject of urgent national study during the period of our work.[1]

Viewed from this wider standpoint it seems that while government policy on *Better Services for the Mentally Ill*[2] has been quite generally welcomed by field agencies, nevertheless its implementation is confronting major barriers. In part these difficulties are political and financial: progress towards improving services has been severely handicapped by resource limitations consequent on national economic circumstances and competition from other priorities. Further difficulties derive from problems in organization and management. The reorganizations of the health and social services in the 1970s have left mental health services fragmented among an extended network of public agencies. Policy leadership is attenuated by the existence of many tiers of management between central government and the staff involved in service delivery; and by the significant role at the periphery played by professions claiming discretion over key aspects of service provision. In addition, the large hospitals which form the core of the old pattern of services are commonly regarded as highly resistant to change.

Understanding each of these factors has been important, therefore, in our work with staff to identify an appropriate strategy for developing the services based on Westville. If this argument suggests what can be described as a 'top down' view, however, it has been complemented by the Assistance Group's strong commitment to a 'bottom up' perspective on change. We recognized from the outset that the main asset available to field agencies is the contribution of staff involved in providing care and that their motivation would be essential to bring about improvements. We believed that efforts to mobilize change would need to begin from a definition of how operational staff saw the situation and help them to enhance their own capacity to achieve innovation.

On the basis of these ideas we shared in staff efforts to establish various elements in a framework for concerted action. In particular we sought to find ways of integrating different components of the total psychiatric services and using more fully the potential contribution of people working in the agencies concerned with these services. Increasingly, that is, we recognized the need for this complex agency network to become a more adaptive *learning system*.[3]

Notwithstanding the attractions of this approach, however, the required transformations in the way public services function are – as readers will recognize – very difficult to achieve. The factors which make such changes necessary are also the factors which make change problematic. Indeed, there are significant forces at work in large organizations which seem to undermine fragile trends in this direction and make the realization of new approaches a continuing struggle. Thus the attempt to mobilize a self-sustaining process of development in the psychiatric services based on Westville encountered significant dilemmas. How, for example, could the local initiative required for creative problem-solving be combined with the central leadership necessary to overcome fragmentation among different contributions to the total pattern of provision? How could the exercise of discretion by professionals involved in delivering services be effectively balanced by an appropriate system of managerial control? How could staff investment in traditional ways of doing things be compatible with their active involvement in a process designed to achieve informed change?

Our experience in this work provided the opportunity to increase our understanding of these dilemmas and to examine in practice how they might be resolved. In turn, reflection on the successes and failures encountered in these efforts suggests some lessons for future strategies to tackle problems of this kind, both at Westville and in other inter-agency systems with complex organizational characteristics like those of the mental health services.

In the rest of this chapter, therefore, I shall first examine the policy and organizational context for any attempts to make improvements in psychiatric provision, pointing to important factors likely to influence the process of change. Drawing on this analysis and further consideration of the situation at Westville, I then describe how the Assistance Group worked with staff there in gradually shaping a relevant local strategy for informed service development. Third, I try to illuminate the nature of this strategy and the difficulties encountered in its implementation by more detailed discussion of the dilemmas involved in adopting new approaches to planning, management and staff participation. In conclusion I hope to show that what has been learnt from this work has wider implications for contemporary challenges in the field of public administration.

The policy and organizational context

The period since the introduction of the National Health Service (NHS) has seen major reforms in psychiatric practice. Changes in treatment, changes in the law and changes in public attitudes have all contributed to the evolution of new approaches most significantly – if ambiguously – represented in the philosophy of 'community care'. However, these innovations have occurred within a pattern of provision still largely based on a set of institutions created with characteristic Victorian enthusiasm a century earlier. Moreover, while in the most favoured situations there has been impressive progress, the Annual Reports of the Health Advisory Service provide a regular reminder of the extent to which the many have lagged behind the few.

Against this background, the 1975 *Better Services* White Paper can be understood as an initiative by central government to draw together what had been learnt from local innovations into a comprehensive statement of good practices. In essence, the White Paper declares the government's commitment to developing a community-based pattern of care in which a local network of facilities and services, both health and local authority, support an integrated range of provision – available through primary care and specialist therapeutic teams, social work and voluntary contributions. Particular features of this policy include the emphasis on multi-professional team work in new district psychiatric services; the need for considerable expansion in social services of various kinds; and the radical shift away from dependence on large hospitals as alternative local services are gradually created.

These aims have been widely adopted as an aspiration and subsequently reflected in government priorities and NHS strategic plans.[4] To date, however, significant progress towards implementation has been quite limited and the promise of new development in community provision remains largely unfulfilled.[5] An enormous range of problems still need to be tackled, therefore, in moving towards this new pattern of psychiatric services.[6]

In understanding these problems and the factors relevant to achieving innovation, a useful starting point is a *pluralistic model* which recognizes that processes of change are likely to reflect the influence of many different interest groups operating in a variety of ways. The results of interaction between these influences will depend on the means available to give weight to different views, the channels through which these views can be expressed and the many aspects of agency structure which affect the distribution of power between groups. Thus, in the case of developing psychiatric services, while government's policy-making role is one significant influence, it has also been important to recognize other relevant contributions. Several levels of management, different professional groupings and trade union organizations, each play a part in decision-making. Less visibly, a number of channels exist to give substance to the public accountability of these services.[7] Interaction between these influences is shaped by a complex set of organizational, planning and management arrangements in the agencies responsible for different components of psychiatric provision.

During the few years prior to publication of the *Better Services* White Paper, each main element in previous arrangements for these services had been subject to radical change as a consequence of the wider reorganizations of both health and social services. In the NHS, the incorporation of psychiatric hospitals into the new multi-tiered administrative structure (led by regional and area health authorities and district management teams) with its emphasis on 'functional management', means that at senior management levels there is no longer special representation of mental health interests and not infrequently a lack of expertise in the needs of these services. This multi-tiered system of administration, with its complex relationships between officers and teams at different levels, has also been widely perceived as causing diffusion of initiative and slowness of response.[8] In the welfare services, the introduction of Seebohm, the incorporation of mental health departments and hospital social workers in the new social services departments, and the initial emphasis on 'genericism', all undermined existing forms of health and social services collaboration. The administrative upheavals of these changes and the reorganization of local government meant that new relationships had to be established between elements of the psychiatric services at a time when many staff had other pressing pre-occupations.[9]

This has also been a period of severe restraint in public expenditure – making the identification of priorities particularly important. Central government has for some time allocated high priority to the development of better services for the mentally ill, but in practice realization of this aim has itself been strongly influenced by the complex organization of these services and competition with other policy objectives. Within the NHS – where the Secretary of State has in principle direct control over area health authorities – it is nevertheless the case that the multi-tiered structure and weakness of existing planning mechanisms have so far meant that the traditional priority given locally to general medical services is only gradually being challenged.[10] A greater complication here is that establishing the new pattern of psychiatric services would require a substantial shift of resources into social services provision in a situation where financing of local authority services (i.e. particularly through the general Rate Support Grant) does not permit central government to allocate funds with the specificity necessary if its policy is to be implemented. The invention of 'joint financing'[11] has partially reduced this problem in the short term – often with direct benefits to mental health services – but this assistance still leaves local authorities ultimately having to pick up the revenue implications of such joint projects. Moreover, social services departments too have other priorities – most obviously, perhaps, in meeting the needs of children – which often make psychiatric services rather a secondary concern. Recent cuts in public expenditure, of course, make all these difficulties more acute.

However, the interdependence of health, social and other local authority services in relating to problems of particular communities has been widely recognized. The need for collaboration in service delivery and joint planning at local level has been a continuing theme of central government guidance since the last NHS reorganization and a range of formal mechanisms has been established for this purpose.[12] Nevertheless, the extensive differences in approach and organization between health and local authorities have made the realization of this intention distinctly problematic.

The role of professions in the health and welfare services is also very significant to any understanding of change. Professional influence in policy-making and professional discretion in service delivery both make an important contribution to shaping psychiatric provision. Professionalism can be a valuable source of commitment and a support to individuals in the necessary exercise of judgement. At the same time, however, the power of professional groups to shape their own activities and the difficulties of managerial scrutiny can pose awkward dilemmas: professional attitudes can also handicap inno-vation and prove a barrier to effective collaboration among those engaged in different aspects of care.

In the mental health services, these issues have given rise to particular debate about the role of the medical profession. Consultant psychiatrists occupy a central position in the development of these services. In recent years these doctors have been confronted by a series of difficulties. As full-time practitioners, they are often overloaded with client demands and the human misery these demands represent. In carrying out their work, they have been challenged to adopt more social approaches to treatment and to acquire new skills in 'community psychiatry'. They have faced disruptions brought about by administrative restructuring and self-doubt prompted by critical enquiries. Perhaps not surprisingly these difficulties have sometimes encouraged responses characterized by retreat and defensiveness: some doctors seem to have withdrawn into a medical world – stressing a traditional view of their prerogatives linked to all-embracing claims for 'clinical autonomy'.[13] These attitudes, the pressures on other professions and the changing relationships between medicine, nursing, psychology, and social work have in turn contributed to widespread problems in multi-professional collaboration.[14]

Alongside recognition of the power of professional organization, it is important to note, too, the growing influence of trade unions – particularly those representing nursing and ancillary staff. Inflation, increasing militancy, and a growing climate of conflict in industrial relations have all contributed to making trade union activity a significant determinant of policy and practice in service delivery.[15]

All these factors are pertinent to the problems of large institutions – most starkly revealed in a continuing saga of ever more costly enquiries. Shortly before our work started in 1976, the report of the St Augustine's Hospital Enquiry[16] provided a searching analysis of inadequacies in management there which were responsible for unacceptable standards of care. This report drew particular attention to the way in which the dependence of nurses on ineffective or absent medical leadership could produce a total lack of purpose in the provision for long-stay patients. More recently, the Normansfield Hospital Inquiry Report[17] has shown even more harshly the deficiencies which can arise from failures in inter-professional collaboration. This report also demonstrated the apparent impotence of the new management bodies at district and higher levels to intervene appropriately in such difficulties. In both these cases there is extensive evidence of the capacity of institutions to resist desirable changes even when the need is widely recognized, thus making external intervention of some kind inevitable.

More generally, considerable problems have been experienced in ensuring high standards of in-patient care in large institutions *and* encouraging integration of institutional provision with the new patterns of local psychiatric services during the lengthy transition period while these new services are being developed.[18] Indeed, the reorganizations of health and local authority services have arguably made management of this transition even more difficult. In a form of health and welfare organization based on geography, profession and the separation of medical and social care, the total psychiatric services seem to have lost their identity as a system.

Towards a local development strategy

As gradually emerged more clearly, many of these wider issues were highly relevant to the psychiatric services based on Westville. Our first impressions of the deficiencies in these services have already been noted. It was these deficiencies and the failure of local management to rectify them which led senior officers of the area and regional health authorities concerned to seek external help. In the event, an experienced consultant psychiatrist, nursing administrator, social worker and I came together to make up the Assistance

Group, each contributing on average three days per month of our time to this work.[19]

Our approach to this task was, of course, influenced by expectations and assumptions derived from our previous experience. In my own case, I was just completing a substantial action research study of change in another psychiatric hospital. The main theme of this study is that whatever the benefits of 'top down' approaches to change represented in central policy initiatives, it is essential that these should be complemented by a philosophy which recognizes the considerable resources of commitment and skill to be found in those who work in field agencies. As the report on this study argues:[20]

> Our own observations suggest that these staff in the 'front line' often have good ideas about how improvements in care can be accomplished: if it is possible to start from the problems these staff experience and work from there, much can be achieved. Aware of the limitations of change for its own sake, we recognise that some systematic examination of these problems together with adequate reflection and conceptualization is necessary to provide the basis and motivation for change. We also believe that managers have crucial roles to play in providing the leadership required to facilitate and encourage genuine participation in such initiatives.
>
> Accordingly we take seriously the view that substantial change is possible from the 'bottom up' in the health and welfare services if only the potential contribution of staff at all levels can be more fully realised.

My experience elsewhere also suggested that while any deficiencies in in-patient care could easily make the institution a focus for anxieties, it is usually inappropriate to view these deficiencies in isolation. Institutional problems are intrinsically bound up with those of developing new patterns of community-based services. The management issues confronting higher levels of the health and local authority agencies concerned with these services can be at least as difficult as those within the institution. For maximum impact, therefore, it could be anticipated that strategies of change would need to engage with the *total system* of services in a given catchment area of which the institution is a part.

These views were consistent with the professional experience of my colleagues and shaped our common stance on this new work. In defining our role, we were also strongly influenced by what we learnt about staff attitudes to our involvement. We quickly discovered in meeting the main management bodies concerned with Westville that, while no one doubted the existence of major problems in the psychiatric services, the nature and cause of these problems was an issue of some controversy. For example, there was evidence of some disagreement between officers at operational levels and those in the higher tiers of the NHS – one consequence of which was that the latter had to apply considerable pressure to persuade local management to accept any outside assistance. This ambivalence about using our help was to continue in some cases – most notably that of some consultant psychiatrists at Westville – throughout the period of our involvement.

Faced with these tensions, we were careful in our early meetings with different sets of officers to insist that we were only prepared to accept this commission if our help was genuinely welcomed by each of the responsible management bodies – at Westville itself, its host district, area and region. We also sought the necessary sanction to examine the total problems of the psychiatric services based on Westville, not just difficulties arising within the hospital. We recognized the vital importance of working in such a way as to restore the capacity of those with full-time responsibilities in this system to solve their own problems: accepting that the authority for change must ultimately be generated from within. We appreciated that the scale of difficulties meant that staff might well require support over a considerable period for this aim to be fully realized. In the light of these conditions, we agreed with relevant management that our role should be to provide extended help to staff working in the Westville system in their own efforts to tackle problems and improve patient care: accordingly we became publicly defined as the 'Westville Assistance Group' (WAG).[21]

In the months that followed we had to tread very carefully in our efforts to establish goodwill towards this initiative: seeking a realistic course between the twin dangers of increasing the defensiveness of those staff most threatened by outside scrutiny or colluding with the expectation of staff most welcoming our presence that we ourselves could produce some magic solutions to their problems. Through a systematic programme of meetings, WAG members made contact with virtually all the different agencies (subsequently extended to include the social services departments), levels of management, professional groups and staff associations primarily concerned with services based on Westville. In individual and group discussions we set out to discover staff views on the strengths and weaknesses of existing services; and to explore what kinds of assistance we might be able to offer. Through these discussions and our own observations we built up an understanding of the issues confronting these services. We also began a *dialogue*[22] with each party about the action they could take in tackling these issues: where appropriate, preparing short working notes on key problems as a basis for exchanging more detailed views with those most concerned.[23]

As we gradually got to know staff at Westville, we were told about difficulties in getting action taken on long-standing complaints and in identifying managerial responsibilities. We saw examples of different professions dealing with common problems in isolation or passing issues up the organization rather than confronting them on the spot. We shared a sense that the outside community was only too ready to leave the hospital alone to cope with its problems. We encountered a pessimistic climate in which staff seemed much more aware of constraints than opportunities. We increasingly recognized how all these points added up to a situation where each individual could feel that this large institution would diffuse or nullify his or her personal efforts to make things better.

At the same time we detected a growing wish to use our assistance and met staff who had good ideas for making changes. Working with these and other staff we began to explore how hospital management could be strengthened and operational policies clarified so as to provide some framework of support for improvements in care. We encouraged the host District Management Team (DMT) and senior hospital officers to initiate consultations on a more appropriate multi-professional management structure for services based on Westville. Through a catalytic contribution to the early meetings of the teams which made up this structure, we sought to help staff learn how to use these new arrangements effectively. We also tried to bring relevant staff together to consider the scope for action to tackle deficiencies in provision for particular sets of clients, like the growing numbers of elderly patients and the institutionalized long-stay population in need of rehabilitation. These efforts then provided the conditions for attempting to involve more fully all staff in reviewing standards and improving services – with WAG underlining wherever possible the notion that everyone has a part to play in achieving innovation.[24]

Similarly, on a wider front, we met representatives of the various agencies concerned with psychiatric services in the Westville catchment area. We were told about the lack of impetus behind development of local services in the more distant districts and the inadequacy of existing mechanisms for ensuring that hospital-based provision was effectively co-ordinated with any such developments. Our attention was drawn to a history of poor collaboration between health and social services. We learnt more about significant gaps between the views of operational staff and those of senior managers in these services.

Accordingly we joined with key staff in the preparatory work for a series of meetings which brought together officers from relevant agencies across the catchment area to examine these problems. Subsequently, we continued to offer support when these meetings divided into small groups to consider the development of services to each district. We encouraged senior officers to formulate clearer plans for the total psychiatric services. We also worked with staff at other levels in the effort to find ways of combining this strategic leadership with more informed participation in the planning process by operational managers and practitioners. We tried to assist staff in examining how better use could be made of the scarce resources available to these services and to help articulate their arguments that extra investment in facilities and personnel was required to facilitate significant changes.

In these and other ways WAG members sought to play their part in stimulating and reinforcing worthwhile innovations, building coalitions of staff able to sustain these efforts, and linking action inside and outside Westville. This was of necessity a lengthy process in which the usefulness of particular ideas had to be tested in practice. Faced with the extent of scepticism about the prospects for improvements, we attempted to mobilize an interlocking range of initiatives so that the momentum for change would accumulate and individual efforts would not falter for lack of complementary movement elsewhere in the system.

Thus, over a period of some two years it proved possible for staff to begin a concerted attack on the problems confronting psychiatric services in the Westville catchment area. The following points briefly summarize main elements in the *local development strategy* which has emerged and give some indication of the progress being made by the time of our departure in 1979:

1 The higher-tier authorities – region and area on the health side – have taken the lead in defining policy for mental health services, with particular reference to planning the future of large institutions. At the same time, joint planning with local authorities has sought to ensure some complementarity in NHS and other forms of provision at least on issues both parties recognize as priorities – although there remains a tendency for this collaboration to rely on consultation after plans have been separately formulated.

2 These authorities have given significant backing to their policies through the commitment of extra resources consistent with the priority allocated to these services, both to improve in-patient care and develop community based services. In the deteriorating economic climate it is proving a struggle, however, to sustain the investments required for major changes in the pattern of provision.

3 Also at this level, a regional and inter-area Steering Group on policy for psychiatric services has been established – able to examine strategic issues and help resolve problems in service development (like redefinition of catchment areas and budgetary changes) which cross existing administrative boundaries. The Steering Group is in a position to monitor whether this policy is realized through the cumulative plans of lower-tier agencies. A parallel initiative has brought together different local authority social services departments. Nevertheless, there are still weaknesses in the region's willingness to exercise this strategic role and in the way these mechanisms link to related operational planning activities.

4 At Westville itself, a Hospital Management Team (HMT) has been created which has increasingly demonstrated the capacity to provide authoritative leadership for the institution as a whole, co-ordinate the work of its component parts and ensure adequate management of central services. This leadership has been handicapped, however, by difficulties which the host and other DMTs in the Westville catchment area – each with their own territorial concerns – encounter in agreeing broad

guidelines for the way hospital management should develop institutional provision.

5 Internally, Westville has been divided so that responsibility for the management of services to each catchment district has devolved to four Clinical Area Management Teams (CAMTs). The multi-professional management arrangements for these CAMTs are helping to facilitate learning about more effective collaboration between the professions in delivery of these services – although with differential success in securing the attitude changes necessary to enhance the utilization of each profession's distinctive contribution.

6 In each part of the catchment area these CAMTs have linked up with representatives of the relevant local health, social services, housing, voluntary and other agencies, to improve operational co-ordination between these aspects of the district psychiatric services and to plan future developments. These Mental Health Planning Groups (MHPGs) are proving to be a valuable tool for joint action to improve services to a defined population, but largely as an *ad hoc* mechanism insufficiently recognized in the formal planning and management systems of the main agencies.

7 In a number of ways these planning and management bodies have gradually attempted to clarify objectives, establish standards and set targets against which the performance of services can be monitored. There have also been systematic efforts to assemble information for planning and monitoring – for example, from the review of clinical practice and from a survey of the in-patient population of Westville.

8 These developments have provided opportunities for widespread staff participation in fresh thinking about the kinds of services to be offered, both through ongoing discussion in clinical and management teams and also through special workshops and task groups on particular problems. In turn, such consideration has supported an extensive variety of individual and group initiatives to improve care. However, this growth in active participation has been unfamiliar to many staff and not always welcomed by those with formal leadership roles.

9 The implications of all this activity for Westville have been drawn together by the HMT in the form of a draft hospital development plan – setting out, with the support of staff concerned, steps necessary to achieve better standards of in-patient care and shape the institution's future role. The HMT has also taken the lead in establishing consultation arrangements with staff associations through which to seek a jointly agreed approach to significant change, although this joint approach at times appears endangered by managerial fallibilities and inter-union competition.

10 Finally, through the work of the independent Assistance Group, a catalytic resource has been available – albeit for a limited period – to sup-

port staff in carrying through this strategy, mediate relevant experience from elsewhere, and help link up initiatives being taken at different levels and in different parts of the total service to the Westville catchment area.

Processes of learning and change

The progress made through this strategy by 1979 and subsequent evidence of further achievements in 1980 give considerable encouragement to the view that with continuing staff commitment successful change *can* be achieved in the services based on Westville. However, this summary has clearly over-simplified what are necessarily complex issues, and the reservations noted give ample reason for caution in this judgement. To date, important problems – like the need to explore the scope for more preventive approaches in the field of mental health – have hardly been addressed. Considerable difficulties have been encountered in the implementation of this strategy, often making progress at best patchy and difficult to maintain. Significant dilemmas arising in these efforts undoubtedly necessitate persistent staff attention.

Reflection on this experience now provides the basis for analysing further the dynamics of learning and change in the mental health system. By *extrapolation* from this analysis, the approaches to planning, management and staff participation required for effective service development can be identified in more detail.

The recent history of public administration has seen increasing emphasis on *planning* as a main instrument of policy-making and implementation. In health and local authority services this has involved a particular stress on the importance of joint planning and collaboration: the aim being that inter-related services should be planned, developed and managed so as to make the best use of resources in meeting the needs of those being served. A variety of organizational arrangements, instructions and inducements have been established to achieve this purpose.

However, general experience of these efforts has widely been judged disappointing. Joint planning seems to have encountered extensive handicaps. In part this can be understood as reflecting inadequacies in the conceptions of planning which have been adopted. Some distinctions between 'strategic' and 'operational' planning and the separation between planning and implement-ation have themselves introduced difficulties. The tendency to regard planning as concerned with the use of extra resources has been less than appropriate in a period of severe financial constraint: this weakness has been magnified where attention has focused narrowly on creating new facilities rather than develop-ing services.

Further handicaps to joint planning have arisen from important differences between the health and local authorities involved. Government exhortation towards the adoption of comprehensive joint planning may well have assumed too readily that shared goals and priorities can easily be arrived at locally. More realistically it might be expected that agencies with different tasks and professional influences would have different perspectives on community problems. The extensive organizational mismatch between authorities – represented in different structures, links with central government, financial and planning systems, forms of professional involvement, and member/officer relations – also contribute considerably to the problems of establishing productive inter-organizational relationships.

In addition, these problems often appear to be accentuated by latent tensions in the network of relationships between agencies and tiers involved in the total psychiatric services. To overstate the case, it sometimes appears that the fragmentation of responsibilities in these services lends itself to a pattern of mutual scapegoating and defensive rigidity among the parties concerned, in which having someone else to blame if things go wrong may become more important than trying to get things right.

Nevertheless, experience has demonstrated that in developing psychiatric services based on large institutions, joint planning is essential not only between health and local authorities, but also between similar local agencies (e.g. health districts) in different parts of the total catchment area. In the work at Westville, therefore, it has been vital to find innovative ways of overcoming these handicaps.

As has been seen, the general approach adopted has involved attempting to give stronger identity to the total psychiatric services as a system: then seeking to combine strategic leadership with the maximum participation of field staff through encouragement to both lateral and vertical interaction in the network of agencies concerned. The main 'nodes' in this network are the regional Steering Group, providing overall leadership for the psychiatric services; at area level the Joint Care Planning Teams, involved in refining strategy and mobilizing organizational support for local proposals consistent with this strategy; and at operational level the MHPGs, bringing together representatives of the parts of Westville and local health and welfare services to consider how the needs of each district population can best be met through joint action.

The nature of this approach can be illustrated by further examination of the innovation in inter-organizational linkage represented by the MHPGs. Although employed in administratively separate parts of the health and local authorities, the managers and practitioners in these groups are working within a common task boundary provided by their shared concern with mental health services to a defined population. The success of this local collaboration then depends on the capacity of these staff to represent their part of the service and gain agency support for initiatives thus generated. For example, such joint work has identified extensive problems affecting long-stay patients at Westville and led to the instigation of a co-ordinated package of measures from different agencies to improve prospects for rehabilitation and resettlement.[25]

In the longer term, these Groups also provide a means for ensuring that contributions from Westville are integrated with community-based services in each district as these develop in the coming years. Again, it seems essential that all elements of the district services are considered within a common task boundary if this lengthy transition is to be effectively managed. Here supporting work by the regional Steering Group also assumes importance, particularly in making the financial adjustments necessary to facilitate these changes.

What is emerging, therefore, is a process whereby, through negotiation at the interface between such local service development groups and leadership on policy from higher-tier authorities, it is increasingly possible to combine both 'top down' and 'bottom up' approaches to planning in such a way as to foster co-ordinated movement towards new patterns of services.

This experience is leading to a fresh conception of planning as a continuous process of problem-solving. Interaction around problems provides opportunities for learning and adjustment among participants with different perspectives. At the same time it is accepted that agency interests may differ, making negotiation and bargaining relevant modes of transaction. In this network each level of management is involved in making and interpreting policy. Similarly, information about needs and opportunities, expertise on forms of provision, and views on priority issues for attention, are widely sought and utilized.[26]

Many of these innovations, of course, run counter to wider trends in the organizational context for this work which were described earlier. Even with outside assistance, therefore, it is taking a long time for participants in the Westville system – especially those with only very part-time involvement in psychiatric issues – to acquire the requisite perspectives and skills, and to gain the confidence in their application which comes from seeing useful results.

Much of this analysis has further relevance for developing appropriate approaches to *management* and *staff participation* in the mental health services. Wider criticisms of the reorganized health and welfare services have pointed to a number of difficult dilemmas. Bureaucratic preoccupation with role definition within a pattern of prescriptive superior/subordinate relationships has seemed less than adaptive to the complex and changing problems confronted by these services. Paradoxically, perhaps, this emphasis on 'line' relationships has failed to provide for adequate monitoring and accountability in relation to standards of care. Attention to the need for management control has to come to terms with the discretion required in service delivery and the extent to which control may itself damage the initiative required from 'front line' workers. Management also has to find ways of integrating different professional contributions in the total pattern of provision.

These dilemmas can easily appear unresolvable when seen from a traditional viewpoint. Rather, experience at Westville suggests that new thinking about the nature of management and professional work is required. The division of labour in psychiatry is such that patient treatment entails drawing on the skills of different practitioners, each organized into professional specialisms claiming some right to control their own work. Therapeutic organization must, therefore, be built on a matrix arising from the interaction of different professions and client groups in such a way as to superimpose some unifying boundary on the total service to patients. This requires that at each level of management multi-professional teams be established in which different professions recognize the inter-dependence of their respective roles in providing care to particular sets of patients. This co-operation entails the development of participative ways of working to ensure that various contributions are appropriately mobilized and to encourage the maximum commitment of staff to realizing the objectives shared by the team. These teams also need sufficient autonomy for staff to use their knowledge and initiative in responding to problems which arise and to establish collaborative working relationships with other services contributing to the total pattern of care: entailing a considerable measure of decentralization in management so that these teams become largely self-managing groups within broader policy frameworks.

Implicit here is a view which identifies the main function of the management of any system as being to define, jointly with participants, the task of this system: then to provide the boundary conditions within which relevant staff can manage their own work so as to perform this task most effectively.[27] What is evolving, therefore, is an 'organic' form of organization characterized by increasing responsiveness to multiple in-puts of ideas and information, changing demands from the environment and new policy objectives: encouraging informed innovation through processes of reciprocal problem-solving by managers and professionals in different parts of the structure.[28]

As in the case of the related approaches to planning, however, creating new management forums is not in itself enough: it is also necessary for participants to acquire complementary attitudes and skills – sometimes requiring significant shifts in orientation over a lengthy period of development.

Successful multi-professional collaboration entails that the dual accountability of staff to management teams and their own profession is recognized, with clarification of the individual's authority to represent his profession in the team context. In a pluralistic setting, some diplomacy is necessary to confront and resolve, rather than avoid, the conflicts which inevitably arise in these relationships between teams, professions and levels of management. A climate is required in which traditional practices can be openly examined. It also seems important that managers become pro-active in trying to anticipate problems and influence change rather than just reacting to imposed demands.

In turn this entails widespread willingness to offer purposeful leadership and take initiatives in the light of explicit attention to the values served by different activities.[29]

Particularly at Westville itself, the long history of intertia has made it essential not to underestimate the considerable difficulties of securing and maintaining such changes. Managers and staff alike lack experience of genuine participation in which individuals recognize their own authority to actively bring about innovation. Still too readily, there is a tendency for managers to rely on inviting comment on previously formulated proposals and for staff to depend on direction from 'above'. A common stance is that of delaying any action until a 'master plan' has been produced. There is a reluctance to accept that the future is necessarily uncertain and staff must be prepared to back their own best judgement of a situation – learning more as they go along.

These difficulties can be illustrated by the case of nursing and medicine. Nursing organization is characterized by many levels of management in a hierarchical system. Nursing management is concerned both with the control of subordinate behaviour in the interests of upholding professional standards and also with encouraging initiative in achieving therapeutic developments. However, the culture and traditions of nursing often seem to emphasize the former at the expense of the latter: a range of more-or-less subtle sanctions are available to foster conformity. In addition, as noted earlier, the pressures on doctors have led some towards a retreatist stance which can easily be expressed in hostility to multi-professional teamwork. As a consequence, staff in contact with clients may become preoccupied with maintaining the rules and the provision of services may become inflexible.

Successful change, by contrast, is likely to entail that nursing managers take every opportunity to demonstrate through their own exercise of authority that new ideas and experiment are highly valued. Similarly, medical leadership is required in which at least some doctors are prepared to take on the role of innovators – sharing with other professional staff in finding better ways of problem-solving. In both professions, these efforts will be enhanced to the extent that it is possible to come to terms with less rational elements of the relationships of dependency between patients, nurses and doctors which typically arise in caring services.[30]

More generally it seems important to appreciate that attitudes to significant social changes are likely to be characterized by *ambivalence*: even where reforms are widely supported, they still lead to anxieties about the disruption of familiar patterns of activities and relationships.[31] These conflicts need to be faced in successfully working through the process of change. Moreover, not uncommonly, where many people are affected by the same developments, aspects of internal conflicts may be projected into external relationships such that groups take up opposing positions around the questions at issue – usually in ways which reflect previous divisions.[32]

Policy and Action

Where appropriate forums exist for negotiation, these social conflicts can be a means for gradually moving towards reconciliation of the rival forces to which they give expression. This requires, however, that complete polarization between competing camps is avoided: individuals retain some capacity to recognize and hold on to their own hopes and anxieties. Similar arguments apply to the introduction of specific innovations which challenge existing practices. Innovating groups can easily become isolated from their colleagues and their innovations put at risk unless it is possible to sustain a dialogue between 'progressives' and 'traditionalists' within a wider management structure which both supports and contains open debate.

This analysis of the dynamics of change has further implications, therefore, for management and participation in service development. Changes imposed from 'above' which do not provide participants with the chance to relate new practices to their own experiences are likely to be resisted or undermined. Implementing even the most desirable proposals requires considerable opportunities for discussion. Sensitivity is needed to the depression which is likely to be associated with most real change, and time should be allowed for adjustment. An essential task of leadership, therefore, is to provide support for staff in coping with the anxieties generated during these transitions. It follows that successful change is likely to be facilitated where participants learn to exercise greater detachment in examining their own contributions to organizational processes and become more aware of these sometimes unrecognized aspects of relationships between individuals and groups.

Further implications

This understanding of strategies and processes of change in the Westville system emerged from our continuing struggle as an Assistance Group to find appropriate ways of helping staff engage with significant problems confronting the psychiatric services. As has been noted, our role was to make available our professional experience in encouraging review of existing practices, identifying possibilities for change and giving support to local initiative, so as to stimulate a co-ordinated programme of service development across the whole Westville catchment area. Less overtly, we also increasingly recognized that our unique access to all the parties in the Westville system conferred on WAG important functions in fostering inter-organizational learning and providing transitional support. In our contacts with different groups of staff, we sought to develop and share our understanding of how the total system works and their part within it. In the light of this understanding we tried to help staff work through the difficulties involved in changing roles and relationships.

Throughout this work we kept in mind the need to contribute in such a way as to maintain the autonomy of staff and develop their own capacity to continue the programme of change. In planning for our gradual withdrawal we sought, therefore, to build these WAG functions into the mental health system and transfer our learning to those with full-time responsibilities within it. In particular, we tried to invest our main catalytic and support roles in the evolving network of multi-professional groups and to ensure that individuals in a wide range of key roles had developed skills in the new approaches seen to be necessary.

Returning in 1980, the review of progress provided considerable evidence of the appropriateness and effectiveness of this approach. Despite major financial difficulties and continuing weaknesses in strategic co-ordination, much of what we saw was encouraging. Particularly at Westville itself, earlier initiatives were showing considerable resilience, successful efforts were contributing to growing staff confidence in their own capacity to achieve change, and a new climate of hopeful realism was developing. After two or more years of management and staff commitment to joint problem-solving, visible benefits could be identified in improved care, not least for long-stay and elderly patients who in the past had been most neglected.

In the light of this experience and further extrapolation from what has been achieved, it seems possible to articulate a clearer vision of the processes of problem-solving appropriate to an inter-agency system with the complex organizational characteristics of the mental health services. Rather than the prevailing 'top-down' view of change in which policy-making is separate from implementation, action is compartmentalized according to existing agency divisions and control mechanisms are biased against local initiative, the elements of an alternative perspective are emerging. Building on Donald Schon's classic analysis,[33] this new approach recognizes that while 'higher' management needs to provide a framework of support and encouragement for change, innovation often occurs primarily near the periphery of large organizations. Creative problem-solving involves concerted action through judiciously selected networks – bringing together different parts and different levels of public agencies according to task requirements. Thus organization itself becomes a tool for action and the prospect can be envisaged of creating learning systems capable of bringing about their own purposeful transformation. Most important, the conditions are sought where, through the exercise of greater *autonomy*, participants are more able to realize their own potential in contributing to valued objectives.

This is, however, an optimistic vision. The difficulties encountered in developing services based on Westville and the still fragile nature of some achievements leave uncertain how far it will be possible to build on the work of the last four years. While staff at all levels are committed to making further progress, it remains to be seen whether these efforts have acquired sufficient potency to become self-sustaining in the face of material deficiencies and wider political constraints. The resilience of this local strategy will certainly be seriously tested by the effects of further cuts in public expenditure and another major reorganization in the NHS.

Nevertheless, it is precisely because of the scale of problems to be overcome that radical innovation – both in the Westville system and more widely – continues to be necessary. In current circumstances health and welfare agencies confront a major challenge in trying to meet more effectively the changing needs of the clients and communities they serve. What has been learnt from our experience provides, I hope, some guide to the further action required if this challenge is to be fully grasped.

Acknowledgements

I am greatly indebted to many other participants in the Westville system with whom I have had the privilege to work and learn so much over the last four years. I am particularly grateful to my colleagues in the Westville Assistance Group – Ann Davis, Fred Forder and Tom Riordan – who have shared the experiences on which this essay is based and been a source of strong support throughout the period of this work.

Notes and references

1 DHSS 1980.
2 DHSS 1975.
3 This concept is developed in Schon 1971.
4 See, for example, *Priorities for Health* (DHSS 1976a).
5 Thus *The Way Forward* (DHSS 1977) reports that all regions continue to foresee slow progress in providing district-based psychiatric services and in closing large hospitals. In 1980 it is still the case, for example, that over 90 per cent of mental illness beds are in large institutions, mostly built in the last century and under-resourced for their current role.
6 These problems include the ambiguities, weaknesses and inherent difficulties which run through the White Paper prescriptions. For example, the nature of 'mental illness' is itself problematic: there is considerable scope for argument about the most appropriate forms of help to people in different situations and the potential for more preventative approaches. The concepts and skills required for new forms of professional practice are proving hard to develop. There are also doubts about how far these prescriptions will lead to a different pattern of psychiatry rather than merely the provision of traditional services in a new location. For elaboration of these points, see National Association for Mental Health 1977 and Baruch and Treacher 1978.
7 The Secretary of State's accountability to Parliament for the National Health Service; the different roles of members in the Health and Local Authorities; and the new form of local monitoring represented by the creation of Community Health Councils each provide potentially important channels of public influence. It is difficult to resist the impression, however, that the effectiveness of these channels in the political struggle necessary to gain greater priority for the psychiatric services

is constrained by continuing public ambivalence about 'mental illness' and the kinds of services which should really be offered.

8 These and related issues have, of course, been the subject of detailed comment in HMG Cmnd 7615, 1979 and are now among the foci for the further reforms in the National Health Service proposed in *Patients First* (DHSS 1979).

9 These points are well argued in Jones 1977: 3–10.

10 The intention to give priority to mental health has also been complicated by the impact of another central government concern – the greater equalization of health resources between geographical areas. See DHSS *Report* 1976b. Quite commonly the local development of psychiatric services in urban areas runs counter to the shift of revenue away from the cities necessitated by this attempt to improve the distribution of expensive general medical services.

11 An ear-marked allocation of NHS funds which area health authorities can make available to their counterpart local authorities to finance social services schemes of direct benefit to health. See DHSS *Joint Care Planning* 1977.

12 Notably the Joint Consultative Committees and Joint Care Planning Teams – see DHSS *Joint Care Planning* 1977.

13 See for elaboration, Jones 1978: 321–32.

14 Particular difficulties have arisen at the points of collaboration between hospital and community services. See, for example, Tibbit 1975; Central Health Services Council/Personal Social Services Council 1978.

15 See, for discussion, ACAS 1978. See also, for example, Mersey Regional Health Authority *Report* 1978.

16 South East Thames Regional Health Authority *Report* 1976.

17 DHSS Cmnd 7357, 1978.

18 See, for elaboration, DHSS 1980 and, for further discussion, Towell 1980: 87–90.

19 As perhaps can be inferred from the perspective adopted in this essay, my own contribution to the Group became particularly concerned with the overall strategy guiding our interventions and the problems facing planners and managers in the Westville system.

20 Towell and Harries 1979: 12.

21 In adopting this title and in other ways, we explicitly sought to distinguish our approach from that adopted by Health Advisory Service visiting teams, where on the basis of intensive study over a short period a report is prepared with recommendations for subsequent officer implementation.

22 The approach here and our conception of dialogue has drawn particularly on the work of Paulo Freire. See Freire 1972.

23 At the beginning of this work, we described our intended role and offered our assistance in a Note circulated to Westville staff with a covering letter from their District Management Team. Subsequent Working Notes reported our impressions, identified progress being made and set out ideas which might be useful in tackling further problems. Altogether, over the following three years, ten such Notes were circulated among groups of staff – at Westville and in related agencies – concerned about the problems in question.

24 We also took the view that if staff at all levels were able to express ideas and take initiatives, then many patients too might be able to assume less dependent roles. Where treatment involves providing support for patients in their personal growth

and exercise of autonomy, it seems essential that staff should be able to demonstrate confidence in self-development and learn in an open, questioning way from their own experiences.

25 Thus a hospital survey has identified several hundred longer-stay patients judged potentially capable of being discharged and the CAMTs, together with a working party on rehabilitation, are organizing the best use of the institution's resources in preparation for this end. Outside, relevant housing departments and social security offices have been approached for assistance. Agreement has been reached on the importance of increased local support to discharged patients in the form of extensions to community psychiatric nursing, day care and voluntary contributions. Appropriate liaison arrangements have also been established between rehabilitation teams in the hospital, the social work team there and social services in each district.

26 This approach to participative planning has been strongly influenced by the work of my Tavistock Institute colleagues; see particularly Miller 1979a; Friend, Power and Yewlett 1974.

27 For example, at Westville itself a multi-disciplinary management structure has emerged which builds up from the basic units of treatment teams serving defined sets of patients or geographical sectors of the catchment area, through the CAMTs concerned with the management of services to each district population, to the HMT responsible for representing the interests of the institution as a whole. At each level, management is involved in negotiating relationships with adjacent levels of management: seeking to provide the optimum conditions for constituent parts of the service to carry out their work while representing the opportunities and constraints that derive from wider considerations.

28 The essence of these approaches can be illustrated by drawing again on the work being done to improve rehabilitation at Westville. Here the HMT's rehabilitation working party established a small team of staff (incorporating members with different professional skills and assisted for some time by the social work member of WAG) to visit individual long-stay wards and explore interest in strengthening the ward-based rehabilitation programme. Where such interest is found, the team works in a support role to ward staff in extending the range of rehabilitative activities and opportunities. At the same time, the team identifies problems and constraints affecting these ward initiatives and reports these back to the working party. The working party then seeks to clarify and resolve the policy issues at the root of these problems. In this way, institutional management both learns from, and becomes a facilitative resource to, the staff taking initiatives directly to benefit patients. In turn, through lateral exchanges of experiences among such staff and patients, the wards where progress is being made become a stimulus and resource to other wards where interest is growing in these possibilities.

29 This argument is developed in Trist 1976.

30 Experience suggests that the stresses associated with psychiatric provision typically give rise to a pattern of socially structured defences against anxiety in which powerful psychological forces encourage patients to become dependent on nurses and make nurses similarly dependent on doctors. In this situation, both 'leaders' and 'followers' may resist any movement towards more participative approaches which require the exercise of greater autonomy. For elaboration, see particularly

Miller 1979a. See also Rosenberg 1970: 21–35.

31 This discussion of ambivalence and the social processes for its resolution has been strongly influenced by the illuminating work of Peter Marris. See Marris 1974. See also Sofer 1961.

32 For example, as has already been implied, in changing the pattern of services based on Westville there has been a continuing tendency for higher tier officers and operational staff (particularly senior doctors) to see each other as the main source of difficulty: with both groups reluctant to see much of positive value in the other's contribution to a comprehensive development strategy.

33 Schon 1971.

9

The policy-implementation distinction:

a quest for rational control?

Michael Hill

As the author has developed his thinking about the study of implementation, he has become increasingly convinced of the view, set out by Sue Barrett and Colin Fudge in the introduction to this volume, that much of the earlier literature works with or implies a distinction between policy-making and implementation which is unsatisfactory and misleading. Yet that distinction expresses a view of the world of government action which accords with a widely cherished model of rational behaviour and of democratic control. Two issues thus emerge from the traditional debate about the relationship between policy and implementation. Are there some situations in which such a distinction can be meaningfully made? And, whatever its connection with the real world of action, what is it about the distinction which leads both practitioners and students of public policy to attach importance to it?

This chapter will attempt to address these issues by means of an analysis of those factors which affect the extent to which real situations may come close to or diverge from the 'rational model' in which policy and implementation are logically separable. The factors to be considered will be grouped as follows:

1 the influence of different topics or issues
2 the influence of political and administrative structures
3 the impact of different interests

The influence of topics or issues

At one level the point to be made in this section is perfectly simple, that the issues with which policies are concerned differ from each other in complexity and thus, on this basis alone, we may be able to make predictions about implementation. If we take an issue like decimalization, which has occurred in Britain, or a shift to driving on the right, as took place a few years ago in

Sweden, it is relatively clear what policy implementation involves. Such clarity is not nearly so evident in relation to, say, planning and land policy.[1] We find it easier to specify the steps necessary for a change in the system of currency than we do for a system of municipalization of development land. Or perhaps we should take two examples closer together in character. It seems *prima facie* to be easier to implement a system to pay all parents £x per week for each dependent child, than to put into practice a scheme to guarantee the unemployed a minimum income. In the former case parents merely need to prove the existence of dependent children; in the latter case evidence is required (a) of unemployment and (b) of other income (if any). The author has elsewhere explored some of these variations in complexity within the British social security system.[2]

However, there are difficulties about this line of argument once it gets beyond a really rather trite level of analysis. Of course, some of the things the state tries to do are instrinsically more difficult than others. But in many cases policies are developed in ways which create implementation difficulties. Proof of penury and unemployment is, in practice, made very much more difficult than proof of responsibility for a child dependent. The reverse could logically be the case. The author and his colleagues[3] have elsewhere looked at the many factors which produce policy complexity. Even the so-called simple issues can be made complex by political processes; imagine decimalization or driving on the right with a local option to retain the older system (not so silly – limited harmonization of policies within the EEC involves just the equivalent of this).

Hence, once a start is made in an attempt to analyse the impact of topic complexity, one comes up against some of the factors in the other groups outlined above – the influence of structures and interests – which in fact seem to mould the forms in which real implementation issues are received.

What also makes it difficult to work with the concept of issue complexity is that a great deal depends upon the level at which our analysis takes place. In earlier, more naïve formulation of this point the author tried to talk of policy complexity. Immediately this brought him up against the problem of the definition of policy. This has, of course, been explored by many other writers.[4] The particular difficulty for the present argument is that if one is to say that some policies are easier to implement than others one has to be able to identify the point at which they are packaged up ready for implementation. We may be able to say some commitments in political party manifestos are easier to implement than others. We may equally be able to say that some Acts of Parliament are easier to implement than others. But in both cases such generalization may be heavily dependent upon the extent to which aspirations have been concretized. In as much as this has occurred it may be argued that implementation – a process of interaction and negotiation with those necessary to make the policy a success – has already begun.

This section has, however, evaded this difficulty by talking of 'issues' and 'topics' rather than policies. But this has merely avoided using the emotive concept of 'policy' while still leaving the problem of concretization. Dunsire[5] has developed a very thorough analysis of an implementation process in the classic mode by examining a railway closure. Yet almost all his analysis is concerned with the relatively clear cut steps taken after closure, when perhaps the more interesting and complex steps occurred between the generalized political commitment to the closure of selected 'unprofitable' railway lines and the specific final decision about the lines Dunsire studied. Implementing the transport policy involved here was highly complex and unpredictable. What followed after specific lines ceased to carry trains was by contrast relatively straightforward. It all depends where you slice such a policy implementation chain[6] whether the issues seem complex or not.

This discussion has begun to shift our analysis away from the concept of the issue to the notion that any particular topic is handled within an extended process which may, while we cannot identify a point within it where policy-making stops and implementation begins, nevertheless be said to be a policy-implementation chain within which issues are increasingly solidified. Such chains, however, occur within structures, and perhaps hierarchies. To what extent therefore do these structures provide a basis for making the distinction between policy-making and implementation? To what extent is our missing 'cut-off point' provided by a structural division or discontinuity?

The influence of political and administrative structures

Several references have already been made to the parallel between the policy-implementation dichotomy and the politics-administration dichotomy, suggesting that the latter is as problematical as the former. As recently as the Bains Committee on *The New Local Authorities: Management and Structure*[7] a prescriptive model has been offered which sees these two dichotomies as related. Similarly, formal official statements about the structure of British central government suggest that a similar split occurs at that level, and 'radical' attacks on the civil service angrily stress that although it currently does not occur it should.[8] It is not the intention here to look at the evidence which suggests that the relationship of these statements to what actually happens is highly tenuous.[9] What is still significant, however, is that the recognition and assimilation of these two dichotomies has an important place in liberal democratic political theory. Hence the large numbers of statements which allege that they are important, or argue that they should be the basis for some division within the policy-making system. Moreover, we also find that actors often feel that they need to explain their behaviour when they violate the distinction. Civil servants will stress that their policy-related advice to ministers is based solely upon practical considerations of feasibility in implementation. Politicians will stress that they only concern themselves with implementation when policy goals are being distorted in day-to-day practice. The proposition here, therefore, is that however sceptical we may feel about the relationship between these two dichotomies, it must remain an important topic for consideration by students of public policy because actors assert that it is significant and try to relate their behaviour to it. This suggests a number of relevant empirical questions: about the influence of this ideal upon behaviour, about the attempts to assimilate structures and roles to the formal distinction, and about the strategies and justifications used wherever it is disregarded.

These comments have drawn upon two widely discussed British examples: the distinction between the roles of politicians and civil servants in central government, and the similar distinction between councillors and officers in local government. But many instances of policy-making and implementation involve both these levels of government. Thus the study of implementation is closely tied up with issues of inter-governmental relations. Furthermore, in many countries this issue is further complicated by a 'federal' relationship between levels of government in which the capacity of one level to require action from another level is severely limited. This had led some writers to see inter-government relationships within states as somewhat similar to relationships between states.[10]

Once we are concerned with inter-governmental relations we must rightly assume that we are likely to face problems in operationalizing our policy-implementation dichotomy. Yet in practice we must give attention to two rather paradoxical findings. One is that many of the leading American studies of implementation have dealt with the problems which have arisen precisely because attempts have been made to evade the complications of inter-governmental relations within a federal system. The other is that where implementation does involve inter-governmental relationships we tend to find the most explicit attempts to define policy and distinguish it from implementation, precisely because of the need for formal devices to govern 'boundary' relationships.

The study of implementation has grown up because of a concern with 'problems' – defined, we suggest, as failures by top level actors to get lower level actors to conform to their expectations. In the United States the difficulties to be faced by federal governments committed to active interventions in society when the states have the major responsibilities for domestic policy have long been recognized. At the centre, government can only give powers and allocate money to those prepared to use the powers. At the state level, particularly when the federal government's commitments are not shared, the response may be inactivity or token activity which enables resources to be acquired but then used for locally determined purposes. Hence the federal government has sought ways to by-pass the states, relating directly to local governments or, in some cases, to grass-roots groups. In the 1960s the Poverty Programme was a noted example of the latter, the Model Cities

Programme an example of the former.[11] Both, but particularly the Poverty Programme, ran into difficulties as it was discovered that, while at the outset intervening agencies of government may be by-passed, once a programme moves into its detailed intervention phase it is likely to find that it needs the co-operation of many of those agencies.[12] This issue, it is contended, lies at the very core of the development of theory about implementation in the United States. Certainly it is fundamental to Pressman and Wildavsky's[13] analysis of the problems of multiple-agency clearances, and to Bardach's[14] emphasis on 'games' as informal devices to deal with potential formal barriers to progress. What, then, does this experience tell us about the role of structures in relation to the policy/implementation distinction? It suggests that American strategies like the Poverty Programme were devised to secure some degree of unification between policy-making and implementation. Agents of the federal government were to go out into localities committed to translating new policies into practice. Situations were to be avoided where local implementers substituted new policy goals for the original ones. What happened in practice was that implementers were faced by a dilemma. Either they must accommodate 'policy' to local interests, or they must experience implementation failure. A new central-local dichotomy emerged, but it would be misleading to simply characterize what happened in the field as implementation failure as if it bore no relation to the inadequacy or unpopularity of the original 'policy'.

In Britain there have been similar attempts to by-pass or evade intervening agencies of government, about which similar tales can be told.[15] Moreover, many more services are directly provided by central government. In this case implementation may be seen much more as an intra-organization issue than as an inter-organizational one. In such a case a unitary structure makes the drawing of a policy/implementation distinction rather less of an issue, involving merely questions about roles, autonomy and discretion within an organization. By contrast in Britain it is where implementation entails a relationship between central and local government that the drawing of the distinction may become an issue of some consequence. The British central-local relationship clearly involves separate autonomous organizations. Yet the separation is not as complete as in a federal system. Attempts to conceptualize the relationship simply in terms of inter-organizational bargaining theory need to face the fact that such bargaining as occurs is between unequal organizations.[16] The powers possessed by local government have been granted to them by central government, and may be similarly taken away. In particular, as is only too evident at this time, the revenue sources of local government are closely regulated by central government.

An earlier paper has rejected the view that the policy/implementation dichotomy may be equated with the distinction between central and local government, identifying the many ways in which local authorities are clearly policy-makers in their own right. But, where conflict between central government and local authorities does occur over policy goals, very clear examples may be seen of central attempts to assert their prerogatives as *the* policy-makers. Comprehensive education and council housing provides perhaps the clearest recent examples of this.

Thus, in Britain, at the boundary between central and local government, there are identifiable attempts by central government to assert its role as policy-maker. Precisely because there is a distinct structural discontinuity within the policy-implementation chain at this point, the clearest examples of phenomena which the outside observer may identify as policy statements tend to be found particularly in Acts of Parliament and government circulars. While this is not necessarily the same as the policy-implementation divide, since local governments are very often significant policy-makers, it is neverthe-less one of the most significant links in the chain. Or to use another analogy, in this seamless web there is the nearest semblance of a seam here.

But even here there is a danger of being misled by the visible. The system formally requires that local activities be legitimized by Acts of Parliament. Inside either level of government such publicly visible sets of rules are less likely to exist. Similarly, the formal separation of local from central govern-ment gives the communications between them, and particularly the com-munications 'downwards' from one government to many, a formality, particularly in the shape of the circular, that other communications within the system are unlikely to have.

This part of the discussion has raised an issue that will increasingly dominate the rest of this paper, the issue of power. What the discussion of central assertion of 'policy' suggested is that the policy-implementation distinction will tend to be more clearly drawn when, at some point in the chain, one of the parties asserts a right to prescribe goals for those at subsequent points in the chain. It has been suggested that this is likely to occur where one party regards itself as having a legitimate right to lay down 'policy' for others, and where it has powers to do so. Such powers may derive, as in this example, from a legal structure. They will doubtless be reinforced by other factors, and are particularly likely to be influenced by a capacity to control the flow of financial resources. They may also be affected by the nature of the issue at stake. If the centre wishes to prevent some local action it is likely to find this very much easier than promoting some innovation, for example.

But three crucial reservations must be made about these generalizations about the central-local relationship. One is that underlying bargaining may well have occurred. It is misleading to take it for granted that an apparent manifestation of hierarchically determined 'policy-making' is not the product of bargaining between the agencies concerned. Hence, again there is a danger of being deceived by a formal device which seems to be a unilateral communication into disregarding the negotiation which may have occurred to shape that device.

212

The second reservation is that assertions of policy may occur at precisely the point at which implementation through inter-organizational relationships have broken down. It may be, therefore, that at such a time there are two distinct and different policies at either side of the divide. This has clearly been the case in Britain with both education and housing policy. It then may be the case that central government is, when asserting policy, establishing authority. It may be able to take a coercive step as the next act, the withdrawal of powers or the reduction of a grant for example, and thus be able to change local 'policy'. But it may be asserting its position in order to convince the electorate or its supporters that it has a 'policy' when it is nevertheless still powerless to act. It may be suggested that some of the things the present government says about the sale of council houses are of this kind, since perhaps this is one of our areas in which influencing implementation is *de facto* extremely difficult.

The third reservation is perhaps the most important of all. It has been suggested that asserting 'policy' is associated with a power relationship, and is a particular characteristic of inter-organizational interaction. But it has also been suggested that there are good reasons why it is most visible in this situation. Therefore it must not be forgotten that similar assertions may occur, often very much less visibly, at other links in the chain. The author and Robin Means are currently engaged on research on the character of discretion in implementation, with particular reference to the British central-local government relationship. We have deliberately chosen to examine some rather different kinds of policy issues – meals on wheels, the control of industrial air pollution, and the administration of rent rebates. The work on meals on wheels suggests that here is an issue where what the public get is greatly determined by discretionary powers exercised at various points in the policy-implementation chain, but that very little attempt is made by central government to influence policy. The legislation under which meals are provided is permissive rather than mandatory, and there has been little attempt at central government direction 'by circular'. Even at the local policy-making level, the council committee, this service has a low visibility. Hence perhaps the most important links in the chain concern attempts by social services managers to lay down criteria for the rationing of meals. Even here, however, the really significant determinants of what we may still call 'policy' are in many areas the personal preferences of staff or volunteers who deliver meals. In particular such people are reluctant to deprive old people of meals once the service is established, and are thus resistant to the application of 'rational' entitlement criteria.

However, the argument that follows from this example must not be pushed too far. This highly localized, even individualized, decision-making occurs within a framework that has been set by statute, and which is significantly influenced by the availability of financial resources. Again and again, therefore, any discussion of the relationship between the policy-implementation dichotomy and the central-local dichotomy comes back to these two considerations, the legal framework and the financial relationship. Of course, neither of these are fixed, nor totally dominated by the central partner, but they are products of a political system in which, as far as Britain is concerned, the local authorities face a power balance which is largely tipped against them.

If, however, we accept that the nature of this central-local relationship is not one in which only the central government is the policy-maker, we want a rather more satisfactory way of describing how the 'top-level' partner can limit the context in which the lower level partners operate other than the policy-implementation dichotomy. One such conceptual device which has already been used in this essay is the 'chain' analogy. The weakness of this, however, is that is suggests a linear model of implementation. Issues are treated as if they come singly, and the implementation process is implied as occurring smoothly and progressively over time. An alternative approach is to talk of programmes, which may have larger and distinguishable dimensions. Knoepfel and Weidner[17] approach the problem in this way, substituting a relatively loose terminology for the rigidity of the policy-implementation distinction but acknowledging the importance of seeing action within a system in which individual activities may be constrained by previous, and perhaps hierarchical, decisions. But they do not translate that approach into a 'top down model', seeing that often the key decisions are made at local levels.

Knoepfel and Weidner have developed their approach for the analysis of air pollution control programmes. They identify these as having the following dimensions: administrative instruments and processes, organization and financing, the setting of emission and product norms, measuring and evaluation methods, and the setting of ambient air quality norms. They then relate the various levels of government – three in the federal systems of Germany and Italy, for example – to these two distinctions within programmes. Hence any particular level of government can be seen as:

1 concerned to regulate in greater or lesser detail (involving different layers in a programme)
2 dealing in different ways with the various control dimensions

To revert to our British meals on wheels example, we may see central government playing a core role in setting the administrative structure within which this activity occurs and an increasingly dominant role in relation to the provision of financial resources, although in this case largely setting a context for the 'core programme'. By contrast its role in relation to the determination of provision norms is a relatively weak 'outer' one, offering general guidelines in circulars.

Knoepfel and Weidner have as one of their main concerns the study of the impact of interest groups upon air pollution control activities. Their approach, therefore, facilitates the discussion of the various points within the total system at which interests may intervene. This is of particular value in cross-national comparative studies, since levels of interest group intervention will relate to the programme structure. In countries such as Germany, where central government has tried to set rigid emission norms, the economic interests have been particularly active in endeavouring to secure that they are fixed at sufficiently high levels to have little impact on their behaviour. In Britain, by contrast, where much control activity rests upon discretionary decision-making within the Alkali Inspectorate, the major concern of the emitter interests has been to maintain a close working relationship with the regulatory agency. The Italian system looks like the German one but works like the British one: practical men in Italy know that formal policies must be judged by their implementation. The 'implementation gap' is often so large in that country that it provides some of the clearest examples for the argument that 'policy-making' really occurs in the implementation process. The Knoepfel and Weidner approach has been emphasized here because of this concern to make links between what goes on within the political and administrative system and the wider 'interests' to which it relates. This, then, must be examined in more detail.

The impact of different interests

In the earlier part of the previous section it was suggested that the policy-implementation distinction seemed to be most useable in situations in which some actors in a chain sought to exercise power over other actors. These situations are often described as ones in which policy is made for others to implement. But then in the later part of the section, with particular reference to the work of Knoepfel and Weidner, it was acknowledged that, in relation to any particular topic, it is likely to be necessary to identify a number of different programme setting (or policy-making?) activities. In addition the impact of different interests was mentioned, acknowledging that what had been left out of the earlier analysis was the fact that assertions of power by actors within government must be seen in relation not only to other government participants but also to non-government interests affected by the policies.

At this stage this whole analysis is open to the accusation that, even if it has avoided the top-down bias, it contains another perhaps even more fundamental bias in seeing governmental activities as its central concern and the world to which they relate as somehow peripheral. Indeed, it has been put to the author that an earlier discussion of implementation by himself and his colleagues[18] treated in a rather weak late section, as a residual topic, the social, economic and political environment within which implementation takes place.

There is always a danger in studies which take (as the study of implementation does) the activities of government as central that the society outside government will merely be treated as that to which things are done. Sometimes it hits back in the form of pressure group activity or some form of political action, but even these categories suggest a view of outside intervention contained within neat, easily handled boxes.[19]

This is not a mistake which Marxist analyses of government activity make. Rather they tend to shift to the other extreme of treating relations within or between governments as really rather uninteresting since they are primarily determined by economic and social factors.[20] One of the challenges for the author of working on the study of implementation with a team of people of varied disciplinary backgrounds and varied stances on the challenge to conventional liberal democratic political science offered by Marxism, is to explore issues of this kind. The discussion here can only just touch on this major topic, but it is important to look at the implications for the policy-implementation distinction of the impact of analyses which take the relevance of the behaviour of 'interests' as paramount for the understanding of administrative behaviour.

In the section of this chapter dealing with the influence of topics or issues, it was concluded that while it may be the case that some policies are intrinsically more difficult to implement than others, it seems likely that the differences detectable between issues have more to do with the extent to which they attract controversy. It will be suggested here that we may perhaps identify four categories of government activity, distinguishable in terms of the kinds of interaction between government and significant interests (and thus in terms of the kinds of controversy involved) and of the levels at which such interaction is likely to occur. These four categories are of course not watertight, indeed one is explicitly a kind of activity which is attached to almost all government action in the modern state. What is offered is a tentative typology, of an 'ideal type'[21] kind which will facilitate further discussion of the policy-implementation distinction. It thus bears some relation to other attempts to typologize government activity [22] but must be primarily interpreted in relation to the task of this paper. The categories are:

1 entrepreneurial activity
2 provision of a minimum framework of services and social control
3 provision of social and welfare services
4 control over economic activities

The category 'entrepreneurial activity' is listed first because it overlaps with all the other categories, and needs explaining as an important limitation upon the generalizations in relation to them. As soon as governments begin to carry out any activities on any significant scale they become large employers and large buyers of goods and services. This generalization applies whether or not they choose to run economic activities. Defence and police activities, which belong in the second of the categories, may clearly have a large economic impact alongside their social control impact. Health, education and social security services, in the third category, equally often become big business.

What this means is that the day-to-day running of these 'enterprises' becomes, whatever they actually do, a matter of wide public concern. Hence attempts will be made to influence pay policies, manpower policies, procurement policies and so on within these government enterprises. Since these will often be seen by government as 'implementation' issues, involving inter-organizational managerial decisions, this is one of the most significant areas of public policy in which the policy-implementation distribution will break down.

It is, in particular, true that in respect of government activity categorized in this way there is the most extreme difficulty in identifying those phenomena which are the conventional indicators of policy decisions – statements in party manifestos, Acts of Parliament, regulations, circulars – since the issues are conceived of as internal managerial ones not requiring legal instruments. The author recently sought, for a European comparative study, to identify the ways in which television broadcasting is regulated in Britain. In the case of independent television he was able to itemize a considerable body of statutory regulations defining the relationship between a quasi-autonomous regulatory agency, the Independent Broadcasting Authority and the independent companies. In the case of the British Broadcasting Corporation he was able to find no more than two very brief documents, a Royal Charter and a Memorandum of the Licence and Agreement between the BBC and the Home Secretary. Was there here a contrast between a highly politicized regulatory situation and the non-controversial provision of a public service? Such an interpretation would be clearly rendered nonsensical by the vast literature on the politics of broadcasting.[23] The formal mechanisms differ in a way which makes policy issues more visible in the case of the IBA, but it would be foolish to argue that by contrast the running of the BBC is all a matter of 'implementation'.

This example is a little away from the basic issues of procurement or wages policy listed above, but the same general point applies – the relative 'formal' invisibility of this by comparison with the government attempts to influence such policies when undertaken by private enterprise, but nevertheless their enormous political importance. Governments which professs to have no 'incomes policies' nevertheless always do have them in respect of the employment sections they control, hence 'private' 'managerial' issues of this kind within the public sector are increasingly politicized. Once the government also becomes the provider of goods and services – be it television, health care, energy or any consumption goods – then it also finds that the nature of what it provides can be a matter of political controversy as can the way in which it provides it. Again and again attempts to make the policy-implementation distinction break down, as many a nationalized industry chief who believed he had 'managerial autonomy' has discovered.

The second category of government activity is, within the broad reservations implied by the first category, the one where the policy-implementation distinction can be most clearly made. What the 'provision of a minimum framework of services and social control' is taken to imply is that basic structure of state activities to which the followers of Milton Friedman would have government retreat. That is the maintenance of external and internal security, the provision of certain indivisible goods such as roads, and the protection of certain conventions which facilitate economic enterprise (a unified currency, systems of weights and measures, etc.). These are the things without which the concept of the unified nation state is in jeopardy. In arguing, therefore, that these are the policies whose implementation is least controversial, and in respect of which the policy-implementation distinction is most clearly made, we recognize that an assumption has to be made about national consensus. These are the policies whose implementation powerful economic interests are most likely to cheerfully leave to the government. However, high levels of civil dissidence, as the Northern Ireland police force could well testify, will make even their implementation a highly politicized activity. It is in this general sense that the overall generalization may be made that the policy-implementation distinction will be totally unworkable in a society where there are very low levels of consensus. Studies of implementation in Italy are suggestive on this point. In some parts of the world the policy-implementation distinction may be regarded as an irrelevant European obsession.

The third category of government activity has many features in common with the second, particularly in its relationship to political consensus. The literature on social policy has, in recent years, become very concerned with the role social and welfare services play in relation to social control. The Marxist literature[24] on this subject has stressed two 'functions' of social policy – the reproduction of a healthy, efficient and educated labour force and the maintenance of order through ameliorative measures and welfare 'concessions'. These arguments have been developed to attack the liberal theory that sees welfare as attributable to a caring society, and concessions from rich to poor as motivated by humanitarian considerations. Clearly, ingredients of humanitarianism are perfectly feasible alongside more calculated and controlling responses to welfare demands. The other line of argument developed to explain social policies is what has been described as the 'social democratic' one which emphasizes the concessions the working class have been able to win as opposed to those they were given.[25]

These different macro-sociological interpretations of the way in which social policies have developed may lead to rather different conclusions about the policy-implementation relationship. Therefore the author cannot develop his own argument without making his own position rather more clear. Those who differ from him may therefore find the argument about the third category of policy the most controversial. It is the author's view that the social democratic perspective is right in drawing attention to the high levels of political controversy which have attended the births of key social policy changes, particularly in the years just before 1914 and in the mid-1940s. On the other hand there is a great deal of strength in that part of the Marxist view which emphasizes the benefits to the capitalist order which some of these social policy changes have brought. The basic framework of social policies as provided in Britain – subsistence level social security, universally available health and education services – does little to challenge economic prerogatives. While there could be policies which are very much more threatening to economic interests – social security measures which are more effectively redistributive or manpower policy measures to ensure full employment – political action has effectively eliminated this possibility. By contrast, the policies we have do contribute to such economic goals as the provision of a healthy and effective labour force. Moreover they play an important role in the maintenance of social order, since they are regarded as the major means by which working-class interests and political demands are accommodated within the system.

Hence it is suggested that the major economic interests in our society are satisfied to take little interest in social policy implementation. Surprisingly, this is as true of trade union interests (unless their members are employees of the services) as it is of other economic elites. This has the effect of making it appear rather easier to make the policy-implementation distinction in respect of social policy than in respect of economic policy. These two policy areas are clearly distinguished in both political debate and academic policy studies, a feature the author has criticized elsewhere.[26] Social policy is seen as settled at a political level, in a way which makes it largely residual to economic policy, and then facing a series of implementation issues which are internal to the policy system. These issues are primarily associated with the power of implementing staff, and particularly the dominance of professional interests, and secondarily with the impact of specific, social policy oriented, pressure groups. They are often perceived as 'top down' managerial issues, particularly where – as in both health and social security – central government has eliminated local authority involvement.

Hence, to summarize this rather complicated argument, it is contended that the group of public policies which are generally known as social policy are characterized by a split between the kinds of controversy which arise at the political level, in which economic interests have been prominent, and the issues which arise in connection with their day-to-day administration, to which economic elites give little attention. This line of argument should not be taken to suggest either that day-to-day issues are not of considerable significance or that this split corresponds with any kind of policy-implementation distinction which appears meaningful to the author.

The line of argument about the fourth category of government action, control over economic activities, has been foreshadowed in the discussion of the third category. This is that when any direct attack is involved, or suspected, upon economic interests it is to be expected that political conflict will extend far, and in a very clear way, into implementation. Powerful interest groups, amongst which must be included both capitalist interests and trade unions, will seek to intervene at every stage in the policy-implementation chain, basing their strategies, as Knoepfel and Weidner have suggested, upon those parts of the chain which seems most open to influence. In this last respect the involvement in the chain of distinct organizations or levels of government which may have some competing interests or perspectives particularly provide opportunities for this influence process.

Hence activities like pollution control, land and planning policy, and all efforts to plan or regulate the behaviour of the economy or levels of income and wealth will be ones where the policy-implementation distinction becomes particularly problematic. It is also instructive to look at those activities which are part social policy, part economic regulation – like manpower and housing policy. These are interesting because in each case three different kinds of policy option seem to be open which fit with categories two, three and four. Such policies can be seen as largely concerned to facilitate the working of a free market by increasing labour mobility and aiding the purchase of houses. Or they can be seen as residual to the working of the market, providing houses or 'sheltered' work activities on a limited basis for the casualties of the market system. Or, third, they may be seen as government attempts to divert the working of the market to social goals, to secure employment protection or the redistribution of housing resources, for example. Hence, inasmuch as efforts are made to push such activities out of categories two or three into four, they will be met by an intensification of conflict over the implementation of policy. In an earlier paper the author has shown how the aspirations of the 1974–9 Labour government to develop an active manpower policy which would be really effective in reducing unemployment came up against implementation problems which reduced much that was done to either token policies for the disadvantaged or implicit subsidies for private enterprise.[27]

The line of argument developed here is supported by much of the present wave of theorizing about 'corporatism'. This has been described as 'an economic system in which the state directs and controls predominantly privately-owned business'.[28] Marxists dispute this notion that the state 'directs and controls', seeing the state as very much in the control of capitalism rather than vice versa.[29] However, many modern Marxist interpretations of the state are at one with the corporatist theorists in seeing a deep interpenetration of government and economic interests in the day-to-day running of the economy. This co-operation and co-optation within economic implementation processes is seen as a way of handling and channelling conflicts of interest. Who co-opts who is a matter of dispute, the interpenetration within day-to-day economic activities is not. The use of *ad hoc* bodies or 'quangos' where both sides of industry are involved along with government to deal with economic management issues, the use of indirect economic levers to enforce incomes policy, the notion of the planning agreement as an instrument of government and so on represent ways of tackling implementation problems in which policy conflicts are settled away from the scrutiny of the direct political process. Hence, as Middlemas argues,

> the concept of democracy needs to be modified much further to account for participation by institutions in the governing process, and for the pheno-menon of opinion management by the state in its bureaucratic aspect. As institutions cross the threshold separating pressure groups from a share of the state's powers and authority, they enhance the tendency already present among governments to categorise political choices in terms of the national interest, over and above class or sectional interests, and to accept as necessary an interdependence almost as binding as the medieval doctrine of organic society.[30]

That formulation by Middlemas is interesting as he expresses the issue of the corporate state as a problem for traditional democratic theory. It is in a similar vein that this paper has argued that the policy-implementation distinction is an important ingredient of that theory, and that therefore evidence that it is not particularly meaningful suggests the existence of a problem for democratic control over policy. This, it may be suggested, is what gives a particular flavour to the top-down search to bring implementation problems under control. To suggest that the only way to do that is to become involved in the imple-mentation process, as writers like Bardach have done, seems to violate democratic theory.

Moreover, this is particularly the case when it is shown, as seems to be the case, that policy issues are best settled by bargaining during the implemen-tation process. This is an issue that has particularly worried lawyers committed to the concept of the rule of law. Thus Jowell[31] has seen the development of discretionary powers in the implementation process as involving a threat to citizens rights. He recognizes the fact that this may involve a community gain at the expense of an over-powerful citizen but is fearful of the private governmental process involved. In this respect an administrative system in which policies are enshrined in laws, and implementers can be brought to account through the courts for the disregard of those laws, represents a lawyer's view of the way the policy-implementation distinction ought to work in a democratic society.

There are, of course, other contributors to the discussion of this issue who express scepticism about this concept of the rule of law, seeing it as essentially protective of established interests.[32] In this sense their voices are joined with those who ask, does the separation between policy and implementation really matter? Is it the important problem for contemporary society that the adherents of the traditional liberal top-down democratic control model suggest it is? Or is this an ideological veneer closely associated with a view that state action should be minimal and should certainly not interfere with the free working of the market? In this way the search for ways of distinguishing policy from implementation comes up against the major ideological controversy in our society. This analysis suggests that it is unrealistic to expect the two phenomena to be clearly distinguishable, and suggests that the search for ways to distinguish them is fundamentally bound up with the quest for rational and democratic control over administration. The dilemma is whether that quest must be essentially an attempt to push back the frontiers of government involvement with society, or whether – as most democratic socialists *must* believe – we can have both more government and more readily influenced implementation processes. Is the demand for active government bound to lead in corporatist directions, which may be totalitarian or at best paternalist or elitist in character? Or can concepts of democratic intervention in the policy process be developed which come to terms, as the standard radical attack on the civil service does not,[33] with the inherently inter-related character of policy-making and implementation?

Notes and references

1 See Barrett, Boddy and Stewart 1979.
2 Hill 1976: 55–7.
3 Hill *et al.* 1979.
4 See particularly Smith 1976: 13.
5 Dunsire 1978a.
6 The chain analogy is particularly developed in Pressman and Wildavsky 1973.
7 DoE 1972.
8 See Sedgemore 1980.
9 The author has earlier explored this in Chapter 10 of Hill 1972.
10 See Simeon 1972.
11 See Higgins 1978.
12 Moynihan 1969.
13 Pressman and Wildavsky 1973.
14 Bardach 1977.
15 Hill and Issacharoff 1971; Higgins 1978.
16 Rhodes 1979, appendix to the SSRC report cited in (3).
17 P. Knoepfel and H. Weidner 1980.
18 See (3).
19 This is an issue with which system models in political science have struggled (see, for example, Easton 1973).
20 See, for example, Poulantzas 1973.
21 See Weber 1949.
22 For example, see Lowi's four categories of 'distributive policy', 'constituent policy', 'regulative policy', and 'redistributive policy' in Lowi 1972: 298–310.

23 See, for example, Whale 1977 and Wyndham Goldie 1977.
24 See, in particular, Gough 1979.
25 These varied competing views are well assessed in Room 1979 and in Higgins 1980: 1–24.
26 Hill 1980b: Chapter 1.
27 Hill 1981. These are issues which are being studied much more fully at present by my colleagues T. Davies and C. Mason.
28 Winkler 1976: 103.
29 See Gough 1979.
30 Middlemas 1979: 381.
31 Jowell 1979.
32 Bankowski and Nelken 1979, another contribution to the Workshops in Discretionary Decision-Making. Michael Adler and Stewart Asquith are editing a collection of these papers for publication.
33 See Sedgemore 1980, and the speeches of Tony Benn.

10

Implementing the results
of evaluation studies*

Randall Smith

Introduction

The term 'evaluation' embraces a wide range of activities. Joseph Wholey, from the Program Evaluation Group of the Urban Institute in Washington, has commented that the word 'seems to cover everything from multi-million dollar social experiments to one-day site visits'.[1] 'Evaluation' as an activity can be briefly described as a procedure which appraises the worthwhileness of an activity, whilst 'evaluation research' is distinctive in so far as it uses the tools of social science research to undertake the appraisal.[2] In this chapter, evaluation refers to judgements about the effectiveness of past actions, not appraisal of possible future alternative strategies.

In a review of the aims and approaches of evaluation research in social policy, Grant and Gallagher list five approaches, while pointing out that they are not mutually exclusive, and most research in social policy calls for a mixed strategy, drawing together elements of each to meet the particular problem under consideration. The five approaches are:

1 The *experimental* or *quasi-experimental* approach, which attempts to quantify success in achieving initial policy objectives, based on some form of before and after study of those involved in the experiment in comparison with a control group.
2 The purely *comparative* study of success in achieving policy objectives using quantitative measures and based on a comparison between those affected by the policy or programme and those who have not been involved.
3 A *social indicator* approach based on the regular collection of quantitative indices which demonstrate the success in achieving policy objectives over time.

* An earlier version of this paper was given at a conference of the Scottish Branch of the Social Services Research Group at Pitlochry in February 1979.

4 A *process evaluation* approach, which is concerned with recording and interpreting programmes and policies as they unfold and employing a mixture of qualitative and quantitative data.
5 *Cost-benefit analysis* and similar less comprehensive approaches (e.g. cost effectiveness, cost minimization) which involve the use of economic concepts to identify and measure the costs and benefits of policies and programmes.[3]

Much of the literature cited in this chapter is drawn from American sources, and most of it is broadly based on the experimental or quasi-experimental approach. It focuses primarily on the external review of particular policies or programmes, rather than on the (usually internal) process of regular or cyclic review, such as is suggested above, for instance, by the social indicator approach.

As well as concern about the diffuse nature of the term 'evaluation', the literature also addresses the problem of using the results of research, whether evaluation research or any other kind. 'The whole notion of what research utilization means is complex and fuzzy.'[4] American commentators have expressed no little anguish about the role, legitimacy and impact of evaluation studies, while also pointing out that 'converting evaluation into a technical speciality has permitted evaluation to be seen by program administrators as an optional activity, something to choose to do or not to do, as if the administrator had a choice. But evaluation is a standard, not an optional feature in program practice.'[5]

This chapter begins by examining the reasons for the apparent lack of use of evaluation studies, and this is followed by suggestions which could improve 'take up' under certain circumstances. In particular, recognition by evaluators, their subjects and their customers (frequently administrators) that *commissioning*, *participating in* and *undertaking* evaluation work is as much a political act as a technical act, may also lead to better opportunities for *using* the results of evaluation studies, through the realization that utilization of research is also a political act.

It is, then, further suggested that evaluation studies and evaluation research may make an impact, but in ways different – and more diffuse – from that anticipated by evaluators and evaluation researchers. During the argument taken from some American literature on evaluation, consideration is given to the relevance of this debate for social researchers in British governmental settings.

Much of the US literature focuses on evaluation endeavours undertaken in organizations separate from government, although in recent years more work has been undertaken in-house at both the state and federal level. In addition, evaluation requirements have been built into recent US legislation. A General Accounting Office survey in 1974 uncovered forty legislative acts – directed at health, education, transportation, law enforcement, housing, the environment, economic opportunity and agriculture – which included varying stipulations for evaluation. Six mandated that a fixed percentage of programme funding should be set aside for evaluation, and eight even specified methods of data collection.[6]

This contrasts strongly with the occasional weak requirement to undertake monitoring in British social legislation, despite the rhetoric about accountability and value for money. In times of economic difficulties and scarce resources, effective policy review, soundly based in tested research techniques but responsive to the political environment in which it is taking place, is crucial. It is therefore important to consider why the results of evaluation studies have been said not to have been implemented in the past.

The non-use of evaluative data

The frequent assertion in the American literature that evaluation work lacks impact is summarized in the following extended quotation:[7]

> The problem of the non-utilization or the under-utilization of evaluation research has been discussed frequently in the evaluation literature. There seems to be a consensus that the impact of evaluative research on program decision making has been less than substantial. Carol Weiss (1972) lists underutilization as one of the foremost problems in evaluation research: 'Evaluation research is meant for immediate and direct use in improving the quality of social programming. Yet a review of evaluative experience suggests that evaluation results have not exerted significant influence on program decisions.'
>
> Other prominent reviewers have reached a similar conclusion. Ernest House (1972) put it this way: 'producing data is one thing. Getting it used is quite another.' Williams and Evans (1969) write that '. . . in the final analysis, the test of the effectiveness of outcome data is its impact on implemented policy. By this standard, there is a dearth of successful evaluation studies.' Wholey (1970) concluded that '. . .the recent literature is unanimous in announcing the general failure of evaluation to affect decision making in a significant way.'

This quotation could have been even longer, citing several more references and ending with the common complaint of evaluators that their findings have been ignored.[8]

But why was the air so thick with complaints? When Carol Weiss wanted to visit a sample of evaluators to discuss methodological problems, she found that they wanted to discuss their problems of personal relationships, not methodological issues.[9] The reasons for the non-implementation of the results of evaluation studies are numerous, and only some of them concern the personal relationships of the evaluator. Others are to do with methodology and measurement, the quality of the investigation, the organizational constraints within which evaluators (and their customers) work, and the customers' own responses to research of this kind. In 1977 Carol Weiss asserted that 'most research studies bounce off the policy process without making much of a dent on the course of events'.[10]

Reasons for the non-use of evaluative data

First, non-use of the results of evaluation studies can be attributed to the *researcher or evaluator* himself, to the nature of the research, or to the nature of the research endeavour. 'The posture of scientific skepticism, which the researcher must assume in the evaluation, may irritate and antagonize dedicated program staff.'[11] It may be that the results of the research are ambiguous or unclear. 'Social science knowledge (compared with the physical sciences) is not apt to be so compelling or authoritative as to drive inevitably toward implementation.'[12] Indeed, Jeffrey Pressman concluded that 'most evaluations are inevitably inconclusive',[13] though he did not suggest that this was necessarily always the fault of the researcher. However, the latter may be very cautious in drawing out the implications of his investigations, on the grounds that the evidence does not permit this according to the canons of traditional academic investigation.[14] In addition, the presentation and dissemination of research results may not encourage their use. The evaluator may not have thought through the best means of transmission of the evidence. Written or other kinds of reports may not be offered in a suitably readable or comprehensible form, and may not be available at the right time.

Undertaking the evaluation may lead to a redefinition of the nature of the problem, such that the results do not address the problem as originally conceived, and so the investigation is labelled irrelevant or peripheral and lacks impact. The research results may be rejected on the grounds that the quality of the investigation was poor, perhaps because the evaluators themselves were of mediocre ability, because of lack of time and other resources, or because of the instability of the research team. Carol Weiss reported that

> the one finding of our study that previous writing in the field had not prepared us for was the tremendous instability of evaluation staffs. Part-time directors were the rule rather than the exception. Turnover in evaluation staff at all levels was phenomenal. It was not uncommon for a three-year study to have had three or four different directors and three complete turnovers in research associates.[15]

It is somewhat chastening to realize that in Britain it is not very clear whether social research, undertaken inside government or extra-murally, suffers from problems of turnover, though Jenny Platt does vividly illustrate the career and personal needs of social research workers, and comments that eight of the fifty-five projects in her sample (mostly university-based) were affected by researchers leaving significantly early.[16]

Second, the results of evaluation studies may be ignored or rejected by *individuals within the organization* whose policy or programme has been studied. If the findings of the research suggest that the impact of the programme or service under investigation has been minimal in relation to expectations or stated intentions, those associated with the programme may not welcome the implications of the evaluation, particularly if they come as a surprise. The research results appear as a challenge to the experience of, for instance, the manager or the fieldworker, and, if the conclusions are not supported by other related studies, they are labelled suspect.

Apart from questioning the results of evaluation studies on the grounds that they do not match the knowledge and experience of managers or fieldworkers, individuals may wish to discredit challenging evaluations in order to maintain their own position in the organization, and the organization as a whole may see the outcome of the investigation as threatening its purpose or even its survival in its existing form. Powerful vested interests may combine to counter the impact of the research. In other words, those responsible for or working in the policy area under scrutiny may conduct their own 'meta-evaluation' of the evaluation study, basing their campaign on knowledge through experience or intuition on the one hand, or resentment and fear on the other. As social policies and programmes tend to have goals which are multiple, conflicting and vague,[17] it may not be too difficult to discredit a piece of evaluation work on the grounds of its irrelevance or lack of focus, whether the motivation for the challenge be disbelief or self-defence. It should, however, be added that the results of evaluation studies may also be available to longstanding opponents of the programme under scrutiny, and they too may be tempted to go beyond the evidence in their campaign to discredit a policy initiative which they have always believed to be misconceived.[18]

Many evaluation studies, according to the American literature, do come up with negative findings, and this provides another opportunity for ignoring the research results. Such negative findings, it is argued, merely indicate what should not be done. As they cannot demonstrate what should be done instead, they are of little help to the manager or the fieldworker and are therefore ignored. They do not pass the 'utilization test', and do not provide a direction for feasible change.[19] If the researcher's job in the context of evaluation is to help the implementer of policies and programmes to reduce the amount of uncertainty in decision-making and yet no ways forward are identified, then the evaluation has proved to be a waste of time. Finally, research results may be ignored because the implementation of the findings would require (or are believed to require) resources at a level far beyond those which are available.

In attempting to pinpoint some of the reasons that lead to the non-implementation of the results of evaluation studies by isolating the responsibilities of the evaluator and the customer of the study, some artificiality has inevitably resulted. Many of the issues raised in the preceding paragraphs reflect in part the nature of the inter-relationships between the evaluator and the customer. This may be couched initially in terms of the distance between the customer and the researcher, particularly marked when the latter works in a separate organization on an extra-mural contract. But the problem remains even when the study is undertaken on an in-house basis, for instance a governmental setting. Even here the distinction needs to be drawn between those operating in a centralized unit with an agency-wide remit and those working in a department with its own executive responsibilities, such as social services, planning or housing in a local authority.

If relationships are not close and continuous, the 'program administrator' (to use American terminology) may not be involved in the design of the proposed evaluation, and the researcher(s) may have a blinkered view of the meaning to the administrator of implementing the research results. Alternatively, researchers may feel powerless and marginal to the process of implementation, particularly if they do recognize that the results of an evaluation study play only a modest part in the highly political game of decision-making, in which many other influences are present. 'There must, in the nature of things, be other considerations that prevail over evaluation, even where the powers that be would like to follow its dictates.'[20]

> At best, evaluators and social researchers can be in a position to pool their work with others in order to develop effective policies. Social scientists are one set of participants among many. Seldom do they have conclusions available that bear directly and explicitly on the issue at hand. More rarely still do they have a body of convergent evidence. Nevertheless, they can engage in mutual consultations that progressively move closer to potential policy responses.[21]

It would be a rare organization in which there were not conflicts of interest between administrators and managers, and between administrators and practitioners or fieldwork staff. Government, for instance, whether central or local, is not a monolith. These conflicts make relationships between evaluators and managers and/or practitioners more complex, and there may be a lack of clarity in the mind of the researcher about the identity of the customer of the results of his study. Who will be affected, and how, by the findings? Glaser and Backer[22] identified at least four distinct audiences:

1 commissioners – whoever commissioned the evaluation and are paying for it
2 programme staff
3 various publics – especially when their tax monies are supporting a project

4   theorists – those concerned with knowledge about concepts and variables related to the programme and its operation

In an English local authority social services department (to take an arbitrary example), this categorization can be substantially elaborated. The 'commissioner' could be central government, the EEC, an independent grant-giving body, the Social Science Research Council, the local authority itself, or a combination of these institutions. The 'programme staff' could include the elected members on the social services committee, the chief executive of the authority in his capacity as a leader of a corporate management team, corporate planning staff with inter-service concerns and responsibilities, the director of social services, his senior management team with policy planning responsibilities, departmental staff in charge of management policies to do with either resource control or service delivery, or professional and other operating staff with fieldwork responsibilities in residential, day care or domiciliary contexts.

Particularly problematic could be the tensions between 'commissioners' and 'programme staff'. Do 'commissioners' knowingly commission research into their own activities? If a piece of evaluation work undertaken within or for a social services department is clearly intended *for* managers, but is *about* operating staff, e.g. home helps, social workers, residential care staff, trouble can result. For instance, if researchers aim to convince social workers that the implementation of a case review system is equally helpful to them, their clients, their supervisors and higher management – the assumption of consensus – the result, unless great care is taken,[23] may be to heighten suspicion. There are no grounds for believing that there is not a conflict of interest. Rational, calm discourse is not an automatic winner – witness the dissent over fluoridation of water supply and placing tachographs in the cabs of lorries. Even if the 'intellectual' case for developing a case review system (to pursue the example) is not challenged, it does not mean that the support of the social workers has been gained. An appeal to intellect can be construed as a threat.

The third of Glaser and Backer's distinct audiences is labelled 'various publics'. They can include actual or potential recipients of services, their families, neighbours or friends, voluntary organizations and pressure groups, the media, as well as ratepayers and taxpayers. The fourth category, 'theorists', could embrace other researchers in the social services department or elsewhere in the local authority, fellow members of the social services research group, researchers elsewhere in the public sector or voluntary organizations, plus academics. This is, admittedly, a somewhat extended list of possible audiences, but it underlines the possibility of lack of clarity in respect of the identity of the customer of a piece of evaluation or any other kind of research work.

In relation to 'programme staff', the outcome may be that the research results may be reported to the 'wrong decisional level'.[24] In other words, the results of the evaluation may be made known to individuals or groups who either do not have the power to take the necessary actions suggested by the results of the research, or who are too far removed from the arena under scrutiny to know what the appropriate actions might be and how to implement them without undesirable consequences which might otherwise have been foreseen. Even if the results of research do go in at the 'right' level, they may not be well received if relationships have not been sustained during the course of the investigation, as the original programme administrator may have been replaced consequent upon promotion, transfer, resignation, retirement, death or, less likely, dismissal. During the course of the investigation, programme priorities may have shifted substantially or the office may have been re-organized, even abolished. None of this aids the receptivity of research results, if the research-customer relationship has been distant.

All this shows that evaluation studies, like other pieces of research and other kinds of investigations, are highly political acts. As Carol Weiss has succinctly pointed out,[25] developing, reducing, maintaining or changing social policies and programmes is a political act, so evaluation research reports on these policies and programmes enter the political arena and therefore evaluation is also a political act. The evaluator has, consciously or otherwise, a political stance. Aaron Wildavsky refers to evaluation as 'manifestly a political activity'.[26] Peter Rossi has asserted that 'no good evaluation goes un-punished',[27] recommended that it was 'useful to sensitize fledgling evaluators to the fact that their findings will often be greeted with skepticism, suspicion and hostility'[28] and concluded that 'the problem presented by evaluation research lies not in research methodology but in the politics of research'.[29] Howard Freeman is in agreement:[30]

in a large number of cases, evaluation studies still are not utilized or are underutilized in policy development and program implementation. The major reason is that we have not fundamentally solved the organizational and orchestrational problems that currently limit the potential of evaluation research. The extensive time requirements to do sound studies, resource constraints, political blockages to conducting work, and administrative barriers are much more serious defects than the extant limitations in methods . . . the plea now is for addressing the political and contextual problems that inhibit successful completion and utilization of (evaluations of social action programs). This is the contemporary challenge to evaluation researchers as well as, of course, to our colleagues in policy, planning and program implementation. To rephrase a line from a general discussion of the responsibilities of science, we must get up and face the wind, confront the future.

Increasing the use of evaluative data

So, what is to be done? Many of the reasons given for the non-implementation of the results of evaluation studies suggest possible solutions to or ameliorations of the problem as defined by the spokesmen of the American evaluation industry. The prescriptions suggested may not always neatly fit the political and organizational context of evaluation studies in Britain, but they should hint at some of the issues faced by researchers in local government and elsewhere, and may even result in the avoidance of some difficulties if those involved in 'policy, planning and program implementation' are able and willing to engage in the debate.

This provides, in fact, the first and possibly most important theme in bringing about effective implementation of the results of evaluation studies, namely, a close relationship between the evaluation researcher and a clearly identified customer (or customers) of evaluation studies, plus a sensitivity to the impact on others in the organization, if research results are acted upon. This suggests that, at the very least, the researchers need to be aware of their own 'assumptive worlds'[31] and to check them against those of their customers and of the subjects of research, to see if the research findings appear meaningful to either customers or the subjects of research. 'Theories of under-utilization with the greatest degree of explanatory power are those emphasizing the existence of a gap between social scientists and policy makers due to differences in values, language, reward systems, and social and professional affiliations.'[32] In a recent study of teams of social workers in British local authority social services and social work departments, the researchers built in (and emphasized) feedback to the social workers. 'We wanted to check the factual accuracy of our presentation and our respondents' reaction to the overall picture of the team's activity – was it "fair" in their eyes? . . . We agreed to consider any points they raised and alter the report if, on reflection, we thought their criticisms fair.'[33]

A close relationship with the customer of the evaluation may also imply a value stance on the part of the evaluator that is consonant with, though not necessarily subordinate to, that of the customer (if not the subject) of the research. 'Acceptance of evaluation requires a community of shared values.'[34] A shared outlook of this kind is probably particularly helpful when the evaluation is undertaken on an in-house basis and implies that 'in the final analysis, the program administrator must take the primary responsibility for the evaluation and subsequent use of the information'.[35] Evaluation research, in this context, is seen as providing a service, performing a confirmatory role, reducing uncertainty, helping to get things started, bringing about change gradually without threatening key interests. The idea of the evaluator as a close colleague of the programme administrator in order to aid the latter achieve policy goals is strongly advocated by Michael Patton in developing the idea of active-reactive-adaptive interactions between evaluator and administrator,[36] and is strongly reinforced in Jack Rothman's study of the circumstances in which research is likely to be successfully applied in English local authority social services departments. In the foreword and introduction to this study, Ronald Havelock and Jack Rothman suggest that the proposed guide to successful application is based on a linkage model of research utilization which focuses attention on effective communications between administrators and researchers.[37]

However, there is a strong case for not adopting this value stance if the purpose of the evaluation endeavour is to challenge the assumptions of those responsible for the programme being investigated. In these circumstances those responsible for the service under scrutiny are not 'customers', at least in the 'customer-contractor' principle sense.[38] Some commentators have argued that the research endeavour should be completely independent of agencies responsible for planning, managing or delivering services. Jim Sharpe indeed concludes that 'an increase in the contribution of social science to policy-making may depend as much on the number and quality of social science academics who stick to their lasts, but take a rigorously critical interest in public policy, as it does on the number who decamp to research institutes and to Whitehall.'[39] This view appears rather exclusive to those social scientists who might well wish to undertake research in academic settings, but who find that the available jobs are in government, other parts of the public sector, or research institutes. 'As . . . in-house research staffs have grown and the academic job market has declined, more people well trained in the social and behavioral sciences have gravitated toward research jobs in public agencies.'[40] In any case, 'the socially conscious researcher, having reported findings in the usual way, cannot rest comfortably in the protective sanctuary of the University, confident that the research will speak for itself if it has social utility. . . . Utilization occurs instead as the result of ingenuity, resourcefulness, and commitment.'[41]

In a commentary on research and policy-making in English local authority social services departments, Tim Booth argues that while the researcher must obviously understand the concerns of policy-makers, it does not automatically imply that he must assume their view of the world. 'The greatest danger facing the in-house researcher . . . is that he identifies himself too closely with the values and priorities of the administrator.'[42] Rather, the researcher has to recognize the political or pressure-group nature of his activity and that the results of his work will serve some of the interests or groupings in the department more than others. Research, in this sense, is not a service activity, producing answers to predetermined problems, but is part of the process by which problems are identified. The researcher's political role is to negotiate the legitimacy of this activity – somewhat easier said than done. The outcome, as elaborated later in this chapter, is likely to be compromise through negotiation between administrator and researcher.

Barry McDonald[43] labels the kind of research activity that is responsive to the perceived needs of the administrator 'bureaucratic evaluation' and contrasts it, on the one hand, with 'autocratic evaluation' undertaken in the 'prestigeful groves of academe'[44] and, on the other hand, with 'democratic evaluation', which he describes as 'an information service to the whole community about the characteristics of a . . . programme . . . . The democratic evaluator recognises value pluralism and seeks to represent a range of interests in his issue formulation.' Wise, in discussing the evaluator as educator, argues that 'the utilization task is to see that various audiences have opportunities to learn about the program and to draw out implications for the future of the program and their place in it. The evaluator can therefore consider different strategies that would provide appropriate opportunities for each audience to come to terms with new knowledge about the program.'[45]

If this last style of evaluation is not perceived as legitimate by powerful interests within a British local authority, it is probably an unhelpful stance for a local authority researcher, who needs the confidence of both the customer and the subject of research to get access to data in order to undertake good quality research, and to have an opportunity to help implement the results of the research. Likewise, the customer wants to have confidence in the researcher in order to avoid the disputes which tend to be associated with sudden, unexpected and challenging research results.

Thus, one possible stance is to create close and sustained links between customer and researcher from the outset of the investigation, with a particular focus on anticipating the possible outcomes of the evaluation. 'Evaluators cannot wait until a report is written before they think about how evaluation information will be disseminated and utilized. Concern for utilization must begin with their initial meeting with the program director and staff members.'[46]

If the customer is involved in the design and conduct of the research, as many commentators advocate,[47] then 'an anticipatory strategy' can be developed: 'all the experiments that we have examined suggest that experimental results are more likely to be used if clear and acceptable strategies are developed beforehand to facilitate the use of negative as well as positive findings.'[48] Such a strategy (a) provides an opportunity for the researcher to negotiate a role in the dissemination and implementation of research results, perhaps by suggesting alternative proposals for action, (b) tends to commit the customer to the outcome of the investigation, and (c) reduces distortion of findings and resistance to their implications.

The researcher may help to reduce resistance further by suggesting trials for a new procedure, by not ignoring resource constraints in research recommendations, by avoiding suggestion of personal criticism,[49] and by reporting in time and yet timing suggestions for change to coincide with expressions of dissatisfaction from elsewhere. Evaluators 'must be prepared to hold back the results of evaluation if the times are not propitious; they must be ready to seize the proper time for change whether or not evaluations are fully prepared or wholly justified'.[50]

All this implies a close reading of the organizational environment by the evaluator, that is, to develop an understanding of the political context in which he is working. 'If evaluation results are expected to affect policy or program management decisions, then an analysis of the *planning-management-control* process to be affected and the development of realistic models of this process must become integral parts of evaluation planning and design.'[51] 'Improving utilization is not going to be so much a matter of training managers in the subtleties of research methodology and interpretation of results as it will be training evaluators in organizational and political realities and communication skills and having them placed in organizations so that they are in extensive contact with relevant administrators.'[52]

An informal contract between researcher and customer can have other beneficial effects in the eyes of the evaluator. It reduces – though it does not eliminate – the possibility that a programme manager or a practitioner will misuse the results, either deliberately or because there has been a distortion of the findings in the course of transmission.[53]

Most of the quotations just cited from the American literature to illustrate the process of 'bureaucratic evaluation' assume that the mode of evaluation study is likely to be experimental or quasi-experimental. Other modes of evaluation work undertaken by social researchers in governmental settings may approximate to McDonald's idea of 'democratic evaluation', which would be congenial in ideological terms to substantial numbers of social researchers as it would take account of the rights of the subjects of research without unduly antagonizing the customer of the research. For instance, Grant and Gallagher comment favourably on a 'process evaluation' approach which is concerned with recording and interpreting programmes and policies as they unfold, using a range of research techniques.[54]

A number of investigators have suggested that there is a range or spectrum of relationships between research and the policy process.[55] All of them include insights, and all of them have their limitations. The use of these commentaries to evaluation researchers in, for instance, governmental settings is as a device by which to increase understanding of the nature of the existing relationship (if any), and to consider what possibilities exist for negotiating a preferable relationship.

The idea of negotiation, increasing understanding and creating informal contracts is crucial not only to improving researcher-administrator relationships, but also to using an improved relationship to achieve a better understanding of the policy, practice or problem to be evaluated. Albert Cherns, assuming that research should be used to solve problems, has stressed the importance of the process of 'negotiating the problem' so that its nature can be discussed, as can the type of acceptable solution and the methods to be adopted by the researcher.[56] If the would-be researcher has no negotiations about the problem, the solution or the research method to be adopted, Cherns labels him a 'subordinate technician'. If he has discretion over research method alone, he is an 'engineer'. If the type of solution is also negotiable and is not predetermined, the researcher plays a 'consultant' role. Finally, if the nature of the problem is also on the agenda for discussion and reconsideration, then the evaluator has full 'collaborative' status with the administrator.

This fourfold categorization suggests that even in a local government context where evaluation tends to be regarded as a problem-solving service industry, there is a range of possibilities for greater or lesser influence by the researcher over shifts in policies, programmes and practice. What Cherns omits to consider is the further negotiation required in respect of the interpretation, dissemination and implementation of findings, when the evaluation is not undertaken in an action research or experimental framework; indeed, Cherns might well argue that a full collaborative relationship can only operate in an action research context, where there is an implied consensus on goals.

Clear identification of the customer of the evaluation and an understanding of who else may be affected by possible changes are necessary if helpful mutual respect is to be established, and may increase the researcher's influence over the implementation of research results. In turn, identification of the customer becomes easier if the purpose of the evaluation is unambiguous. Tripodi, Fellin and Epstein[57] show clearly that it is the job of the programme administrator to ask: who is the consumer of evaluation? Where a researcher already exists in the same organization, he could aid the administrator in addressing this question, and in so doing make an effective evaluation more likely. 'The usefulness of any information can never be decided without considering "for whom" and "to do what".'[58]

The evaluation researcher can increase his influence on the implementation of research results by improving his own procedures and practices. The first issue, quite evidently, is 'better' communication of research results. Agarwala-Rogers[59] argues for heavy emphasis on 'receiver orientation' and this is accomplished by multiple channels of communication, including oral presentation (which implies personal contact), short written reports and films. Statistics tables should be accompanied by short explanations and texts. Davis and Salasin[60] draw on literature from communications research and, in the context of selecting alternative ideas for possible action, suggest the following unsurprising practices:

1 the communicator identify himself with his audience;
2 pretesting of presentation for readability, coherence and understanding

from the viewpoint of the audience for whom it is intended;

3 presentation of factual report that has been agreed, if possible, by people of prominence and influence;

4 emphasize positive reinforcements or benefits that can result;

5 ensure any risks involved are discussed;

6 combine logical and non-exaggerated emotional appeals;

7 use pictorial and other illustrative material, where appropriate;

8 take account at once of any objections that are likely to arise;

9 the essential information is repeated, reiterated and said again when practicable. 'In other words, repetition of a message from different communication sources is often necessary for effective transmission.'[61]

The result of all this is persuasive communications!

Suggestions have also been made that increasing the knowledge base of managers by effective communications can be aided by 'professional information experts, librarians, abstractors, editors and others (who) are employing a variety of hardware-oriented techniques for making information more readily available to those who engage in even minimal information-seeking behaviour'.[62] Such services may well be as helpful to the researcher as to the programme administrator, but the former can be part of the information-processing system for the latter. Richard Rose has proposed that evaluation research teams might sometimes be advised to hire a writer, so that their results could subsequently be understood.[63] Jack Rothman has summarized a variety of linking procedures and mechanisms between administrator and researcher 'in order to bring about appropriate coupling'.[64]

In Britain, some of the reports from the Community Development Projects were influenced by advice to increase their appeal to and impact on particular audiences, and the Centre for Environmental Studies appointed a professional journalist to edit their review, which first appeared in July 1977. In Whitehall itself, the Central Policy Review Staff found that the problems they faced in the collective briefing of Cabinet ministers on evaluations over a range of policy developments and initiatives lay in the mode of presentation as well as in the substance of their comments.

Perhaps more important, at least in the American context, is Rose's suggestion of further development of a brokerage function between policy-makers and researchers in order to bridge the user-evaluation gap. 'Instead of repeating the admonition to both public officials and researchers to understand each other's perspective, Rose preferred to work on the strengthening of a specialised brokerage function that could mediate between the groups.'[65] Agarwala-Rogers, too, refers to the linking system 'which performs the functions of translating practitioner needs to researchers and of diffusing research results to practitioners', and taking examples from a number of fields, such as agriculture, public technology and education, concludes that experience shows that 'some type of linkers is essential if research is to be effectively utilized'.[66]

In the United States linkers may be found in separate institutions, particularly where the evaluation work is undertaken in an organization distinct from the one whose programmes are being studied. In a governmental context in Britain, a linker would be more likely to be an individual within the organization than a separate institution, perhaps a research manager with other administrative responsibilities, e.g. an assistant director of a local authority social services department in charge of training as well as research. He (or she), rather than directly undertaking investigations, could develop a number of 'networking' activities likely to increase the use of research results. Following some of the suggestions of Tony Tripodi,[67] he could (a) negotiate staff time and other resources for working on 'research utilization'; (b) set up working parties to review research knowledge on a particular topic, or buy in reviews of research from the academic world for local discussion; (c) persuade the local school of social work to pay more attention to issues related to the use of research results; (d) encourage the social services research group (or other appropriate bodies) to mount conferences and arrange workshops on the same theme; and (e) try to organize the 'simultaneous publication of research and utilization articles in professional journals'. The key issues are (1) that the linker himself has a legitimacy in all the sub-systems he is trying to bring closer together and (2) that he has a personal style which aids him in bringing off this 'networking' or 'reticulist' role. Personal factors are seen to play a key role in the use of evaluation research results.

For lack of a better term, we have simply called this . . . variable the personal factor. It is made up of equal parts of leadership, interest, enthusiasm, determination, commitment, aggressiveness and caring. Where the personal factor emerges, evaluations have an impact; where it is absent, there is a marked absence of impact.[68]

But are evaluative data not used?

This chapter has reached the point where it has outlined a number of prescriptions on how some of the problems which are said to result in the non-implementation of the findings of evaluation studies can be overcome. It is high time to make the simple point that there may be more implementation of evaluation studies than some spokesmen of the American evaluation industry in the past would have us believe. First, it is worth pointing out that 'decisions contrary to the recommendations of an evaluation do not necessarily imply nonutilization'.[69] Second, if the evaluator begins with 'an ideal-typical construct of utilization as immediate and concrete effect on specific decisions and program activities resulting directly from evaluative research findings',[70] it is not very surprising that instances are few and far between.

The problem-solving model of research utilization has been characterized as very limited.

It probably takes an extraordinary concatenation of circumstances for research to influence policy decisions directly: a well-defined decision situation, a set of policy actors who have responsibility and jurisdiction for making the decision, an issue whose resolution depends at least to some extent on *information*, identification of the requisite informational need, research that provides the information in terms that match the circumstances within which choices will be made, research findings that are clear-cut, unambiguous, firmly supported, and powerful, that reach decision-makers at the time they are wrestling with the issues, that are comprehensible and understood, and that do not run counter to strong political interests. Because chances are small that all these conditions will fall into line around any one issue, the problem-solving model of research use probably describes a relatively small number of cases.[71]

However, if immediate results are not seen as the sole or main criterion by which to judge the effective implementation of evaluation studies, then a different picture begins to emerge.

What we found in response to . . . questions on impact was considerably more complex and less dismal than our original thinking had led us to expect. We found that evaluation research *is used* by decisionmakers but not in the clear-cut and organisation-shaking ways that social scientists sometimes believe research should be used. The problem we have come to feel may well lie more in many social scientists' overly grand expectations about their own importance to policy decisions than in the intransigence of . . . bureaucrats. The results of our interviews suggest what is typically characterized as underutilization or nonutilization of evaluation research can be attributed in substantial degrees to a definition of utilization that is too narrow and fails to take into consideration the nature of actual decision-making processes in most programs.[72]

Davis and Salasin indicate that 'the evidence of effective utilization of evaluation becomes much clearer if one maintains observation over a sufficiently extended period'. In particular, they quote a personal communication from James Ciarlo in which, despite his earlier belief that evaluation results were generally ignored, he reported that, 'after continued close observation of the careers of his findings, he is learning that a time period of about nine months must pass before things begin to happen that can be traced to the evaluation effort'. Even that time scale may seem rather short, though longer time scales may give rise to the problems of obsolete research results having a continuing effect. Davis and Salasin suggest that 'better tracer evaluations of evaluation utilization itself would offer more reinforcement to evaluators'.[73] In addition to extending the time scale for observing the effects of the results of evaluation studies, it is also important to be sensitive to the timing of evaluation studies in relation to the short-run and long-run impacts of particular policy initiatives. Salamon pointed out that the New Deal land reform experiments in the United States in the late 1930s and early 1940s were judged to have failed in the early years of the programme, but have had very significant long-run effects, 'transforming a group of landless black tenants into a permanent landed middle class that ultimately emerged in the 1960s as the backbone of the civil-rights movement in the rural South'.[74]

Further reinforcement for evaluators is provided by another suggestion of Davis and Salasin that evaluators should widen their roles and become change agents, taking on the explicitly political function outlined earlier. 'If evaluation is not political in the sense of party partisanship, it is political in the sense of policy advocacy. . . . Evaluative man seeks knowledge, but he also seeks power.'[75] It is a matter of faith (values, if the term is preferred) whether better policies or services emerge from a successful bid for more power through negotiation with other powerful interests, widening the range of network contacts and good timing and style in the presentation of material.

Carol Weiss has suggested for social science research in general, not just evaluation research, that 'use' is an exceedingly ambiguous concept.

> Officials interpret using research to mean anything from adoption of the recommendations of a single study all the way to a general sensitivity to social science perspectives . . . . And not only are interpretations of use highly variable, but also the *phenomenon* of use is an amalgam of diverse activities. People can use social science research to clarify the relative advantages of alternative choices, but they also use it conceptually: to understand the background and context of program operation, stimulate review of policy, focus attention on neglected issues, provide new understanding of the causes of social problems, clarify their own thinking, re-order priorities, make sense of what they have been doing, offer ideas for future directions, reduce uncertainties, create new uncertainties and provoke rethinking of taken-for-granted assumptions, justify actions, support positions, persuade others, and provide a sense of how the world works.[76]

In particular, Weiss has argued that social science research has an 'enlightenment' function.[77]

> It encompasses a range of conceptual contributions, from helping to 'establish new goals and bench marks of the attainable', to helping to 'enrich and deepen understanding of the complexity of problems and the unintended consequences of action', to guiding the 'effort to interpret and structure the social world by establishing languages and symbolic universes used in comprehending and carrying on social life'.[78]

The argument is that government officials, for instance, use research less to arrive at solutions than to orient themselves to problems. 'It was found that utilization frequently took the form of having gradual influence on administrator perceptions of the evaluated program and that evaluative information was interactive with other data sources in becoming utilized.'[79]

In his analysis, Tim Booth concludes that the purpose of research in local authority social services departments is 'to stimulate new thinking and open up new ways of looking at things which help to introduce or foster a new emphasis or direction in the political debate about policy'.[80] However, Jack Rothman's guide to the successful application of research in social services departments concludes from the opinions of both managers and researchers that support of existing policies and legitimation is a more central activity than challenge to current programmes.[81] Robert Wise characterizes challenge as the role of the evaluator as teacher; performing an educative function, compared with the evaluator as servant, judge or scientist.[82]

This may well be an indirect process, not easily discernible. The process of 'enlightenment' is a mode of research utilization. Carol Weiss would agree with Ciarlo and with Davis and Salasin that it is important to examine the career of research findings over time. What is less than clear is how this is to be satisfactorily undertaken and by whom. It sounds like a clarion call for the growing breed of meta-evaluators, who review the activities and impact of evaluators. In the US governmental context, Weiss argued that the 'enlightener' role is only to be found in the upper reaches of a bureaucracy. 'Staff in most analytic offices work under such pressure of time, client demand and limited access that opportunities for wide-ranging analysis are limited.'[83] Surely the research endeavour does not have to be wide-ranging to be enlightening? Peter Rossi and his colleagues suggest an even longer time scale than implied by a gradual influence on current administrators.

> One of the major lasting effects of evaluation, we believe, is to increase the sophistication of our knowledge about how social programs operate. This general rise in knowledge has filtered first into the administration of social programs, to some degree into legislative bodies, and possibly to a lesser degree to the general public. It has made special inroads into the curricula in universities and may well serve as the knowledge base for the decision-makers of the future, whose training will be undertaken in those institutions.[84]

Throughout this chapter there has been a deliberate conflation of the terms evaluator and researcher, evaluation and evaluation research, not because a distinction cannot be made between them, but because, in a governmental context, social researchers are as likely to engage in a procedure for judging the worthwhileness of an activity (evaluation) as to use the tools of science to make the judgement (evaluation research).

In both circumstances the individual may, if he wishes, try to exercise and develop political nous and become a change agent within and on behalf of the governmental agency. Drawing upon primarily American literature may have given a spurious precision or rationality to the process of implementing (or not) the results of evaluation studies, as experienced in Britain. Sharpe points out that 'American culture is more predisposed than most to believe in the beneficial effects of rational enquiry as an aid to decision-making.'[85] But no harm is done, and some good may be achieved, by applying some of the arguments in the US literature about the researcher-administrator relationship to British governmental settings, in the light of the need to undertake effective reviews of policies and to use effectively the resources available through the increasing number of social science graduates who have moved into government posts in the 1970s.

Notes and references

1 Wholey 1976: 679.
2 Freeman 1975: 145, quoting Suchman 1967.
3 Grant and Gallagher 1977: 6.
4 Weiss 1977a: 533.
5 Wise 1980: 14.
6 Rein and White, Spring 1977: 240–1 and Fall 1977: 120.
7 Patton *et al.* 1977: 141. See also Patton 1978: 18. The references within the quotation are as follows: Weiss 1972: 10, 11; House 1972: 412; Williams and Evans 1969: 453; Wholey *et al.* 1970: 46.
8 Weiss 1972: 319.
9 Weiss 1973a, quoted in Davis and Salasin 1975: 625.
10 Weiss 1977a: 532.
11 Goldstein, Marcus and Perkins Rausch 1978: 35.
12 Weiss 1979: 426.
13 Pressman 1975: 201.
14 Argyris 1971: chapter 9.
15 Weiss 1973a: 53.
16 Platt 1976: 153.
17 Wildavsky 1972: 20. See also Wildavsky 1980: 215–17.
18 Suchman 1967: 143 lists the major techniques of distortion and classifies them into six major types.
19 Rothman 1980: 134.
20 Wildavsky 1972: 46. The relationship between evaluators and politicians is not examined in this chapter on the grounds that in most British governmental settings, hierarchical relationships are such that 'program administrators' mediate between politicians and in-house evaluation researchers.
21 Weiss 1979: 428.
22 Glaser and Backer 1972: 58.
23 Goldberg and Fruin 1976; Goldberg, Warburton, McGuinness and Rowlands 1977; and Goldberg, Warburton, Lyons and Willmott 1978.

24 Barton 1976: 232.
25 Weiss 1973b: 37, 38.
26 Wildavsky 1980: 228.
27 Rossi 1973, quoted in Agarwala-Rogers 1977: 331.
28 Rossi, Freeman and Wright 1979: 295.
29 Rossi 1971: 99.
30 Freeman 1977: 48–9.
31 Young 1977: 3.
32 Caplan 1977: 194.
33 DHSS, *Social Service Teams* 1978: 6, 7.
34 Wildavsky 1980: 234.
35 Tripodi, Fellin and Epstein 1971: 137.
36 Patton 1978: 127–9.
37 Rothman 1980: 12, 21–2.
38 HMG, Cmnd 4814, 1971.
39 Sharpe 1975: 11.
40 Polivka and Steg 1978: 704.
41 Caplan 1980: 3–4, 9.
42 Booth 1979: 183. In summarizing his study of the views of senior research officers and chief administrators in twelve social services departments in England, Jack Rothman concluded that challenge to the *status quo* was less emphasized as a central function of researchers than support for current programmes and careful incremental change (Rothman 1980: 137–8, 150).
43 McDonald 1976.
44 Rossi 1971: 97.
45 Wise 1980: 17.
46 Brown and Braskamp, 'Summary' in Braskamp and Brown (eds) 1980: 92.
47 Among many others, Davis and Salasin 1975: 645–7; Larsen and Nichols 1972: 40; Rich 1975; Tripodi 1974: 87; Weiss 1971: 141; Freeman 1975: 157.
48 Riecken and Boruch 1974: 242.
49 Davis and Salasin 1975: 643–4, 646–7.
50 Wildavsky 1980: 229.
51 Wholey 1972: 364.
52 Cox 1977: 507.
53 Tripodi 1974: 81–2.
54 Grant and Gallagher 1977: 12–13.
55 Among others, Freeman and Sherwood 1970: 17–20; Cherns, Sinclair and Jenkins 1972: chapter 2; Donnison 1972; Shipman 1972: 165–7; Platt 1976: 64; Cherns 1976: table 1, 907; Weiss 1977: chapters 1, 3, 5, 10, 12–15; Bulmer 1978: chapters 1–3, 15.
56 Cherns 1976: 906.
57 Tripodi, Fellin and Epstein 1971: 119.
58 Grant (n.d.), 9.
59 Agarwala-Rogers 1977: 332. See also Rothman 1980: 76–7 and especially chapter 5, Reports and Products of Research.
60 Davis and Salasin 1975: 641. See also Brown *et al.* 1978: 331–41 and, for a more general, and equally naïve, commentary on the importance of good communications, Newman *et al.* 1980: 29–35.

61 Tripodi 1974: 82.
62 Schulberg and Baker 1968: 1254.
63 Pressman 1975: 204.
64 Rothman 1980: 21, 49–51.
65 See (63).
66 Agarwala-Rogers 1977: 328, 330.
67 Tripodi 1974: 188–97.
68 Patton *et al*. 1977: 155, and Patton 1978: 64. This view is strongly reinforced by the results of naturalistic research on evaluation and utilization at five local school sites, undertaken by Marvin Alkin and his colleagues. See Alkin 1980: 23–6; also Alkin, Daillak and White 1979.
69 Alkin 1980: 21.
70 Patton *et al*. 1977: 158 and Patton 1978: chapter 2.
71 Weiss 1979: 428.
72 Patton *et al*. 1977: 144, and Patton 1978: 20.
73 Davis and Salasin 1975: 622, 626.
74 Salamon 1979: 129.
75 Wildavsky 1972: 43, 49 and 1980: 231.
76 Weiss and Bucuvalas 1980: 305.
77 Weiss 1977a. She has also pointed out that 'there are no procedures for screening out the shoddy and obsolete . . . . The indirect diffusion process is vulnerable to oversimplification and distortion, and it may come to resemble "endarkenment" as much as enlightenment.' Weiss 1979: 430.
78 Weiss 1980: 309. The three quotations cited by Weiss are: (1) Robert K. Merton, 'The role of applied social science in the formation of policy: a research memorandum', *Philosophy of Science*, vol. 16, 1949: 170; (2) Henry J. Aaron, *Politics and the Professors: The Great Society in Perspective*, Washington, The Brookings Institution, 1978: 166; and (3) David K. Cohen and Michael Garet, 'Reforming educational policy with applied social research', *Harvard Educational Review*, vol. 45, 1975: 42.
79 Alkin 1980: 27.
80 Booth 1979: 185.
81 Rothman 1980: 137–8.
82 Wise 1980: 11–18. The multiple roles of the evaluator are briefly outlined in Anderson, Ball, Murphy and Associates 1975: 147–51.
83 Weiss 1977a: 545.
84 Rossi, Freeman, Wright 1979: 307–8.
85 Sharpe 1975: 11.

Part Three
Policy and Action

Reconstructing the field of analysis

Colin Fudge and Susan Barrett

Introduction

What can we learn from the individual contributions? What main points and issues emerge from the cases? And how do the contributors' views accord with those we reviewed earlier in the introduction? In this concluding chapter we present our own view of the main themes raised in the book, and suggest ways in which the material may be interpreted to further the understanding of the policy-action relationship.

We have presented ten case studies of policy implementation, ranging from macro-negotiations between central and local government over the implementation of public expenditure cuts to transactions between individual professionals over the design of a school. The immediate and overriding impression (for us) is one of variety and complexity. But what do we mean by this? In clarifying the meaning, it seems important to decide whether we mean that implementation is complicated in practice or whether we are talking about the complexity of theorizing from variety in practice. It is important to make this distinction. It may be difficult to get things done, to implement public policy, but it is certainly also difficult to provide general explanations which hold in a variety of situations.

When we set out to produce this book, we were concerned that there seemed to be a paucity of British case material on policy implementation. One of our aims, then, has been to contribute to filling this gap. However, in the context of this book, and our emphasis on practice as the starting point for the development of understanding, we are very conscious of the problems and dangers of using case material. The issue of case study versus a comparative focus is a central methodological problem, not just for those trying to understand policy and implementation, but in many other areas of the social sciences. The issue, in a nutshell, is that in attempting to formulate a theoretical perspective or useful steps towards that goal, severe methodological problems have to be faced, one of which is the decision concerning the level of analysis on which to operate.

We would contend that much which passes for explanation in the policy world is inadequate for a number of reasons, of which two are relevant here. Some theoretical work, for example the political economy tradition, exists at present at too broad a level to relate clearly to actual practices or to be subject to empirical tests. It fails to explore the micro-structure of the political and social system, which we believe is necessary for explanation. On the other hand, much of the material which describes practice and seeks explanation (for example, much of the case study literature on implementation already cited)[1] fails where the political economy tradition is strong – it fails to make links with wider aspects of societal structure and lacks explicitness on the values and interests of the actors involved.[2] Nevertheless, we would argue the need for detailed study to pick up the variety in practice and to develop theory from an empirical base – a 'grounded theory' approach to the study of implementation,[3] accepting, of course, the impossibility of collecting and interpreting empirical material with theoretical neutrality. This approach, however, leaves us with the problem of trying to make sense of and locating the results of a detailed level of analysis within the wider socio-historical structure. To meet this problem, we would argue that the study of implementation at this time needs to consider a linking of levels of analysis, a synthesis of different theoretical positions and viewpoints and yet be grounded in practice. In developing our analysis we have favoured, therefore, the combination of case study and comparative work set against the background of existing bodies of theory or hypotheses.

In this chapter we begin by reminding ourselves of the main points which emerged from our review of the mainstream implementation literature in the introduction. Having done that, we then consider a number of new themes and issues raised by the case study chapters which, we feel, need to be addressed in an analysis of public policy implementation. The case studies have made us particularly aware of both the multiplicity and complexity of linkages within the policy implementation process and the impact on that process of the resolution or non-resolution of different values, interests and intentions held by individual actors, or agencies. Thus, in the remaining part of the chapter, we examine a number of dimensions of analysis: linkages and the idea of 'implementation structure';[4] interactions and the idea of negotiated order;[5] the actors themselves, their values and interests; and the nature of policy itself in relation to questions about the distribution of power within and between organizations and in society. By examining these issues, we point to areas for further work and attempt to reconstruct the field of analysis.

Review

The introduction attempted three things: to review some of the approaches to policy analysis and the study of implementation, with reference to existing literature; to raise questions about how well the 'conventional wisdom' seems to fit with what goes on in reality; and to suggest alternative views of the implementation process. To summarize, on the *study of policy*, four points emerged. First, we identified three elements of the policy process: an environmental system, the political system and the organizational system. The problem, we suggested, was how to understand and explain the way in which these dynamic systems operate and interact. Second, we found that interpretations of case material were limited in use and did not hold in a wide variety of circumstances, and evidence showed that it is even more difficult to prescribe in a way which accommodates reality without merely mirroring its ineffectiveness. Third, given the complexity of the policy-action relationship, and the view, from Allison,[6] that what you see depends on where you are and which way you are looking, then a pluralistic approach in the use of conceptual models or theories and in the types of studies undertaken (comparative as well as case studies) seems an essential prerequisite to understanding what is happening. Fourth, until recently policy decisions have been equated with action by many policy analysts. Only lately have they started to turn their attention to what practitioners are only too aware of – 'the implementation gap'.

On the *study of implementation* and action, we agreed with the view taken by those who have written from the basis of detailed case studies that agencies or organizations, be they public or private, fulfil a variety of roles; as policy-makers and implementers carrying out their routine or innovatory activities; as agents, in the sense of executing the policies and wishes of other organizations; and also as part of the environment affected by the policy outcomes of others. Following from this we proposed that, in agreement with some of the literature, the relationship between policy and action could not be regarded as a simple transmission process but rather must be viewed as a complex assembly job involving the fitting together of different interests and priorities. Furthermore, we argued that the policy-action relationship is not a linear step-by-step progression by which a policy is translated into anticipated consequences, but is better described as interactive and recursive. Holding to this view, individuals' and organizations' actions and reactions may determine policy as much as policy itself determines action and response. We considered interactions between actors as crucial arenas for understanding the policy-action process and emphasized the importance of examining the particular organizational and administrative linkages used for implementation, and the negotiations and negotiative activity taking place. Finally we suggested that policy cannot be regarded as a constant. It is mediated by actors who may be operating with different assumptive worlds[7] from those formulating the policy, and, inevitably, it undergoes interpretation and modification and, in some cases, subversion.

This view raised a number of questions about the nature of policy. How and where is policy 'made' and who 'makes' it? How far is action influenced by policy decisions emerging from a political decision-making process, or is what happens more a reflection of the behaviour of the implementers, combined with the repetition and routinization of tasks? And what is the influence of the political, social and economic environment in which policy is made and its implementation takes place? We will return to these questions in the final part of this chapter.

The introduction, in reviewing some of the approaches to policy analysis and the study of implementation, dealt in some detail with the 'rational model' of the policy-action relationship and used this analysis for identifying key issues for understanding the process of implementation: the multiplicity and complexity of linkages, questions of control and co-ordination, and issues of conflict and consensus. From this, we suggested that the policy-action relationship must be considered in a political context and as an interactive and negotiative process, taking place over time between those seeking to put policy into effect and those upon whom action depends.

Relating the case chapters to the introductory review has reinforced two groups of issues in particular, the multiplicity and complexity of linkages, and that of conflict and consensus. It is to these issues that we now turn.

Multiplicity of linkages, conflict and consensus

Conventional wisdom suggests that successful implementation rests on achieving consensus in the policy process. As we have shown, both Pressman and Wildavsky[8] and Dunsire[9] emphasize the importance of making and maintaining a variety of links in the implementation chain and co-ordinating the resources available. The reality, we would argue, is somewhat different, with conflict likely to occur at various stages throughout the policy process. This conflict may arise because of different interests and value systems, which may in turn reflect the impact of differences in the power structure in society and differences in values concerning the policy direction and content. However, conflict must not be interpreted solely as a macro-power struggle related to broad class interests, but also as a question of relative autonomies within and between organizations or, as Williams suggests,[10] as issues of 'performance' versus 'conformance'. Even if it is possible to achieve a measure of consensus about policy objectives, or at least compromise around a particular form of policy, conflict may still occur in terms of the interpretation of what is meant to happen and the application of policy directives or rules. If we take the land example (case three), we can see the broad, societal interest-power struggle underlying the whole issue, and also the administrative struggle, particularly between the centre and the locality within the public sector, about whose interpretation should prevail. Even agencies apparently sharing a similar view about public intervention and the land market differ markedly about the roles of the central and local state. Again in this example we can also see the different interpretations of societal needs and priorities, for example, which sector should be the beneficiary of public investment – industry and employment, or housing. The complexity of this and many of the other cases makes it difficult to unravel how far the policy-action relationship can be explained by the influence of the interest-power structure in society, how far it is the product of 'bureaucratic politics'[11] and how far it is formed by professional and administrative values, and in what sense and in which ways all three are interrelated. This kind of analysis supports Geertz'[12] argument for an approach which sees as its first task the understanding of the 'lives' of ideologies from their origins to their destruction. The interests and values at work within the policy process will be shaped by these ideologies or dominant belief systems which, in themselves, are a reflection of the broad power relationships in society. Ultimately, then, it is necessary to go beyond the identification and analysis of ideologies and investigate the relationship between these ideologies and the power structure in society.

We have identified two fundamental issues: that of the multiplicity of linkages in the policy process and the recognition that consensus is often not achieved and that conflict occurs for a number of reasons. How does the discussion help us in addressing the policy-action relationship? How can we approach the analysis? In this perceived complexity what should we concentrate on?

If we are dealing with a process characterized by a multiplicity of linkages between actors and agencies in a variety of administrative divisions and interorganizational dependencies, and with a variety of interests and ideologies, then first we need to understand these linkages, how and why they have arisen and how and why they are maintained or broken. We would argue that much of the theoretical work on organizations and administration is inadequate for explaining both the informal network of linkages and the broader social relations. What is needed is an analysis that accepts the importance of the micro-structure and world of the actors' interactions and the interests and values involved, but can locate this understanding within the broader interest-power structure within society. Burrell and Morgan, in examining Allen's[13] significant attempt at the construction of a radical organization theory, have argued that what is needed 'is a perspective which emphasises the importance of looking at actual empirical situations, identifying structures and superstructures, and identifying the contradictions and their repercussions'.[14] There are similarities between our suggested reconstruction and what has been termed radical organization theory in which two approaches can be identified: Marxian structuralist and radical Weberian. It is not our intention to examine these in detail here,[15] merely to state the similarity between our approach and the radical Weberian approach which 'offers a mode of analysis which in focusing upon the totality of contemporary social formations, allows one to transcend the insights which emerge from an exclusive preoccupation with the middle-range level of analysis characteristic of functionalist organisation theory'.[16] In developing our analysis we suggest that interactions between actors need to be examined in some detail to identify the interests, stakes and power bases at play. Further we suggest that the dominant value systems influencing the policy process should be examined to find out their derivation, how they construct reality and their relationship with different interests in society. Finally, we need to look at the nature of policy itself and the relative influence of different policy fields on the behaviour of actors and agencies. This involves examining the nature of policy intervention, what it represents, or appears to represent, to promoters and recipients, embracing such aspects as 'real' or 'symbolic' intervention,[17] policy as change, and not least, the question of how far, and when, it can be regarded as separate from implementation.[18]

Our approach to restructuring the analysis of policy implementation reflects the main themes coming out of the practice cases, but also offers a way of conceptualizing issues so that ideas and bodies of theory can be utilized to interpret practice. In the rest of this chapter we explore some ideas which may provide a way forward on these issues and a basis for further work.

Linkages and the idea of implementation structure

We have already pointed to the importance of recognizing the cross-cutting nature of linkages between groups and agencies involved in implementing policy. We have suggested that the group of people involved in implementation does not necessarily reflect formal organizational structures or hierarchies. We have also noted that in many cases actors and groups from several agencies are involved and do not have any 'formal' relationship with each other. The way in which these individuals, groups or agencies work together in implementing policy has been variously described as 'creating' or 'forging' new 'chains' between policy and action. This kind of understanding of the implementation process has been taken further by Hjern and Porter[19] in a comparative study of the implementation of manpower policies in Sweden, Germany and the UK. They argue that if there is interest in finding out and understanding what is going on in the policy-action relationship, then it is necessary to adopt a new unit of administrative analysis which reflects the *actual* linkages between individuals and groups involved in different parts of the policy process: planning, mobilizing resources, effecting action and evaluating action. They have called their unit of analysis, 'implementation structure'.

They define implementation structures as 'bundles of programme related activities and *parts* of organisations'.[20] In other words, they are defining networks of activities and actors that interact to carry out a programme of action. Their key argument is that the organizational reality to which actors carrying out a particular policy or programme refer is not the formal individual organization or groups of organizations but the implementation structure. The organizations involved at face value ('the pool of organizations') derived from an analysis of a programme imperative,[21] they argue, should be carefully separated from the description of implementation structures.

A description of the pools provides information on the resources, constraints and rules of individual organisations. It gives objective background data but should not be confused with the characteristics of implementation structures. Implementation structures may form out of a pool of organisations. But their composition is not determined by the organisations represented, and the behaviour of the persons involved cannot be simply inferred from the rules of 'their' organisation.[22]

Hjern and Porter see the concept of implementation structure as both a way to avoid a 'one-motive rationalisation of purposive collective action'[23] and as an alternative way of addressing the complexity of linkages involved in implementation without assuming hierarchy (the 'top down' approach we referred to earlier). Their main arguments for adopting this kind of 'unit of administrative analysis' follow many of our criticisms of conventional organizational wisdom:

1 The need to distinguish between 'organizational rationales' and 'programme rationales'.
2 The tendency of organizational theory to focus on *formal* organizations and make assumptions about effectiveness of organizations in terms of co-ordination and control – the 'top-down' kind of perspective.
3 The tendency to treat some research evidence, pointing to the importance of informal organization, social norms, leadership styles, modes of negotiation, as deviant and unacceptable features upsetting organizational performance or resulting in 'policy failure'.

Their final criticism of the organizational rationale is that it 'denies the possibility of behaviour which is good for implementation, but bad for the organisation'.[24]

One way of coping with the perceived complexity of organizational linkages is to adopt a hierarchical organization model where complicated tasks are managed by divisions of labour and mechanisms for co-ordination and control. Hjern and Porter argue that this is not a good model for policy related research. They agree that hierarchical relations exist, but their impact can be over-emphasized and stereotyped, whereas the reality is more subtle and even less relevant where actors involved in programmes of action belong to several distinct hierarchies. In other words, they are arguing that the idea of hierarchical organization is limited in two ways: for defining the relationships of actors and for explaining the motivation for collective action. Hjern and

Porter go on to suggest that implementation structures are not 'designed' through hierarchical relationships but form through a process of self-selection by individuals committed to a programme or policy. Hence, the identification of implementation structures must follow the programme rationale *as defined by the participating individuals*. The processes by which membership of the implementation structure form may then offer a clue to understanding how complexity is reduced and managed in practice. In this context, the idea of implementation structure represents a methodological tool as well as an alternative unit of analysis. Implementation structures will only be identified by detailed empirical research tracing the individuals and groups with whom individuals actually interact to carry out different parts of the policy process.

Implementation structures are formed from pools of organizations and their formation is based largely on processes of self-organization. 'In contrast to other theories which deal with the formation of groups for purposive collective action it is postulated that many motives are at play when implementation structures form.'[25] Hjern and Porter identify two interrelated motivational assumptions in the inter-organizational literature: resource exchange – mutual benefits from interacting, and, power dependency – relationships form when one party is powerful enough to force or induce the other to interact. They assume that these motives may both be at play in the formation of an implementation structure. They discard a third motive, individual self-interest, but they do this cautiously, particularly bearing in mind Olsen's work.[26] Finally, they suggest that members of an organization may be motivated to get involved in an implementation structure to protect 'their organization'. That is, active involvement to either prevent action or to ensure that their organization does not suffer as a result of the collective action of other participants. This fourth motivation is akin to Bachrach and Baratz' idea of 'non-decision making'.[27] They thus argue that in practice actors participating in implementation structures perceive them as administrative entities, perhaps as important to them as their employing organizations. They concede that commitment to a programme may vary from person to person, organization to organization, but nevertheless the implementation structure *is* perceivable and is perceived.

As a conceptual approach we think the idea of implementation structure is useful because it addresses the complexity and variety of linkages and interactions involved in 'getting something done'. It is persuasive because it is grounded in a substantial body of empirical work examining manpower policy implementation dealing with a whole range of quasi-governmental, voluntary and private sector actors and agencies in formal and informal relationships. It is a good model for describing the process of getting something done without falling into 'top down traps', for example it addresses issues of co-ordination without recourse to hierarchical concepts. It also, therefore, bridges the (perhaps) false polarization of 'top down' versus 'bottom up' perspective. The 'top down' perspective falsely assumes that all initiative is from the top or centre, along with the ability to control the periphery or subordinate actors. The 'bottom-up' perspective tends to assume that action is spontaneous. However, in reality there is also a trap in assuming that no network of influence or co-ordination is necessary within the policy-action relationship. Implementation structure is free from assumptions about where action is initiated, but rightly points to a process of creating networks of interaction that are essential to achieving action or performance. It is, then, a useful methodological tool and offers a way of studying what is going on without making assumptions about linkages.

Our acceptance of the idea does not mean that we are uncritical of it. The two authors argue that implementation structures are self-defined and self-organized and that a variety of motivations may affect or inform this process and presumably the implementation structure created. However, their tendency to treat the programme as a fix to which all participants subscribe – for example, their statements about participants viewing the implementation structure as an administrative entity and action being focused on a consensually agreed upon programme rationale – does not ring true for us. If there are a variable degree of motivation and a variety of rationales for participating, then it is difficult to accept the implementation structure as the coherent entity they describe. There may be some wishful thinking here. Perhaps it is only the initiator who really sees an implementation structure as an entity, the totality of which achieves action. What about a situation in which a mixture of power-dependence and desire for non-action is coupled with very strong organizational or individual self-interest? From this set of forces you could imagine an unholy alliance of groups and individuals that can be identified and 'mapped' as an implementation structure but where the outcomes bear very little resemblance to the 'programme imperatives' or initiatives that generated the action.

In conclusion we think that this approach still leaves questions about value systems and interests around policy issues, and the effect that lack of *consensus* (and differences of interest) have on the basic processes at work. This takes us back to the question of the nature of policy and how far there are different sorts of implementation forces at work, one essentially 'apolitical' and administrative, and one a continuing struggle over the direction of policy itself. This leads us on to our next set of ideas – about the nature of interactions between actors and agencies, and the degree to which this focus helps us to analyse the wider setting of interests and power relations.

Interactions and the idea of negotiated order

The idea of implementation as a negotiating process came from our earlier discussion (Part One) of the relevance of 'control' and 'compliance' as functions of policy-makers and implementers, respectively, within the policy process. Part of the literature we reviewed suggests that control over policy execution or the ability to ensure compliance with policy objectives is a key factor determining the success or failure of the policy. This material treats problems of control and compliance as purely administrative – lack of compliance is seen as recalcitrant behaviour, a deliberate and natural reaction to authority. The assumptions, therefore, behind successful implementation are that control or compliance can only be achieved by providing the 'right' incentives or through the application of sanctions. In opposition to this line of argument, we suggested that compliance is not only a matter of control but also needs to be distinguished from the issue of consensus – the degree to which different actors and agencies are willing to share value systems, objectives and resources, and thus are willing to support and execute particular policies and programmes. If we accept the argument about control and compliance, and if implementation is defined as putting policy into effect, then *compromise* by the policy-makers would be seen as policy failure. However, if implementation is seen as 'getting something done', then performance rather than conformance is the main objective and compromise a means of achieving it. The emphasis, we argued, then shifts away from a master/subordinate relationship to one where policy-makers and implementers are more equal and the *interaction* between them becomes the focus for study. In examining interaction we find that *negotiation*, *bargaining* and *compromise* form central elements in the process. In this approach implementers are not seen as passive agents on the receiving end of policy but as semi-autonomous groups that are actively pursuing their own goals. Bardach[28] characterizes the interactions between agencies as a struggle for control or self-determination, whereas both Dunsire[29] and Pressman and Wildavsky[30] assume a degree of interdependence and understanding of the need to work together between those negotiating. In practice this distinction between power dependency and resource exchange may not be so clear cut. If we turn to our contributions we can see that in some cases they illustrate and in others confound these interpretations or models.

In case one, which examined the implementation of the 1975–6 public expenditure cuts, Stewart and Bramley concluded that local authorities, in spite of being basically opposed to the cuts, had complied with central policy guidance (in so far as the policy was identifiable) even though the prevailing system of control over local expenditure was inadequate to ensure compliance with central policy. This example suggests that interdependence is relevant but needs to be defined in more subtle terms. Local authorities, whilst complaining bitterly about the proposal to cut expenditure, did not use their apparent power potential to resist the cuts. It could be argued that authorities were taking account of some wider and longer-term power potential of central government to change 'the rules of the game'. Resistance to the cuts might provide an excuse for central government to increase its controls and reduce local autonomy, whereas compliant or co-operative behaviour would be 'rewarded' in the sense that local authority autonomy would remain intact. Equally, it might be argued that the collective power-potential of the local authorities to resist cuts could not actually be realized since no adequate mechanisms exist to mobilize effective collective action. In this case each local authority was responding in terms of its perception of its individual power in relation to that of central government rather than in terms of the potential of collective action by a number or all local authorities. Boddy's analysis, in case three, of the relationship between central government and the building societies during the same period indicates a similar process at work, though in an entirely different context. Although the building societies are not subject to direct government control or dependent on government for resources, they did agree to participate in the Local Authority Support Lending Scheme (SLS), introduced during 1975 following the cutback in direct local authority lending. Under the SLS individuals applied to a local authority for a loan and, if the authority considered that it would have granted a loan had it had funds available, it nominated the applicant for a building society loan under the Scheme. Boddy argues that the agreement to co-operate was a product of the building societies' desire to remain autonomous. In the face of a growing mortgage famine caused by rising interest rates and cutbacks in local authority lending, non-cooperation might be regarded by the public at large as anti-social behaviour and provide government with a mandate to intervene and take more direct control via legislation.

In both these examples it could be argued that compliance was obtained from agencies hostile to the policy, despite the absence of mechanisms to enforce compliance. In both cases, the agencies perceived compliance to be in their own interests because non-compliant behaviour might upset the *status quo* to the extent that government would seek to reduce their autonomy.

However, the authority of central government to change the power-dependency relationship is also dependent on obtaining a mandate. The behaviour of the agencies concerned could thus be argued to be limited not so much by the existing power-dependency relationship as by a broader perception of 'social acceptability' within the overall social, economic and political environment. This suggests that the policy environment plays an important part in the dynamics of power relations[31] in setting the rules of the game or determining how and when the rules get changed. To take another example, the Conservative party until the early 1970s was fundamentally opposed to the taxation of development gains. However, the boom in property speculation of the early 1970s provoked such a hostile public reaction to the development industry ('goodies' and 'baddies' alike) that the Conservative government felt obliged to intervene and introduce a development gains charge. The development industry was felt to have 'gone too far' in exploiting its autonomy to the point where Edward Heath (then Prime Minister) described the behaviour of some speculators as 'the unacceptable face of capitalism', and the need for government to assert itself by altering (or being seen to be altering) the balance of power overrode ideological concerns.

There are many parallels between what we have described and Strauss's analysis of negotiation.[32] He considers negotiation as one of the possible means of 'getting things accomplished' when different individuals, groups or organizations need to consider each other's viewpoints to get things done. In his work he suggests that social orders – the framework of norms and rules within which groups and individuals operate, including their organizational context – are changing all the time and argues that negotiation plays a large part in this change process.[33] Thus he refers to inter-organizational relationships as 'negotiated orders'. His work on negotiation stems from studies of psychiatric institutions undertaken a decade ago, from which he came to the following conclusions:

(1) We stated that social order was negotiated order: in the organisations studied, apparently there could be no organisational relationships without accompanying negotiations.

(2) Specific negotiations seemed contingent on specific structural conditions: who negotiated with whom, when, and about what. So the negotiations were patterned not accidental. They could be studied in terms of their conditions, character, and consequences for persons and organisations.

(3) The products of negotiation (contracts, understandings, agreements, rules, and so forth) all had temporal limits, for eventually they would be reviewed, reevaluated, revised, revoked or renewed.

(4) Negotiated order had to be worked at, and the bases of concerted action needed to be continually reconstituted. Not only were negotiations continually terminated, but new ones were also made daily.

(5) The negotiated order on any given day could be conceived as the sum total of the organisation's rules and policies, along with whatever agreements, understandings, pacts, contracts and other working arrangements currently obtained. These include agreements at every level of the organisation of every clique and condition, and include covert as well as overt agreements.

(6) Any changes impinging on the negotiated order – whether something ordinary such as a new member of staff, a disrupting event, or a betrayed 'contract', or whether more unusual, such as the introduction of a new technological element or a new ideology – called for renegotiation or reappraisal. This meant consequent changes in the negotiated order.

(7) We went on to suggest that the reconstitution of social or organisational order (which was our central concern) might be fruitfully conceived of in

terms of a complex relationship between the daily negotiation process and a periodic appraisal process . . . .

(8) We suggested, finally, that future studies of the complex relationships that exist between more stable elements of organisational order and more fleeting working arrangements might profit by examining the former as if they were sometimes a background against which the latter were being evolved in the foreground, and sometimes as if the reverse obtained.[34]

More recently, he has taken this work further. In his book, entitled *Negotiations*, he presents eleven cases, drawn from various research publications, with the aim of bringing out features utilizing a paradigm with an emphasis on both the structural context or social setting and the negotiation itself. Within these cases, a considerable variety of social settings and associated types of negotiation are examined.[35] The paradigm he uses includes the following terms:

Subprocess of negotiation   e.g. 'making trade-offs, compromising, paying off debts, reaching the negotiated agreements'.
Structural context   'the context "within which" negotiations take place in the largest sense'.
Structural properties   e.g. 'in each case of negotiation it is necessary to bring out some of the salient structural properties of the social setting'.
Negotiation context   e.g. 'the structural properties entering very directly as conditions into the course of negotiations itself'.

Using these key terms, Strauss suggests that

the many specific kinds of negotiation contexts pertaining to interaction among negotiating parties are related to permutations of the following properties of any negotiation context:

— The number of negotiators, their relative experience in negotiating and whom they represent.
— Whether the negotiations are one-shot, repeated, sequential, serial, multiple or linked.
— The relative balance of power exhibited by the respective parties in the negotiation itself.
— The nature of their respective stakes in the negotiation.
— The visibility of the transactions to others: that is, their overt or covert characters.
— The clarity of legitimacy boundaries of the issues negotiated.
— The options to avoiding or discontinuing negotiation; that is the alternative modes of action perceived as available.[36]

In a nutshell, Strauss is arguing two points. The first is that *consideration of social order* is crucial to any analysis of negotiation (and any other mode of interaction). By social order we mean the bases of concerted action in organizations, which must be reconstituted continually. Contracts, understandings, agreements, rules are not binding but must be worked on to retain some kind of order. The second is that any one interaction has both a *past* and a *future* which must be considered in any analytical work. Outcomes of negotiation may well contribute to changes in negotiation contexts relevant to future interactions, and negotiations may have already been affected by the nature of previous negotiations.

In addition, he is suggesting that the structural context is much wider than the negotiating context. That is, there are different levels of framework constraining or providing the context for particular negotiations which themselves interact. The influence of one on the other might run in either direction, although he argues that the structural context is less likely to be affected by the outcome of individual negotiations except where serial, repeated negotiations or combinations of negotiations and other modes of action might produce a cumulative effect.

How then is this work useful to the study of implementation? How can Strauss's paradigm be useful when our main concern is not necessarily with negotiation itself?

Four reasons seem important to us. First and foremost, the concept of negotiations and negotiated orders has provided us with another way of interpreting our data. It has, to use Strauss's term, 'sensitised' us to possibilities that may have gone unnoticed, for example, to the negotiations themselves, actors, interactions, tactics, subprocesses of negotiation and consequences that we might have overlooked. Reference here should be made to Bishop's case study on the interaction of education and design professionals in the production of a school, and Towell's case study on the negotiations between various actors in action-research work to change the approach to caring for the mentally ill. Second, focusing on negotiation and systematically pursuing negotiation data should lead us to consider the relationship between the negotiations under study and the major substantive matters under study. That is, in analysing a situation, we need to relate the negotiation properties to other substantive properties. Third, it can help in the understanding of which contextual properties of negotiation are salient to the different fields of interest covered in the case studies. And fourth, it has drawn our attention to an aspect of the concept of structural context – the negotiating parties' or actors' 'theories of negotiation'. By this we mean the actors' ideologies and beliefs and how these affect their perception of the policy debate and thereby influence their objective for involvement, negotiation stance and tactics. This fourth point reinforces our earlier statement about the need to focus on values and interests as the basis for understanding how and why conflict exists.

In accepting and utilizing the mode of analysis suggested by Strauss, we have not done so uncritically. Indeed, in many of our cases the important things do not seem to be negotiable or are limited by other negotiations or interactions. For example, as Barrett explains in case two, the criteria for obtaining loan sanction to purchase land under the Community Land legislation were in theory advisory rather than mandatory, but in practice were used as 'rules' within which negotiation was strictly limited. These limits to negotiation between local authorities and regional offices on individual loan sanctions could be regarded as the result of negotiations between the Department of the Environment and the Treasury over the allocation of public money to the scheme.

Both Benson and Day and Day have reviewed much of the negotiated order work and have developed a critical stance toward it. Benson, in commenting on the work of Day and Day, says

> They are particularly critical of its failure to deal with historical origins and larger institutional arrangements and of the consequent implications that everything of importance is currently negotiable. Thus, while the negotiated order analysts have effectively challenged the static view, they have fallen into the error of disregarding structural limits. They have emphasized the small-scale adjustments possible within the limits imposed by more encompassing structural arrangements and have not dealt convincingly with the latter. The negotiated order theorists have a basic difficulty in grappling with social structure which in their framework concerns the relations between distinct contexts wherein negotiation occurs. While it may be true, as they contend, that negotiation is present in all social situations, the structural problem is to grasp the relations between situations – the ways in which some negotiations set limits upon others.[37]

These criticisms have been developed further by Benson in an examination of public policy. He argues that

> the policy sector is multilevelled in the sense that its patterned practices may be divided into several partially autonomous levels which are related to each other as limits within limits. At each succeeding level, using a metaphor of depth, we encounter a set of limits upon the level just above. Thus, the practices at the surface level follow a set of rules specific to that level and are limited by sets of rules at deeper levels.[38]

The major objection in our minds to the 'negotiated order' approach relates to our uncertainty of its ability to come to grips with matters of relevance to social structure. In other words, those advocating negotiated order have tended to fail to come to grips with the concept of *power* and the power structure in society and thereby make assumptions about the freedom of action and the 'action space' of actors in the policy or negotiating process. In doing this perhaps too little attention has been given to the wider contextual impingements on negotiations, and historical as well as contemporary influences. In other words, too little attention to the *limits of negotiation*.

Nevertheless, we have found the focus on negotiations and the negotiated order perspective useful in helping us to understand the policy-action relationship. We have to be careful here not to assume that negotiation explains everything, for generally it is found in conjunction with other alternative 'modes of action', for example, coercion, persuasion, manipulation, regulation and the like. Both Strauss and others[39] have listed different varieties of modes of action used by agreement in attempting to get things done.

In trying to understand the policy-action relationship, we need to examine the various modes of action that are alternative to negotiation. For, as Strauss suggests, 'wherever there are social orders, there are not only negotiated orders but also coerced orders, manipulated orders and the like.'[40] At least three questions for research remain. First, why, in what circumstances, and with what assumptions are the various modes of action utilized? Second, is there a relationship between the utilization of the different modes and the differential power relations between the interacting parties? If there is, what is the nature of that relationship? And third, are there connections between the different modes of action?

We want to leave the idea of negotiation and the negotiated order perspective and move on to examine the actors themselves and the influence of their ideologies, beliefs and practices in the policy-action relationship.

Actors, values and interests

Heclo and Wildavsky's study of 'village life in Whitehall', referred to by Bramley and Stewart in the first case study, argued that 'Cabinet government is only the insignia on the coach; we wish to know what goes on inside. Inside political administrators are at the wheel, or more accurately, scrambling over the seats to find maps, brakes and steering devices to help them organise policy advice and make decisions about spending public money.'[41] Heclo and Wildavsky have been able to penetrate the world of political administrators and the role of ideology, beliefs and culture within Whitehall, thereby providing significant insights into the working of a part of government. It is the actors' *use of scope*, involving the perceptions of the scope and need for action, and their motivation to act that is important here. In the introductory review we referred briefly to the different ideologies, attitudes, values and 'perceptions of the situation' held by different groups of actors thereby shaping their approaches to problem definition and action. We argued that these kinds of consideration open up the whole field of theories and ideas about perception, motivation and ideology, and also lead back to political theories concerning the determinance of action and non-action.[42] The way that different 'actors' perceive and make sense of the world helps to explain organizational behaviour and response. Individuals and groups of actors, via the rules they establish (or absorb) for their own behaviour and the roles they occupy in organizations, not only influence the specific decisions of those organizations but also 'embed' institutional structures with certain values and norms which will result in a distinctive organizational 'culture' and a tendency to promote certain interests rather than others. This phenomenon is illustrated in Davies's description of the attempt to introduce and implement a workers' co-operative within a district authority (case study four). Whilst the policy was 'legitimized' at a political level and a co-operative was established, in practice the estates department was extremely reluctant to let local authority-owned premises to the co-operative. The co-operative could not pay as much rent as an alternative user from whom an offer had been received. They took the view that their basic responsibility and *duty* was to obtain the highest financial return possible for any letting, and that this responsibility overrode any other considerations such as social criteria or even, in this case, the specific policy decision to establish the co-operative. Davies explains this in terms of the prevailing ideology of that department, i.e. professional values and ideology combined with a view of their role and responsibility within the organization. Similar illustrations can be found in Underwood's case study on development control, Bishop's case on the briefing of architects for educational building, and the case study by Towell on the implementation of improved services for the mentally ill.

These chapters support our view that in attempting to understand the policy-action relationship it is necessary to go beyond the policy analysis of, say, Allison,[43] which utilizes organizational process and bureaucratic politics models, and thereby undervalues by omission the actors' perceptions of their organizational setting and purpose. Jenkins, for example, has argued that 'to understand the emergence of policies and the processes that surround them one must probe the internal structures of the political system and expose the *pattern of ideologies* operating there'.[44] Our argument here is that it is important to look at actors' definitions of the situation and the subjective meaning they attach to their actions.

While many commentators in the public policy field have stressed the importance of actors' ideologies, beliefs and opinions, there have been relatively few attempts to go beyond either assertions that they are important or fairly crude ideological distinctions. Vickers and Young have both attempted to develop the conceptual basis of 'value analysis'. Young has been, and still is, developing a more sophisticated approach utilizing the term 'assumptive worlds'.[45]

This formulation is based on 'the assumption that reality is construed differently by different people; every individual has a need to impose order on experience and does so by developing out of his personal experiences a model of the world which incorporates all his perceptions, values and beliefs'.[46] The function of the assumptive world is to allow the individual to cope with the events of everyday life by providing a 'map of problematic social reality'.[47] Assumptive worlds can be seen as a hierarchically organized system of hypotheses or constraints.

> Lower level opinions, beliefs or percepts, those through which the world is known, derive in part from and may be validated by appeal to the more fundamental aspects of culture or personality. At an intermediate level these will include the contructs with which we manage the world as it is presented to us. At a higher level of generality are the symbolic, taken-for-granted and virtually untestable representations of the world which we might think of as the ideology of the individual.[48]

Young and Mills relate the different levels by suggesting that 'while the higher level attributes (ideologies) are more enduring, those at the lower level are more malleable and fragile and open to continuous revision in the light of experience'.[49] The basis of Young and Mills's argument is that 'an understanding of the assumptive worlds of governmental actors is essential to successful policy analysis, for it enables us to interpret events in the light of the meaning which the actors involved ascribe to their own actions, rather than interpret these actions in terms of postulated motives, interests or goals.'[50]

One of the problems with this perspective is the treatment of the 'assumptive world' as the property of the individual. For our purposes we need to examine the individual response but in relation to peers and the institution. Interactionist sociology deals with the formation of common definitions of reality from the separate but socially aligned definitions of individuals.[51] By drawing on this work, Young and Mills[52] suggest that it would enable us to take as our focus what Blumer terms 'the acting unit' – 'agents acting on behalf of a group or organisation'.[53] Thus we are interested not only with actors as individuals and their formulations of reality but also with how their reality is constructed. If we accept the basic contention that reality is socially constructed, then to understand the reality of society or, in our terms, those parts of society involved in the policy-action relationship, we require an enquiry into the manner in which this reality is constructed. It is not our intention here to develop any further the theoretical field known as the sociology of knowledge.[54] However, it does lead us to consider the processes by which ideas, beliefs and definitions of situations are constructed within and by organizations, as clearly they are important to the analysis of actors' interpretations and responses to their perceived situation and environment. Through their education and their position in society, governmental actors are already acculturized and socialized into holding certain ideologies, beliefs and opinions before they join a governmental agency. On top of that, however, professional training and organizational socialization provide further experiences that define reality and set institutional and social norms, behaviour and modes of operation.

266

The influence of professionalism

Because of the scale, complexity and impact of public policy-making, the policy implications of professionalism become central, in our minds, to any analysis of policy-making and implementation. However, in many approaches to the study of policy this dimension is missing or barely mentioned. In the Introductory Review we pointed to increasing attempts to introduce rationality into the policy process, associated with the gradual bureaucrat-ization and technicalization of policy determination and political processes. This change creates a tension between the pursuit of rational processes and the maintenance of highly valued goals of western democracy, political represen-tation, autonomous action and decision.[55] The tension is also reflected in the apparent conflict in the conceptualization of implementation as, on the one hand, a step in a rational process following policy formulation, or, on the other hand, a more political bargaining process. It is thus very important to understand the influence of administrative and professional ideologies and the way they impinge on the policy process. But what is a profession and what is its influence? Traditionally, the defining characteristics of a profession have been a skill based on theoretical knowledge, the provision of education and training examined and certificated by the professional qualifying institute, a relationship with the client regulated by codes of professional ethics, and an ideology which incorporates altruistic service to the community. Johnson,[56] more recently, has been critical of this approach. He argues that the traditional 'collegiate' model of the profession, regulated internally by the 'peer group' of its members, no longer corresponds to contemporary society. For our purposes in examining professional actors involved in public policy-making, the 'state mediation' model of a profession provides a more accurate description. Those working at the local agency level, as opposed to central government, argues Underwood,[57] have an additional element with which to contend, which in some cases gives them more of the characteristics of a 'corporate patronage' model, with the focus of their attention being given to locally determined needs and a duty to the employing organization. Dunleavy[58] argues that there is a significant similarity between the new pluralist theory and the ideology of many professionals and administrators in government. This is particularly borne out in their resistance to political control and public involvement and participation.[59]

This argument is supported by a considerable body of literature on the impact of such ideologies on clients' experience of contact with state agencies.[60] Clearly, then, professional and administrative ideologies are very influential in local and central government and the health service. What is often ignored, or at least downgraded, is the much more specific influence of the profession in linking the public sector with the private sector, in influencing the context of national level debate, and in defining a detailed intra-departmental process of policy formation.[61]

Policy and Action

Organizational socialization

Whilst vocational education and professional training equip people with a particular way of seeing the world, it is not the only process through which reality is socially constructed. It is also constructed by the experience of joining an organization and of being 'new'. Organizational socialization is the process through which an individual comes to appreciate the values, abilities, expected behaviours and social knowledge essential for assuming an organizational role and for participating as an organizational member. The discussion of organizational socialization can be organized around four main themes: characteristics of socialization, stages of socialization, content of socialization, and the characteristics and impacts of socialization practices.

The experience of being 'new' is characterized by disorientation, foreignness and a kind of sensory overload. In taking on a new role the newcomer is typically given some time in which to 'get up speed', that is, to master the basics of the job and to perform at or above some minimum level.[62] The newcomer must also 'learn the ropes', as socialization is frequently termed by those going through it. Learning the ropes is necessary in each new organizational culture, since by definition cultures differ between organizations and even between roles within the same organization.[63] What is important for us in all this is the power of the formative experience to 'shock' people into conforming to the *culture* of the organization, bringing with it ideology, beliefs, opinions and ways of behaviour and doing things that distinguish between what is acceptable and what is unacceptable.

The second theme concerns stages through which newcomers pass during organizational socialization. When beginning work, the individual passes from outsider to newcomer and enters the encounter stage. Experiences during this stage are critical in shaping the individual's long-term orientation to the organization. During the encounter stage, newcomers' anticipations are tested against the reality of their new work experiences. The individual's adaptation to the organization occurs with the passage from newcomer to insider. Socialization models suggest that the adaptation process is a state rather than a stage, i.e. states of being adapted, of having assumed an insider role, are indications of the completion of socialization. Newcomers become insiders when and as they are given broad responsibilities and autonomy, entrusted with privileged information, included in informal networks, encouraged to represent the organization and sought out for advice and counsel by others.

In order to perform adequately in a new role an individual needs ability, motivation and an understanding of what others expect. That is, the individual needs a base of knowledge and a sense of strategy, direction and mission, and an understanding of critical organizational values to identify essential or pivotal role behaviours. For example, 'this is how *we* do things, this is what matters around *here*' are two expressions that emphasize and instruct the

268

newcomer in organizational culture. When newcomers are learning the ropes they are in part learning the culture. In organizations, as in societies at large, culture conveys important assumptions and norms governing membership, values, activities and aims. The norms and assumptions are collectively shared and interactively emergent; they are enacted rather than spoken. What culture *is* aside from what it conveys is more difficult to identify. In anthropology, where culture has been most directly and extensively studied, a variety of views have been advanced. For our purposes a semiotic view seems appropriate for examining culture in regularly convening organizations such as government. On the semiotic view Geertz has written: 'it denotes an historically transmitted pattern of meanings embodied in symbols of inherited conceptions expressed in symbolic forms by means of which men communicate, perpetuate and develop their knowledge about, and attitudes towards, life.'[64]

Thus, if we examine different organizations, and, to a lesser extent, different units of the same organization, we will find different cultures. Membership of these different organizations will lead to different orientations, roles and goals. Thus in learning the culture, newcomers develop a definition of the situation and a scheme for interpreting everyday events in the particular social setting.[65]

To summarize the argument so far: we have been trying to make sense of the variety in practice and in doing so have chosen to focus on specific approaches to analysis that we consider do help to tie things together without losing sight of reality in the process. First, we looked at the *complexity of linkages*. Hjern and Porter's idea of 'implementation structure' was introduced as an alternative way of interpreting the reality of implementation, in preference to the literature on the study of organizations examined in the introductory review. We then examined *interactions*, and drew on Strauss's work on negotiations and the idea of negotiated orders. We turned next to the actors themselves and their *values and interests*, and looked at Young's formulation of actors' 'assumptive worlds' before moving on to consider the influence of both professional and organizational socialization.

Edwards and Batley[66] have also commented on the importance of actors' perceptions and values in the development of the Urban Programme. Although they do not use the 'assumptive world' formulation their 'insiders/outsiders' commentary on the Urban Programme policy process helps the exploration of the issues raised by this approach. For as well as arguing that actors' perceptions and values are important in the policy process they also suggest a link between 'assumptive worlds' and the power structure. Thus they contend that 'certain parallels can be drawn between conceptions of welfare as either institutional or residual, of the power structure of society as predominantly élitist or pluralist, of poverty as an inherent part of either the economic infrastructure or the culture of poverty, of the comparative wisdom of universal or selective welfare benefits, and of social problems (including urban deprivation) as being structural or pathological'.[67] Although, to our minds, their argument is somewhat incomplete and not pursued to its logical conclusion, they seem to be suggesting that actors' values and ideologies will be shaped by dominant belief systems which themselves are a reflection of the power structure. These points by Edwards and Batley pick up some of our own criticisms of Hjern's concept of implementation structure and Strauss's negotiated order perspective, that is, neither recognizes that conflict as well as consensus exists in the policy-action relationship and that much of this comes from a lack of recognition of the impact of different interests and values.

Ultimately, then, we feel it is necessary to go beyond the detail of implementation activity and examine the relationship between ideologies, values and actions with the interest-power structure in society. If certain groups within society can get their construction of reality accepted and imposed on others, we need to know more about how this is achieved.

Developing this idea a little further, there is a need to analyse the social construction of the state. Schattschneider's term 'mobilisation of bias' has been used by Bachrach and Baratz to refer to the 'set of predominant values, beliefs, rituals and institutional procedures (rules of the game) that operate systematically and consistently to the benefit of certain persons and groups at the expense of others.[68] It is the operation of these values, beliefs, rituals and procedures that sets the policy agenda.[69] More specifically, discussion of the mobilization of bias draws attention not only to why certain policy discussions are acceptable and others apparently out of favour, but also to the importance of examining the nature of the policy discussion and the content of policy in relation to the interest-power structure in society. It is with these points in mind that we turn to our final section on the politics of policy.

The politics of policy

The different conceptualizations that have been the focus of both this chapter and Part One do not necessarily introduce entirely new variables from those, say, identified by Van Meter and Van Horn. But different perspectives give more or less emphasis to particular variables and thereby help to widen avenues for exploration. By taking different perspectives, different questions get asked about the process itself; indeed, some interesting and difficult methodological questions also arise about what is actually being studied as well as the best way to go about it.

However, throughout the discussion we keep coming back to the question of policy in the whole debate about implementation. Policy has variously been seen as a starting point for action, the focus of negotiations, or the whole complex framework of attitudes, values and practices that frame organizational activity. Given the complexity of inter- and intra-organizational linkages it may only be possible to define policy in terms of something that one group of actors wish to see carried out by others – which embraces the whole continuum of intentions, decisions, programmes and procedures that variously feature or are perceived as 'policy' in the sense of frameworks that guide or constrain activity. However, this definition leaves out the important issues of *negotiation* and *discretion*.

If we take a view of inter- and intra-organizational relations as a series of negotiations, then policy becomes the focus of negotiations, the issues around which different kinds of negotiation take place. This perspective (as we have discussed earlier) has repercussions on the way in which success and failure are defined, and leads to the view that implementation cannot be separately defined as a process distinct from the continuous reformulation of 'policy' that occurs in these negotiations.

Another way of looking at policy is to regard it as *property*, something owned by one group, with which they identify and feel a sense of possession. The issue of control over implementation can then be seen as the degree to which policy is retained by the policy-makers or how far they are giving it away to others. 'Giving away' can be seen as a chain process of transformation (or watering down) through negotiation and compromise. Negotiation is then all about discretion or autonomy – the degree to which policy becomes the property of the implementation agency to do with what they like.[70]

Policy has also been seen implicitly throughout the chapter as *innovation*, something new that requires new 'links in the chain', that requires change. Strauss's concept of negotiated order leads to questions about the nature of change; whether negotiation involves changing *policy* or changing *social orders* – and thereby the redefinition of the negotiative process as, perhaps, the way of resolving the tensions between them.

Our emphasis on inter- and intra-organizational aspects of implementation has pointed to another gap. Analysis of organizational relations tends to be 'policy free' in the sense of disregarding the specific subject matter and intentions of policy as a factor affecting the outcome of relationships and interactions. Yet much of the literature on implementation *starts* with policy and sees 'problems' in terms of putting a specific policy into effect. How far does the nature of policy – subject matter, intention, implications for change – an important factor in itself, influence the 'game that is being played' or the rules of the 'game'?

It could be argued that the substantive subject area sets the scene in terms of the groups of actors, agencies and interests involved and the attitudes, values and stances that they bring with them, originating from their roles within organizations and from their disciplines or political ideologies.[71] For example, the Community Land Scheme was all about public versus private control of the land development process involving the wider and highly polarized ideological issues of property 'rights', public versus private ownership of land and the 'rent' derived from its scarcity value. The Scheme therefore automatically brought into play not only the specific public agencies through which the policy was formulated and implemented (mainly central and local government) and the landowners upon whose activities the scheme was designed to impinge, but also a whole range of actors involved in the development process – developers, contractors and exchange professionals.

Each of these groups of actors brought with them distinct values, interests and priorities deriving in part from their roles and interests (or 'stakes') in the land development process, and in part from their ideological stances on the wider political issues involved. The same implementation agencies dealing with a different policy – for example, rent and rate rebates – would find themselves involved with a different set of actors, agencies and interests, but perhaps more importantly, a different range and set of values and attitudes associated with the ideological debate on welfare policy and those interests involved in it.

The origins and history of policy may well be a crucial factor in shaping attitudes, since *expectations* of what the policy will be about and its likely effects may derive from past debate, experiences and practice. In the case of the Community Land Scheme, this represented the third attempt by a Labour government since World War II to deal with the issues concerned. Many of the professionals involved in its implementation had been through it before and were sceptical about both its feasibility in view of past experience and its longevity in political terms. This generated caution even amongst those basically in agreement with the intentions; over-enthusiasm towards what was seen as highly political policy might be 'punished' under a change in political direction.

Thus the history and political identification generated by that history are likely to produce stances and attitudes towards policy issues that may not be directly related to the specific policy being promulgated, but nonetheless have an important effect on reactions and responses to the policy itself. The development industry attitudes to the Land Scheme are interesting in this respect. The scheme was generally regarded as a threat to their autonomy if not to their livelihood, even though a close look at the legislation and operational policy shows that the greater proportion of the industry, i.e. medium to small builders and developers, would not necessarily have been adversely affected and indeed could have benefited substantially from the continuity of land supply and reduction of risk resulting from the public sector taking on the responsibility of providing a supply of development land.

The point is that attitudes and values are not necessarily generated by a specific policy but are more deeply ingrained by virtue of the subject matter itself, the polarization of issues surrounding the subject and the antecedents of the policy currently under debate. In addition, we saw earlier how actors may be socialized into accepting both professional and organizational values and ways of thinking and doing. This socialized behaviour may also be specific to each policy field. The degree and nature of polarization, whether ideological (in a party political sense) or to do with specific material interests affected, clearly affects the way in which inter- and intra-organizational negotiations take place. This brings us back to the question of policy as change. The degree to which policy represents change can be seen both as a *function* of the polarization of ideologies, attitudes and value systems participating within the existing social order and as a *determinant* of the degree and type of negotiation likely to be necessary if it is to be implemented.

Two aspects of change, then, need to be considered. First, the extent of change in terms of ideology, values and attitudes. Does the policy issue 'fit' with prevailing ideologies and priorities or is there a mismatch? If change would be required in order to get the policy accepted, is it a matter of incremental shift or would it represent a 'paradigm shift' on the part of the actors concerned? For example, one of the important factors found in practice to determine the level of proposed land scheme activity among local authorities was their existing attitude towards compulsory purchase of land. Authorities, both Conservative and Labour controlled, that already used compulsory purchase as a means to effect their own goals found it much easier to accept the idea of the Land Scheme than those who were intrinsically opposed to compulsory purchase, for whom implementing the Land Scheme meant a dramatic shift in their value system as well as changes in practice.

Second, change may be considered in terms of Pressman and Wildavsky's 'links in the chain' and the idea of specific policy requiring new linkages between different actors, and new structures and practices from those already existing within and between organizations. Here a policy-oriented view helps to link together ideas about co-ordination (highlighted by the 'putting policy into effect' perspective) and negotiation (highlighted by the 'interactive' perspective). If 'policy' is viewed as anything which guides, constrains or limits actions, then change must be considered also in terms of administrative autonomy. The implications of practice or procedural changes must be considered of as much significance as ideological value shifts. These can be regarded as simply problems of the new or unfamiliar which just 'take a bit of getting used to', but in practice the degree of resistance to such changes implies that there is more to it than that. Again, perhaps a distinction can be drawn between changes which 'fit in' to the existing social orders within and between organizations, and those which involve a major shift in relations, that is, raise more fundamental questions of political and organizational autonomy. For example, the introduction of housing investment programmes could be regarded as a procedural matter – establishing a new planning and financial allocation procedure for dealing with housing finance. But even at this level there seem to be major inter- and intra-organizational issues involved. From a local authority viewpoint, the procedures have been seen to represent a restructuring of central-local relations and a reduction of local autonomy. Within local authorities problems have arisen about who operates the system and what this means in terms of a shift in departmental power relations.[72]

Thus, on the one hand, the subject matter of policy may set off reactions apparently out of all proportion to the specific issues being promulgated. On the other hand, an apparently uncontentious procedural change may have wider implications for inter- or intra-organizational relations – and spark off a different set of reactions which again seem out of proportion to the procedure involved.

This leads us back again to the nature of policy in relation to the *status quo*. If difficulties with accepting change derive from the nature of change in relation to the *status quo*, then attention needs to be focused on the kinds of frameworks, contracts and relationships that make up the *status quo* and how these evolve over time. We have referred to the idea of Strauss, and this seems a useful avenue to pursue in attempting to explore the nature of policy in terms of its role in the 'negotiated order', as well as in attempting to understand the role and nature of negotiations in organizational relationships. Similarly, we have not yet explored the question of time in the policy-action relationship which we raised earlier. There is a substantial body of literature in the field of evaluative studies involving the kinds of issues outlined above – and in particular focusing on time-scales of attitudinal change. How do actors shift their definitions of the situation? How does the time-scale of attitudinal change fit with political time-scales? How far are institutional responses to change to do with personal or organizational insecurity or uncertainty rather than purposive resistance? These are all questions which we consider to have a bearing on the understanding of the policy-action relationship, some of which are addressed by Smith in case study ten. Smith, for example, points to the failure of those addressing the role of evaluative research to make the distinction between hostility or resistance to change with the time needed for change to take place.

Last but not least, we turn to the question of policy *intentions*. We have argued and tried to show in this chapter that implementation is ultimately bound up with political behaviour – not just in party political terms, but in terms of individual actors' ideologies and values, of intra- and inter-agency politics and of the wider political environment. We also argue that it is very difficult to isolate implementation as a process distinct from policy-making. So we inevitably come back to the politics of policy formulation as an integral part of the study of 'implementation'. We have already noted the tendency in the implementation literature to de-politicize the policy-action relationship. This is best exemplified by Sabatier and Mazmanian's first two 'conditions' for effective implementation:

  i. the programme is based on a sound theory relating changes in target

group behaviour to the achievement of the desired end-state (objectives).
ii. the statute (or other basic policy decisions) contains unambiguous policy
    directives and structures the implementation process so as to maximise
    the likelihood that target groups will perform as desired.[73]

The idea that 'sound theory' should be the starting point for policy just does
not fit the political world we live in. Quite apart from the difficulty in
formulating theories that explain social cause and effect, this kind of statement
takes no account of political ideology or political decision-making processes. In
a sense the whole purpose of political action is to influence the ordering of
society according to value judgements about how it *ought* to be. Policy, in this
context, represents the expression of political intention.

Coming to the second 'condition', again it hardly needs saying that policy is
often very unclear, confused or ambiguous. Why is this so? The 'rational'
approach to policy analysis would assume that this is due to bad policy design.
But if we look at policy formulation in a political context, several possible
explanations emerge. First there is ambiguity born of uncertainty. In
situations of imperfect understanding or where policy-makers have little
control over action, the temptation is always present to leave policy as vague as
possible. This can be argued to be a virtue – in leaving a maximum of discretion
for 'performance' rather than 'conformance' to a specific directive that might
be inappropriate when applied in particular circumstances. Equally, vague-
ness can be seen as abdication of responsibility; non-performance can be then
'blamed' on implementers rather than policy-makers.

Second, ambiguity may often arise because of a multiplicity of goals or
intentions, some of which may be in conflict with one another. In particular,
ambiguity is likely to arise out of the political process by which intentions are
translated into decisions and procedures. If policy is formulated, modified and
translated into frameworks for action in a series of negotiative processes
between groups of actors and agencies, it is hardly surprising that the resultant
compromises produce 'policy' that is less than coherent and may appear to
have several conflicting objectives. For example, Banting[74] has examined the
way in which the 'fair rents' formula was developed for the 1965 Rent Act out
of a compromise between the Labour party commitment to return to rent
control and the advocates of the interests of landlords. The 'policy' which
emerged was something more complicated and ambiguous than the original
Labour aspiration to reimpose a rigid formula for rent determination.

Whilst not denying the validity of the problems and constraints deriving
from attempting to manage complexity and uncertainty, observation of what
actually happens in practice leads to the inescapable conclusion that certain
individuals, groups or governments tend to find a way of doing, or getting
done, what they *really want to do* while others do not. Thus consideration of
policy intention merges with the question of strength of *will*. How far are

'implementation problems' really a function of lack of political will or positive direction by powerful interests against the policy line?

In several of the case studies we have looked at it is difficult to assess the degree to which what happened to the policy can be ascribed to the relative lack of power of policy-makers to assert their will on other agencies – hence compromise, goal displacement, policy subversion – or whether there was no genuine intention behind the stated policy objectives and it actually *suited* policy-makers to be able to 'blame' implementers for policy failure. In the case study on the implementation of the Brent Manifesto there was discussion of the difficulty of achieving the abolition of corporal punishment. The politicians as a group blamed the officers within the education department. Reflecting on this, it is not clear to us whether the political leadership was really interested in achieving this manifesto commitment or whether its main purpose was to 'buy off' the left of the party during the formulation of the manifesto and after that to remain as a political symbol of action or intention to act.[75]

In this sense policy may become a substitute for action, to demonstrate that something is being done without actually tackling the real problem. There are many reasons why this might be the case. For example, most usually quoted are 'electoral' reasons; governments or policy-makers wish to be seen to be responsive without necessarily really wanting to take responsibility for intervention. Equally, policy-makers wish to be seen as powerful. Symbolic policy also serves to avoid tackling the real issue of attempting to change the 'negotiated order' or upsetting powerful groups which might show up only too clearly the limits of the policy-makers' power. There may also be concern about the ability to cope with the unforeseen consequences of intervention which will cause policy-makers to draw back from a 'real' intervention.

This kind of analysis results in a somewhat pessimistic and sceptical view of the policy-action relationship, particularly from the point of view of those groups in the community at large that *depend* on elected representatives to further their interests via public interventions of different kinds. Certainly these issues start to raise very fundamental questions about a pluralistic system of government whereby public policy is trying to be all things to all people.

Notes and references

1 We are referring here to the mainstream case study material reviewed in the Introduction; see (18) in the Introductory Review (p. 30).
2 For a more developed debate between the present plurality of theoretical positions in planning, see Healey, McDougall and Thomas 1980.
3 Glaser and Strauss 1967.
4 The idea of 'implementation structure' has been introduced by Hjern and Porter 1981.
5 The idea of 'negotiated order' is set out in Strauss 1978.

6 Allison 1971.

7 For discussion of 'assumptive worlds', see Young 1977; Young and Mills 1980.

8 Pressman and Wildavsky 1973: xv.

9 Dunsire 1978a: 85.

10 Williams 1971: chapter 8.

11 The idea of 'bureaucratic politics' is introduced in Allison 1971: 162–81.

12 Geertz 1964: 47–76.

13 Allen 1975.

14 Burrell and Morgan 1979: 384.

15 For a more detailed discussion of the two approaches, see Burrell and Morgan 1979: 365–92.

16 Burrell and Morgan 1979: 388.

17 Edelman 1971.

18 The question of how far policy can be regarded as separate from implementation is discussed by Michael Hill in case 9.

19 Hjern and Porter 1980.

20 Hjern and Porter 1980: 2.

21 The expression 'programme imperative' used by Hjern and Porter refers to the main objective or intention of a programme.

22 Hjern and Porter 1980: 14, 15.

23 Hjern and Porter 1980: 15.

24 Hjern and Porter 1980: 7, 8.

25 Hjern and Porter 1980: 15.

26 Olsen 1965.

27 Bachrach and Baratz 1970.

28 Bardach 1977.

29 Dunsire 1978b: 106.

30 Pressman and Wildavsky 1973: 134.

31 See, for example, Rhodes 1980: 289–322.

32 Strauss 1978.

33 Strauss 1978: 12.

34 Strauss 1978: 5 and 6.

35 Eleven case studies were presented to bring out similar or contrasting features around a central issue raised by a paradigm, with an emphasis both on structural or social setting considerations and on the negotiation itself: (1) negotiating working relations in organizations, (2) legal and illegal negotiations in the political arena, (3) negotiating co-operative international structures, (4) negotiating compromises within social orders, (5) antagonistic negotiations and changing structural contexts, and (6) organizational functioning and the silent bargain.

36 Strauss 1978: 238.

37 The negotiated order approach has been criticized by a number of writers, notably Benson and Day 1976; Benson 1977: 3–16; Day and Day 1977: 126–42. This particular summary of the critique is from Benson 1977: 14.

38 Benson 1980.

39 See, for example, Lewis and Flynn 1979: 123–44.

40 Strauss 1978: 262.

41 Heclo and Wildavsky 1974: 13–14.

277

42 Bachrach and Baratz 1970.
43 Allison 1971.
44 Jenkins 1978: 40.
45 The term 'assumptive world' was formulated first by Cantril in 1950 as 'assumptive form world', but other psychologists have elaborated the concept further. Essentially it builds on Lewin's earlier concept of 'lifespace': Cantril 1950; Lewin 1948; Lewin 1952.
46 Young and Mills 1980: 6.
47 Geertz 1975.
48 Young and Mills 1980: 7.
49 This formulation is similar, although inversed, to Benson's metaphor of depth concerning levels of analysing practice and the rules that govern operations at each level. Benson 1980.
50 Young and Mills 1980: 8 and 9.
51 See Rose 1962a: 3–19; McHugh 1968.
52 Young and Mills 1980: 8.
53 Blumer 1962: 179–92.
54 For further development of the sociology of knowledge see Berger and Luckman 1966. They argue that society possesses 'objective facticity', and society is 'built-up by activity that expresses subjective meaning'. This duality in the character of society, they argue, makes up reality, and therefore to understand reality requires an inquiry into the manner in which this reality is constructed. This inquiry into how 'subjective meanings become objective facticities' is the task, they maintain, for the sociology of knowledge.
55 Habermas 1971.
56 Johnson 1972.
57 Underwood 1980: 11.
58 Dunleavy 1980: 112.
59 See Lipman 1969: Harrison 1975: 259–74; Davies 1972.
60 See Hill 1972: chapter 8; Davies 1972.
61 Dunleavy 1980: 113 and developed further on 113–19.
62 Becker and Strauss 1956: 253–63.
63 Berger and Luckman 1966: 70–85.
64 Geertz 1975: 89.
65 Berger and Luckman 1966.
66 Edwards and Batley 1978.
67 Edwards and Batley 1978: 240.
68 In a useful article on social policy-making, Ham draws on the work of Bachrach and Baratz and their use of Schattschneider's term the 'mobilisation of bias': Ham 1980: 55–71; Bachrach and Baratz 1970: 43; Schattschneider 1960.
69 Solesbury 1976: 379–97.
70 See, for example, Young 1981.
71 See, for example, Edwards and Batley 1978 and Malpass 1975: 82.
72 Bramley *et al.* 1980.
73 Sabatier and Mazmanian 1979.
74 Banting 1979.
75 Edelman 1971.

Bibliography

Adler, M. and Asquith, S. (eds) (1981) *Discretion and Welfare*, London, Heinemann.

Advisory Conciliation and Arbitration Service (ACAS) (1978) *Royal Commission on the National Health Service: ACAS Evidence*, London, ACAS.

Agarwala-Rogers, R. (1977) 'Why is evaluation research not utilized?', in Guttentag, M. and Saar, S. (eds) *Evaluation Studies Review Annual*, vol. 2, Beverly Hills, Sage Publications.

Aldred, K. (1979) 'The Treasury financial information system', *Management Services in Government*, 34(4).

Alkin, M. (1980) 'Naturalistic study of evaluation utilization', in Braskamp, L. S. and Brown, R. D. (eds) *Utilization of Evaluative Information*, New Directions for Program Evaluation No. 5, San Francisco, Jossey-Bass.

Alkin, M., Daillak, R. and White, P. (1979) *Using Evaluations: Does Evaluation Make a Difference?*, Beverly Hills, Sage Publications.

Allen, V. L. (1975) *Social Analysis: A Marxist Critique and Alternative*, London, Longmans.

Allison, G. T. (1971) *Essence of Decision*, Boston, Little, Brown.

Ambrose, P. and Colenutt, B. (1975) *The Property Machine*, London, Penguin.

Anderson, S. B., Ball, S., Murphy, R. T. and Associates (1975) *Encyclopaedia of Educational Evaluation*, San Francisco, Jossey-Bass.

Apter, D. E. (ed.) (1964) *Ideology and Discontent*, New York, Free Press.

Argyris, C. (1960) *Understanding Organisational Behaviour*, London, Tavistock.

Argyris, C. (1971) 'Creating effective research relationships in organizations', in Caro, F. G. (ed.) *Readings in Evaluation Research*, New York, Russell Sage Foundation.

Armstrong, R. H. (1969) 'The approach to PPBS in local government', *Local Government Finance*, August.

Ashworth, W. (1954) *Genesis of Modern British Town Planning*, London, Routledge & Kegan Paul.

Bachrach, P. and Baratz, M. (1970) *Power and Poverty: Theory and Practice*, New York, Oxford University Press (reprinted 1977).

Bacon, R. and Eltis, W. (1976) *Britain's Economic Problem: Too Few Producers*, London, Macmillan.

Bakke, W. E. (1950) *Bonds of Organization*, New York, Harper Bros.

Bankowski, Z. and Nelken, D. (1979) 'The problem with discretion', paper presented at the Social Science Research Council sponsored Workshops in Discretionary Decision-Making in Law and Social Policy, April.

Banting, K. (1979) *Poverty, Politics and Policy*, London, Macmillan.

Bardach, E. (1977) *The Implementation Game: What Happens After A Bill Becomes A Law*, London, MIT Press.

Barrett, S., Boddy, M. and Stewart, M. (1979) *Implementation of the Community Land Scheme: Interim Report April 1978*, SAUS Occasional Paper 3, Bristol, School for Advanced Urban Studies.

Barton, A. H. (1976) 'The limits of evaluation: problems of evaluation of techniques, programmes, institutions and social systems', in Cherns, A. and Sinclair, R. (eds) *Sociotechnics*, London, Malaby Press.

Baruch, G. and Treacher, A. (1978) *Psychiatry Observed*, London, Routledge & Kegan Paul.

Battersea Redevelopment Action Group (1975) *Land Nationalisation* (mimeo).

Becker, H. S. and Strauss, A. L. (1956) 'Careers, personality and adult socialization', *American Journal of Sociology*, 62.

Beer, S. (1971) *Decision and Control: The Meaning of Operational Research and Management Cybernetics*, New York, Wiley.

Beer, S. (1974) *Designing Freedom*, New York, Wiley.

Beer, S. (1975) *Platform for Change*, New York, Wiley.

Benington, J. (1973) *Local Government Becomes Big Business*, London, CDP Information and Intelligence Unit.

Benn, C. (1974) 'Education in committee', *New Society*, 28 February.

Benson, J. (1977) 'Innovation and crisis in organisational analysis', *Sociological Quarterly*, 18.

Benson, J. (1980) 'Interorganisational networks and policy sectors', unpublished mimeograph.

Benson, J. and Day, R. (1976) 'On the limits of negotiation: a critique of the theory of negotiated order', paper presented at the annual meeting of the American Sociological Association, New York.

Berger, P. and Luckman, T. (1966) *The Social Construction of Reality*, New York, Anchor Books. Reissued in Peregrine Books 1979.

Blackburn, J. S. (1979) *Presentation and Interpretation by Local Government of the White Paper on Public Expenditure*, Birmingham Institute of Local Government Studies.

Blumer, H. (1962) 'Society as symbolic interaction', in Rose, A. M. (ed.) *Human Behavior and Social Processes*, New York, Houghton Mifflin.

Boddy, M. (1980) *The Building Societies*, London, Macmillan.

Bolam, R. *et al.* (1976) *Local Educational Advisers and Educational Adminis-*

tration, report on research funded by DES, University of Bristol, School of Education.

Boléat, M. (1978) 'Co-operation between building societies and local authorities: origins, methods and effects', *Co-operation between Building Societies and Local Authorities*, London, BSA.

Boléat, M. (1979) Memorandum of Agreement: Building Society Mortgage Finance, 8 October 1973, Appendix to *The Building Societies Association*, London, BSA.

Booth, T. A. (1979) 'Research and policy making in local authority social services', *Public Administration*, 57, Summer.

Bramley, G., Leather, P. and Murie, A. (1980) *Housing Strategies and Investment Programmes*, SAUS Working Paper 7, Bristol, School for Advanced Urban Studies.

Braskamp, L. A. and Brown, R. D. (eds) (1980) *Utilization of Evaluative Information*, New Directions for Program Evaluation No. 5, San Francisco, Jossey-Bass.

Brent Borough Council (1978) Labour Group Minutes, 10 August.

Brent Borough Labour party (1978) *Forward Together with Labour*, London, 4 May.

Brittan, S. (1975) 'The economic contradictions of democracy', *British Journal of Political Science*, 5(2), April.

Broadbent, G. (1973) *Design in Architecture*, London, Wiley.

Brocklebank, J. *et al.* (1973) *The Case for Nationalizing Land*, London, Campaign for Nationalizing Land.

Brown, R. D. and Braskamp, L. A. (1980) 'Summary: common themes and a checklist', in Braskamp, L. A. and Brown, R. D. (eds) *Utilization of Evaluative Information*, New Directions for Program Evaluation No. 5, San Francisco, Jossey-Bass.

Brown, R. D. *et al.* (1978) 'Evaluator credibility as a function of report style: do jargon and data make a difference?', *Evaluation Quarterly*, 2(2), May.

Building Societies Association (BSA) (1978a) Evidence Submitted by the Building Societies Association to the Committee to Review the Functioning of Financial Institutions, London, BSA.

BSA (1978b) Co-operation between Building Societies and Local Authorities, London, BSA.

Building Societies Institute (1970) *Building Society Management*, London, Franey & Co.

Bulmer, M. (ed.) (1978) *Social Policy Research*, London, Macmillan.

BURISA (1979) 'Development control data in policy making and management', report of a BURISA/SAUS workshop October 1978, *BURISA Newsletter*, 37 (January) and 38 (March–April).

Burns, T. and Stalker, G. M. (1961) *The Management of Innovation*, London, Tavistock.

Burrell, G. and Morgan, G. (1979) *Sociological Paradigms and Organisational Analysis*, London, Heinemann.

Butler, F. E. R. and Aldred, K. (1977) 'The financial information systems project', in *Management Services in Government*, 32(2).

Cantril, H. (1950) *The 'Why' of Man's Experience*, New York, Harper & Row.

Caplan, N. (1977) 'A minimal set of conditions necessary for the utilization of social science knowledge in policy formulation at the national level', in Weiss, C. H. (ed.) *Using Social Research in Public Policy Making*, Lexington, Mass., D. C. Heath & Co.

Caplan, N. (1980) 'What do we know about knowledge utilization?', in Braskamp, L. A. and Brown, R. D. (eds) *Utilization of Evaluative Information*, New Directions for Program Evaluation No. 5, San Francisco, Jossey-Bass.

Caro, F. G. (ed.) (1971) *Readings in Evaluation Research*, New York, Russell Sage Foundation.

Central Health Services Council/Personal Social Services Council (1978) *Collaboration in Community Care – a discussion document*, London, HMSO.

Chandler, J. A. and Templeton, J. (1980) 'Implementation: local authorities and job creation', paper given to the Public Administration Committee Conference to the Joint University Council for Social and Public Administration, University of York.

Chapman, R. (1975) 'The role of central or departmental policy and planning units: recent developments in Britain', *Public Administration* (Sydney), 34(2), June.

Chartered Institute of Public Finance and Accountancy (CIPFA) (1980) *Expenditure Control*, London, CIPFA.

Chase, G. (1979) 'Implementing a human services program: how hard will it be?', *Public Policy*, 27(4), Fall.

Cherns, A. B. (1976) 'Behavioural science engagements: taxonomy and dynamics', *Human Relations*, 29(10).

Cherns, A. B. and Sinclair, R. (eds) (1976) *Sociotechnics*, London, Malaby Press.

Cherns, A. B., Sinclair, R. and Jenkins, W. I. (eds) (1972) *Social Science and Government: Policies and Problems*, London, Tavistock.

Cherry, G. E. (1972) *Urban Change and Planning: History of Urban Development in Britain Since 1750*, Yeovil Foulis Books, International Textbook.

Cockburn, C. (1977) *The Local State*, London, Pluto Press.

Community Land Act 1975, Chapter 77, London, HMSO.

Community Land (Expected Development) Regulations 1976, S.I. 1976, no. 331, London, HMSO.

Cox, A. (1980) 'The limits of central government intervention in the land and development market: the case of the Land Commission', *Policy and Politics*, 8(3), August.

Cox, G. B. (1977) 'Managerial style: implications for the utilization of program evaluation information', *Evaluation Quarterly*, 1(3), August.

Crenson, M. (1972) *The Unpolitics of Air Pollution*, Baltimore, Johns Hopkins University Press.

Crozier, M. (1964) *The Bureaucratic Phenomenon*, London, Tavistock.

Cullingworth, J. B. (1975) *Environmental Planning, Vol. 1: Reconstruction and Land Use Planning, 1939–47*, London, HMSO.

Davies, J. G. (1972) *The Evangelistic Bureaucrat*, London, Tavistock.

Davis, H. R. and Salasin, S. E. (1975) 'The utilization of evaluation', in Struening, E. L. and Guttentag, M. (eds) *Handbook of Evaluation Research*, vol. 1, Beverly Hills, Sage Publications.

Day, R. and Day, J. (1977) 'A review of the current state of negotiated order theory', *Sociological Quarterly*, 18.

Department of Education and Science (DES) (1979) *The Briefing Process in School Design*, Occasional Paper No. 5, Architects and Building Branch, London, DES.

Department of Health and Social Security (DHSS) (1972) Circular 35/72, *Local Authority Social Services: 10 Year Development Plans 1973–1983*, London, DHSS.

DHSS (1975) Cmnd 6233, *Better Services for the Mentally Ill*, London, HMSO.

DHSS (June 1976) Health Circular (76)30, *Health Services Management, The NHS Planning System: Planning Activity in 1976/77*, London, DHSS.

DHSS (1976a) *Priorities for Health and Personal Social Services in England*, London, HMSO.

DHSS (1976b) *Report of the Resource Allocation Working Party*, London, HMSO.

DHSS (May 1977) HC (77) 17, LAC (77), *Joint Care Planning: Health and Local Authorities*, London, DHSS.

DHSS (1977) *The Way Forward*, London, HMSO.

DHSS (1978) Cmnd 7357, *Report of the Committee of Enquiry into Normansfield Hospital*, London, HMSO.

DHSS (1978) *Social Service Teams: The Practitioner's View*, London, HMSO.

DHSS (1979) *Patients First*, London, HMSO.

DHSS (1980) *Report of the Working Group on Organisation and Management Problems of Mental Illness Hospitals*, London, DHSS.

Department of the Environment (DoE) (1972) *The New Local Authorities: Management and Structure*, London, HMSO.

DoE (1973) Circular 104/73, *Local Transport Grants*, London, HMSO.

DoE (1973) *Making Towns Better: The Sunderland Study*, vols 1 and 2, London, HMSO.

DoE (1975) Circular 121/75, *Community Land – Circular 1, General Introduction and Priorities*, London, HMSO.

DoE (1976) Circular 66/76, *Capital Programmes*, London, HMSO.

DoE (1976) Circular 26/76, *Community Land – Circular 6, Land for Private Development: Acquisition, Management and Disposal*, London, HMSO.

DoE (1976) Community Land Notes: GNLA/12, *Effect of Public Expenditure Cuts*, London, DoE.

DoE (1976) Circular 45/76, *Local Authority Current Expenditure*, London, HMSO.

DoE (1976) Circular 84/76, *Local Authority Expenditure, 1976/78*, London, HMSO.

DoE (1976) Circular 120/76, *Rate Support Grant Settlement 1977/78*, London, HMSO.

DoE (1977) Circular 63/77, *Housing Strategies and Investment Programmes: Arrangements for 1978/79*, London, HMSO.

DoE (1978) Circular 44/78, *Private Sector Land: Requirements and Supply*, London, HMSO.

DoE (1978) Community Land Notes: GNLA/19, *Programmes and Block Allocations, Distribution of Land Account Surpluses and Interest Rate for Financial Forecasting*, London, DoE.

Derthick, M. (1972) *New Towns In-Town*, Washington D.C., the Urban Institute.

Deutsch, K. W. (1966) *The Nerves of Government: Models of Political Communication and Control*, New York, Free Press.

Development Land Tax Act 1976, Chapter 24, London, HMSO.

Dobry, G. (1975) *Review of the Development Control System*, London, HMSO.

Donnison, D. (1972) 'Research for policy', *Minerva*, 10(4), October.

Dower, M. and Rapoport, R. (1977) 'Portrait of an urban borough', *Leisure Provision and Human Need*, Research working paper no. 1, July.

Drewitt, R. (1973) 'Land values and the suburban land market', in Hall, P. et al., *The Containment of Urban England, Vol. 2: The Planning System: Objectives, Operations, Impacts*, London, Allen & Unwin.

Dror, Y. (1968) *Public Policy Making Re-examined*, Scranton, Penn., Chandler.

Dror, Y. (1971) *Design for Policy Sciences*, New York, Elsevier.

Dubin, R. (ed.) (1976) *Handbook of Work, Organization and Society*, Chicago, Rand McNally.

Dunleavy, P. (1978) *The Politics of High Rise Housing in Britain: Local Communities Tackle Mass Housing* (D.Phil. thesis, Oxford).

Dunleavy, P. (1980) *Urban Political Analysis*, London, Macmillan.

Dunsire, A. (1978a) *Implementation in a Bureaucracy: The Execution Process*, I, Oxford, Martin Robertson.

Dunsire, A. (1978b) *Control in a Bureaucracy: The Execution Process*, II, Oxford, Martin Robertson.

Durlak, J. et al. (1972) 'Observations of user activity patterns in open and traditional plan school environments', in Mitchell, W. (ed.) *Proceedings of the EDRA 3 Conference*, University of California Press.

Easton, D. (1973) *The Political System*, New York, Knopf.

Eddison, T. (1973) *Local Government: Management and Corporate Planning*, London, Leonard Hill Books.

Edelman, M. (1971) *Politics as Symbolic Action*, Institute for Research on Poverty Monograph Series, Chicago, Markham.

Edwards, J. and Batley, R. (1978) *The Politics of Positive Discrimination*, London, Tavistock.

Etzioni, A. (1967) 'Mixed scanning: a "third" approach to decision making', *Public Administration Review*.

Etzioni, A. (1968) *The Active Society*, New York, Free Press.

Fay, B. (1979) 'Criticisms of the positivist view of social science and politics', in Pollitt, C., Lewis, L., Negro, J. and Patten, J. (eds) *Public Policy in Theory and Practice*, London, Hodder & Stoughton and the Open University.

Faludi, A. (1973) *A Reader in Planning Theory*, Oxford, Pergamon.

Forrester, J. W. (1969) *Urban Dynamics*, Cambridge, MIT Press.

Freeman, H. E. (1975) 'Evaluation research and public policies', in Lyons, G. M. (ed.) *Social Research and Public Policies*, Hanover, New Hampshire, Dartmouth College Public Affairs Center.

Freeman, H. E. (1977) 'The present status of evaluation research', in Guttentag, M. and Saar, S. (eds) *Evaluation Studies Review Annual*, vol. 2, Beverly Hills, Sage Publications.

Freeman, H. E. (ed.) (1978) *Policy Studies Review Annual*, vol. 2, Beverly Hills, Sage Publications.

Freeman, H. E. and Sherwood, C. G. (1970) *Social Research and Social Policy*, Englewood Cliffs, N.J., Prentice-Hall.

Freire, P. (1972) *Pedagogy of the Oppressed*, Harmondsworth, Penguin.

Friedman, J. (1973) *Retracking America: A Theory of Transactive Planning*, New York, Anchor Books.

Friend, J. K. and Jessop, W. M. (1969) *Local Government and Strategic Choice*, London, Tavistock.

Friend, J., Power, J. M. and Yewlett, C. (1974) *Public Planning: The Intercorporate Dimension*, London, Tavistock.

Fudge, C., Murie, A. and Ring, E. (1979) *First Steps to a Career? – the problems of being a newly elected member in an English local authority*, SAUS Occasional Paper 4, Bristol, School for Advanced Urban Studies.

Gazzard, R. (1978) 'Community Land Act and the environment', *Town and Country Planning*, November.

Geertz, C. (1964) 'Ideology as a cultural system', in Apter, D. E. (ed.) *Ideology and Discontent*, New York, Free Press.

Geertz, C. (1975) *The Interpretation of Cultures*, London, Hutchinson.

Glaser, B. G. and Strauss, A. L. (1967) *The Discovery of Grounded Theory:*

Strategies for Qualitative Research, Chicago, Aldine.

Glaser, E. M. and Backer, T. E. (1972) 'Outline of questions for program evaluators utilizing the clinical approach', *Evaluation*, 1(1), Fall.

Goldberg, E. M. and Fruin, D. J. (1976) 'Towards accountability in social work: a case review system for social workers', *British Journal of Social Work*, 6(1), Spring.

Goldberg, E. M., Warburton, R. W., Lyons, L. J. and Willmott, R. R. (1978) 'Towards accountability in social work: long term social work in an area office', *British Journal of Social Work*, 8(3), Autumn.

Goldberg, E. M., Warburton, R. W., McGuinness, B. and Rowlands, J. H. (1977) 'Towards accountability in social work: one year's intake to an area office', *British Journal of Social Work*, 7(3), Autumn.

Goldman, S. (1973) *Public Expenditure Management and Control*, London, HMSO.

Goldstein, M. S., Marcus, A. C. and Perkins Rausch, N. (1978) 'The non-utilization of evaluation research', *Pacific Sociological Review*, 21(1), January.

Goodenough, W. H. (1964) *Exploration in Cultural Anthropology*, New York, McGraw-Hill.

Gordon, I., Lewis, J. and Young, K. (1977) 'Perspectives on policy analysis', *Public Administration Bulletin*, 25, December.

Gough, I. (1979) *The Political Economy of the Welfare State*, London, Macmillan.

Grant, R. A. (n.d.) *Evaluation Research*, Edinburgh, Housing Research Unit, Scottish Development Department (mimeo).

Grant, R. and Gallagher, J. (1977) *Evaluation Research in Social Policy: A Review of Aims and Approaches*, Edinburgh, Central Research Unit, Scottish Development Department.

Green, G. (1972) 'National city and ward components of local voting', *Policy and Politics*, 1(1), September.

Griffiths, J. A. G. (1966) *Central Departments and Local Authorities*, London, Allen & Unwin.

Griggs, N. (1976) Report of an address to the Northumberland and Durham Building Societies Association, *Building Societies Gazette*, May.

Gunn, L. (1978) 'Why is implementation so difficult?' *Management Services in Government*, November.

Guttentag, M. and Saar, S. (1977) *Evaluation Studies Review Annual*, vol. 2, Beverly Hills, Sage Publications.

Gyford, J. (1976) *Local Politics in Britain*, London, Croom Helm.

Habermas, J. (1971) *Towards a Rational Society*, London, Heinemann.

Ham, C. (1980) 'Approaches to the study of social policy making', *Policy and Politics*, 8(1), January.

Harloe, M. (1975) *Swindon: A Town in Transition, A Study in Urban Develop-*

ment and Overspill Policy, London, Heinemann.

Harloe, M., Issacharoff, R. M. and Minns, R. (1974) *The Organisation of Housing*, London, Heinemann.

Harrison, M. L. (1977) 'The local authorities/building societies support scheme in Leeds', *Housing Research Paper*, no. 1, University of Leeds, Department of Social Policy and Administration.

Harrison, W. (1975) 'British town planning ideology and the welfare state', *Journal of Social Policy*, 4.

Healey, P., McDougall, G. and Thomas, M. (1980) 'Theoretical debates in planning: towards a coherent dialogue', a position paper prepared for the conference, Planning Theory in the 1980s, Oxford Polytechnic, October.

Healey, P. and Underwood, J. (eds) (1976) *The Organisation and Work of London Borough Planning Departments*, CP 18, London, Centre for Environmental Studies.

Healey, P. and Underwood, J. (1978) *Professional Ideals and Planning Practice*, Oxford, Pergamon.

Heclo, H. H. (1972) 'Review article: policy analysis', *British Journal of Political Science*, vol. 2.

Heclo, H. and Wildavsky, A. (1974) *The Private Government of Public Money*, London, Macmillan.

H.M. Government (HMG) (1962) Cmnd 1432, *Control of Public Expenditure*, London, HMSO.

HMG (1968) Cmnd 3638, *The Civil Service*, vol. 1, Report of the Committee 1966–68, London, HMSO.

HMG (1969) Cmnd 4040, *Royal Commission on Local Government in England 1966–69*, London, HMSO.

HMG (1970) Cmnd 4506, *The Reorganisation of Central Government*, London, HMSO.

HMG (1971) Cmnd 4728, *Fair Deal for Housing*, London, HMSO.

HMG (1971) Cmnd 4814, *A Framework for Government Research and Development*, London, HMSO.

HMG (1973) Cmnd 5280, *Widening the Choice: the next steps in housing*, London, HMSO.

HMG (1974) Cmnd 5730, *Land*, London, HMSO.

HMG (1975) Cmnd 5879, *Public Expenditure to 1978–79*, London, HMSO.

HMG (1976) Cmnd 6393, *Public Expenditure to 1979–80*, London, HMSO.

HMG (1977) Cmnd 6721, *The Government's Expenditure Plans*, London, HMSO.

HMG (1977) Cmnd 5851, *Housing Policy*, London, HMSO.

HMG (1977) *Housing Policy Technical Volume*, London, HMSO.

HMG (1978) Cmnd 7049, *The Government's Expenditure Plans 1978/79 to 1981/82*, London, HMSO.

HMG (1979) Cmnd 7439, *The Government's Expenditure Plans 1979/80 to*

1982/83, London, HMSO.

HMG (1979) Cmnd 7615, *Royal Commission on the National Health Service, Report*, London, HMSO.

HMG (1980) Cmnd 7937, *Final Report*, Committee to Review the Functioning of Financial Institutions, London, HMSO.

H.M. Treasury (1972) *Public Expenditure White Papers: Handbook on Methodology*, London, HMSO.

Heydebrand, W. V. (1977) 'Organisational contradictions in public bureaucracies: towards a Marxian theory of organisations', *Sociological Quarterly*, 18, Winter.

Higgins, J. (1978) *The Poverty Business*, Oxford, Basil Blackwell.

Higgins, J. (1980) 'Social control theories of social policy', *Journal of Social Policy*, 9(1).

Hill, M. J. (1972) *The Sociology of Public Administration*, London, Weidenfeld & Nicolson.

Hill, M. J. (1976) *The State, Administration and the Individual*, Glasgow, Fontana.

Hill, M. J. (1980a) 'The role of British local government in the control of air pollution – a growing gap between policy and implementation?', paper presented to the European Consortium for Political Research (ECPR) Workshop on Environment Politics and Policies, Florence.

Hill, M. J. (1980b) *Understanding Social Policy*, Oxford, Martin Robertson.

Hill, M. J. (1981) 'Unemployment and government manpower policy', in Showler, B. and Sinfield, A. (eds) *The Workless State*, Oxford, Martin Robertson.

Hill, M. J. and Issacharoff, R. M. (1971) *Community Action and Race Relations*, London, Oxford University Press.

Hill, M. J. *et al.* (1979) 'Implementation and the central-local relationship', Appendix II in *Central-Local Government Relationships*, A Panel Report to the Research Initiatives Board, Social Science Research Council.

Hjern, B. and Hull, C. (1980) 'Central-local relations in the broader perspective of the mixed economy: implementation structures as an analytical device for approaching the mixed economy', paper prepared for the Conference on Central-Local Government Relations, held at the Institute for Local Government Studies, Birmingham, 14–16 March.

Hjern, B. and Porter, D. O. (1980) 'Implementation structure: a new unit of administrative analysis', paper prepared for a conference, Institute for Advanced Studies, Vienna. Unpublished mimeo, International Institute of Management, Berlin.

Hood, C. C. (1968) *Public Policy Making Re-examined*, Scranton, Penn., Chandler.

Hood, C. C. (1976) *The Limits of Administration*, London, John Wiley.

House, E. R. (1972) 'The conscience of educational evaluation', *Teachers*

College Record 73, 3.

House Builders Federation (1977) *Land for Housing*, discussion paper, London, HBF.

House of Commons (1976) HC 69-11, *The Financing of Public Expenditure: First Report of the Expenditure Committee*, vol. II, session 1975–6, London, HMSO.

House of Commons (1976) HC 718, *Planning and Control of Public Expenditure: Thirteenth Report of the Expenditure Committee*, session 1975–6, London, HMSO.

House of Commons (1977) HC 395-1, *Planning Procedures: Eighth Report from the Expenditure Committee*, session 1976–7, London, HMSO.

House of Commons (1978) HC 661, *Fourteenth Report from the Expenditure Committee*, session 1977–8, London, HMSO.

House of Commons (1978) HC 299, *Fourth Report from the Committee of Public Accounts*, session 1977–8, London, HMSO.

House of Commons (1978) HC 257, *The Government's Expenditure Plans 1978/79 to 1981/82; Second Report from the Expenditure Committee*, Session 1977–8, London, HMSO.

Hudson, K. and Maverick, J. (1978) *A Proposed Method of Expenditure Forecast*, DHSS, QSR and I Branch, unpublished.

Jackman, R. (1979) 'Monetarism and local spending', *CES Review* 7, London, Centre for Environmental Studies.

Jackman, R. and Sellars, M. (1977) 'Rate support grant: the hows and whys of the new needs formula', *CES Review*, 1, London, Centre for Environmental Studies.

Jenkins, W. I. (1978) *Policy Analysis: a political and organisational perspective*, London, Martin Robertson.

Johnson, T. J. (1972) *Professions and Power*, London, Macmillan.

Jones, G. W. (ed.) (1980) *Central-Local Government Relations in Britain*, Farnborough, Saxon House.

Jones, K. (1977) 'Mental health administration: reflections from the British experience', *Administration in Mental Health*, 4(2).

Jones, K. (1978) 'Society looks at the psychiatrist', *British Journal of Psychiatry*, 132.

Jowell, J. (1979) 'Official discretion: problems, trends and influences', paper given to Social Science Research Council sponsored workshops in Discretionary Decision Making in Law and Social Policy, London, January.

Keeling, D. (1972) *Management in Government*, London, Allen & Unwin.

King, A. (1975) 'Overload: problems of governing in the 1970s', *Political Studies*, 23.

Knoepfel, P. and Weidner, H. (1980) 'Normbildung und Implementation: Interessenberücksichtigungsmuster in Programmstrukturen von Luftreinhaltepolitiken', in Mayntz, R. (ed.). Also IIUG – Preprint 79/25: 'The formation and implementation of air quality control programmes: patterns of interest consideration', Berlin, International Institute for Environment and Society, Science Centre.

Lambert, C. (1978) 'Building societies, surveyors and the older areas of Birmingham', Working paper no. 38, Birmingham, Centre for Urban and Regional Studies.

Lancashire Education Authority (n.d.) 'Plans and people', Lancashire County Council.

La Porte, T. (1975) *Organised Social Complexity*, Princeton, NJ, Princeton University Press.

Larsen, J. K. and Nichols, D. G. (1972) 'If nobody knows you've done it, have you . . .?', *Evaluation*, 1(1), Fall.

Lawrence, W. G. (ed.) (1979) *Exploring Individual and Organisational Boundaries*, London, Wiley.

Levitt, R. (1980) Implementing Public Policy, London, Croom Helm.

Lewin, K. (1948) *Resolving Social Conflicts*, New York, Harper & Row.

Lewin, K. (1952) Paper in Cartwright, D. (ed.), *Field Theory in Social Science: Selected Theoretical Papers*, New York, Harper & Row.

Lewis, J. and Flynn, R. (1979) 'The implementation of urban and regional planning policies', *Policy and Politics*, 7(2), April.

Lindblom, C. E. (1959) 'The science of muddling through', *Public Administration Review*, Spring.

Lindblom, C. E. (1965) *The Intelligence of Democracy*, New York, Free Press.

Lipman, A. (1969) 'Architects' belief systems', *British Journal of Sociology*.

Litwak, E. and Meyer, H. J. (1974) *School, Family and Neighborhood: The Theory and Practice of School-Community Relations*, New York, Columbia University Press.

Local Government, Planning and Land Act 1980, Chapter 65, London, HMSO.

London Borough of Brent (1977) *Brent – A Statement of Forward Planning Policies – Position Statements 1977*, London Borough of Brent.

Long, J. *et al.* (1974) *Designing for Human Behaviour*, Stroudsberg, Penn., Dowden, Hutchinson & Ross.

Lowi, T. A. (1972) 'Four systems of policy, politics and choice', *Public Administration Review*, 32.

Lyons, G. M. (ed.) (1975) *Social Research and Public Policies*, Hanover, New Hampshire, Dartmouth College Public Affairs Center.

McDonald, B. (1976) 'Evaluation and the control of education', in Tawney, D. (ed.) *Curriculum Evaluation Today: Trends and Implications*, London, Macmillan.

McDonald, J. and Fry, G. K. (1980) 'Policy planning units – ten years on', *Public Administration*, 58.

McHugh, P. (1968) *Defining the Situation: The Organization of Meaning in*

Social Interaction, New York, Harper & Row.

McIntosh, N. (1978) 'Mortgage support scheme holds the lending lines', *Roof*, March.

McLoughlin, B. J. (1969) *Urban and Regional Planning: A Systems Approach*, London, Faber & Faber.

McLoughlin, B. J. (1973) *Control and Urban Planning*, London, Faber & Faber.

Majone, G. and Wildavsky, A. (1978) 'Implementation as evolution', in Freeman, H. E. (ed.) *Policy Studies Review Annual*, vol. 2, Beverly Hills, Sage Publications.

Malpass, P. N. (1975) 'Professionalism and the role of architects in local authority housing', *Royal Institute of British Architects Journal*, 9.

March, J. G. and Simon, H. A. (1958) *Organizations*, New York, Wiley.

Marriott, O. (1967) *The Property Boom*, London, Hamish Hamilton.

Marris, P. (1974) *Loss and Change*, London, Routledge & Kegan Paul.

Massey, D. and Catalano, A. (1978) *Capital and Land*, London, Edward Arnold.

Mersey Regional Health Authority (1978) *Report of a Committee of Enquiry, Liverpool Area Health Authority*, Liverpool, MRHA.

Meyerson, M. and Banfield, E. C. (1955) *Politics, Planning and the Public Interest*, New York, Free Press of Glencoe.

Middlemas, K. (1979) *Politics in Industrial Society*, London, André Deutsch.

Miller, E. J. (1979a) 'Autonomy, dependency and organisational change', in Towell, D. and Harries, C. (eds), *Innovation in Patient Care: An action research study of change in a psychiatric hospital*, London, Croom Helm.

Miller, E. J. (1979b) 'Open system revisited: a proposition about development and change', in Lawrence, W. G. (ed.) *Exploring Individual and Organizational Boundaries*, London, Wiley.

Ministry of Housing and Local Government (1965) *The Future of Development Plans: A Report by the Planning Advisory Group*, London, HMSO.

Mitchell, W. (ed.) (1979) *Proceedings of the EDRA 3 Conference*, Berkeley, University of California Press.

Montjoy, R. S. and O'Toole, L. J. (1979) 'Towards a theory of policy implementation: an organisational perspective', *Public Administration Review*, 39(5), September/October.

Moynihan, D. P. (1969) *Maximum Feasible Misunderstanding*, New York, Free Press.

Murie, A., Niner, P. and Watson, C. (1976) *Housing Policy and the Housing System*, London, Allen & Unwin.

National Association for Mental Health (1977) *MIND's Evidence to the Royal Commission on the NHS with Regard to Services for Mentally Ill People*, London, NAMH.

NEDO (1976) *A Study of U.K. Nationalized Industries: their role in the economy and control in the future*, London, HMSO.

Newman, D. L. *et al.* (1980) 'Communication theory and the utilization of evaluation', in Braskamp, L. A. and Brown, R. D. (eds), *Utilization of Evaluative Information*, New Directions for Program Evaluation No. 5, San Francisco, Jossey-Bass.

Olsen, M. (1965) *The Logic of Collective Action: Public Goods and the Theory of Groups*, Cambridge, Mass., Harvard University Press.

Orren, K. (1974) *Corporate Power and Social Change: the politics of the life assurance industry*, Baltimore, Johns Hopkins University Press.

Patton, M. Q. (1978) *Utilization-Focused Evaluation*, Beverly Hills, Sage Publications.

Patton, M. Q. *et al.* (1977) 'In search of impact: an analysis of the utilization of federal health evaluation research', in Weiss, C. H. (ed.) *Using Social Research in Public Policy Making*, Lexington, Mass., D. C. Heath & Co.

Perrow, C. (1972) *Complex Organisms: A Critical Essay*, Glenview, Illinois, Scott Foresman & Co.

Platt, J. (1976) *The Realities of Social Research: An Empirical Study of British Sociologists*, London, Chatto & Windus for Sussex University Press.

Polivka, L. and Steg, E. (1978) 'Program evaluation and policy development: bridging the gap', *Evaluation Quarterly*, 2(4), November.

Posner, M. (ed.) (1978) *Demand Management*, London, NIESR/Heinemann.

Poulantzas, N. (1973) *Political Power and Social Classes*, London, New Left Books.

Prentis, B. (1979) 'Cash limits: the problems for local government', *Public Finance and Accountancy*, July.

Pressman, J. (1975) 'Decision makers and evaluators: some differences in perspective and possible directions for the future', in Lyons, G. M. (ed.) *Social Research and Public Policies*, Hanover, New Hampshire, Dartmouth College Public Affairs Center.

Pressman, J. and Wildavsky, A. (1973) *Implementation*, Berkeley, University of California Press.

Purdue, M. (1977) 'The scope of planning authorities' discretion – or what's material?', *Journal of Planning and Environmental Law*, August.

Rein, M. and White, S. H. (1977) 'Can policy research help policy?', *The Public Interest*, 49, Fall.

Rein, M. and White, S. H. (1977) 'Policy research: belief and doubt', *Policy Analysis*, 3(2), Spring.

Revell, J. (1973) *The British Financial System*, London, Macmillan.

Rhodes, R. A. W. (1979) 'Research into central-local relations in Britain: a framework for analysis', Appendix I in *Central-Local Government Relationships*, a panel report to the Research Initiatives Board, Social Science Research Council.

Rhodes, R. A. W. (1980) 'Analysing intergovernmental relations', *European*

Journal of Political Research, 8.

Rhodes, T. and Bailey, S. (1978) 'Equity, statistics and the Rate Support Grant', in the Proceedings of the Research and Intelligence Annual Conference, Birmingham, Institute for Local Government Studies.

Rich, K. F. (1975) 'Selective utilization of social science related information by Federal policy makers', *Inquiry*, 13(3).

Riecken, H. W. and Boruch, R. F. (eds) (1974) *Social Experimentation: A Method for Planning and Evaluating Social Intervention*, London, Academic Press.

Roberts, N. A. (1976) *The Reform of Planning Law*, London, Macmillan.

Room, G. (1979) *The Sociology of Welfare*, Oxford, Martin Robertson.

Rose, A. M. (1962a) 'A systematic summary of symbolic interaction theory', in Rose, A. M. (ed.) *Human Behavior and Social Process*, New York, Houghton Mifflin.

Rose, A. M. (ed.) (1962b) *Human Behavior and Social Process*, New York, Houghton Mifflin.

Rose, M. (1978) Reply to Rhodes, T. and Bailey, S. 'Equity, statistics and the Rate Support Grant', in the Proceedings of the Research and Intelligence Annual Conference, Birmingham, Institute for Local Government Studies.

Rose, R. (1978) 'Ungovernability: is there fire behind the smoke?', *Studies in Public Policy*, no. 16, Strathclyde, Centre for the Study of Public Policy.

Rosenberg, S. D. (1970) 'Hospital culture as collective defence', *Psychiatry*, 33(1).

Rossi, P. H. (1971) 'Evaluating educational programs', in Caro, F. G. (ed.) *Readings in Evaluation Research*, New York, Russell Sage Foundation.

Rossi, P. H. (1972) 'Testing for success and failure in social action', in Rossi, P. H. and Williams, W. (eds) *Evaluating Social Programs: Theory, Practice and Policy*, Seminar Press.

Rossi, P. H., Freeman, H. E. and Wright, S. R. (1979) *Evaluation: A Systematic Approach*, Beverly Hills, Sage Publications.

Rossi, P. H. and Williams, W. (eds) (1972) *Evaluating Social Programs: Theory, Practice and Policy*, Seminar Press.

Rothman, J. (1980) *Using Research in Organizations: A Guide to Successful Application*, Beverly Hills, Sage Publications.

Royal Institute of British Architects (RIBA) (1962) *Handbook of Office Practice and Management*, London, RIBA Publications.

Royal Institute of Chartered Surveyors (1979) 'The unacceptable face of development control', *Estates Gazette*, 13 January.

Royal Town Planning Institute (1978) *Development Control: The Present System and Some Proposals for the Future*, London, RTPI.

Royal Town Planning Institute (1979) *Making Planning More Effective: A Discussion Document: Report of the Implementation in Planning Working Party*, London, RTPI.

Sabatier, P. and Mazmanian, D. (1979) 'The conditions of effective implementation: a guide to accomplishing policy objectives, *Policy Analysis*, Fall.

Salamon, L. M. (1979) 'The time dimension in policy evaluation: the case of the New Deal land reform experiments', *Public Policy*, 27(2), Spring.

Sapolsky, H. (1972) *The Polaris System Development*, Cambridge, Mass., Harvard University Press.

Savon, R. (1973) *Policy Making in Secondary Education*, Oxford University Press.

Schattschneider, E. E. (1960) *The Semi-Sovereign People*, New York, Holt, Reinhart & Winston.

Schon, D. A. (1971) *Beyond the Stable State*, London, Temple Smith.

Schulberg, H. C. and Baker, F. (1968) 'Program evaluation models and the implementation of research findings', *American Journal of Public Health*, 58(7), July.

Sedgemore, B. (1980) *The Secret Constitution*, London, Hodder & Stoughton.

Selznick, P. (1966) *TVA and the Grass Roots*, New York, Harper & Row.

Sharpe, L. J. (1975) 'The social scientist and policy-making: some cautionary thoughts and transatlantic reflections', *Policy and Politics*, 4(2), December.

Shipman, M. D. (1972) *The Limitations of Social Research*, London, Longman.

Shore, P. (1978) 'The housing policy review and the role of the building societies', *The Housing Policy Review and the Role of the Building Societies*, BSA.

Showler, B. and Sinfield, A. (eds) (1981) *The Workless State*, Oxford, Martin Robertson.

Simeon, R. (1972) *Federal-Provincial Diplomacy: The Making of Recent Policy in Canada*, Toronto, University of Toronto Press.

Simms, A. G. (1978) *The Effect of Consultation on Delays in Development Control*, Building Research Establishment Note 9–78, London, DoE.

Skitt, J. (ed.) (1975) *Practical Corporate Planning in Local Government*, London, Leonard Hill Books.

Smith, B. (1976) *Policy-Making in British Government*, Oxford, Martin Robertson.

Sofer, C. (1961) *The Organisation from Within*, London, Tavistock.

Solesbury, W. (1976) 'The environmental agenda', *Public Administration*, Winter.

South East Thames Regional Health Authority (1976) *Report of Committee of Enquiry, St. Augustine's Hospital, Chatham, Canterbury*, Croydon, SETRHA.

Spalding, J. (1978) 'The building society support scheme for local authorities', *Co-operation Between Building Societies and Local Authorities*, BSA.

Stewart, J. D. (1969) 'Programme budgeting in British local government', *Local Government Finance*, August.

Stewart, J. D. (1970) *Management in Local Government*, London, Charles Knight.

Strauss, A. (1978) *Negotiations*, San Francisco, Jossey-Bass.

Struening, E. L. and Guttentag, M. (eds) (1975) *Handbook of Evaluation Research*, vol. 1, Beverly Hills, Sage Publications.

Suchman, E. A. (1967) *Evaluative Research*, New York, Russell Sage Foundation.

Tawney, D. (ed.) (1976) *Curriculum Evaluation Today: Trends and Implications*, London, Macmillan.

Temperance Permanent Building Society (1973) *Into the Future*.

Tibbitt, J. (1975) *The Social Work/Medicine Interface: a review of research*, Edinburgh, Social Work Services Group, Scottish Education Department.

Towell, D. (1975) *Understanding Psychiatric Nursing*, London, Royal College of Nursing.

Towell, D. (1980) 'Large Institutions reconsidered: an approach to the management of transition', *Hospital and Health Services Review*, March.

Towell, D. and Harries, C. (1979) *Innovation in Patient Care: An action research study of change in a psychiatric hospital*, London, Croom Helm.

Town and Country Planning Act 1968, Chapter 72, London, HMSO.

Town and Country Planning Act 1971, Chapter 78, London, HMSO.

Town and Country Planning (Structure and Local Plans) Regulations 1974, S.I. 1974, no. 1486, London, HMSO.

Tripodi, T. (1974) *Uses and Abuses of Social Research in Social Work*, New York, Columbia University Press.

Tripodi, T., Fellin, P. and Epstein, I. (1971) *Social Program Evaluation*, Itasca, Illinois, F. E. Peacock.

Trist, E. (1976) 'Towards a post-industrial culture', in Dubin, R. (ed.) *Handbook of Work, Organization and Society*, Chicago, Rand McNally.

Underwood, J. (1980) *Town Planners in Search of a Role*, SAUS Occasional Paper 6, Bristol, School for Advanced Urban Studies.

Van Meter, D. and Van Horn, C. E. (1975) 'The policy implementation process, a conceptual framework', *Administration and Society*, 6(4), February.

Vickers, G. (1965) *The Art of Judgement*, London, Methuen.

Vickers, G. (1970) *Value Systems and the Social Process*, Harmondsworth, Penguin.

Weber, M. (1949) *The Methodology of the Social Sciences*, New York, Free Press.

Weiss, C. H. (1971) 'Utilization of evaluation: towards comparative study', in Caro, F. G. (ed.) *Readings in Evaluation Research*, New York, Russell Sage Foundation.

Weiss, C. H. (1972) *Evaluation Research: Methods of Assessing Program Effectiveness*, Englewood Cliffs, NJ, Prentice-Hall.

Weiss, C. H. (1973a) 'Between the cup and the lip . . . .', *Evaluation*, 1(2).

Weiss, C. H. (1973b) 'Where politics and evaluation research meet', *Evaluation*, 1(3).

Weiss, C. H. (1977a) 'Research for policy's sake: the enlightenment function of social science research', *Policy Analysis*, 3(4), Fall.

Weiss, C. H. (1977b) *Using Social Research in Public Policy Making*, Lexington, Mass., D. C. Heath & Co.

Weiss, C. H. (1979) 'The many meanings of research utilization', *Public Administration Review*, 39(5), September/October.

Weiss, C. H. and Bucuvalas, M. J. (1980) 'Truth tests and utility tests: decision-makers' frames of reference for social science research', *American Sociological Review*, 45(2), April.

Whale, J. (1977) *The Politics of the Media*, Glasgow, Fontana.

Wholey, J. (1972) 'What can we actually get from program evaluation?', *Policy Sciences*, 3(3), September.

Wholey, J. (1976) 'The role of evaluation and the evaluator in improving public programs: the bad news, the good news and a bicentennial challenge', *Public Administration Review*, 36(6), November/December.

Wholey, J. *et al.* (1970) *Federal Evaluation Policy*, Washington, The Urban Institute.

Wildavsky, A. (1972) *Evaluation as an Organisational Problem*, University Working Paper 13, London, Centre for Environmental Studies.

Wildavsky, A. (1975) *Budgeting: A Comparative Theory of Budgetary Processes*, Boston, Little, Brown.

Wildavsky, A. (1979) 'Rescuing policy analysis from PPBS', *Public Administration Review*, March/April.

Wildavsky, A. (1980) *The Art and Craft of Policy Analysis*, London, Macmillan.

Williams, L. (1978) 'The role of building societies in the housing market', *Co-operation between Building Societies and Local Authorities*, London, BSA.

Williams, P. (1976) 'The role of financial institutions and estate agents in the private housing market', Working paper no. 39, Birmingham, Centre for Urban and Regional Studies.

Williams, W. (1971) *Social Policy Research and Analysis*, New York, Elsevier.

Williams, W. and Evans, J. W. (1969) 'The politics of evaluation: the case of Headstart', *Annals of the American Academy of Political and Social Science*, September.

Winkler, J. (1976) 'Corporatism', *Archives Européenes de Sociologie*.

Wise, R. I. (1980) 'The evaluator as educator', in Braskamp, L. A. and Brown, R. D. (eds) *Utilization of Evaluative Information*, New Directions for Program Evaluation No. 5, San Francisco, Jossey-Bass.

Wyndham Goldie, G. (1977) *Facing the Nation: Television and Politics 1936–76*, London, Bodley Head.

Young, K. (1977) 'Values in the policy process', *Policy and Politics*, 5(3), March.

Young, K. (1979) 'Values in the policy process', in Pollitt, C. *et al.* (eds) *Public Policy in Theory and Practice*, London, Hodder & Stoughton.

Young, K. (1981) 'Discretion and implementation: a framework for interpretation', in Adler, M. and Asquith, S. (eds) *Discretion and Welfare*, London, Heinemann.

Young, K. and Mills, L. (1980) *Public Policy Research: A Review of Qualitative Methods*, London, Social Science Research Council.

Biographical notes

Susan Barrett, B.Sc., M.A., is Senior Lecturer at the School for Advanced Urban Studies. Before joining the School she worked for several years as a professional town planner in both local and central government. Since being at SAUS she has undertaken research supported by the Department of the Environment on the implementation of the Community Land Scheme and on the role of local authorities in the supply of land for private development. She has recently been involved in an SSRC-supported study of policy implementation in the context of central/local government relationships.

Colin Fudge, B.Arch., M.A., is Lecturer at the School for Advanced Urban Studies with special interest in public policy-making, political processes and the 'world' of the representative, behaviour in organizations, environmental planning and the impact of EEC policies on British local government. He recently undertook research at SAUS on the role of the elected member in English local authorities. Before joining the School he worked for several years as a professional planner in local government. He is currently engaged in research on local planning.

Jeff Bishop, A.A. DIP., is Lecturer at the School for Advanced Urban Studies. He trained as an architect and worked in private practice on a variety of projects including public housing and a football stadium. He taught architecture and undertook research on environmental psychology at Kingston Polytechnic before moving to SAUS. His interests lie in the boundaries of architecture – where and how it meets social, economic and political policy-making.

Martin Boddy, M.A., Ph.D., is Lecturer at the School for Advanced Urban Studies. He graduated from Cambridge with a degree in geography, and subsequently carried out postgraduate research into aspects of the British housing system, particularly housing finance in the private sector. At SAUS he has been involved in research on the implementation of the Community Land Scheme, and local authorities and industrial development. He is author of *The Building Societies* (1980). His main interests are British land policy, financial institutions and the urban development process.

Glen Bramley, B.Sc., is Lecturer at the School for Advanced Urban Studies with special interests in public finance at central and local levels, the economy and employment, and housing markets, finance, needs and programmes. He gained a B.Sc. from Bristol University in Economics and Economic History (1970), undertook graduate studies and research at Sussex University in the urban and regional studies field (1970–3), and worked as economist on the Lambeth Inner Area Study (1973–6).

Tom Davies, M.A., is Lecturer at the School for Advanced Urban Studies. He has carried out research and teaching in the field of employment and regional planning at the Building Research Establishment and the Polytechnic of Central London. Before taking up his post at SAUS he was a forward planner dealing with employment policy in a district authority. Recent research includes implementation in manpower policy at the local level, labour market problems in a new town, and inner city policies.

Michael Hill, B.Sc. is Senior Lecturer at the School for Advanced Urban Studies. He has written extensively both on policy studies and on social security policy. In the early 1960s he worked in the National Assistance Board. More recently he has undertaken research sponsored by the Department of Health and Social Security on the unemployed and on the task of social workers in local government. He has recently been involved in an SSRC-supported study of policy implementation in the context of central/local government relationships.

Randall Smith, B.A., is Senior Lecturer at the School for Advanced Urban Studies, previously at the Civil Service College, Centre for Urban and Regional Studies, University of Birmingham, Department of Social and Economic Research, University of Glasgow and Acton Society Trust. Current interests are the place of research in the policy process, inter-organizational relationships in social policy-making, social planning in new communities, policies for elderly people and the impact of EEC policies on British local government.

Murray Stewart, M.A., is Professor of Urban Government and Deputy Director at the School for Advanced Urban Studies. He worked as an economist in the civil service for five years on transport policy and regional planning as well as holding posts at the universities of Glasgow and Kent. He is generally concerned with processes of planning and resource allocation and is currently collaborating in research on the extent to which formal planning systems incorporate a concern for implementation. His recent specific interest has been the development of inner cities policy, and he is currently engaged in SSRC-sponsored research in this area.

David Towell, M.A., Ph.D., is Senior Research Fellow at the School for Advanced Urban Studies and also Assistant Director, responsible for work on long-term and community care, at the King's Fund Centre, London. He is currently involved in a programme of action research studies of policy and practice in health and welfare agencies. His disciplinary background is in sociology and organisation theory. He is also author of *Understanding Psychiatric Nursing* and co-author of *Innovation in Patient Care*.

Jacky Underwood, B.A., M.Phil., is Lecturer at the School for Advanced Urban Studies. She is a town planner by background and worked for several years in a London borough before carrying out research on the role of professionals in local government. At the School she is currently involved in teaching and research on planning and on the inner cities initiative.

Index